THE COSMIC FAMILY

Volume II

THE COSMIC FAMILY

Volume II

SECOND EDITION

as transmitted through
the Audio Fusion Material Complement

Gabriel of Urantia/TaliasVan of Tora

Global Community Communications Publishing

Tubac / Tumacácori, Arizona, USA

© 2009 by Global Community Communications Alliance

First Edition published February 1993

All rights reserved. No part of this book shall be reproduced, translated, or transmitted in any form or by any means, electronic, mechanical, magnetic, photographic including photocopying, recording, or by any information storage and retrieval system, without prior written permission of Global Community Communications Publishing. No patent liability is assumed with respect to the use of the information contained herein. Although every precaution has been taken in the preparation of this book, the publisher and author assume no responsibility for errors or omissions. Neither is any liability assumed for damages resulting from the use of the information contained herein.

ISBN 978-0-9822423-3-9

Global Community Communications Publishing
P.O. Box 4910, Tubac, Arizona 85646 USA
(520) 603-9932
e-mail: info@GlobalCommunityCommunicationsPublishing.org
www.GlobalCommunityCommunicationsPublishing.org

ABOUT THE PAPER USED IN THIS BOOK

According to our printer, Lightning Source, Inc. has 'Chain of Custody' certifications with The Sustainable Forestry Initiative, The Forest Stewardship Council, and The Program for the Endorsement of Forest Certification that permit Lightning Source to complete the custody chain from the stump, to the mill, to the paper, to the finished books. No papers used in Lightning Source books are sourced from endangered old growth forests, forests of exceptional conservation value, or the Amazon Basin.

CONTENTS

Titles of the Papers viii

Foreword xiii

Continuing Fifth Epochal Revelation Terminology xv

Copyright from a Cosmic Perspective xxiii

Preface from the Author's Heart xxvi

Introduction 1

Papers 229–261 16

Notes 455

Glossary 462

About the Audio Fusion Material Complement 547

Concerning Van 549

Global Community Communications Alliance and Divine Administration 551

Index 557

TITLES OF THE PAPERS

Introduction — *Machiventa Melchizedek, Planetary Prince* 1
The Audio Fusion Material Complement in Relationship to the Mandate of the Bright and Morning Star, Clarification of Other Material Complements Who May Reach Reflectivity Status and Mandate Potential, All Relative to the Adjudication Process of the Bright and Morning Star versus Lucifer Now Being Implemented on Urantia in and Through the Machiventa Melchizedek Administration

Paper 229 — *Paladin, Chief of Finaliters* 16
Thought Adjusters in Relationship to Indwelling the 170,000,000 Interuniversal and Intrauniversal Ovan Souls in Relationship to the Present Adjudication of the Bright and Morning Star versus Lucifer in the System of Satania and Incorporating Various Other Universes Affected by the Extension of the Lucifer Rebellion

Paper 230 — *Paladin, Chief of Finaliters* 25
Kinetic Energy in Relationship to Auhter Energy in Relationship to Mind-Gravity Circuits in the Implementation of the Divine Administration in Correlation with the Present Planetary Prince, Machiventa Melchizedek, and in Further Relationship to the Cosmic Reserve Corps and the Urantian Reserve Corps of Destiny

Paper 231 — *Paladin, Chief of Finaliters* 34
Mandates, the Power of Recognition in Relationship to Circuit Reflectivity and Other Interuniversal Headquarters Circuits of Deotonic Reality Pertaining to the Administrative Organizational Flow of Grand Universe Functional Procedure

Paper 232 — *Paladin, Chief of Finaliters* 42
The Three Meridian Circuits in Relationship to the Morontia Body Correlated with the Seven Circuits of the Lower Body in Reference to Clairvoyant Telepathic Planetary Function and Intrauniversal and Interuniversal Circulatory Administrative Broadcasts

Paper 233 — *Paladin, Chief of Finaliters* 59
The Seven Circuits of the Third-Dimensional Body in Relationship to the Seven Superuniverses, the System of Satania, and the Eighth and Ninth Meridian Circuits in Relationship to the Fourth Dimension and Above, and the Salvington Circuit

Paper 234 — *Paladin, Chief of Finaliters* 84
Personalities in Relationship to Human Mortal Ascenders with Coexistent Nonrealized Contact with the Energy Circuits of the Seven Superuniverses and the Central Circuit of the Morontia Light Body

Paper 235 — *Paladin, Chief of Finaliters* 93

Titles of the Papers

Astralology Reconstruction in Relationship to the Seven Circuits of the Lower Body Which Incorporate the Glandular Systems and the Eighth and Ninth Circuits of the Morontia Body and Above Corresponding with the Seven Superuniverses

Paper 236 — *Paladin, Chief of Finaliters* 105
The Appointments of Mandates by Celestial Overcontrol to Human Personalities at Varying Levels Including Nonmandated Positions Such as Supervisory Capacities in Various Services, Construction, and all Other Areas That Are Overseen by Various Mandated Personalities in Relationship to the Staff of the Present Planetary Prince, Machiventa Melchizedek—A Philosophical Addendum to a Constellation Survey of a Similar Fallen Planet of Interuniversal Nonhuman Mortals Entering the First Stages of Light and Life

Paper 237 — *Paladin, Chief of Finaliters* 115
Transpositional Visualization Sequence in Relationship to Common Prayer; Individual and Corporate Force of Activation Coordinating with Divine Mind and Divine Purpose on Any Evolutionary Plane or Higher Spiritual, Morontial or Above Reality

Paper 238 — *Kumatron and Kalacortex, Finaliters* 122
Post-Change-Point Realities in Relationship to Individual Talents, Family Life, and Destiny Purpose Within the Divine Administration of the First Stages of Light and Life on Urantia

Paper 239 — *Paladin, Chief of Finaliters* 131
Morontia Magnetic Field Flows in Relationship to Auhter Energy Correlating with Cosmic Family as a Form of Sequential Force-Energy in Dyad Units in Relationship to Interconnecting Links in Various Geographic Locations on Urantia Pertinent to the Formation of the Divine Administration of the Present Planetary Prince and in Meeting Cosmic Family Members and Trusting One's Own Open Circuits by Sensing These Magnetic Fields One to Another

Paper 240 — *Paladin, Chief of Finaliters* 140
The Seven Evolutionary Races of Urantia Plus the Nodite and Andite Amalgamations in Relationship to the Seven Cosmic Families and Some of the Present-Day Strains Pertinent to Certain Offshoots of the Seven Primary Ones, Their Historical Influences, and the Present-Day Responsibilities of Those Reservists, Both Cosmic and Urantian, Within Those Races in Relationship to the Implementation of the Divine Administration

Paper 241 — *Paladin, Chief of Finaliters* 154
The Fallacy of the Statement "All Paths Lead to the Same God" in Relationship to the Ascension Process of Nebadon, Avalon, Fanoving, and Wolvering, Accelerated Due to the Adjudication of the Bright and Morning Star Versus Lucifer in Respect to Each of the 170,000,000 Fallen Ovan Souls Presently on Urantia

Paper 242 — *Paladin, Chief of Finaliters* 163
Body Chemistry in Relationship to Deo-Atomic Inheritance of Both Individuals and Pair-Unit Classifications Pertinent to Higher Functions in Destiny Purpose in Social and Divine Administration

Paper 243 — *Paladin, Chief of Finaliters* 174
Human Mortal Reproduction in Relationship to Genetic Inheritance and Circle Attainment on Post-Rebellion Urantia Incorporating Interuniversal Diotribes Influencing the Reproduction Process and the Productivity of Deo-Atomic Genes Causing a Form of Gene Splicing

Paper 244 — *Paladin, Chief of Finaliters* 182
The Seven Cosmic Families and the Seven Root Races of Urantia in Relationship to the Interuniversal Enzymes and the Digestion Techniques of Those Various Bodies Due to Post-Rebellion Amalgamation

Paper 245 — *Paladin, Chief of Finaliters* 197
Oxidation and the Air We Breathe in Relationship to the Paradise Trinity as Manifested in Form in Pair-Unit Classifications and Complementary Polarities on the Evolutionary Worlds of Time and Space by Ascending Sons and Daughters of Procreation Ability

Paper 246 — *Paladin, Chief of Finaliters* 211
Helper (Helpmate) Molecules, Magnesium and Iron, in Fusion with Protein Enzymes in Relationship to Pair-Unit Classifications or Higher Spiritual Complements in the Activation of Healing Force Energies on the Lower Worlds of Time and Space and in the Ascension Process to Higher Spiritual Bodies

Paper 247 — *Paladin, Chief of Finaliters* 218
Vitamins and Their Relationship to the Physical and Spiritual Bodies and in Turn Their Relationship to Paradise-Origin Personalities and the Reflectivity Sources That Create These Vitamins, Pertinent to Physical and Spiritual Health Based Upon Free Will in Relationship to Cosmic Law and Destiny Purposes, and in Particular to Ovan Souls of the Cosmic Reserve Corps

Paper 248 — *Paladin, Chief of Finaliters* 237
The Glands of the Body in Relationship to Physical and Spiritual Health and the Appropriation of the Morontia Body with the Coordination of Deo-Atomic Hormones More Resonant with Paradise-Origin Energies and the Seven Superuniverse Families of Reflectivity

Paper 249 — *Paladin, Chief of Finaliters* 248
Hormones in Relationship to the Paradise Circuits of the Universal Father, the Eternal Son, and the Infinite Spirit; the Design Factors in Body Programming of the Cellular Structure and Other Third-Dimensional and Lower Body Functions

Paper 250 — *Gabriel, the Bright and Morning Star of Salvington* ... 264

Titles of the Papers

Reflective Cellular Magnetic Motion Polarity in the Beginning Morontia Body and its Relationship to Celestial Mechanics and Planetary Administration in the First Stages of Light and Life Pertinent to the Cosmic Families and Electromagnetism on a Third-Dimensional Level

Paper 251 — *Paladin, Chief of Finaliters* 286
Sound Waves and Celestial Harmonics in Conjunction with Primal Absolute Paradise Circuit Waves in Correlation with Pre-Designed Patterns of the Grand Universe and Master Designs Including Personality Formations, and in Particular, Pair-Unit Classifications of Various Evolutionary and Descending Levels in Cosmic Scope Coordinate with Quantum Physics—A Beginning Treatise

Paper 252 — *Paladin, Chief of Finaliters* 307
The Mortal Ear, in This Case the Human Ear, Has the Receiver Unit of All Energies of Paradise Circuitry; the Paradise Circuits From Upper Paradise and Energy Circuits of Nether Paradise in Relationship to Cosmic Absolute Paradise Virtues, Perfected Harmonic Frequencies, and the Understanding of This Audio Sensor Unit in Relationship to the One-, Two-, and Three-Brained Types as Transmitters to the Body of the Commands, the Creations, and the Laws of the First Source and Center, Receiving from Other Human or Mortal Personalities and/or Interdimensional and Interplanetary Personalities, All in Some Capacity Tapping Into the Primal Absolute Paradise Circuit Wave

Paper 253 — *Paladin, Chief of Finaliters* 321
The Inner Ear, the Third Ear, or More Appropriately, the Morontia Ear in Relationship to the Causal Body Coordinating with the Light or First Morontia Body in the Lower Realms, and Specifically on Urantia, the Fourth Dimension, Pertinent to Interdimensional Reception of Auditory Circuitry in Alignment with the Primal Absolute Paradise Circuit Wave

Paper 254 — *Paladin, Chief of Finaliters* 339
Psychophysics and Virtue Sensors in Relationship to Dimensional and Innerdimensional Understanding, the Sound and Hearing Abilities Which Regulate Deo-Atomic Structuring of the Next Body of Ascension, and in Particular the Third Dimension to the Fourth—the Main Subject of this Transmission

Paper 255 — *Paladin, Chief of Finaliters* 350
Universal Ontology and Otology in Relationship to Sensing Sensors at the Various Locations Within the Evolutionary Body, the Morontia Body at the First Level, and the Various Diseases and Malfunctioning Circuitry to the Binaural Hearing of Evolutionary Mortals with Two Outer Ears

Paper 256 — *Paladin, Chief of Finaliters* 364
Deo-Atomic Generics in Association with Psychobiology, Psychophysics, and Ascension Science; Psychospirituality in Relationship to the Cosmic Reserve Corps of Starseed, Second-Time

Urantians, and First-Time Urantians Pertinent to Brain Functioning and the Central Nervous System—A Beginning Study

Paper 257 — *Paladin, Chief of Finaliters* 380
The Four Divisions of the Urantian Human Brain in Relationship to Interuniversal Cellular Formation of the Human Brain, Corresponding to Specific Functioning Sensory Positions in Relationship to Universal Reflectivity of Various Personality Bestowals Pertinent to a Particular Universe

Paper 258 — *Paladin, Chief of Finaliters* 397
Psychochemical Behavior Responses of the Brain in Relationship to Deo-Atomic Mind–Soul Causal Current, Deo-Atomic Receptor Units, and Causal Memory Circuits Within the Family of Neurotransmitters

Paper 259 — *Paladin, Chief of Finaliters* 414
The Present Planetary Administration of Machiventa Melchizedek in Interuniversal Personality Representation in Administrative Function on Urantia

Paper 260 — *Paladin, Chief of Finaliters* 431
The Clarification of the Process in the Use of an Audio Fusion Material Complement Pre-Level One as Opposed to Deo-Audio Coupling (Pre-December 1989) and Dio-Audio Coupling (Channeling)—Reflectivity Personality Pattern and Higher Levels of Audio Fusion

Paper 261 — *Paladin, Chief of Finaliters* 443
Similectic (Semi-electric) Genetic Alignment Transference in Relationship to the Aquarian Age, Which is the Alignment of Urantia with Planets in the Highest Stages of Light and Life in the System of Satania Within the Context of the Adjudication of the Bright and Morning Star Versus Lucifer Which in its Upstepped Energies Has Occurred Since the Arrival of the Planetary Prince in December of 1989

FOREWORD

The Cosmic Family volumes[1] are unlike any writings you have ever encountered. They are the Continuing Fifth Epochal Revelation to this planet and contain the succeeding papers of revelatory information begun in *The URANTIA Book*[2] (the Fifth Epochal Revelation), which was first published in 1955. To truly comprehend the information presented, it is best understood when studied sequentially or simultaneously—beginning with *The URANTIA Book*, then *The Cosmic Family* volumes—to build a foundation of information based precept upon precept, concept upon concept. All Continuing Fifth Epochal Revelation terms are set off in a unique font the first time they are used within each paper (except in the titles and sign-offs of the papers), to enable the reader to more easily identify these new concepts. They are also defined in the Glossary in the back of the book.

Since *The Cosmic Family* volumes are the continuation of the first 196 papers found in *The URANTIA Book*, we have retained capitalization styles similar to *The URANTIA Book's* style for orders of beings and certain other Fifth Epochal Revelation terms. Throughout *The Cosmic Family* volumes the editing team has retained Celestial Overcontrol's wording of the transmissions. Celestial Overcontrol's very unique language style and presentation technique often create a braid of information that weaves throughout a transmission. We have learned that any given sentence may have multiple meanings on multiple levels. We would like to note that it was the human editors and not Celestial Overcontrol who determined punctuation, paragraphing, capitalization, and other stylistic formats.

Throughout this book, statements regarding personalities transcending from mortal life without experiencing death are statements that have to do with the reality of a higher planetary mass consciousness understanding and practicing the concepts of Divine Administration—which as of the publishing of this volume (2009) has not yet happened. There is only one planetary Divine Administration sector at this time.

To truly benefit the most from this volume, we suggest you first (or simultaneously) read and study *The Cosmic Family, Volume I* and *The Divine New Order* (the autobiography of Gabriel of Urantia/TaliasVan of Tora).

A variety of study aids—including an extensive glossary, diagrams and charts, and cosmic paintings and drawings—are continually being developed. Many students of this revelation have found such tools to be invaluable in their attempts to grasp the many new concepts presented in *The URANTIA Book* and *The Cosmic Family* volumes. Please contact Global Community Communications Publishing or Global Community Communications Alliance for more information on how to obtain these study aids.

Autumn 2009

The Editors

Niánn Emerson Chase	Graduate Studies, Education — Arizona State University
	B.A., English — Arizona State University
Marayeh Cunningham	Ph.D., Psychology — University of Texas
Landau Lawrence	M.D. — University of Texas
	B.S., Physics — University of Texas
Rafeel Coenenberg	M.A., Library Science — UC Berkeley
	B.S., Business — University of Oregon
LaTaYea Calviero	B.A., English — Pennsylvania State University

CONTINUING FIFTH EPOCHAL REVELATION TERMINOLOGY

Continuing Fifth Epochal Revelation, transmitted through the Audio Fusion Material Complement Gabriel of Urantia[1]/TaliasVan of Tora, is the continuation of the Fifth Epochal Revelation (*The URANTIA Book*). During a twenty-year span, from 1989–2009, Gabriel of Urantia/TaliasVan of Tora received and transmitted more than 135 technical transmissions, 158 community transmissions, and 635 personal transmissions—all of which provide continuing revelation to the planet. Although more than 130 papers for *The Cosmic Family* volumes have been transmitted, only *The Cosmic Family, Volumes I* and *II* have been published; *Volumes III* and *IV* are being finalized for publication.

Continuing Fifth Epochal Revelation introduces many new concepts, referred to in Divine Administration as Aquarian concepts. The physics of rebellion is a fundamental concept addressed in Continuing Fifth Epochal Revelation. As was indicated in the Foreword, all Continuing Fifth Epochal Revelation terms are set off in a unique font the first time they are used within each paper (except in the titles and sign-offs of the papers), to enable the reader to more easily identify these new concepts.

Below are some frequently used significant terms found in *The Cosmic Family, Volume II*. A glossary defining many more terms is located in the back of this text.

audio fusion material complement

An audio fusion material complement is a unique mortal vessel among interdimensional and interplanetary receivers. The process involves a fusion between a celestial being and a mortal, a fusion of one entity with another in the complete subatomic-to-cellular reality of the lower being. The fusion takes place within the particle reality of the life force of the existing soul. They co-exist within the life force, and the existing soul does not leave. It is a gradual process over many years, and the higher the virtue of the chosen mortal vessel, then the higher the fusion, the higher the celestial being, and the higher the level of revelation that can be brought through.

Since Gabriel of Urantia/TaliasVan of Tora became an audio fusion material complement in 1989, he has gradually reached higher and higher levels in this fusion process. It was announced at a community transmission on April 11, 2007 that in March 2007, coinciding with Gabriel of Sedona becoming Gabriel of Urantia, he became a level eight audio fusion material complement. He is the only audio fusion material complement on Urantia (Earth). The Bright and Morning Star fuses with Gabriel of Urantia/TaliasVan of Tora periodically to teach for a few hours. Paladin, Chief of Finaliters, often fuses with Gabriel of Urantia/TaliasVan of Tora several times per day.

Celestial Overcontrol

Celestial Overcontrol on Urantia (Earth) is the term designating orders of beings who function on higher levels of universe administration, guiding and overseeing the human mandated personalities on a planetary level of functioning in cooperation with the Planetary Prince, Machiventa Melchizedek (who is in spirit form). These beings typically reside in the fourth and fifth dimensions (and above) here on Urantia, and include—but are by no means limited to—the Bright and Morning Star (Gabriel of Salvington) and the Chief of Finaliters on Urantia (Paladin). Throughout this book the terms Celestial Overcontrol and Overcontrol have been used interchangeably when referring to this administrative body of celestial beings.

change point

The term change point used throughout *The Cosmic Family* volumes can have multiple meanings. The reader should understand that there is not just one particular moment, day, or

Continuing Fifth Epochal Revelation Terminology

year that is the change point, but rather the change point unfolds over time, with many smaller change points (both personal and collective) contributing to the ultimate shift of the planet into the first stage of light and life. For further clarification see the June 24, 2001 Global Change Teaching by Niánn Emerson Chase titled "The Change Point: The Continuing Saga," available from Global Community Communications Publishing.

On August 2, 2005 Paladin gave this explanation of change point: "It should be understood at this time that there are obviously several change points—a series of change points that work up to a final change point. For instance, 1989 was a change point with minor change points working up to that date, and May 5, 2001 was another change point. These are two major change points, and there have been minor change points between these two major ones. This will continue until the final change point. That could be the return of Christ Michael to Urantia, the coming of a Trinity Teacher Son, or the materialization of Machiventa Melchizedek. What this means is a complete taking over by the light forces over the dark forces. After all, a rebellion on any world must end eventually, and so the final change point on this world is approaching. So, the many meanings of the change point that are mentioned in *The Cosmic Family* volumes need to be understood in that context."

Christ Michael
Also known as Michael of Nebadon and Jesus Christ Michael. He is the Creator Son of our local universe of Nebadon, who bestowed as Jesus of Nazareth approximately two thousand years ago. He is a Paradise-origin personality of the order of the Michael Sons and one of 700,000 Creator Sons.

cosmic family
A cosmic family is astrally related through cosmic genetics. At present there are seven cosmic families on Urantia (Earth) from four different universes. Each cosmic family is headed by

a different finaliter. The highest destiny of each member of these cosmic families is to align with Divine Administration.

In a broader sense, the concept of cosmic family also presents the fact that we are all related as one spiritual family under God, the Universal Father, and this family extends throughout the cosmos, beginning in Paradise and reaching down to the lowest evolutionary worlds. Cosmic family includes all seen and unseen beings—celestial, mortal, and many unrevealed types of beings.

Deo

Deo is a term that refers to something that is within God's divine pattern.

dio

Dio is a term that refers to something that is outside of God's divine pattern.

First Planetary Sacred Home

Celestial Overcontrol has consistently clarified that the First Planetary Sacred Home is the spiritual planetary headquarters of Urantia (Earth). Planetary Headquarters is the centralized location where epochal revelation is received, implemented, and disseminated, and it is the administrative center of celestial and human divine administration on Urantia. The two terms First Planetary Sacred Home and Planetary Headquarters can be used interchangeably.

Throughout the history of Urantia there have been five different planetary headquarters: the first Planetary Headquarters was Dalamatia at the time of Caligastia, 500,000 years ago; the second was the Garden of Eden at the time of Adam and Eve, 38,000 years ago; the third was the schools of Salem at the time of Machiventa Melchizedek, approximately 4,000 years ago; the fourth was wherever Jesus of Nazareth was, 2,000 years ago. (For further information about these four epochal revelations see *The URANTIA Book*, Papers 66, 74, 93, and Part IV.)

Presently, Planetary Headquarters is located in Arizona, USA, where the Planetary Prince, Machiventa Melchizedek, resides in a higher dimension in spirit form; where the archangels' headquarters is situated; where all loyal angelic and non-angelic orders as well as revealed and unrevealed midwayers assemble for the performance of planetary, interplanetary, universal, interuniversal, and interdimensional administration; and where mortals aligned under the Mandate of the Bright and Morning Star are cooperating within Global Community Communications Alliance to implement Machiventa Melchizedek's Divine Administration on this planet. These combined unique aspects of Planetary Headquarters are what draw people spiritually there and make the area and its energy feel so special and sacred.

Gabriel of Salvington

Gabriel of Salvington, also known as the Bright and Morning Star, is the firstborn son of Christ Michael and the Universe Mother Spirit. He serves as the chief administrator of this local universe, Nebadon. Since 1989 Gabriel of Salvington has fused with Gabriel of Urantia/TaliasVan of Tora through the audio fusion material complement process on an ongoing basis to bring continuing revelation, as part of the adjudication of the Bright and Morning Star versus Lucifer. (For further information about Gabriel of Salvington see *The URANTIA Book*, "Gabriel—The Chief Executive," pp. 369–370)

Lucifer Rebellion

The Lucifer Rebellion is a rebellion initiated 200,000 years ago by Lucifer, who was then the Sovereign of the system of Satania. Thirty-seven of the then 607 inhabited worlds in the system of Satania participated. (Currently there are 619 inhabited worlds, with others soon to be thus designated.) The rebellion involved many personalities of various celestial orders as well as mortals. On Urantia (Earth) the adjudication of the Bright and Morning Star versus Lucifer is bringing an end to this rebellion.

The Fifth Epochal Revelation and Continuing Fifth Epochal Revelation play a major part in re-opening the universe circuits. The adjudication on Urantia is now in progress under the Mandate of the Bright and Morning Star in and through the Divine Administration of Machiventa Melchizedek and his staff, both celestial and mortal. Many fallen starseed and some second-time Urantians have had to repersonalize on Urantia at the present time for this adjudication. (For further information about the Lucifer Rebellion see *The URANTIA Book*, Papers 53 & 54 and *The Cosmic Family, Volume I*, Papers 213 & 227)

Machiventa Melchizedek

Machiventa Melchizedek has been Planetary Prince of Urantia (Earth) since December 1989. He exists in a higher dimension in spirit form on the planet, residing at Planetary Sacred Headquarters. This same Melchizedek, who belongs to the highest order of local universe Sons, incarnated in the likeness of mortal flesh and lived on Urantia for 94 years during the time of Abraham and was known as the Prince of Salem. At that time Machiventa Melchizedek came on an emergency mission when the spiritual light on Urantia was almost extinguished, and he taught the one-God concept. (For further information about Machiventa Melchizedek see *The URANTIA Book*, Paper 93)

One-mile, Three-mile, and Five-mile Radii

In August 2000 a change in nomenclature for certain geographic areas was given by Celestial Overcontrol, as the use of the word radius in these instances refers to "an area of influence." At that time the then "one-mile radius" became the "First Radius," the "three-mile radius" became the "Second Radius," and the "five-mile radius" became the "Third Radius." The change was based on the anticipation of the continued growth of auhter energy. For example, the First Radius could grow to be a one-hundred-mile radius rather than the initial one-mile. These radii are not necessarily perfectly circular but rather are more amoeba-like in shape, with valleys and peaks reaching out in various directions simultaneously.

ovan souls

Ovan souls are mortals who have had at least one previous life. On Urantia, both second-time Urantians and starseed are ovan souls.

Paladin

Paladin is a finaliter—an evolutionary mortal who ascended from his planet of origin to Paradise. Paladin became Chief of Finaliters on Urantia (Earth) in January 1992. He is the head of the First Cosmic Family and the cosmic father of Gabriel of Urantia/TaliasVan of Tora. Paladin—who fuses with and speaks through the Audio Fusion Material Complement Gabriel of Urantia/TaliasVan of Tora—is the chief spokesperson for celestial personalities bringing Continuing Fifth Epochal Revelation to the planet. (For further information about finaliters see *The URANTIA Book*: "Glorified Mortals" pp. 347–348; "Transitional Culture Worlds" pp. 509–510; and "The Finaliters' World" pp. 530–531. For further information about Paladin see *The Cosmic Family, Volume I*.)

second-time Urantians

Second-time Urantians are ovan souls who have had one previous mortal life, and this life was on Urantia (Earth). Some second-time Urantians have spent time on the mansion worlds before returning to Urantia for a second human mortal life. Since the transmissions in this volume of *The Cosmic Family* came through in the early 1990s, new information is being given now that there are more second-time Urantians than the original 2,000 spoken of. As of June 1998, another 1,500 have been assigned to Urantia and this number will be increasing. It was stated at that time that by the year 2005 there could possibly be 10,000 second-time Urantians.

starseed

Starseed are evolutionary mortal ascending sons and daughters whose soul origin is on another planet, usually in another universe. Starseed children are born of human parents through the repersonalization technique. There are seven orders of starseed on Urantia (Earth). Many starseed are presently repersonalizing on this planet as part of the adjudication of the Bright and Morning Star versus Lucifer. (For further information about starseed see *The Cosmic Family, Volume I*, Paper D)

Urantia

The cosmic name of the planet Earth.

Copyright from a Cosmic Perspective

Paladin, Chief of Finaliters

This transmission is mandated by Christ Michael, Universe Sovereign of Nebadon, for the implementation of the Divine Administration of the present Planetary Prince, Machiventa Melchizedek, and for the calling forth of the Cosmic and Urantian Reservists within the present adjudication of the Bright and Morning Star versus Lucifer that is now taking place on Urantia

As transmitted through
the Pre-Level-One Audio Fusion Material Complement,
Gabriel of Urantia/TaliasVan of Tora

PREFACE
FROM THE AUTHOR'S HEART

I would like to give my human perspective on being an audio fusion material complement of the Bright and Morning Star and Paladin, a finaliter, and the process over the years. Presently I am functioning as a level-eight audio fusion material complement according to Celestial Overcontrol and am working on *The Cosmic Family, Volume IV*. All of *The Cosmic Family, Volume II* was transmitted when I was basically at what Overcontrol calls pre-level-one.

If you really compare this information with channeled material, it should be easy to understand why Celestial Overcontrol states that bringing through Continuing Fifth Epochal Revelation is the only audio fusion process on the planet. As you read the highly technical information that comes through at pre-level-one audio fusion, it may be difficult to understand how information could be much higher, as *Volumes I* and *II* of *The Cosmic Family* are quite astounding in themselves.

As I was drawing near level-one, which happened in March 1993, after my cosmic daughter Delphéus arrived from Australia, the information began to get a little more technical—technical in the sense of incorporating very difficult-to-understand scientific terms from physics that I, as the human Gabriel of Urantia/TaliasVan of Tora, do not understand.

The importance of Cosmic Reservists and cosmic family members aligning with Divine Administration is absolutely invaluable, for as often as certain past cosmic family members came to Arizona and aligned, my level of reception in relation to particle reflectivity to these beings increased. So, when Santeen my cosmic son arrived, I became level-two, which was in September 1993. My own personal ascension, as well as being complemented by past repersonalization cosmic family members, creates a union of souls not only in our dimension

Preface

with each other but in the higher invisible dimension with our angels of enlightenment and other ministering celestial personalities.

When I re-read *Volumes I* and *II* I was amazed at the quality of information that combines scientific knowledge with spiritual truths (ascension science). As an artist I am more "right-brained" than "left-brained," and in high school and college, science and mathematics were not my favorite subjects. Yet Celestial Overcontrol is able to bring this information through me when I myself have little or no understanding of many scientific concepts; this does not happen in "channeling." [See Paper 209 of *The Cosmic Family, Volume I* for clarification of the differences between a channel and an audio fusion material complement.]

In the understanding of the Lucifer Rebellion as it relates to our everyday lives here at the First Planetary Sacred Home and the evil, sin, and iniquity in the world, I certainly have learned much in relation to what Celestial Overcontrol calls the physics of rebellion and ascension science.

As Van [see the section "Concerning Van" at the end of this book]—the oldest soul on the planet, who has had countless repersonalizations—it should be clear to see by the keen spiritual observer why Celestial Overcontrol has chosen the soul of Van to bring through Continuing Fifth Epochal Revelation. My experience on Urantia and with Continuing Fifth Epochal Revelation has truly trained me to be a soul surgeon and morontia counselor. (I realize that my statements of knowing who I am and the global importance of my destiny can sound like extreme arrogance. I have no choice but to try to be understood. Self-confidence can often be misinterpreted.)

This process has not been easy for me or my highest spiritual complement, Niánn Emerson Chase, who co-shares the Mandate of the Bright and Morning Star. From the very beginning, when personal transmissions were given that dealt with the error, sin, and iniquity in the people who requested those transmissions, we discovered that many of those who did not want to deal with their own dio (evil) rejected us and the work, and some even chose to act as our enemies. Many of those in rebellion only accepted the parts that suited them.

It was interesting to watch the process of their defaults. Some of them kept the cosmic names that were given to them or names of their past lives of more notoriety, but they rejected Continuing Fifth Epochal Revelation on the whole. They wanted to believe the only truth that came out of their personal transmission was their cosmic name or point of origin, not the confrontational truths.

Some claim to still be doing Christ Michael's (Jesus') will. Many of these once-chosen souls could have become Destiny Reservists, for many are called but few are chosen. Celestial Overcontrol cannot choose you until you agree to be chosen. As a vessel being used for personal transmissions, the hardest part for me is to let Celestial Overcontrol say what needs to be said. Niánn and I lost cosmic children, siblings, and many others we loved. It was and is very painful.

Over the years there have been many changes at the First Planetary Sacred Home, mostly in administration. People who had mandates in the earlier years may not have them in the later ones. People who were perhaps Vicegerent Second Assistants years ago may be First Assistants or even Elders now. Presently, according to Celestial Overcontrol, more than 60% of those aligned in Divine Administration have reached the third psychic circle and stabilized. The serendipities that we realize here everyday can best be understood and believed by being here. We are so blessed.

In the pain that I do feel in being so misunderstood—even by those who are just in error in the Urantia movement or the New Age movement or my brothers and sisters in the Christian world—I want you to know that I forgive you and that in my heart I desire to help bring peace to this planet, the first stage of light and life, and, hopefully, the return of Jesus Christ Michael, my beloved Master when I was Peter and my present Universe Father who adopted me 500,000 years ago as His son from Avalon.

Preface

In the seriousness of these times on Urantia,

Gabriel of Urantia/TaliasVan of Tora
Mandate of the Bright and Morning Star

Autumn 2009

INTRODUCTION

The Audio Fusion Material Complement In Relationship To The Mandate Of The Bright And Morning Star, Clarification Of Other Material Complements Who May Reach Reflectivity Status And Mandate Potential, All Relative To The Adjudication Process Of The Bright And Morning Star Versus Lucifer Now Being Implemented On Urantia In And Through The Machiventa Melchizedek Administration

THESE processes in administration by celestial personalities in liaison with human mortal personalities, be they cosmic personalities in human form from another universe or cosmic personalities in human form from the universe of Nebadon, are a unique phenomenon, so unique that the using of the audio fusion material complement to be the voice of many of us is most difficult. It is continually and increasingly difficult to relay higher cosmic truth and administrative procedure and policy to imperfect creatures, as has always been the case, but particularly now on Urantia because so much absolute information has to be brought through and processed in such a short period of time.

It should be understood by all concerned that the first part of the Fifth Epochal Revelation, which has now become known as *The URANTIA Book*, was brought to this planet over a period of time. The transmissions began in 1906, became much more clear in 1911, and even more so in the early 1930s. All of this information brought great turbulence to those who received it. All of this information had to be set aside and corrected, organized and reorganized, edited and re-edited, and even sometimes changed for human understanding.

The process was not perfect, and the process now is even more difficult. This is because we are now dealing with a vessel who has to hear what is being said at a high level, not a subconscious level, but at the level of conscious hearing so that he himself can assimilate what is being said in an awakened state. In order for him to be a teacher of these concepts he must not learn in retrospect; he must learn in the now. This has to do, as far as this particular individual is concerned, with **memory circuits**. The first vessel who was used to bring the first one-tenth of the Fifth Epochal Revelation was not a **material complement**. I repeat, he was not a material complement. It was much easier to bring information through in the process that we used with him because he was very much unaware of what was brought through him, and it was a process that had nothing to do with information he had accumulated within his own mind.

This is not the case with **Gabriel of Urantia/TaliasVan of Tora**. He is, and it should be noted, a higher vessel. He is an **ovan soul**, and he is meant to be a teacher of this information and a leader and one in authority. He cannot be indifferent to the material brought through him, nor can he be indifferent to his cosmic identity, which is the reality of his being an audio fusion material complement in reflectivity to the Bright and Morning Star of Salvington. The process in which we began contact with Gabriel of Urantia/TaliasVan of Tora, and continually maintain contact, is based upon many criteria. Please read Paper 209 of *The Cosmic Family, Volume I*.[1] It may be best to do so now, before continuing to read this one, if you are not familiar with it.

It is stated in Paper 209 that many factors must take place for celestial personalities, including midwayers, in the administration of Michael of Nebadon, to speak to your side from ours. The most important of these criteria is that there must be a complementary polarity of the opposite sex of proper **pair-unit classification** paired with the vessel. Without this pair-unit classification, higher revelatory absolute truth simply cannot come through. If the vessel is an ovan soul, what will come through is a mixture of possibly a higher self and the lower self, and, if he or she is a lower ovan soul, all of the stupidity that that soul has incorporated in his or her time–space experience of the past. A fallen entity can also come through. All three of these things can happen and usually do.

From the time that Michael has allowed this process to take place on Urantia, not only in this century but for the last 200,000 years since the fall of Caligastia, countless channels have been used in this manner for many reasons. Basically, it is because since the circuits were cut off on Urantia, even if some higher truth comes through, it is better than none at all. When you read five pages of information, if two of them represent some cosmic absolutes, it is better to read the five pages and get two pages of cosmic absolutes than it would be not to read anything at all. However, this is not, and I repeat, not the highest will of Christ Michael, nor of those in administration under Him, to teach. It is a way that has been used.

The Audio Fusion Material Complement with the **Mandate of the Bright and Morning Star** does not receive his mandate over one lifetime. It takes countless repersonalizations, countless trials and errors. Basically, in using an imperfect vessel, one criterion, and one criterion alone, must rise to the high probability status, and that is the criterion of fear before God. Let me extrapolate a little upon this.

It is good to have a healthy respect for one's elders. It is good to have a little bit of healthy fear of your human father. Respect and fear are very close to one another. Sometimes a healthy respect and fear can keep a child out of danger if that child realizes the repercussions that will happen if he or she is caught doing something that he or she should not do. So the child can avoid doing something wrong because of the respect and fear of the discipline of the father. This does not apply to an imbalanced fear or the abuse of the child by the father. It has to do with a sense of security. The child knows that the father is right, and the child would rather do what is correct in order to avoid the punishment of the father. It is a wise decision.

The cosmic absolutes are written in time and space so that at whatever level you can adhere to them to avoid the punishment of God (self-imposed by your choices)—and there is punishment—then you must make the decision based upon a healthy fear and respect, knowing that if you break these rules, cause and effect will happen to you, and, in that sense, the Eternal Father will discipline you. These laws were written in the beginning of time, not just time as you know it, but long before you were ever a living, breathing, thinking entity. These laws were understood and adhered to by others long before you, in worlds that have become settled in light and life, because they have adhered to the rules of the Father of all. They wished not to be spanked, and therefore they ascended into a time-and-space mode of reality, free from the pain and suffering they would have gotten themselves into had they not had a healthy respect for God.

The vessel who was chosen to be the mandated audio fusion material complement of the Bright and Morning Star has this healthy respect. Oh, it is a hard thing to deal with, for it brings about many questions, turmoil, and inner pain; but if all of the doubt, all of the turmoil, all of the questions, concerns, and responsibilities that he feels were not there, we would not be there either. It is as simple as that. Over a period of many hundreds of years, this healthy respect must be a part of the reality of these souls, and it is observed and measured.

Secondly, they must learn to hear at the highest level possible from their own Thought Adjuster, the Spirit of Truth, and the Holy Spirit within, and the fusion of all three. They must learn to hear the inner voices in whatever way the threefold reality of God is speaking to them at any one moment at any one point in time and space.

Thirdly, in order for higher celestial personalities to speak through them, they must be complemented by other complementary polarities around them in a physical geographic location. **Cosmic wives, cosmic husbands, cosmic brothers and sisters, cosmic sons and daughters** must live within a one-mile radius of them and be in the same exact spiritual work. They must have a union of souls.

This was not the case with the first vessel used to channel through the information in the first one-tenth of the Urantia revelation. Yes, there had to be a certain goodness about the first vessel used to bring the beginning revelation, but we could have used anyone if we had so chosen. It was not the vessel's great spirituality; it was a number of circumstances based upon others nearby who could be used to bring the transmissions to publication in paper form. So, the reason the vessel was chosen was not because of the quality of the vessel himself.

With Gabriel of Urantia/TaliasVan of Tora, it is just the opposite. It is his ascension, and the ascension of others around him, that brings us through in a continual manner for the purposes of the adjudication of Urantia. It is not just for epochal revelation or to have a study book handy. Gabriel of Urantia/TaliasVan of Tora, Niánn Emerson Chase, and others who will be mandated are walking representatives; some are potential material complements. They have to walk into the material complement of their reflectivity in the universe of Nebadon. No matter if they are of another universe, they reflect the celestial personalities of the administration of Christ Michael in this universe of Nebadon.[2]

Yes, confusion can enter in trying to understand interuniversal reality, based upon the reality of the universe in which you are presently residing, and we are trying to do so much with so few harvesters. You do well to observe any contradictions you may find in **Continuing Fifth Epochal Revelation** and to point them out to those at the **First Planetary Sacred Home**, for they receive so much material daily and process it and get it out to certain individuals in a time span that took decades for the first forum to do. You would do better to come to **Planetary Sacred Headquarters** and to help them get this information out so that these mistakes would not be made or would be lessened.

When we began to work with Gabriel of Urantia/TaliasVan of Tora, he had a loyal mind, heart, soul, and spirit; but he did not have his former cosmic higher mind, that is, a mind of Continuing Fifth Epochal Revelation terminology reality. We had to bring that mind to him, and we had to do so by placing new terminology and new concepts within his mind at a rate that most individuals on Urantia would not be able to handle, and that would probably drive them insane. But because he is who he is, a thinker, he was and is able to process all of this and still maintain his sanity. We admire his faithfulness, and we understand his unhappiness at times, for he, more than anyone else on the planet at this time, understands the potential of true freedom for himself and for so many others. But he, like so many others on the planet, cannot actualize that potential based upon the many problems that exist on Urantia, all due to the fact that you are not used to living in perfection and self-actualization or in interuniversal absolute reality based upon your **point of origin**.

So we bring transmission after transmission through with new terminology and new conceptual realities, all challenging the ones who receive it. Trying to synthesize all of this and to understand Continuing Fifth Epochal Revelation while living in your boxes based upon third-dimensional realities, conforming to the wills and wishes of others (even others lower and lesser than you), under the thumbs of religious systems, governments, and corporate employers of the Caligastia system, it is no wonder that all of you feel so frustrated. It is hard enough for the Eldership to understand Continuing Fifth Epochal Revelation. We can certainly understand why many of you, who are far away in other parts of the world, have difficulty with it.

For those of you who can somehow fuse your heart with your mind, it becomes a little easier to comprehend, and that is the key. If you try to understand Continuing Fifth Epochal Revelation at the state in which it is now, with transmissions coming to you in bits and pieces, and even the transmissions themselves seemingly not consistent in part, it is not because the truth is not the truth, but because those bringing this truth through on this human level simply do not have the necessary help to bring the accuracy needed to suit your own analytical minds.

Thank you for pointing out what needs to be pointed out. Thank you for seeing some of these inconsistencies, for they will be corrected and changed, for truth is truth and there should be no inconsistencies. But when you are trying to learn a new science, do not think that you can learn everything there is to learn about astrophysics, for example, in a week or two, a month, or even a year or several years' time. Try to write about it yourself without inconsistencies. In order for you to become a writer of astrophysics without inconsistencies, you would need help, and that is just a human science.

Consider cosmic science that we are trying to bring through one individual who has to wipe the faces of his children at times, change their diapers, listen to them whining and crying most of the day when his complement has to go out to help earn a living,[3] worry about the financial needs of others also in the community, try to publish books for which there is no money to publish them, worry about the housing of others who come to the community when they at times have no roof over their heads, and on and on.

So, in using this vessel who has this real concern for others (and if he did not, we would not use him), we go ahead at times and allow certain errors[4] with the full knowledge that if we stop the transmission every time, his mind will get into something else and we would get so far off track that we would not be able to bring the full transmission through in the context in which we would want it. That is just the way it is when using a mind in transmissions like we do. In order for it not to happen in this way, he would have to be in a trance and would have to read everything there is to read, and learn after the fact. There is much that is impressed upon his mind, coming through us to him, that helps him to learn at a higher rate far beyond the human potential, for we are able to synthesize much within his mind by him being conscious. If he were unconscious he would lose much.

It is hard to explain what we are trying to say. It is hard to give even the slightest of examples. Sometimes human words are simply inadequate, and that is another problem we have. It is not just the English language; any of the human languages are inadequate for explaining cosmic absolutes. Right now, we have chosen the English language because we know that it is the highest language on the planet of Urantia to present cosmic realities, but it is still incomplete and leaves much to be desired. Realizing the imperfection of this language, we work with it.

Another reality is that in the beginning, at a certain time on Urantia, we were not allowed to reveal some things concerning universal absolutes or cosmology correlating various universes and their names with your astronomy. Therefore, we allowed certain error to happen simply because we were not allowed to give certain information. We still are not allowed to give certain information. This will continue until the final **change point**, which means that there will continue to be inconsistencies, not because it is the human Gabriel of Urantia's/TaliasVan of Tora's fault, or the Elders' in transcribing; it is simply because this is the adjudication, and certain information will be given at certain levels, and various people will have various levels of understanding based upon what we choose to give them.

When the time comes for all of this information to be put into a book form such as *The URANTIA Book*,[5] it may well be after the final change point, and any inconsistencies that remain, whatever they may be, will be corrected. That will only be because any of the material corrected will then be allowed to be given for all on all levels on the planet, because all will then be deserving of this information. But at this time this is not the case on Urantia.

Speaking of contradictions, a Melchizedek states regarding the Caligastia One Hundred:

> In conformity to their instructions the staff did not engage in sexual reproduction, but they did painstakingly study their personal constitutions, and they carefully explored every imaginable phase of intellectual (mind) and morontia (soul) liaison. [*The URANTIA Book*, p. 744]

And again:

> The Prince's staff lived together as fathers and mothers. True, they had no children of their own, but the fifty pattern homes of Dalamatia never sheltered less than five hundred adopted little ones assembled from the superior families of the Andonic and Sangik races; many of these children were orphans. [*The URANTIA Book*, p. 750]

Yet a secondary Lanonandek Son of the reserve corps states:

> Many of the offspring of the ascenders of the Prince's materialized staff remained loyal, deserting the ranks of Caligastia. These loyalists were encouraged by the Melchizedek receivers of Urantia, and in later times their descendants did much to uphold the planetary concepts of truth and righteousness. The work of these loyal evangels helped to prevent the total obliteration of spiritual truth on Urantia. These courageous souls and their descendants kept alive some knowledge of the Father's rule and preserved for the world races the concept of the successive planetary dispensations of the various orders of divine Sons. [*The URANTIA Book*, p. 576]

You might also wish to refer to page 574 of *The URANTIA Book*.[6] I would appreciate knowing what conclusions you draw from these three statements and their seeming contradictions.

You should also know at this time that *The URANTIA Book* contains other contradictions. If you have not found them it is because you are not as good a student of *The URANTIA Book* as you think you are, for they do exist. These inconsistencies can be explained to those who would find these contradictions long before they would come to Continuing Fifth Epochal Revelation, by the statement made on page 1109 that indicates that *The URANTIA Book* is an incomplete revelation.[7]

It also should be noted at this time that reincarnation as it is understood in Eastern theology and philosophy is not a reality in Continuing Fifth Epochal Revelation. We tried to introduce an explanation of ovan souls and **repersonalization** procedures to the forum of souls in 1934–35 in preliminary papers, but they were already divided over many issues and further papers could not be given. Had we done so, it could very well have compromised the acceptance of many other key absolutes that we taught, which contradicted the Christianity that many of them had accepted. They were simply not able to handle any more changes in their thinking, and that could have actually caused the abandonment of the 196 papers they already had.

It was difficult for them to remain in some form of agreement as to the continuation of putting these papers into publication. It took another twenty years until there was enough synthesis among the members to even print what has become known as *The URANTIA Book*, and so there were certain statements made based upon the inability of those who resonated to accept what they read, and certain sentences were phrased by the Revelatory Commission with that in mind.

You are children, and you have to be treated as such. If you want higher cosmic absolute truth, then grow up. So long as you wish to stay in your boxes and keep your loved ones in their boxes, you will get what you deserve, and no more.

The First Planetary Sacred Home and the Eldership will always have the highest information, and even certain transmissions that may go out with inconsistencies, we will later correct in and through the Eldership. They will know the higher truth, but others may not, and they may not be allowed to correct the transmissions that others may have, or to notify them of the correction. Why? Because these others are not deserving to know. If you think that all higher truth and absolute truth is available to all on fallen worlds, you are absolutely incorrect. Truth in the hands of individuals with wrong motives, or who are iniquitous, or who are just ignorant is a very dangerous thing.

Some of the reasons why we have allowed some partial or incorrect statements to come through Gabriel of Urantia/TaliasVan of Tora and Niánn Emerson Chase are because they were so loving, so willing to give of what they learned that they gave it away freely, sometimes even though we warned them time and time again not to give this information to others. Even now, *The URANTIA Book*, which is published and can be acquired in the bookstores around the planet, should not be given to just anyone. We, in our own way, block the doors many times and block the minds of those who pick it up and do not deserve to have its contents. If it was the sole function of one of the higher personalities, such as seraphim, to just wait around in a metaphysical bookstore at a certain place on Urantia to do just that, as you might realize, it would be very boring. How would you like to work in a metaphysical bookstore on Second Avenue in Chicago? I think you get the idea.

So, we from our side ask for your very-much-needed human help in this case. We have our work to do on our side, and you have yours to do on yours. That is what cooperation from one side to the other is all about. It is a very serious business that there are personalities who are undeserving of the pearls that you may so easily cast before them. Did not Jesus call them swine?

Today on Urantia these swine have increased into herds, and they are all around you. They sit in positions of authority, and they are very active in the Urantia movement, in the other religious movements, and in the political arena; so you must be wise, and when you are not, we have to be.

The inconsistencies in the Continuing Fifth Epochal Revelation are, at this point, not as inconsistent as you may think. We do this to protect all of you, but we thank those who do notice these things for being students of Christ Michael and the Universal Father, for if you did not notice them it would mean that you are unconcerned, and it is good that you have gone this far to notice them. Most of the ones you point out, Eldership is already aware of, and it is they who have been in turmoil about these things long before you have noticed them, because they have to process all of this first.

How do you think the first readers [of *The URANTIA Book*] felt when the information came that Jesus was not born of a virgin? How do you think the Protestants and Catholics felt, who, in spite of all of their other disagreements, had come to agree on this one particular dogma, that Jesus was born of a virgin? How do you think that affected those devout Christians?

Even the fact that Jesus did not die for the sins of the world caused turmoil after turmoil and argument after argument as to the validity of *The URANTIA Book*. The fact that the apostles, as indicated in the papers indited by the Midwayer Commission, were not saints but such imperfect human personalities continually caused many disagreements and arguments. Why do you think that it took so long for the first part of the Fifth Epochal Revelation to be published? Why did it take almost fifty years?

At the present time we are asking four Elders to process information in a matter of weeks from when we bring through a transmission.[8] So if you receive a transmission that may have some inconsistency in it, forgive them and us please, and then make all appropriate moves in your life to come to Planetary Sacred Headquarters and help them. That would be what Christ Michael would want of you.

The answer to the question of whether the Pleiades are in the universe of Avalon or in the universe of Nebadon is simply information that we did not want anyone to have at that time. The information that the Pleiades are in the universe of Avalon was given to certain individuals for a reason. However, there will be those who still believe that the Pleiades are in Nebadon. These are individuals who we do not want to know where the Pleiades are, so we will not make this information available to them. They will not receive the literature from **The Starseed and Urantian Schools of Melchizedek** [now called the **Global Community Communications Schools**] concerning this statement or the teaching of these truths, for they will remain on the level of reality-acceptance where their lack of loyalty to Christ Michael has placed them.

Can they mistakenly be given information of higher truth by undiscerning givers such as yourself? Yes, they can, and when they do, other measures must be taken by us to confound them. Why do we do this? Because the adjudication is now taking place on Urantia and the good seed is being separated from the bad seed, the wheat from the chaff, for it is time for this to happen and you are part of it. If you are not a part of it on the level that we are trying to make you a part of it, then you do need prayer, because you are still part of the problem, and we will confound you. You can work within the clarity and loyalty of God, and yet you have a right to question, and you should, but be ever so careful in your judgment of what is happening at the First Planetary Sacred Home, for you will be so judged yourself.

The events that are about to happen on Urantia, and are already happening at a more rapid rate since my appointment in December 1989 as your present Planetary Prince, will continue to cause confusion on Urantia at all levels and to all people. We hope you can realize at this time the turmoil that is about to begin on Urantia, regarding the earth changes and other upheavals, which some speculate about and prophets to some degree have begun to warn about at various levels. Some of you who have read Paper 215 of *The Cosmic Family, Volume I* have doubts that this is true. You say that since God is a loving God and so are the representatives of God, how can this be? It is a loving God who has allowed these things to transpire. It is a loving God who does indeed correct and spank His children when they are disobedient, and to whatever degree that cause and effect places you over the knee of the Eternal Father, it is you yourself who have allowed it and you yourself who have asked for it.

When you are in a dark room and turn the light on, depending upon the quality of that light, you will see more or less. If it is a small 10-watt bulb, you will see little. If it is a bright bulb of 100 watts, you can see more. But if it is too bright—say 1,000 watts—you will be blinded, and you will actually see less than you would have with the 10-watt bulb. Many of you would like to have me, Machiventa Melchizedek, walk in personally. You would like to see Jesus come back and be able to see Him personally, or perhaps the Trinity Teacher Sons, or whoever you feel should appear in front of you to help you to become less the agondonter. The truth of the matter is that you do not see the serendipities that take place right before your very eyes, and if one of us did walk in, we would blind you. You are not ready for the 1,000-watt bulb. You can barely handle the 100-watt one. So, in whatever manner of reflectivity we speak to you, you still are not ready.

Do you not remember that it was Jesus who was crucified? The Creator Son of this universe you put on the cross, and now you say, "Come back again." You say you are ready for Him, or you are ready for me to materialize in my fullness as a Melchizedek, not as a human man as I did in Salem. Well, my friends, you are not ready, for even now you do not see the love of the human personalities of reflectivity who stand before you.

You are sent a picture of Gabriel of Urantia/TaliasVan of Tora in reflectivity of the Bright and Morning Star, you look at it, and what do you think? If you do not understand what is before your very eyes, what makes you think you will understand the brightness that will blind you? If you cannot see the love of God in those brothers and sisters who stand next to you, whom you can touch, why do you ask for the higher reflection of it? You do not treat the ones in front of you with admiration and respect.

We suggest you get a mirror and look at yourself. Take a long, long look and hopefully come to some conclusion as to your own imperfections, your own inadequacies, and your own inability to humble yourself to accept authority in your life; and that is the authority of mandated humans who have ascended to a higher reflectivity than what is in the mirror you are looking into. You want to be a material complement? Then I suggest that you respect the reflectivity of the ones who are presently on the planet. So be it.

July 9, 1992

Machiventa Melchizedek
in cooperation with the Bright and Morning Star of Salvington, for the implementation of the Divine Administration as ordered and assigned in purpose for the calling forth of the **Cosmic and Urantian Reserve Corps** by Christ Michael Himself

As transmitted through
the Pre-Level-One Audio Fusion Material Complement,
Gabriel of Urantia/TaliasVan of Tora

PAPER 229

Thought Adjusters In Relationship To Indwelling The 170,000,000 Interuniversal And Intrauniversal Ovan Souls In Relationship To The Present Adjudication Of The Bright And Morning Star Versus Lucifer In The System Of Satania And Incorporating Various Other Universes Affected By The Extension Of The Lucifer Rebellion

> . . . There are many interesting details which might be presented, but I withhold them upon the advice of your immediate planetary supervisors. But within the limits of my permission I can say this much: [*The URANTIA Book*, p. 1234]

IN the neighboring universes of time and space affected by the Rebellion, many of the ascending sons and daughters, who had been persuaded through mental telepathic communication into Luciferic reality, had already reached the first circle of attainment. Many of them had supreme self-acting Adjusters. Some of them had Adjusters that functioned in an unrevealed manner but were quite advanced. Many of them, who had reached the equivalent of Nebadon survival status, were eternalized (a partially unrevealed type of fusion that has to do with time-and-space memory activation and is completely different from Thought Adjuster fusion in that it is not a personality reality but a time–space factor). The implications of these statements are massive in context in relation to cosmic ascension science fact. Transitional reality in ovan soul experience had already begun for many of these souls. Ovan soul identification had developed. Again, we clarify, we are not speaking of the Nebadon experience.

An interuniversal meeting took place between the Creator Sons of each respective universe and the Ancients of Days of Orvonton, along with various Paradise-origin supervisors, as well as Divinington collaborators. Because of inherent cosmic laws in relation to the grand universe as it is known, similarity of rules had to be decided upon as a result of the Lucifer Rebellion in relation to what was transpiring in the mind factors of evolving mortals, influenced now by uncircuited and unresponsive reflectivity coordinations within the choice arena of these evolving free-will God realities. Here we are not just talking about evolutionary mortals in third-dimensional flesh forms. We are talking about morontia and higher body forms that are nonmaterial and more presently eternal.

A complete analysis of the factors of will needed to be augmented in relation to analysis of past eternity relationships as close as possible to the present set of circumstances caused by this particular rebellion. There were unknown factors. The divine presence within these evolving souls did not default. The evolving mortals themselves were not in rebellion by choice, but error eventualized, and to rectify and eliminate the situation it was decided that Satania would become the laboratory, as it was the source of the problem.

As has been previously stated [in *The Cosmic Family, Volume I*], many of the mortals were sent to satellite worlds, but upon transcendence from those worlds, nonphysical and spiritual reality—in relation to the ascension process of that particular Creator Son and the various Thought Adjusters involved—had to be correlated in a unique way with the overall plan and with the total harmony of all planets and systems where interuniversal damage took place.

Since the Thought Adjusters themselves did not default, and since many of the mortals themselves actually were not in default, great care was taken so that the mortals involved could more totally benefit without falling into default when presented with choices that they normally would not be presented with, due to the rearrangement not only of certain ascension processes, but the diversion of indwelling Thought Adjusters, and also the taking away of Thought Adjusters temporarily from some of them.

The majority of the 170,000,000 **starseed** on Urantia are of the fourth-order type, meaning that they fell into rebellion on another planet in a universe other than Nebadon but had supermortal ancestors who had been on Urantia. Many of the pre-personal Thought Adjusters who had become advanced Adjusters did not indwell these repersonalized mortals until at a certain point on Urantia the mortals came near to regaining the first estate of their former ascension before error entered their mind circuits. The seven adjutant mind spirits worked very closely with these individuals, as did the Holy Spirit, and after Pentecost, the Spirit of Truth. But except for a few of them, they did not regain their Thought Adjusters until after the year 1955 of the present era on Urantia. The majority of the 170,000,000 still have not received their former Thought Adjusters, although they communicate by an unrevealed process working with seraphim, as far as the ministry of indwelling goes. This cosmic fact also applies to **second-time Urantians** who are here because of the adjudication. Even the apostles who are presently back on Urantia must re-receive their Thought Adjusters as well as the Holy Spirit and the Spirit of Truth. Those who have aligned themselves with the Machiventa Melchizedek Administration thus far have re-received their Thought Adjusters.

> In varying degrees and increasingly as you ascend the psychic circles, sometimes directly, but more often indirectly, you do communicate with your Adjusters. But it is dangerous to entertain the idea that every new concept originating in the human mind is the dictation of the Adjuster. More often, in beings of your order, that which you accept as the Adjuster's voice is in reality the emanation of your own intellect. This is dangerous ground, and every human being must settle these problems for himself in accordance with his natural human wisdom and superhuman insight. [*The URANTIA Book*, p. 1208]

Many ovan souls on Urantia, who have higher clairvoyant abilities and telepathic power, are beginning to tap into past memory circuits in relation to certain cosmic realities. They misinterpret this as the voice of their Thought Adjuster or even a separate entity speaking to them. This is dangerous ground because they do open the door for rebellious forces who can subsequently influence them in a negative manner. Once the mind/soul tampers with the unknown factors of time and space, it, in a sense, leaves the body and allows another entity to enter the human mind circuit. Even if that individual prays to Christ Michael for protection and is not a mandated personality, he or she is open to certain cosmic accidents that were set into motion when this previously mentioned interuniversal council took place.

> . . . Those mortals who ascend without Adjusters are dependent on the instruction of seraphic associates for the reconstruction of human memory; otherwise the morontia souls of the Spirit-fused mortals are not limited. The pattern of memory persists in the soul, but this pattern requires the presence of the former Adjuster to become *immediately* self-realizable as continuing memory. Without the Adjuster, it requires considerable time for the mortal survivor to re-explore and relearn, to recapture, the memory consciousness of the meanings and values of a former existence. [*The URANTIA Book*, pp. 1236–1237]

Those ovan souls, who are now beginning to re-receive their Thought Adjusters and become more uniquely infused, may begin to have certain memories of past repersonalizations activated. This will happen more precisely to the **First Cosmic Family** of particular pair-unit classification.

> . . . The living cosmos is an all but infinitely integrated aggregation of real units, all of which are relatively subject to the destiny of the whole. But those that are personal have been endowed with the actual choice of destiny acceptance or of destiny rejection. [*The URANTIA Book*, p. 1232]

This brief statement by a Solitary Messenger is in reference to the cosmic family, and more particularly, to **pair-unit classifications** that are more genetically linked to the Material Sons and Daughters of their respective planets of origin. Some of these pair units are genetically linked, not only to the Adam and Eve of this planet, Urantia, but to Material Sons and Daughters of other planets. This **Deo-atomic** inheritance and interuniversal ovan-soul reality creates the morontia oversoul of unique characteristics.

> ... In the physical life, mortals may be outwardly beautiful though inwardly unlovely; in the morontia life, and increasingly on its higher levels, the personality form will vary directly in accordance with the nature of the inner person. On the spiritual level, outward form and inner nature begin to approximate complete identification, which grows more and more perfect on higher and higher spirit levels. [*The URANTIA Book*, p. 1236]

As Urantia comes closer to the final **change point**, those **complementary polarities** and those ovan souls now joined in integrated relationships, in the union of souls within the present Machiventa Melchizedek Administration on the human side, will begin to exhibit physical changes now more inherent to the inward spiritual selfhood. This light-body manifestation is, in Nebadon, an inheritance of the first mansion world and above. Those ovan souls of other universes also will begin to incorporate within the mind circuits certain behavior patterns that are more indigenous to their respective universes and to the cultures on their particular planets of origin. This realization of identity transition is the birth of the ovan soul.

> ... And thus does the material and mortal reality of the self transcend the temporal limitations of the physical-life machine and attain a new expression and a new identification in the evolving vehicle for selfhood continuity, the morontia and immortal soul. [*The URANTIA Book*, p. 1218]

The Mystery Monitors are not thought helpers; they are thought adjusters. They labor with the material mind for the purpose of constructing, by adjustment and spiritualization, a new mind for the new worlds and the new name of your future career. [*The URANTIA Book*, p. 1191]

Many ovan souls are now beginning to come into a cosmic consciousness, and coming into this cosmic consciousness, they also begin to experience memories in relation to past repersonalizations on Urantia. Many of them begin to adopt names suitable to those persons they were in the past or adopt names that are more resonant with who they were before their cosmic fall; and in going backward they eventually create, in their mind circuit, a forward process as they tap into an essence of their cosmic selfhood before the fall.

Only the **Mandate of the Bright and Morning Star** can determine the spiritual identifications of those individuals. The individuals themselves can resonate with various names that may be very close in sound or feeling to that cosmic identification, and some psychics can be used at various levels for these purposes. But only the Mandate of the Bright and Morning Star can properly spiritually identify the cosmic identification name.

As an Adam becomes the firstborn seed of a higher genetic linkage through his offspring and begins to properly name animal and plant life in relation to cosmic identification, incorporating cosmic physics and biology, so does the Bright and Morning Star Mandate incorporate spiritual identification in ascension science ovan-soul reality.

As ascending sons and daughters, mortals of various universes are classified in pair-unit classifications as to ancestral identification, both spiritually and quite physically as to **famotor movement**, so too, the ancestry of the Thought Adjusters in relation to those mortals is classified. This is a classification of absoluteness in relation to the Supreme and Absolute Being in experiential time and space.

The absoluteness is part of the divine mind—the First Source and Center, the Universal Father—and separate from the Second and Third Sources and Centers. It is pre-existent reality in relation to experiential reality. It is the fusion of the past and the present in relation to the evolutionary realms of time and space. It is time factor in relation to evolutionary ascension within the union of souls of evolutionary creatures and Divinington fragments. It is the romance of the Father with the evolutionary creatures of time and space, in separate but coordinately classified groupings of these various fragments of advanced Adjusters in the first beginning stages of light and life and above, and onward into semi-spirit and spirit reality and then finaliter reality.

> And yet, while the Adjusters utilize the material-gravity circuits, they are not subject thereto as is material creation. The Adjusters are fragments of the ancestor of gravity, not the consequentials of gravity; they have segmentized on a universe level of existence which is hypothetically antecedent to gravity appearance. [*The URANTIA Book*, p. 1183]

On the lower evolutionary worlds of time and space—particularly on defaulted worlds, and in particular Urantia, with its vast array of interuniversal varieties of mortals with ovan-soul reality, intermingled with transitional administrative entities (beings who more or less are now resident in a higher dimension from another world as part of the Planetary Prince's staff)—the uniqueness of experience can be more perfectly romanced, in relation to cosmic reality, when each individual begins to realize perfection as opposed to coincidence, Providence as opposed to chance, and divine choice as opposed to happenstance.

Perfection is a pre-existent reality. Imperfection is a freewill choice of incorrect decision. Perfection is inner harmony with divine prerogative; imperfection is disharmony with pre-existent choice in divine matters. Moment-to-moment positive choices create moment-to-moment perfection. Moment-to-moment bad choices create moment-to-moment imperfection and unreality. Future transmissions will incorporate Thought Adjuster perfection and divine reality in relation to the First Cosmic Family, relative to all seven cosmic families.

When ascending sons and daughters can become integrated at any one level, particularly in liaison with Celestial Overcontrol, factors of pure energy, pure spirit, and single-mindedness, coordinating with divine perfection, can become actualized. The fusion of the perfection of Divinington becomes coordinate with mortals of cosmic discretion working in cooperation with other universe associates of Deity.

That union of souls who are no longer fragmentized begins to create the factual presence of God the Threefold, and on Urantia, begins to create the ethereal city. They begin to create the ethereal throne; they begin to create the ethereal administration that, on Urantia, becomes the **Planetary Sacred Headquarters** or the **First Planetary Sacred Home** that will totally embrace and receive the **New Jerusalem**, in which Michael Himself will reign. The cooperation within the union of souls of evolutionary mortals on an evolutionary world of time and space calls forth first the higher orders of beings from the various headquarters worlds of the system and universe, or universes, and then, when this **auhter** community is on a cosmic level, it calls forth the very Creator Son who is closest in light-years distance. In this case, Urantia beckons Michael; and the arrival of Christ Michael is very much dependent upon the integrated choices and decisions of those starseed on Urantia and Urantians alike, who cooperate together under cosmic law and cosmic absolutes, in which the Creator Son Himself can integrate and transcend.

March 19, 1992

Paladin, Chief of Finaliters
in cooperation with a Solitary Messenger of Orvonton, and in liaison with a Universal Censor of Havona. This transmission is

given to further awaken the Cosmic Reserve Corps, for the implementation of the administration of the present Planetary Prince, Machiventa Melchizedek, and to call forth those personalities who need to be mandated for various administrative functions

As transmitted through
the Pre-Level-One Audio Fusion Material Complement,
Gabriel of Urantia/TaliasVan of Tora

PAPER 230

Kinetic Energy In Relationship To Auhter Energy In Relationship To Mind-Gravity Circuits In The Implementation Of The Divine Administration In Correlation With The Present Planetary Prince, Machiventa Melchizedek, And In Further Relationship To The Cosmic Reserve Corps And The Urantian Reserve Corps Of Destiny

IN previous transmissions auhter energy is described as the force created by the alignment first of ovan souls with the purposes of the Creator Son to usher in the first stages of light and life on Urantia or on any other fallen planet. This measurable energy can also be defined in a human scientific manner as a form of kinetic energy.

> Kinetic: of or relating to the motion of material bodies and the forces and energy associated therewith

> Kinetic energy: energy associated with motion

> Kinetics: **1 a**: a branch of science that deals with the effects of forces upon the motions of material bodies or with changes in a physical or chemical system **b**: the rate of change in such a system **2**: the mechanism by which a physical or chemical change is effected

> Kinetic theory: either of two theories in physics based on the fact that minute particles of a substance are in vigorous motion: **a**: a theory that the particles of a gas move in straight lines with high average velocity, continually encounter one another and thus change their individual velocities and directions, and cause pressure by their impact against the walls of a container—called also *kinetic theory of gases*

b: a theory that the temperature of a substance increases with an increase in either the average kinetic energy of the particles or the average potential energy of separation (as in fusion) of the particles or in both when heat is added—called also *kinetic theory of heat*[1]

Kinetic fusion in the **ascension science** process is the fusion of the union of souls of the third or fourth dimensions from one side to another. It is a closer link in the communication process between the seen and unseen personalities of time and space. Just because something is not seen does not mean it is not there. The atoms exist, but they are not seen. Personalities exist who are not seen, and yet they are totally present; but because you are not accustomed to visualizing them on this planet, your reality factor is void of encompassing them into your decision-making and your reality field. On planets where default has not occurred, normal communication exists even with unseen presences of personality status.

In the communication from one side to the other, from a higher dimension to a lower one, a form of motion needs to take place that combines the unseen atoms into certain groupings that create a certain kind of usable energy communication field. These fields have been labeled by some in metaphysical realities of the past and the present as band fields. Of course they did not understand what a communication band truly is. Some have improperly interpreted these bands as star routes. It has nothing to do with interplanetary communication. Interplanetary communication is another topic.

Interdimensional communication is a fusion of auhter energy with kinetic energy that creates motion, and in this motion, communication can be received by those ascended souls capable of such transmission, either by pure impression, or, as in the case of this transmission, **audio motion**. The process functioning in such communication is done in and through a scientific process called **automaton communication**, which includes such aspects as **automaton** *sounding, automaton sequence,* and *automaton coding,* the details of which are not the subject of this transmission. This automaton communication can happen to hundreds of thousands, and even to millions, of individuals on any one planet where default has not occurred. It is just as normal as present-day Urantians picking up a telephone and talking to someone on the other side of the planet.

I will give a general definition regarding automaton communication. In relation to the higher orders of creatures, those in administrative positions and process, it is the ability to tap into an automatic transmitting circuitry of inter- and intraplanetary, system, universal, and superuniversal broadcasts, much like tapping into a computer network, such as the Internet. It is not direct communication from personality to personality, as is mental telepathy.

Certain mandates from universe headquarters are given in relation to very specific decision-making, having to do with major decisions and their outworking in individual lives, from evolutionary worlds to universe headquarters worlds and upwards. Because God the Supreme is evolving, this automaton communication is also ever changing, ever active, and necessary, particularly for lower beings, to make available another link with universe administration that is untouchable, unseen, yet ever present in the realm of authority. However, higher administrators such as Lanonandek Sons could override the automaton communication within their jurisdiction but not outside of it.

For most people, sound may be heard but not felt, but to the more spiritual, sound can also be felt, and this reflective sense is available to transfigure a body form into visual observation where a sound becomes visual to the eyes through a higher nonmaterial thought communication. It is also sound, for thoughts vibrate and resonate at a measurable and discernible sound level. This is why certain psychic clairvoyants are able to ascertain certain things. They actually are picking up sound patterns, and it is being registered in the interpretation circuits through the ears and to the central nervous system. The pineal gland incorporates a certain kinetic motion, which to the higher sensitive who is also the higher spiritual, registers as a very clear image.

Sound, again, is visual, and this is why great musicians create images with their music compositions. In the orchestras of time and space at higher levels, sound can create physical matter, and when it is used by higher spirit personalities in conjunction with divine mandates, it proceeds from the First Source and Center in conjunction with alignment with the Conjoint Actor to one of the Seven Master Spirits, then to specific personalities of Paradise origin (presently located in any of the seven superuniverses), and then to any of the universes in which architectural worlds are to be engineered and established. This construction is all done through the use of Paradise sound. Many implications of this process take place as to color and substance of organic matter. The force of auhter energy created by the **First Cosmic Family** can be a force to change kinetic motion of the masses of individuals on an entire planet.

The Master Architects of time and space are not just architects, they are also artists. One cannot be one without the other. The higher Master Architects (and there are levels) are the great composers of physical matter.[2] They incorporate the harmonious melodic patterns of **Deo-atomic reality** and fuse them with pre-existent substance of a nonlife variety. On the lower evolutionary worlds where very few ascending mortals can coordinate one side of the brain with the other, great imbalances occur between artists and engineers when in reality great harmony should occur. This is due to many reasons inherent in the Lucifer Rebellion and in the misuse of talents and abilities outside of one's genetic inheritance, either cosmic or planetary native.

Alignment of thought processes outside of divine mind is self-assertion and operates solely in the process of self-gratification. Therefore, evolution of the soul, which is a kinetic response in relationship to God-purpose, cannot happen. The purposes of God are in relation to the brother-/sisterhood of humankind and the benefit of the whole. Thus, on Urantia you have billions of personalities operating in self-assertion, and even though the majority of them may be good and decent personalities, they have not learned to fuse themselves with the divine mind as opposed to cultural and evolutionary religious practices.

This has created nationalism and various cults within cults, all segregated, down to the individual who cannot even find his or her place within the subgroups of various societies. This becomes more commonplace in civilizations where affluence is prevalent, where more and more recreation is available, and where laziness takes the place of spiritual quest. Where the ease of life is misunderstood to be the luxury of self-indulgence, the divine purposes of God cannot be realized by the mass community and by those individuals who have accepted certain realities and have grown accustomed to believing in them.

The majority of individuals on Urantia would fight and die for their realities, even though they are not happy in them. This has long been the case on Urantia and is a unique phenomenon of ignorance and downright stupidity. Those of higher ascendancy, who for whatever reason are able to break away from the lower standards of lesser minds, may find themselves quite isolated and may even begin to think themselves crazy, as has been the case with many ovan souls in past centuries.

In the educational system of today, particularly in Western civilization and more specifically in the United States of America, genius personalities have often been labeled as slow learners and slow achievers because they do not function within the standards set. The standards set are based upon group variables of a left-brain variety and, to be more exact, are based upon an analytical approach to logical process where the intuitive is not realized, and where the intuitive cannot even find its place in the thought process. Those in the early grades may be quite accomplished in the mathematical process, yet insensitive enough to tear the wings off a butterfly or may not be able to understand a piece of art by a master artist even in its simplicity of approach in the visual.

The coordination of the circuits from the Infinite Spirit with the reception of these circuits by individuals on Urantia at this time on the planet is imperative, but the reality is that the reception of these circuits is being blocked by the "higher education" in the universities of this world. In regard to learning for the higher orders of starseed, the complications are immense. They may be labeled in the early years as slow achievers and be actually held back from their destiny purposes of God, even to the point of never achieving the actualization of their destiny. This has occurred on Urantia with many ovan souls time and time again, all because those in positions of authority did not recognize these children and neither did their own parents, who are themselves either younger souls or souls who were iniquitous or in error and trapped in the system of Caligastia and Lucifer.

Throughout the hundreds of thousands of years since the Lucifer Rebellion, Celestial Overcontrol has not been able to fuse auhter energy with kinetic motion from your dimension to ours, in order to create the first stages of light and life on Urantia, up until now, with the alignment of the First Cosmic Family that is happening at **Planetary Sacred Headquarters**, where these individuals have been brought together.

These same individuals have repersonalized together in other centuries but were not able to step out of the system together long enough, as a group; nor could they create the necessary motion to change the masses while they lived. Usually they would have to separate, and when they separated and went their various ways on the planet, the force of the auhter energy could not be obtained from our side to yours, for even where well-intentioned separation takes place, a form of error occurs; thus was the default of Adam and Eve. It is of utmost importance that those separated units of higher mindal capacities and ascension soul status—who understand these words and can resonate with this kinetic motion that will evolve the morontia soul—help create this auhter energy by aligning themselves spiritually and physically at the **First Planetary Sacred Home** of the Machiventa Melchizedek Administration.

Greatness of purpose for any soul cannot be found outside of the calling of God. Providential reality at this time on Urantia can only be found in the purposes of the present implementation of the planetary administration, and it begins in recognition of the **Continuing Fifth Epochal Revelation** and of those human mandated personalities who are Elders and who function under the overcontrol of celestial personalities on our side. This motion that is taking place is unique on this decimal planet called Urantia and will eventually create the kinetic band that will either bring the Trinity Teacher Sons to this planet or will bring Michael Himself. Here we are not talking about thousands of years, nor are we talking about hundreds of years. We may possibly be talking about just a few years of Urantia time.

You, who may be on the cosmic fence of mind and heart, must fuse the one with the other and give your total loyalty to Christ Michael and His Spirit of Truth, which will most imperatively resonate with the words of this transmission. You are part of a great mechanism and, indeed, of a master plan. The master plan will take place with or without you, but you can greatly hinder the timing of this master plan for easing the pain of your brothers and sisters of Urantia.

As to your suffering on Urantia, in Havona time this may perhaps be a blink of the eye, but we would prefer that this suffering be ended, and the only way it can be done in less time, with less suffering to the people of your planet, is that individuals like yourselves begin to make the right decisions and choose your alignment with the higher purposes of God, wherein your talents, abilities, and material possessions can be used for the greatest good of all on this planet. We very clearly state that this is the calling to the First Planetary Sacred Home where you first must become a student of Continuing Fifth Epochal Revelation and then, perhaps, a mandated personality yourself, for you may also go out to another location on Urantia and help create the motion necessary to reach the hundreds, perhaps millions of individuals, who can only be reached because you first made the right decisions. It is written: "The act is ours; the consequences God's." [*The URANTIA Book*, p. 556]

If you take the steps of faith necessary, you can fulfill your own destiny, and self-fulfillment and self-actualization will be realized in your life. It begins with acting upon the words of this transmission, and it begins a new life that will become a reality when your physical body finds itself at Planetary Sacred Headquarters, where you find yourself to be a student.

Do not think that your present understanding of *The URANTIA Book* as being a complete revelation is sufficient or that your position in the Urantia movement is one recognized by God. The way to self-discovery is through humility. Our prayer to Michael is that you continue your ascension process by recognizing your need to become a student of Continuing Fifth Epochal Revelation, which will not be available to you unless you recognize those who are mandated to be your teachers, both human and nonhuman alike, at **The Starseed and Urantian Schools of Melchizedek** [now called the **Global Community Communications Schools**].

If this transmission finds itself within your eyesight, it is because in some manner you have requested it. You must continue to request or you will not continue to receive. It is that simple. Continuing Fifth Epochal Revelation, although necessary for the masses, is not to be made available to them until individuals like yourselves make it possible. It will be made available to the masses, and it is hoped that millions will benefit from these revelations. It is our sincere and optimistic prayer that these revelations can be given to the masses when enough of you on your side have created the kinetic motion and auhter energy in which the grace of God can be bestowed to anyone on the planet.

March 23, 1992

Paladin, Chief of Finaliters
in cooperation with the Master Physical Controller responsible for the content of this transmission, for the implementation of the architectural design already in motion for the New Jerusalem that will be realized at the First Planetary Sacred Home within the Machiventa Melchizedek Administration some time after the final change point

As transmitted through
the Pre-Level-One Audio Fusion Material Complement,
Gabriel of Urantia/TaliasVan of Tora

PAPER 231

Mandates, The Power Of Recognition In Relationship To Circuit Reflectivity And Other Interuniversal Headquarters Circuits Of Deotonic Reality Pertaining To The Administrative Organizational Flow Of Grand Universe Functional Procedure

TRYING to communicate destiny purpose and destiny function, from higher morontia mota constellation reality and superuniverse **Deotonic** levels, to evolutionary mortals is almost impossible. And particularly on defaulted worlds it is extremely difficult for the higher purposes of divine mandates to be actualized and for divine realities to become common realities on these planets. On these defaulted worlds, **Deontology** (the theory or study of moral obligation) is either an unknown factor or understood by only those who are students of theology and ethics.

Urantia, which has been functioning for thousands of years under principles other than divine, has created a reality within a Luciferic pattern where true beauty and humility are lost to force and power, wealth and prestige. The true ideals of success have been lost to social standards of false values and principles. Morality and spirituality are based upon materialistic values, and because of the use of capital for the transference of goods and services, **Deotonic reality** is almost unknown on Urantia, and where it is understood and practiced, it is out of balance. In the superuniverse of Orvonton, Deotonic reality is a recognition of the spiritual authority of another personality of higher ascension and that individual's reaction to the mandate of the higher personality regarding the acceptance of certain decisions that may be contrary to one's own.

Lucifer, in his fall from authority, lost true authority when he disassociated himself from Deotonic reality. He did not lose all authority, as there were many billions who recognized his self-proclaimed authority. This authority still continues over those in rebellion who do not recognize universal truth and universal law, and so those who are in deception—and on Urantia this includes the majority of Urantians—continue to function in cosmic unreality.

Deotonic authority cannot be implemented, for those on Urantia have grown accustomed to giving their loyalty to false teachers and leaders. They do not recognize true spirituality or true leadership, and in the higher civilizations the problem can actually be intensified. The fact that the Creator Son of your universe was crucified by those who did not recognize who He was is a prime example of the state of your planet.

In the twentieth century great leaders have also been silenced, by assassination (such as Gandhi, Martin Luther King, Jr., and the Kennedys); or their publications have been kept from the general public; or they have not been recognized by their peers; or they are suppressed by others who would keep them from recognition. This is because those who are in power in any field of endeavor are there basically outside of the will of God, for one cannot be in the perfect will of God and remain in that present system.

That is why Jesus set the example 2,000 years ago when He avoided those who wished to place Him in political authority. There is nothing wrong with politics so long as politics are divinely coordinated, for governmental process should be a divine mandate. But when those in the political arena are governed by the wills of corporations based upon profit and greed, the divinely mandated cannot become functional, and whatever good is done within those governments fluctuates and can even be eliminated upon the whims of humans. Food and medicine should be free to all on this planet, provided those who receive these services and substances equally return their talents to the good of the whole.

In societies where capital gain and prestige are the reality, true benevolence is rarely found, and social needs cannot be met. Great revolutions on this planet, particularly since the industrial revolution, have only resulted in governments being replaced by other corrupt governments because there have been no great leaders connected to the divine mind to implement divine administration and because the mass consciousness of the people of those countries were themselves out of the will of God as individuals. Might does not make right, and the majority does not make right. In a democracy where the majority of individuals are in the lower consciousness, the electoral process means very little, for if two men are running, the higher spiritual one will not be elected because the people will vote based upon lower values.

On the lower evolutionary worlds of time and space and even into the stages of light and life, divine administration can only be functional when leaders can be chosen in cooperation with divine mandate. In this sense, divine choosing must be understood by evolutionary choosing. This can only be done when the majority of the masses can properly hear from God and God's messengers. On planets of default this becomes most difficult. Divine authority does not force itself; it just is. It functions.

Throughout the ages on Urantia, individuals with divine authority have continued to be crucified in one way or another. When this begins to cease, Urantia can heal itself. But the problems have become so immense that without an international change in consciousness, where true spiritual leaders can be recognized and all citizens on this planet become less nationalistic and more like planetary citizens who hear from the one Cosmic Father of all, divine administration cannot come to Urantia. Perhaps it can begin to come with a small group first, a subculture, and that is what we are trying to implement at the **First Planetary Sacred Home** where the present Planetary Prince, Machiventa Melchizedek, functions in Deotonic reality.

Most Urantians have grown accustomed to self-assertion, so much so that they question those whom God puts before them in leadership capacity, even when they do recognize these leaders to some degree. Perhaps it may be a godly husband or a godly employer. Urantians have grown accustomed to accepting what they want to hear and not what they need to hear or what displeases them. When something displeases them, all of a sudden the trust they had in their superior yesterday is complete mistrust today. In the present system, trust is bought and paid for. Perhaps your livelihood depends upon your obedience to those you do not trust, and even though you obey, you obey with your minds and not with your hearts.

In the kingdom of God, the heart and mind must join in cohesion with divine authority. In reality, the heart is the circuit of the Father authority, and mind realizes that authority.

On Urantia the majority of employers do not function within the divine mind. Throughout the history of Urantia this could only be done in subcultures or subgroups away from the main structures of society, in certain monastic circles such as monasteries or other religious institutions where ecclesiastic leadership was trusted and obeyed. Because of this respect for ecclesiastic leadership, great strides have been made for humanity, and much good has been done within these religious institutions, according to the degree of spiritual leadership's ability to actually hear from Celestial Overcontrol. At whatever level this communication was the highest, and is now the highest, determines the ability of these groups to do the most good for the people of Urantia.

The highest purpose of any subculture is in the service of all humankind. A subculture that exists primarily for itself cuts itself off from divine prerogative. The power that a subculture will have to do good, even if the subculture is in the highest communication to God and His divine administration, is dependent upon the mass consciousness of the planet.

This is the state of present-day Urantia, and this is why a total change is necessary by the people of this planet within all the governments of this world. The chance of this happening in the way it should happen is very low on the cosmic providence level. It is increasingly an obvious presumption that the mass cleansing must take place on Urantia for true change to come, and the way of cleansing and purification is tribulation, suffering, and death. This has been observable for the last 200,000 years of Urantia time.

It seems that first-time Urantian souls, and even the ovan souls who have had to continually come back here, are stuck in a static spirituality based upon obstinacy, complacency, and misplaced loyalties. True wisdom is a divine gift that can only be given to certain individuals, and then at various levels, those with the highest of mindal capacities are limited in what they can do for their planet, for your planet is not ready to receive them, nor is it ready to receive its Creator Son again.

Many wish Jesus to return to Urantia. Where do they wish Him to sit as King of Kings and Lord of Lords? In Rome? In Salt Lake City? In Tibet? In Israel? In Mecca? In Chicago? To what kind of mass consciousness should the Creator Son now return? And, if Machiventa Melchizedek made himself visible, who would even know who he is? Would not those in the governments of this world try to kill him to keep their power? Should Machiventa Melchizedek command obedience from the masses? Should he force his power upon the people of this planet? What is power to those who do not recognize his beauty?

Beauty is void of form to those who do not recognize goodness, and love has no meaning. Many confuse love with dependency, want love without discipline, and understand love only within the context of false and unbridled liberty and self-assertion. Power and authority of God—although powerful in what it could do to those who would not respect it—usually, and particularly in the superuniverse of Orvonton, is respectful of the ignorance of those who cannot, or choose not to, recognize or perceive it.

Each system within each universe has its timetable for the relinquishment of rebellion. Each planet within those systems can achieve harmony with the divine mandates independent of those other planets of rebellion, and at a more rapid rate than others, but for each planet of rebellion there is a timetable for the end of disobedience. This is so because of cosmic laws of cause and effect, effects that are detrimental not only to the inhabitants of the planet but to the physical structure of the planet itself. Evil, sin, and iniquity will completely destroy a physical planet over a period of time, and one way or another this is a cosmic absolute.

Urantia is very near that absolute. When the majority of ignorant and complacent people of Urantia do not see reality, they think that humans can solve the problems of humankind, and they tear down one government and then follow leaders just as confused or iniquitous as those who preceded them.

When total Truth stood before Pilate:

> ... Then said Pilate: "... Do you not realize that I still have power to release you or to crucify you?" Then said Jesus: "You could have no power over me except it were permitted from above. You could exercise no authority over the Son of Man unless the Father in heaven allowed it." [*The URANTIA Book*, p. 1996]

What authority do you follow? Who gives you your authority? To whom do you give authority? If truth stood before you and asked you to make changes in your life and your reality, how would you respond? Does your loyalty have to be paid for? Do you respect wealth, power, prestige, or higher education? Are you concerned about the suffering of others? Do you feel that you are doing all that you can to ease the pain of the people of this planet, or do you think that there is nothing you can do about it yourself? To whom do you give allegiance? If a god came down from the heavens and pointed his hand toward human leadership, would you follow those human leaders, or would you expect Christ Michael to stay here indefinitely on Urantia? Do you have to be forced to obedience? If so, is that true obedience?

The apostles of Jesus and the first disciples and followers did not follow great wealth, worldly power, or prestige. They followed the Spirit of Truth, the same Spirit of Truth that is available to follow now on Urantia. The people who followed this Spirit of Truth looked to the apostles for leadership, for they had walked and talked with Jesus. Divinely mandated leadership continues on present-day Urantia, but it cannot be found in the religious or political institutions of humans. As it began on Salvington in the headquarters of Nebadon, it begins in the present era preceding the first stage of light and life on Urantia at the First Planetary Sacred Home and with a group of individuals with human leaders.

So it was with Paradise and through time and space with the experiential gods. And so it is on Urantia where the divine mind first proclaims its will to humankind within the supreme mandates of God the Supreme, fused with the Creator Son of Nebadon in cooperation with the Bright and Morning Star—the first creation of the Creator Son and the Universe Mother Spirit—within Deotonic alignment from the Ancients of Days and proceeding to system reality and the System Sovereign, Lanaforge, to planetary reality within the administration of Machiventa Melchizedek, the present Planetary Prince, to the human mortal side where these divine mandates can be implemented on an evolutionary mortal level. This is the way of the master universe.

As all truth is and ever will be, these truths are powerful and self-actualizing and individually adhered to by those obedient to divine ordinances that every Thought Adjuster within the minds of men and women adheres to and communicates to its human subjects to understand and follow. This is a gentle persuasion. It is a persuasion of the heart (the Father circuit) with the Universe Mother (the root circuit) that will bring total and complete balance to each individual who hears this complementary message and coordinate Aquarian reality.

March 30, 1992

Paladin, Chief of Finaliters
in cooperation with a Solitary Messenger in the implementation of the Divine Administration of Machiventa Melchizedek, present Planetary Prince, in the calling forth of the Cosmic and Urantian Reserve Corps of Destiny for the adjudication of Urantia

As transmitted through
the Pre-Level-One Audio Fusion Material Complement,
Gabriel of Urantia/TaliasVan of Tora

PAPER 232

The Three Meridian Circuits In Relationship To The Morontia Body Correlated With The Seven Circuits Of The Lower Body In Reference To Clairvoyant Telepathic Planetary Function And Intrauniversal And Interuniversal Circulatory Administrative Broadcasts

THIS is the first of a series of transmissions that will deal specifically with the circuits within the light body, particularly in the **ovan souls**, which gives more insight into communicative abilities within the ascension process from one personality to another, from one place to another, and from one time zone to another. It is the opening up of the lower circuits with the addition of the three **meridian circuits**, which is now a part of the adjudication process for those sons and daughters of God who are coming out of the third dimension to fourth-dimensional and above reality.

Usually this information is reserved for the morontia sojourn but is available now for those with the mental capacity to understand and the spiritual acquiescence to complement it. The study itself, concerning any one of the ten circuits that we will mention in this series of transmissions, extends to the constellation universities. And even in the Havona worlds, information is known about these circuits at varying levels, and we can only give information to evolutionary mortals at varying degrees of revelatory allowance.

We begin first with a circle, which can be defined as a closed curve where every point is the same distance from the center or a series ending where it began, especially when perpetually repeated, such as a cycle. It has been surmised by metaphysicians and theologians, as well as certain stargazers, astronomers, and astrologers, that the circle is a symbol of infinity, and to many the circle is a symbol of God and completeness. To higher celestial personalities it is a completeness of force or energy that the First Source and Center, the existential God, has manifested to the experiential God in all of the master universe.

To the personalities of the beings created, manifestation of God is circulatory reality, meaning that every entity of time and space discovers itself in relation to the origin of its Creator and the thoughts of that Creator, who was in existence before the entity itself became organic or inorganic matter. There are life forms such that you know not of that are inorganic, not carbon-based.

In a sense, as beings become more God-realized, they become more centripetal in spiritual motion, which creates an interuniversal harmonic pattern that resonates with one of the sacred spheres of Paradise. This study is an eternal one.

Physical planets, although not completely round or circular, are designed to become circular over a period of time during the higher stages of light and life. Although Paradise itself is elliptical in form, the closer to circular exactness a planet becomes, the closer is the linkage to nether Paradise and other physical energies inherent in the grand universe; so the physical shape of a planet is also responsive to the nether Paradise circuits. This has nothing to do with the individuals on a planet, but it can influence the evolutionary process of the mortals of that planet. Architectural worlds are designed in circular perfection and so are the individual circuits within the bodies of all ascending sons/daughters and descending beings of differing orders.

The ancient Tibetans began to receive information about these circuits that they labeled chakras, for they saw them somewhat like a wheel or like a flower with petals. The teachings of the Tibetans about chakras, or circuits, were at the kindergarten level in relation to true cosmic reality for the use of these circuits, and throughout the years on Urantia, very little new information has been given until this transmission. It is true that the seven circuits are attached in some manner to the physical glands of the flesh body and perhaps to the inner body organs, which then correspond in totality to the circulatory systems of the body.

As the grand universe functions within a circulatory system, so do the bodies of all created personalities. To the degree of ascension in the perfection of the first circle of Paradise is the degree of the massive complexity of circuitry in the relationship of one particular body to the First Source and Center and then outward to the grand universe itself.

All of this evolutionary process, ad infinitum, is totally realized within the circle of the reality of God the Ultimate and God the Absolute. In relationship with evolutionary human mortals, each of the seven circuits of the third-dimensional body and the subcircuits within the main seven circuits are related to the seven superuniverses, to individual universes within the seven superuniverses, and to individual systems, particularly to headquarters worlds of the systems. Depending upon circumstantial cosmic reality, which is actually Providential and not coincidental, the use of these circuits is a divine prerogative, yet it is also a divine inheritance. (Notice, please, in the use of various words that I have been transmitting, I have been keeping in harmony with the words circle and circuits. It would, perhaps, benefit you if you read, along with this transmission, the transmission on language.[1])

The word circle is also defined as an administrative division. In cosmic perspective this administrative division of the circle is the circle of the experiential God, God the Supreme, and His experience of the creation from the Paradise center. This administrative circle has its complete and total oneness with each and every individual from its created source. This more complete harmony begins with the fusion of the Thought Adjuster, which more totally incorporates the three meridian circuits with the seven evolutionary circuits.

In astronomy circle refers to the orbit of a heavenly body. In geology a meridian is defined as a great circle of the earth passing through the poles and any given point on the earth's surface. A meridian is also a point or period of highest development, greatest prosperity, splendor, elevation, or the like. In astronomy a meridian circle is a transit instrument provided with a graduated vertical scale, used to measure the declinations of heavenly bodies and to determine the time of meridian transits.

In the pre-stages of light and life certain individuals, particularly ovan souls, begin to develop meridian circuits. These meridian circuits are in relation to God the Father, the Eternal Son, and the Infinite Spirit. They are a Paradise link with lower evolutionary beings. Most evolutionary Urantians do not receive meridian circuits until the higher mansion worlds, although they may begin at the first mansion world. Many of the 170,000,000 ovan souls on Urantia have already developed certain aspects of these meridian circuits. Those higher in spiritual ascension have formulated these circuits to a higher degree. In the morontia worlds these meridian circuits are completely formed before Thought Adjuster fusion. Once they are totally complete, fusion transpires, but there are always exceptions to every rule.

Meridian circuits are universal in their design and technological in function, even though they are nonphysical and nonpersonal. The individual discussion of each of the meridian circuits is a very complex and time-consuming study that extends also to the Havona worlds. There is some speculation that even some higher teachings exist in the twenty-one worlds of Paradise upon which I am not allowed to conjecture or elaborate.

The use of the circle in astronomy in measurement and definition of heavenly bodies correlates with cosmic reason and cosmic philosophy that the astronomers themselves little understand, but they have been able to tap into certain broadcast circuits based upon universal laws of physical acquiescence within mind gravity circuits.

A circuit is a circular journey or one beginning and ending at the same place; a roundabout journey or course; a periodical journey from place to place to perform certain duties. The administration of the grand universe is done through circuit patterns in a circulatory motion, and although physical travel by seraphic transport may be direct and noncircular, it is always done within a circular area. This has to do with cosmic physics in relationship to time travel.

Universe broadcasts and nonpersonality transport are done in the same manner, always taking into consideration circumference/radius definitive of administration spheres, based upon Paradise mandates and Paradise measurements, not corresponding in particular with superuniverse mandates or designs. In this manner higher spiritual authority is kept within divine-origin personality and with those finaliters who have attained certain information based upon the experience of spirit fusion. It is all too complicated and impossible to explain to minds under constellation level. We can only begin to elaborate in generalities to you.

Each personality is a circuit link to Paradise in some manner or another. Father-fused personalities are the more direct link. Those evolutionary mortals, who receive the threefold essence of God within at any one point in the evolutionary process and fuse with a Father-personalized Adjuster and eventually receive finaliter status, become one of the highest entities of interuniversal communication existing within the grand universe. Their ability to communicate from one superuniverse to another and from any universe to Paradise in a matter of seconds is a prerogative known only to these unique and ascending finaliters, which I, myself, have been honored to attain.

In electronics, circuit refers to the complete path of an electric current, including the generating apparatus, intervening resistors, and capacitors. It is known by Fifth Epochal Revelation readers that the circuits were cut off at the time of the Lucifer Rebellion. On a planetary level, such as on Urantia, the short-circuits were within individual bodies. The fallen staff of Caligastia who had acquired meridian circuits were also cut off. These short-circuits were inward and outward: inward in the sense of inner body short-circuiting between creature and Creator, creature and higher created administrators, creature and universe broadcasts; and outward in the sense of messages from higher personalities to lower ones.

With the bestowal of the Spirit of Truth on Urantia, one of the three meridian circuits became available and began to formulate in those individuals who understood who Jesus was at a level that could form a meridian circuit of the Eternal Son. This is a sort of fusion, you might say, between a subcircuit of the heart circuit with the Eternal Son meridian circuit and a subcircuit within it.

Meridian circuits that began to be formed within Urantians are reconstructed in the morontia mortal. Meridian circuits cannot be formed until the personality begins to realize God the Father. Although divinity exists within evolutionary Urantians in the form of a Thought Adjuster, meridian circuitry does not become actualized unless the free will of the bestowal personality becomes linked with circulatory universe laws. The first law is the existence of a First Source and Center—being God the Father, the Eternal Father, the Absolute Personality.

As transistors and capacitors and other transforming devices are used to aid in the generation of electrical force and the circuit path of an electrical force, so too then God the Father uses personalities to bring His message and His voice to those of His creation. Each capacitor and each device along the circuitry from the beginning of the source to the end of it has a function. Take away a capacitor and you can disrupt the entire flow. Each personality is a capacitor. Each personality is an original device used in the design of God to transform His energy, His message, His perfect will to others. The higher the personality in spiritual ascension, the more authority is given that personality transformer. They become, in nontechnical definition, **change agents**.

A change agent is a higher transformer within the circulatory system of the grand universe. Evolutionary mortals who become leaders or change agents within the administration of the Planetary Prince are vital links to transfer the voice of God more clearly to the evolutionary world, in this case, Urantia. It is the procedure on all planets coming into the first stages of light and life.

On Urantia with its uniqueness of interuniversal personalities and where the Planetary Prince, his staff, and other celestial personalities remain invisible, their authority is being made manifest in very visible human personalities whose circuitry is functioning in closer harmony with other celestial personalities in total liaison with the circulatory system of the grand universe. In anatomy, a circulatory system is the system of organs and tissues—including the heart, blood, blood vessels, lymph, lymphatic vessels, and lymph glands—involved in circulating blood and lymph through the body. As each circuit within the body corresponds to these organs, so too do these circuits correspond to higher spiritual mandates, directives, laws, and absolutes. It is impossible to open up any of these higher circuits and obtain higher true spirituality again until you totally realize God the Father as your Creator, and understand your Creator Son of your universe to be your Creator Father.

Another definition of circuit is a league or association. An association of reality will either be in conjunction with divine reality or Luciferic rebellion. If you have not realized God the Father, then your circuits remain cut off. You may be a good person in many ways, but you will transcend this plane through physical death by some disease or perhaps by accident, at which time you will one day be awakened only to discover that you are an eternal being who will then have to discover your Creator Father from that moment on.

In eternity, age has little to do with authority. Although the probability of authority comes with age, it is not necessarily the fact. Many aged personalities have fallen into rebellion and remain there. Many aged personalities have remained cut off from the circuits of God, although they have continued opportunity to realign themselves.

Knowledge is an eternal quest. Wisdom cannot be obtained by a quest outside of God-quest and God-realization in the Father aspect of ascertainment. An ounce of wisdom is worth 100 tons of knowledge. Knowledge passes away; wisdom is eternal.

Within the evolutionary religions of humans on this planet, knowledge has found a place, but very little wisdom exists. Of all these religions, Christianity, if weighed on the scales of godly balance, has acquired wisdom measurement, but only because of its foundations being the recognition of Jesus Christ as a Son of God and the understanding of Jesus Christ in relation to Paradise origin. To the many within Christianity who have not only realized who He is but have begun to some degree to practice what He taught, the meridian circuit of the Eternal Son has begun to formulate.

But unfortunately, if you have remained in institutional Christianity, even though a circuit has opened up for you to certain Paradise truths, you have become short-circuited in most of your spirit bodies, cutting you off from higher spiritual growth. That is why disease and death is still a part of your reality. Those of you who can break free to higher spiritual revelation can now receive the other two living circuits and can actually avoid the death experience as you truly become a new creature in Christ Jesus as written in the New Testament.

Circuitry is a detailed plan of an electric network or circuit. None of your circuitry will totally coordinate with the divine plan of God until you connect with the higher purposes of God, which cannot be found in evolutionary religions, including Christianity, or in fundamentalism of any kind. The Spirit of Truth, which hopefully you have received, must be able to transmit to you continued revelation. The Fifth Epochal Revelation will continue to come to this planet until Christ Michael returns in a very recognized manner where every eye will see Him and every knee will bow and every soul will confess that He truly is the King of Kings and Lord of Lords.

Circular function or trigonometric function is a function such as the tangent or cotangent of an angle, expressed as the ratio of the sides of a right triangle. Trigonometric series are infinite series involving sines and cosines of increasing integral multiples of a variable. Again, here mathematicians have in some manner begun to realize cosmic language in the communicative process incorporating circulatory reality within human English communication.

As we have said over and over again, in transmission after transmission, every human being on this planet is interdependent upon another, and the measurement of individual fulfillment is based upon the ratio of the spiritual ascension of significant others of their pertinent genetic ancestry and in the cooperation of individuals within those families of either Urantian genetic inheritance or cosmic inheritance.

Outside of that ratio you are an isolated amoeba, and as written thousands of years ago, you are "lost sheep" who have gone astray. Although you are a freewill entity and a special personality designed by God, you are also a mathematical equation, and you must realize yourself within that mathematical equation as a part of a whole process. You must learn to define yourself in relation to your God and to your cosmic family, be it from Urantia or from any of the evolutionary planets of time and space.

In geometry trihedral is defined as having, or formed by, three planes meeting in a point: a trihedral angle. Trilateral is having three sides. If you are a god unto yourself or if you think that you can accomplish greatness with the help of your God outside of the authority of others over you who are your elders and cosmic ancestors, you will not be able to be linked with the higher planes of cosmic design, for you have left that design.

Some of you have left it a long time ago and in many **repersonalizations** outside of the trihedral planes of existence. You are somewhere in a subplane of existence, and no matter what you try to accomplish for God you seem to fail, and you wonder why since you have some realization of God-knowingness. Perhaps you have some sense of God-realization and may well have good intentions, but you bounce back and forth like a rubber ball. You are influenced by the pride of this world. Thousands of years ago you would have been recognized as within the Babylonian reality. Now perhaps you have the Hollywood illusion, but you do not see it in yourself because you attach spirituality to this illusion. You also attach other delusions to your illusions, one of which is prosperity, and you think that materialistic acquirement is spiritual bestowal and success.

In cosmic definition you are short-circuited and malfunctioning. You might say you are a defunct soul mechanism, and in this present adjudication process—unless you become realigned with some cosmic absolutes, and find your **cosmic family**, and align yourself with the authority structure of your cosmic circulatory system—you are a candidate for another fallen world very similar to Urantia upon transcendence from this one, no matter how rich you may presently be, no matter how popular you may presently be, or whatever the deception that may be entertained in your mind that you call God's blessings in your life.

Is it not written that you should not form idols or worship them? Yet many of you would rather choose the path of the attainment of an Academy Award than to lend your talents to your spiritual families that you probably did not know existed until this transmission reached you. You may still even deny this transmission until it is re-read to you by the Ancients of Days who will then send you on a "vacation" to another fallen world.

Circularize means to circulate (a letter or memorandum, etc.). Circular velocity is the velocity at which a body must move in order to maintain an orbit at the outer edge of the earth's atmosphere. The universe broadcasts, i.e. letters from God's messengers, in many cases are sent through the meridian circuits of higher celestial personalities to the meridian circuits of others. One is the transmitter, and one is the receiver. On the lower evolutionary worlds, technological devices are still used, but as the individual ascends to higher cosmic reality, all interuniversal and intrauniversal communication can be done within the mind circuits and the meridian circuits. Meridian circuits can be considered part of the morontia mind, and morontia mota begins in these meridian formations.

Within the atmosphere of Urantia, universe broadcasts are greatly distorted. Outside of the earth's atmosphere, communication reception between entities is greatly increased in personalities who have developed meridian circuits. Much of the interference within the atmosphere of the earth is caused by the rebellion of its inhabitants to universal law, and this interference is nonexistent until one reaches another fallen atmosphere, in this case, among the other thirty-six fallen planets of Satania. Even in your own solar system, as your physical body would find itself much lighter on your own moon, so too would your ability to break free of Luciferic deception become much easier outside of the earth's atmosphere. A fallen world consists of fallen individual personalities, and usually they are isolated—either physically through technology or mentally through the mind circuits—from extraplanetary and extrauniversal circuits.

On planets that the Lucifer Rebellion has not touched, interplanetary travel is possible thousands of years before it is on fallen worlds, even though interplanetary communication exists long before physical travel becomes possible. This is because the communicative abilities of the mind supersede the necessity of physical body transport. On planets with three-brained mortals, superuniversal communication between ascending beings is the norm, and intersuperuniversal cultural exchanges occur long before space travel becomes possible.

On your planet, the necessity for technological communication such as the telephone, and before the telephone, the wireless, actually slowed down the process of telepathic abilities. Where technology replaces **meridian telepology**, the Conjoint Actor becomes less discernible, less comprehensible, and less realized.

Meridian telepology is a higher form of clairvoyance and is the forming of the Third Source and Center within the

meridian triad. The forming of the meridian triad, a higher cosmologic vibration pattern, can become individually realized where a group or a circuit of people form their own individual meridian circuits and then together create a subcircuit. This subcircuit is known as a **meridian center**. The first meridian center becomes the planetary headquarters of the Planetary Prince.

The meridian triad is connected to both aspects—the three circuits of the individuals and the higher link to a particular celestial entity. If this particular triad is the highest—for instance, three first circlers, linked directly to the Creator Son and Universe Mother Spirit—then this subcircuit is known as the meridian triad, and it becomes the heart circuit of the meridian triad. It also becomes the heart circuit of the meridian center. It is the heart circuit within the government of the planet in relation to the other six circuits or meridian centers, which eventually become Divine New Order communities. It is the planetary logos; it is the planetary body of the Seven Master Spirits; it is the planetary circuitry of the seven superuniverses existing on any particular planet at any one time.

Depending upon your psychic circle at the time of transition from the planet or your ascension while you are still here on the planet, the eighth, ninth, and tenth meridian circuits will relate first to your seraphim, your angel of enlightenment. If you reach the first circle and remain on it before transition, which few on the planet will, then the link will be to the next administrative level, which would be the administrator of the system, Lanaforge. At that point it gets a little complicated and there are many circumstances, but it is a beginning link also to the Creator Son, the Creative Spirit, and the Bright and Morning Star.

In systems where the first seven planets reach the higher stages of light and life, those planets reflect the Seven Master Spirits in preordinate light patterns. These preordinate light patterns are coexistent within the circulatory system of the grand universe Deity, and as such, become sons in themselves—not suns but sons in reflectivity. The light that is seen is the most natural of lights, for it is of Paradise origin in essence. Sunlight exists because of nonspiritual forces and is unnatural light, though you in your worlds in lower evolutionary reality call it natural light.

All of the higher headquarters worlds resonate with reflective lighting, preordained with Paradise coexistent pattern. These worlds are architectural in design. Some evolutionary worlds that become headquarters worlds are then based upon architectural world design to whatever degree of manipulation is possible by inspirational celestial creators. Many of these evolutionary headquarters worlds are actually visible in the skies with human eyesight on any clear night. One such star system that you call the Seven Sisters is such a headquarters system. There are others.

Urantia is becoming the first planet of the thirty-seven fallen planets in the system of Satania to realign itself, and it is aligning with six others preceding it in higher preordained coexistent light pattern within the **cosmologic vibration pattern** of the Seven Master Spirits, therefore creating in its alignment an activated planetary circuit within a circulatory body of a system of correlated planets.

These seven planets are forming into their own organization of morontia worlds. You might say that the mansion worlds of Satania are giving birth to sister planets. Urantia, now coming into alignment with its six sisters, is forming an integral function in the circulatory system of the grand whole; in this case the grand whole is the universe of Nebadon, which, in itself, is a very young universe and just beginning to form her body parts in relation to the grand circulatory system.

All life is correlated. Every ultimaton, every individual, every planet, all visible and invisible matter, everything that exists, exists within the design; and it is circular in motion and infinite, yet centered within the divine mind of its absolute design and absolute factual existence.

Eventually every substance that is nonliving or nonpersonal will rearrange itself to the design of the First Source and Center, and so too will every living personality who chooses survival status. Fallen individuals, who have not learned to flow in the divine design moment to moment, create their own suffering and the suffering of others on their planet of isolation. Those who begin to align more precisely in perfection, moment to moment within the design of the divine mind, begin to create individual and planetary harmony, peace, and self-fulfillment, which increase the possibility of planetary oneness and corporate cooperation between all other individuals who have aligned themselves to the existing divine administration on that planet.

Such was the harmony with the evolutionary mortals within the Caligastia government before the fall. Such is also the alignment of other Planetary Princes with evolutionary mortals on worlds that have not fallen, such as six of the higher worlds with which Urantia is beginning to align itself. There were many choices for the seventh aligned planet; there were 576 planets other than Urantia that could have been chosen, as the majority of them were more advanced spiritually than Urantia. Because of the uniqueness of Urantia and because Urantia is known as the planet of the cross on which the inhabitants crucified their own Creator Son, it was voted upon in an interplanetary council of Planetary Princes that Urantia be elected to align with the seven mansion worlds of Satania, making it an eighth mansion world. This decision greatly upstepped the process of evil, sin, and iniquity on Urantia, which the previously given Paper 215 discusses.[2]

Implications are massive, not only on the system and universe level but more so on a planetary level, which in actuality can even upstep the forthcoming return of Christ Michael to this planet. It is our speculation that this decision made by the Planetary Princes of Satania, in cooperation with the System Sovereign, was greatly influenced by the wishes of the universe administrator, the Bright and Morning Star of Salvington. Although he personally made no command, his wishes were well known from the beginning of the Lucifer Rebellion. We in Overcontrol are all delighted that his wishes are now beginning to be granted and that they are being granted by lesser personalities than himself, all in tune with the circulatory system of Nebadon and the divine mind of the Creator Son, Christ Michael, whose own wishes seem to be becoming actualized in the here and now on Urantia.

It should be noted that there are various alignments of Urantia with other planets in light and life taking place over a period of time. Urantia is also aligning with six other worlds in light and life closest to it in the neighborhood, but they are not necessarily the highest planets in Satania, and there are also other planets in higher stages of light and life that Urantia is coming into alignment with in various aspects as the planet progresses in consciousness. The alignment with the other six planets closest to us physically that are in light and life will be spiritual as well as physical, but it doesn't mean that Urantia will be as high as those planets, just in the highest alignment. When Urantia comes into that spiritual and physical alignment, it will create many circumstances under universe law that Urantia was not subject to previously.

Another derivative of circular is circumcision, which is defined as spiritual purification. The ancient Jews practiced circumcision in their own way, and many other cultures practiced it in their own way. The Hopi believed, and still believe, in the time of purification of the Earth Mother. The Planetary Princes of Satania have aligned themselves with the divine wishes of Christ Michael and Gabriel of Salvington, who have together begun the spiritual process of the purification of Urantia. Urantia is becoming circumcised!

Circumstance is defined as a condition, detail, part, or attribute, with respect to time, place, manner, agent, etc. that accompanies, determines, or modifies a fact or event; a modifying or influencing factor: Do not judge the act without considering the circumstances. There is a difference between destiny as opposed to chance or coincidence. The person who is totally realized within the divine mind and absolute purpose does not think of himself or herself within coincidence, and all circumstances become part of that absoluteness. Individuals who see circumstance as accident are not God-realized and truly are prone to accident and disease and are chance-oriented. If they create certain successes by their self-asserted charismatic abilities, they do not create divine purpose, rather they create short-circuits within the circulatory system of the divine mind.

Sooner or later in the cosmic circulatory system, all of these blockages and all of these short-circuits must be eliminated from planets whose individuals are beginning to become less resistant to the energy patterns of the divine mind because divine mind wishes the individual fulfillment and total actualization of all of the children of God.

Even in ignorance, resistance of one individual to divine pattern can cause a whole family to suffer. Multiply this 10,000 times or more and you can see that the sufferings of the planet are caused by the people within it who are out of alignment with divine absolutes.

Again we state very strongly that the statement that says that each one has his or her own path may sound relatively innocent and true, but until all individuals are aligned with the direct path within the divine mind of absoluteness, the circulatory system of the experiential God will continue to suffer pain in the various parts of its body. It is not God who causes the pain; it is those who have fallen into evil, sin, and iniquity who caused it within that system.

This transmission is a beginning teaching on the 10 circuits of the morontia light body. Future transmissions will deal with the subcircuits. Please note that the number 10 has a circle within it. The numeral 1 represents oneness and wholeness and cannot be divided within itself except in fractions. With its complement, the zero, the number 10 is divided by 2 which equals 5. 5 represents the 2 halves, the Fifth Epochal Revelation, which began for the circuits of the third-dimensional body and now the **Continuing Fifth Epochal Revelation** that is for the meridian circuits and the morontia body.

With the addition of the balance of the second half of the Fifth Epochal Revelation, the individual ascending son or daughter of Urantia, with the designation of Urantian or **starseed**, becomes more presently a part of the **fourth dimension**—that should have occurred a few thousand years ago on Urantia—and a part of the **fifth dimension** that is now co-existent with the third and fourth on Urantia. The Continuing Fifth Epochal Revelation is to help those ascenders to attain morontia reality even before the death occurrence is necessary. The understanding of the Continuing Fifth Epochal Revelation is an acquiescence to the fifth dimension and above, and it is the ink and the brush that is needed to form the preexistent design of the morontia body.

April 2, 1992

Paladin, Chief of Finaliters
in cooperation with Lanaforge, the System Sovereign of Satania, and Machiventa Melchizedek, the Planetary Prince of Urantia

As transmitted through
the Pre-Level-One Audio Fusion Material Complement,
Gabriel of Urantia/TaliasVan of Tora

PAPER 233

The Seven Circuits Of The Third-Dimensional Body In Relationship To The Seven Superuniverses, The System Of Satania, And The Eighth And Ninth Meridian Circuits In Relationship To The Fourth Dimension And Above, And The Salvington Circuit

THOUSANDS of years ago sixth- and seventh-stage morontia progressors, who were repersonalized on Urantia and had become known as masters, began to teach about the circuits of the body that they called chakras. The process of interplanetary and interdimensional communication is always hindered because of the consciousness of the mind at the time and the language within it.

Even the Creator Son of this universe who bestowed on Urantia 2,000 years ago basically experienced a consciousness in the first-century reality. His language, as Son of Man, although diversified, was still limited to the consciousness of a first-century human. As it was with the ancient Tibetans, so it is with the twentieth-century receiver of this information.

Taking this into consideration, we will build upon what are some of the known characteristics of the seven circuits and give cosmic definitions to the twentieth-century mind nearing the twenty-first century. Actually, it is a fourth-dimensional awakening from a third-dimensional perspective. Fourth-dimensional reality and above incorporates cosmic citizenship and realigns cosmic broadcasts to post-rebellion personalities. If rebellion had not occurred, fourth-dimensional reality would have occurred thousands of years ago to certain individuals of higher evolutionary races of this planet, particularly those of the Adamic seed, including the Adamic seed of the Material Sons and Daughters repersonalized as ovan souls. The reopening of communication broadcasts has been available to certain individuals even before the Spirit of Truth was bestowed on Urantia. Always, these individuals are of a higher spiritual and mindal capacity, and the motive and intent of these personalities are in the service of humankind.

It should be understood by all students of **Continuing Fifth Epochal Revelation** that, in relation to understanding the interconnectedness of the circuitry and the integration of the Trinity circuits at any one primary subcircuit, there will be the problem of the encircuiting of every aspect of the Trinity in any one circuit. Certain subcircuits will definitely have response mechanisms in relationship to the central nervous system and the brain that are more dominant to one Trinity aspect or another. As you ascend within the spiritualized mind, and as you fully begin to understand the Trinity response and how it affects you at your time-and-space moment—be it material, semi-material, or spirit form—these lessons are eternal ones to finality and onward. You will be unable to fully comprehend any one chart or any one transmission on circuitry in totality at any one moment in time and space.

The Heart Circuit

In the **heart circuit** the ancient Tibetans saw 12 flower-like petals, 12 subcircuits. What they did not see were additional subcircuits existing in the middle of the petal, circuits within circuits. A second subcircuit consists of 1,000 circuits; a third subcircuit consists of 10 million circuits. These subcircuits are in direct broadcast linkage to the individual inhabited worlds of Satania that have reached a certain governmental function in the stages of light and life on those particular planets, and to the universe of Nebadon and the projected 10 million inhabitable worlds within it on a same level of governmental function.

The 12 petals represent the 12 Vorondadek Sons who were placed in governmental capacity as the Most Highs in the constellation of Norlatiadek. As we would like for all of you to come into a higher understanding of the Most Highs, we will list these 12 Vorondadek Sons. Those spiritual leaders, change agents, and others involved in the Divine Administration of the present Planetary Prince, Machiventa Melchizedek, must come to know these Most Highs just as commonly as you know the 12 apostles. The 12 apostles must come to know these Most Highs as easily as they know one another.

It is in the complete knowing of something that reality realization is manifest, that communication exists, even on the level of human to human. Misunderstanding and miscommunication occur when individuals do not know one another and misinterpret that which the other says or how they perceive one another. Thus in morontia and above communication, the more you know about celestial personalities, the more authoritative you are and the more authority you obtain. This is also true in your ascension process in relation to your Creator. More authority of divinity is given those individuals who obtain the absoluteness of God.

Representative government on any level becomes possible when individuals ascend in knowingness of the absolute First Source and Center. In many cases individuals can know something but not be able to express it by language communication or by written word. This is a commonplace reality not only on Urantia but on other worlds in time and space. And so it is not possible on your mortal side to accurately discern another person's relationship with his or her Creator. However, within the First Cosmic Family a higher discernment of an individual's God-knowingness can begin to exist.

Even on planets in the higher stages of light and life, a certain understanding exists, of which we can call God the Unexplainable, recognizing the limitation of language at these lower evolutionary levels. Keeping this in mind, a personality in God quest should be absolute in that quest, but relative in certain aspects of the acquirement of God the Absolute. In this manner, a tendency towards false pride of knowledge can be eliminated, and self-contemplation does not lead to self-deception, all-knowingness, and rebellion.

1. Let us start with the first Vorondadek Son. Starting from the top of the circuit going clockwise, from the right side of the center exists the first subcircuit of the *Constellation Father*, the present Most High Ruler number 617,318 of the Vorondadek series of Nebadon. This subcircuit and this personality, once contact mode is linked, can open subcircuits within the other projected 10 million inhabitable worlds of Nebadon to particular personalities of other **Father-circuited** ascension. A coordinate celestial personality, usually a Planetary Prince, must first be contacted in this intrasystem broadcast circuit. Other transmissions will more clearly specify how this is done.

2. Next, on the right of the top center (going clockwise) is the *Senior Most High Associate*. The Senior Most High Associate is in direct communication with the archangels' headquarters (one of which is presently on Urantia) of any particular world and seldom communicates below that level, except when a mortal contact personality is being used, such as the one we are using now.

3. The next on the right is the *Junior Most High Associate*. The Junior Most High Associate is in direct linkage with sanobim and cherubim.

4. Next on the right is the *Most High Advisor*, Michael's representative. Usually he functions as Michael's representative with the System Sovereigns of various systems of worlds.

5. The next one is the *Most High Executive*, who is the representative of Gabriel, the Bright and Morning Star. Usually, as Gabriel's representative, he functions with the Council of Elders of a particular planet, and in the case of Satania, the Council of Twenty-four.

6. Next is the *Most High Chief of Planetary Observers*. This Vorondadek coordinates with the Planetary Prince and very seldom does he personally visit the lower evolutionary worlds.

7. Next is the *Most High Referee*. Interaction between the Planetary Prince and various celestial personalities who may need further counsel as to the actualization of either misunderstood or misinterpreted communications requires further elaboration with a referee son who is more fully aware of what was spoken by the Planetary Prince at the time the order was given.

8. The next Vorondadek Son is the *Most High Emergency Administrator*. In cases where higher genetic strains are in danger of extinction on any particular planet or where the planet itself is in danger, emergency administrators advise and counsel, starting with the staff of the System Sovereign whose specific instructions are then given to the Midwayer Commission of the endangered planet, who in turn advise procedure to the Planetary Prince or the Resident Governor General. This perspective is as close to a material perspective as can be given by nonmaterial personalities.

9. Number nine is the *Most High Mediator*. Mediators perform various mediations between personalities of different views and misunderstandings wherever necessary, where lower mediators have not been able to reach solutions.

10. Number ten is the *Most High Judge Advocate*. The Judge Advocates work directly with the Ancients of Days periodically concerning individual ovan souls and these ovan souls' decisions at any particular moment in time and space, when these ovan souls continue to make decisions that could cause them total extinction.

11. Number eleven is the *Most High Liaison*. The Most High Liaison corresponds with Paradise-origin personalities and transfers higher Havona mandates to universe-level reality.

12. Number twelve is the *Most High Director*, who also works with Paradise-level personalities, but organizes problematic solutions based upon program-oriented procedure as opposed to individual solution or personal counsel. Most High Directors work in group administrative policy and not in individual process.

Usually, but not always, twelve representatives of mortal ascension are picked by the Planetary Prince to coordinate communication with these twelve Most Highs, based upon those particular individuals' ability to activate the twelve circuits of their morontia heart circuitry. It is assumed by myself and others that the twelve apostles of Jesus, presently returned to Urantia as change agents, will be chosen in this capacity.

The heart circuit is also the headquarters circuit of the universe of Nebadon and cannot even begin to be activated at any beginning level until an individual has an understanding of God as Creator. The more the ancient Tibetans began to accept what became known as the Buddhist philosophy of individual divinity, the more they began to lose the power of clairvoyant perception and to short-circuit themselves. They were given the keys but did not know how to use them.

The Crown Circuit

The **crown circuit** is the complement to the heart circuit. The crown circuit was seen by the Tibetans to have 972 subcircuits. Actually, they missed twenty-eight; and even though it came to be known as the thousand-petal lotus, it is a thousand-circuited band that also corresponds to the 1,000 inhabitable worlds destined for Satania. It is located in the higher body on the top of the head, for this is where the soul and spirit enter the next plane, and this is the travel route in transcendence. It is the tunnel seen by those who pass through the death experience.

These particular subcircuits that were visible to the Tibetans are more easily accessible to the premorontia personality who has obtained the third circle of attainment and has received an angel of enlightenment. This angel of enlightenment, working in close liaison with a seraphim of one of the twelve groupings of the Chief of Seraphim, enables clairvoyant reception from Urantia to one of these other planets or to personalities upon them, but it begins in the crown circuit in the third circle of attainment and with a seraphim and not a Vorondadek Son. Imagination and inspiration enter through this circuit. The opening up of this circuit must begin in the mind.

The crown circuit also functions in a clockwise manner. Urantia, being number 606 of Satania, is located approximately between numbers six and seven if the subcircuits were visualized as the face of a watch. The opening up of this subcircuit from Urantia to any of the other 999 subcircuits develops in the ascension process. On the lower evolutionary worlds in a young system or in a young universe, most of these subcircuits have not been activated because the planets themselves have not registered mortal life.

However, the personality carries a formation of these subcircuits with it upon transcendence into the morontia worlds, and they become activated at any time in the ascension process that the point-of-origin system gives birth to a new planet of mortals who have received Thought Adjusters. Any of these particular subcircuits may not become activated until those individuals are hundreds of thousands of light-years away from their planet of origin. Yet when this happens, a certain fullness of cosmic reality begins, which in turn produces countless possibilities of inspirational reception and future administration.

Individuals who have reached the first circle of attainment before transcendence have opened up circuit communication in the crown circuit to every inhabited planet of that system. On a planet of nondefault, those personalities can receive technological and ascension science communication far beyond genius level of present-day Urantia. Because of the default of Urantia, individuals who do receive this level of communication are quite limited as to what they can do with this inspiration for many reasons, all stated in various parts of the Continuing Fifth Epochal Revelation. It is one of the greatest problems of fallen Urantia.

In the past most individuals of this nature have become nonfunctional in the Urantian society of that day, or have become recognized as a genius on some occasions where those in power have used them to benefit themselves. But the majority of those who have attained first-circle attainment on Urantia, and in particular many artists, have lived and died with genius capability unknown by their fellow men and women. Some of them who have been able to incorporate the third eye with the crown circuit have been quite useful in the areas of prophetic clairvoyant capability such as Nostradamus, Edgar Cayce, and Gabriel of Urantia/TaliasVan of Tora, the personality who we presently use.

The Third-Eye Circuit

The third-eye circuit, according to the ancient Tibetans, contained 96 subcircuits, while in actuality there are 100. Each one corresponds to one of the 100 systems within our constellation of Norlatiadek. It was understood that the third-eye circuit could be used for certain clairvoyant prophetic usage in relation to events and interdimensional communication and celestial personality observance. Quite often those who had developed their third eye by developing a relationship with Christ Michael were at times able to see certain of those celestial personalities closest to the human plane such as midwayers, sanobim, and cherubim.

To the **ovan soul** or **first-time Urantian** who has reached the third circle, certain cosmic facts and absolutes begin to be sent in relation to universe procedure and superuniverse administration, but the personality may not even know where this higher insight is coming from. Many in the Urantia movement opened up these subcircuits but cannot totally and fully actualize them for a practical purpose until they understand Continuing Fifth Epochal Revelation that is the key to this activation. This is a process of the beginning activation of morontia mota upwards to constellation level. These cosmic realities are not easy to transmit from our side to the evolutionary mind, but we must begin somewhere.

The third eye is a link to time-and-space reality. Time-and-space reality has not happened, yet it has happened. It is totally future and totally past. It is present in the now and present in the future. It is post-present in the past, yet it is material in all three aspects and is quite physical upon time travel.

These picturizations within the subcircuits are present-sent and never post-sent messages. They are future-oriented and never past-oriented. They can be present-sent and present-oriented but never presently actualized until future tense aligns with present thought.

Circumstantial reality based upon the free will of a certain grouping of mortals of any particular realm designates a certain planetary reality. Individual prerogative can be, and at times is, displaced by Overcontrol if those particular individuals are of a higher ascendancy with divine mind. However, they must be allowed to experience rebellion at any level to the point of human frustration just so long as necessary for the good of the master universe as a whole.

Time-limit prerogatives are in the hands of the Ancients of Days, not in the hands of the Creator Sons. Creator Sons can make decisions based upon the whole in relation to a particular planet within their particular universe so long as that whole does not interfere with the part of another universe and the laws therein. Superuniverse prerogative supersedes the whole and functions in administrative capacity to the individual ascending son or daughter. Individual destiny can be, and has been, rearranged. Planetary destiny remains cohesive with universe design.

Personality bestowal is a Paradise-origin design and functions within the gravity circuits of Paradise. Nonliving matter functions within universe circuits and is destined in other scientific realities that are preprogrammed for specific purposes outside of ascension growth. The fusion of personality ascension with prelife ascension is more totally realized in the developed third eye, which is a relationship between the systems of time and space that have already been aligned with the grand universe.

Each of the 100 subcircuits is a direct link to a System Sovereign. Subcircuit number twenty-four, linked to the system of Satania, is the twenty-fourth subcircuit from the right in clockwise motion. The visualization of this subcircuit in proper alignment with Christ Michael and the present Planetary Prince of Urantia, Machiventa Melchizedek, opens a more direct communication ability between the System Sovereign, Lanaforge, and Urantia.

Inspirational ability becomes more technologically understood to be an ascension science ability. It is the fusion of the ascension of the soul with spiritual technology. It is not supernatural; it is technologically natural and cosmically absolute in prewritten cosmic law. It is mathematically precise and without error. It may be totally unrecognized at various levels, but when totally recognized it is a tool of the divine for the evolutionary son or daughter in the ascension to Paradise.

To the finaliter it becomes something else. It is a gift to the finaliter beyond human words to express. It is a gift of time travel. It is a gift of the remembrance of feelings and emotions. It is a gift of touch in the various sensitivities of various levels that have long been forgotten in spiritual bodies. It is the feeling of a tear, either of joy or sadness. It is the remembrance of mortal life at any level that now becomes a felt reality as opposed to the memory cycle.

The third eye enables higher celestial personalities to complement lower mortal personalities such as the **audio fusion material complement** I am now using at this time. It is a door from our side to yours. It is a door that extends from one particular location to another, millions of light-years away. It opens up a journey for celestial travels to any part of the master universe for finaliters, and for those morontia progressors who learn to activate the circuits of the third eye, to every part of the constellation.

Urantia mortals do not have the necessary information to activate these circuits I am mentioning, but the **Mandate of the Bright and Morning Star** can begin this process, and Continuing Fifth Epochal Revelation will begin to open up the realization of these circuits so that morontia pilgrims can begin time–space travel perhaps thousands of years earlier than they would have if they had not received Continuing Fifth Epochal Revelation and understood it at a necessary level.

As the physical body begins to become more morontial, cosmic knowledge, wisdom, and absolute factuality begin to complement that morontia body. Cosmically absolute information in the mind of the material body is like putting a huge set of wings on an elephant. Unless that elephant develops a lighter body, it will be unable to fly even if it knows how and where to go. However, it is much better to receive the information in the material body, for when the time of the transition comes you then will be able to accelerate instead of drift with the currents. It is our function with the Continuing Fifth Epochal Revelation to help you accelerate.

The third eye, which is nonphysical sight, is divine sight. It is the fusion of the Thought Adjuster with the will of humans. Psychic ability outside of correct motive complements the ego not the spirit. It may seem correct to the ego and may be factually comprehended, for the rebellious personality usually gets what it desires in one way or another. True clairvoyant ability is for the benefit of others and for the recognition of danger to others. It provides safety. It is the protective hand of God seen by the balanced Father-circuited and **Mother-circuited** personalities in cooperation with the System Sovereigns of the respective systems and the Planetary Princes of the planets on which those individuals reside.

The Throat Circuit

The **throat circuit** corresponds to the power and force of the spoken laws of God throughout the universes of time and space where language is used as a mode of communication. It is the power of the word in relation to cosmic absolutes and cosmic law. The ancient Tibetan teachers saw 16 petals; in actuality there are 210 subcircuits that more clearly resonate with the 210 Perfections of Days. The divisional number 16 is the number of perfection that they recognized. In numerology, $6 + 1 = 7$, which is a perfect number, and this correlates to the 7 Reflective Spirits and the 7 Reflective Image Aids of each superuniverse. 210 is also divisible by 7.

Although the throat circuit is attached to the Infinite Spirit, it is more of a triune attachment than it is an independent function. This is why it is negative (–) and positive (+). With ascending sons on the third circle, it is + – because at that point it begins to function as their primary source-center for Deo-subatomic to cellular reality. With ascending daughters, it is – +. For them it also functions as part of a dual source-center after they reach the third circle.

It was understood that this was the circuit of coordination between the will of humans and the will of God. More precisely, it is the correlation of this, plus the hearing of that will as manifested through the personalities of the First Source and Center in reflectivity, starting through the Reflective Spirits to the Reflective Image Aids and the Perfections of Days, through time and space to the evolutionary worlds to the next personality of audio ability. This translates to what has become known as clairaudience. It is the hearing of the will of God through the personality circuits of time and space. It begins from the Paradise level and outward to the evolutionary worlds.

In the human body it is connected to the voice, which also commands authority to fellow mortals. That authority can be God-originated, Lucifer-originated if in this rebellious system, or self-originated, with perhaps error instead of iniquity. The power and authority of God to realms of imperfection comes from Paradise in and through the voices of the Reflective Spirits, the Reflective Image Aids, and the Perfections of Days through correlated and mandated related communication circuits.

Nondivine communication lacks authority. All true authority is divine authority, and all divine authority is encircuited, starting from the Paradise Trinity through the Reflective Spirits to the major sectors of the superuniverses of time and space, in alignment with the purposes of creation. Divine authority does not have to be forceful, it just has to be spoken. Therefore, even the most gentle of Mother-circuited personalities can speak softly the dictates of God's law and will. Here we have the triune Paradise will in action. If it is not understood or adhered to, it is only a temporary disobedience, for ultimately any divine mandate that a Perfection of Days speaks is adhered to sooner or later within the time lag of justice. No Paradise-level mandate that is spoken is ever spoken without the intention of creative purposes and will always carry with it a form of Paradise force.

This pre-existent force out of pre-existent mind eventually actualizes itself in the universes of time and space through the Creator Sons, who become, in a sense, reflective personalities of the Threefold God. The 700,000 Creator Sons create in respective alignment with a Perfection of Days and cooperate with one of their 210 Paradise associates.

The power of Creator Sons consists in their alignment with a Perfection of Days, and the power of evolutionary mortals to create lies in their alignment to their Creator Father, a Michael Son. The subcircuits of the throat circuit are thus related to the Salvington Circuit. None of these circuits can be activated at any level until the realization of the Michael Son or your Creator Son is actualized. You have no authority of God until you speak with your words the knowledge of your Creator Son as your creator and of His absolutes as part of your own absolute reality. Any other kind of authority is self-proclaimed authority. It is written: "And the Word was made flesh, and dwelt among us, and we beheld his glory, the glory as the only begotten of the Father, full of grace and truth."[1]

No cosmic truth spoken is spoken in vain, and each time you present a cosmic truth or thought you are putting these treasures in a cosmic storehouse. These **Deo-atomic** thoughts become visible cellular structure and, in a sense, you are a co-creator of absolute divine reality, and in this divine presence you share your godliness with others and they in turn with you.

In communication where God-presence is void and distorted, power and authority of the divine presence is absent, and confusion, disharmony, and disease exist, which is the state of present-day Urantia. Where the authority of God is strong, divine manifestations and divine serendipities can become commonplace. In the first stages of light and life, where the majority of individuals on any one particular planet begin to speak the language of universal absoluteness, individual self-fulfillment becomes the reality and divine purpose is manifest.

The Solar-Plexus Circuit

Edgar Cayce saw 7 subcircuits in the **solar-plexus circuit**, each connected to 1 of the 7 glands of the body and to 1 of the then known planets of our immediate solar system, which we now know as Monmatia. In reality, there are 10 subcircuits connected to the 10 major sectors of the superuniverse of Orvonton. Our superuniverse, Orvonton, is superuniverse number 7. Our major sector, Splandon, is major sector number 5, and its headquarters world is Umajor the fifth. The solar-plexus circuit is related to the Universe Mother Spirit, not only of the universe of Nebadon but of other universes within the 10 major sectors. It is a vast network of the Infinite Spirit circuit, but there is also a correlation with the Father aspect.

On a human mortal level, it is a circuit of emotions. Emotions are not logical in reception and are more instinctual in thought and appropriation. The solar plexus is associated with intuitiveness and is very strongly connected to the earth energies, which are Mother-circuited. It is known as a nurturing circuit in relationship to children and motherly instinct. Although the subcircuits are connected to the major sectors, until an individual reaches the third psychic circle these subcircuits do not become activated, and only Splandon, the fifth subcircuit, becomes activated, particularly in the female. When a male or female begins to become more balanced within the Mother circuit, the subcircuits to the other nine major sectors begin to become activated and more fully begin to resonate with the Infinite Spirit presence in the superuniverse of Orvonton, and therefore, the soul more totally begins to experience and then express a higher nature of Infinite Spirit reality.

Empathic ability is realized within this circuit, and on some worlds, diseases can actually be transmitted out of one body and redirected to a semimaterial nonmortal body or an inanimate object by certain personalities with the ability to heal in this manner. On Urantia, some have had this ability to some degree but have not truly known what to do with it. The diseases of the stomach begin in the solar plexus area of the body where imbalance occurs within the thinking of individuals who are out of balance with the Infinite Spirit or Mother circuits.

Other problems of discomfort will also arise in that area when unfulfillment occurs in relation to creativity, which is part of the function of the Conjoint Actor registering in the solar plexus region. Nourishment lacking within the body will manifest first in the lower stomach area that, in the female is the birth-of-life area and in both sexes will bloat the stomach due to the lack of vitamins and food supplements. The lack of pure water will also affect the solar plexus as well as the physical area around the circuit.

Although to the first-time Urantian, a developed solar plexus can create a sense of knowingness by feeling, it is not the highest form of discerning the will of God, for the Mother circuit, although in tune with cosmic nourishment, may be out of alignment with divine purposes when an individual does not recognize logical input for the overall good of the situation in regard to the whole. Many females who try to discern the will of God through the solar plexus greatly err in judgment. This is why it is wise for the female to adhere to the advice of a balanced male, for the female functions intuitively within the solar plexus, the navel, and the root circuits.

The Navel Circuit

The **navel circuit** in actuality was the circuit of 619 subcircuits at the time of the first revelation to the ancient Tibetans, and it continues to expand as long as the number of inhabited worlds of a system expands. Although the subcircuits are related to inhabited worlds in relation to administrative purposes, there is also a correlation with the Father/Mother circuits in relationship to the Son/Mother, the Son representing the Father aspects in relation to the Mother and to emotional responses in this circuit.

The Tibetans saw the dominant outer six subcircuits representing six aspects of the yang and yin or Father/Mother reality of God on the lower worlds. The three Father aspects are authority, logic, and decisiveness. The three Mother aspects are creativity, sensitivity, and nourishment. It is in reality a fusion circuit of the Eternal Son and the Infinite Spirit, and both evolutionary men and women base many of their decisions in the area of the emotions through these subcircuits. Females, particularly, are more closely attached to the Mother aspects of the energies of these planets.

It is through this circuit that evolutionary ascending sons can more totally harmonize themselves with the Universe Mother circuit energies. Evolutionary male mortals who have not balanced themselves usually develop some kind of disease in this area of the body that may manifest in weak legs or knees and other lower body disorders. Females who are imbalanced in this area will also develop similar problems, as well as a change in the muscular and the skin tissue surrounding this particular area. Skin problems can also develop throughout the whole body.

This particular circuit in the system of Satania can develop up to 1,000 subcircuits, but it is known as the 606 circuit (Urantia being planet number 606 in the system of Satania). This stems from the fact of the uniqueness of evolutionary Urantians in relation to the threefold Paradise energies and in the reception of these Paradise-origin energies through these subcircuits and to other areas of the body through the adrenal gland.

The Root Circuit

The root circuit, located at the base of the spine, was seen by the ancient Tibetans as having four subcircuits. It is actually a creation circuit, and these four subcircuits represent the Universal Father, the Eternal Son, the Infinite Spirit, and the Creator Son and Creative Mother Spirit of each respective local universe. There is a fusion of the Creator Son and Universe Mother Spirit in one subcircuit. The root circuit is the circuit of birth. It is the circuit of life and the breath of life bestowed upon the soul at the time of decision.

The knowledge of how this is done remains a Paradise prerogative, but we conjecture that the Creator Sons have received the predetermined decision and act upon the wishes of the First Source and Center. For every life that is ever created within any particular universe, the perfect will of the Father is a Paradise-origin creation, and all Creator Sons, as well as all evolutionary mortals and nonmortal descending sons or daughters, align to do that same will.

Instinctual habits and certain behaviors are inherited through this circuit in and through a Deo-atomic exchange. For evolutionary mortals it is the source-center in which Deo-subatomic to cellular reality is stored from various other circuits and then transferred to the other circuits within the body (including the meridian circuits) according to the ascension level of the soul.

All mortals begin with the source-center being the root circuit. When ascending sons reach the third circle, the source-center begins to shift to the throat circuit as they begin to draw more from the Father circuits above. For ascending daughters the root circuit will always remain the primary source-center, although the throat circuit can also function as such in a dual capacity with the root circuit after they reach the third circle.

It is unknown, even by finaliters in my classification, if any of the other circuits are used to transfer Deo-atomic creation prerogatives for whatever particular personality reason. The ancient Native Americans and other cultures saw in this circuit the four directions of the power of God, this particular circuit being the Earth Mother circuit. In a sense this is true, as it more technically resonates with the energies of the Universe Mother Spirit.

Female evolutionary mortals, in particular, react to this circuit in determining many life decisions based upon feeling and intuition at the level of nourishing. It becomes a problem when certain decisions are made by females using this circuit when they cannot see the whole picture and add the influence of the higher circuits to their decision-making. Most Urantia mortals are insensitive to this circuit and resonate more with the throat circuit.

Male ovan souls, particularly those who have reached the third psychic circle and above, begin to use these subcircuits for certain decision-making. When, in their thinking process, they attach themselves to sensitivity, caring, and nourishing alone for decision-making in this circuit, it is quite inappropriate, but in certain situations it can bring a balance.

The Meridian Circuits

The higher meridian circuits, the eighth and ninth, do begin to resonate with a violet and ultra-golden color, the eighth being violet and the ninth being ultra-golden. The eighth and ninth circuits are attached to morontia souls and those beginning to come into the first stages of light and life and above, while the lower circuits correlate more with individual superuniverses. Both meridian circuits resonate with all seven superuniverses at once, as do any continuing circuits from the eighth circuit on. Subcircuits within these circuits are connected first to major and minor sector headquarters and then to system and planetary headquarters. This varies within each subcircuit according to the number of the inhabited worlds in that particular system.

There is a correlation between the growth of the planet and mass consciousness and the ascension of an individual soul. The descending sons and daughters are immediately attached to an inhabited world when it is registered as such. Ascending sons and daughters are not immediately attached; they have to attain this by individual growth. That is why the 606 circuit of the navel circuit was only seen as six. In reality, at the time of this revelation to the Tibetans, there were 619 inhabited worlds. In a sense, subcircuits are built in relation to each individual's spiritual attainment and are activated in the same manner. They are not precreated, but they are predesigned.

Cosmic artists, who have infinite patience, do draw complete circuitry that is massive in concept, consisting of various levels incorporating trillions of subcircuits. However, although it is beyond the scope of mortal artistry, it is within the scope of cosmic artistry, particularly on the Havona worlds, to draw such perfect circuitry. What may seem incomprehensible, even to constellation pilgrims, is quite comprehensible in the Havona worlds. I bring this whole process of reasoning to you to show you that when you think of seven chakras, or even learn about a few subcircuits within them, you are at the kindergarten level of understanding.

The beginning of an eighth circuit is the beginning of a morontia light body. The eighth circuit more properly attunes itself to perfection and is a total eternity circuit. It incorporates the past with the future to more perfectly actualize the present. It resonates with completeness and cosmic law. In its infancy within the light body, it can and does make very real physical changes in an evolutionary body, first within the thoughts and mind, which then transfer to the physical body.

Within an ovan soul it more closely attaches itself to any of the experiences of that ovan soul's reality in higher perfection that it once experienced. It accelerates the opening up of certain circuits to past-memory realities, perhaps not specific visualization but certain experiential feelings, desires, and, hopefully, forgotten virtues.

The eighth circuit deals with administration and cosmic mandates. The eighth circuit is the heart circuit of the morontia body, and again, the subcircuits are built upon individual acquiescence to the Threefold Spirit. And so, each individual will have a unique eighth meridian circuit or morontia heart circuit. It is always and eternally called the eighth circuit or morontia circuit. This circuit is automatically formulated within each surviving soul on the first mansion world. The fact that it can begin to formulate in the third dimension aids all ascending sons and daughters in their placement and responsibility on morontia worlds, or in the first stages of light and life in a coexisting morontia experience, which is now happening on Urantia with the First Cosmic Family.

The ninth circuit will begin to formulate when the eighth circuit remains constantly appropriated for 1,000 Urantian days. The ninth circuit resonates with fifth-dimensional reality and above. It is a transport circuit and has to do not only with seraphic transport but with other means of nonspiritual transportation of body forms. It is not just the mind circuit.

That which has become known as astral travel is done in and through this circuit, but is quite dangerous when those individuals have not aligned themselves with the higher universe realities, particularly with God the Father, for this circuit is not constantly actuated within them, and no grounding of the soul is actually manifest until this circuit becomes actualized by proper alignment with God the Father, God the Son, and God the Infinite Spirit. Astral travel before this is done is out of the will of God and can actually create many problems, not only on your side but on ours.

The Seven Circuits in Relationship to the Seven Superuniverses

Each of these seven circuits is also related primarily to one of the seven superuniverses. The key to understanding this lies in the various combinations of the Paradise Trinity personalities in relationship to the Seven Master Spirits.

1. The **crown circuit** resonates with the *first superuniverse*, which is the universe of *God the Father*. When an individual reaches the first circle of attainment there is a correlation between the crown circuit and the fourth superuniverse and the heart circuit, which also attaches itself to the first superuniverse.

2. The **third-eye circuit** and the **heart circuit** both resonate with the *second superuniverse* of *God the*

Son, particularly within individual evolutionary mortals when they receive the Spirit of Truth and are activated into fourth-dimensional reality and consistent third-circle attainment.

3. The **throat circuit** is attracted to a magnetic-like energy coming from the *third superuniverse*, the universe reflection of the *Infinite Spirit*.
4. The **heart circuit**, the **throat circuit**, and the **crown circuit** reflect the *fourth superuniverse* of the *Universal Father* and the *Eternal Son*.
5. The **solar-plexus circuit** connects itself to the *fifth superuniverse* of the *Universal Father* and the *Infinite Spirit*.
6. The **navel circuit** attaches itself to the *sixth superuniverse* of the *Eternal Son* and the *Infinite Spirit*.
7. The **root circuit** attaches itself to the reflectivity of the natures of the *Universal Father, Eternal Son*, and the *Infinite Spirit* of the *seventh superuniverse* we know to be Orvonton.

Auras

Although these circuits have become known to resonate with a particular color, the colors themselves fluctuate in relation to the soul itself and the individual's ascension and alignment with the perfect will of God. These colors remain constant only when an individual reaches the first circle of attainment and remains there for approximately 1,000 Urantia days. At any time, even then, these colors can change if an individual defaults in mind, will, or character.

The overall color of the ovan soul is a combination of the total colors of all seven circuits when an individual reaches the first circle and remains there for 1,000 days. Very seldom can clairvoyance determine individual circuitry color. Statements to that effect are based upon imagination, hallucination, or guesswork. Usually one dominant color, or perhaps two to three, will manifest around the ovan soul. It will tend to be more black or white or gray.

Activation of the Circuits

When we are activating the circuits in relation to administrative entities, we do so at various levels of administration. For example, the crown, heart, and navel circuits all connect to the 1,000 worlds of Satania, and in each one a different level of administrative entities are involved. The throat and solar-plexus circuits both connect to the major sectors, but in the throat it is to the Perfection of Days and in the solar plexus it is to other administrators.

Since little is known on Urantia about these circuits, and what is known is quite ancient, most ovan souls who are beginning to know of these circuits' existence have begun to activate them; for as energy follows thought, these circuits and the power within them are activated upon thinking of them and understanding them, and when constantly reflected upon, constant reflection equals constant energy. A cosmic equation exists such that R (reflectivity) = EC (energy constant). The more constant the thought, the more powerful the energy to actualize a cosmic law, either physical or spiritual, as long as it exists within cosmic reality and as long as the reason you are using this spiritual power is for the good of others. If not, this is where, on the lower evolutionary worlds, so-called black magic exists as opposed to what is called white magic.

Because of the misuse of spiritual power, Continuing Fifth Epochal Revelation will be short-circuited in the minds of most evolutionary mortals, starseed and Urantians alike, until they can be trusted. In short, they simply will not understand it, and that is because we intend them not to. They may know a few words here and there, enough to fool and influence certain other undiscerning individuals, but they will not have any real spiritual power, for all of these circuits are activated only by pure motive. That is why Lucifer and others in the Rebellion could have been totally stopped at once. And that is why, when it was decided for certain ones to be imprisoned, they were at once imprisoned.

The human heartbeat can artificially be made to beat past the will of the Eternal Father for it to beat, but that heartbeat is not life. On some worlds, even on Urantia, sustained heartbeat does not mean sustained eternal reality for the soul, for certain subcircuits connected to the heart circuit are also connected to the brain, and the working of this circuitry is unrevealed to any evolutionary mortal in time and space.

The physical body, although important to the evolutionary mortal for health purposes, is not an eternal piece of machinery. Even morontia bodies change. Lucifer attached all too much significance to the physical body, and there is some teaching on Urantia and on other fallen worlds that indicates that the same atoms that are now functioning in your physical body will function again on other planes. There is absolutely no truth to this. The only thing that you inherit in transcendence is your Deo-atomic cells, and they are not understood within the same level as atoms. They are part of the ascension science process, and although they are measurable, they are not part of the understanding of your Urantian physical scientists in relation to ascension reconstruction.

Although on Urantia the first seven circuits have become attached to certain planets in the solar system and have been designated by astrologers in certain manners, these teachings are false, which should be realized after reading these higher transmissions. Although they are attached to certain animal-life qualities (with the exception of the dove, which is a representation of the Spirit of Truth and is attached to the throat circuit, which is the word of God made flesh), all other attachments to animals are based upon superstition and guesswork. These circuits, however, do vibrate with certain musical notes, which is the basis of another transmission. They also resonate with body glands, and more information will also be given in another transmission.

Again, not even the lower circuits can be fully activated until God the Father is realized, God the Son is actualized, and the Infinite Spirit becomes eternalized and internalized. Knowledge alone will not activate the spiritual power of these circuits. For both nonmortal and mortal alike, it is right motive and proper alignment, first to God and to the administration of the existing Planetary Prince of Urantia; that is the only way in which the circuits will be activated and totally realized. It is a divine prerogative based upon the will of the Creator. It is not a future prerogative to actualize the divine without first wanting to be in the perfect will of God. Perfect power is perfect will. Throughout time and space, perfection is found and spiritual authority is realized within that perfect will.

April 6, 1992

Paladin, Chief of Finaliters
in cooperation with Physical Controllers, Universal Censors, Reflective Image Aids, and a Solitary Messenger of Orvonton with the cooperation of the present Planetary Prince of Urantia, Machiventa Melchizedek

As transmitted through
the Pre-Level-One Audio Fusion Material Complement,
Gabriel of Urantia/TaliasVan of Tora

PAPER 234

Personalities In Relationship To Human Mortal Ascenders With Coexistent Nonrealized Contact With The Energy Circuits Of The Seven Superuniverses And The Central Circuit Of The Morontia Light Body

IN all the worlds of time and space, evolutionary mortals resemble in some manner—materially and nonmaterially—a particular fusion of the threefold Trinity, from physical body form and **famotor movement** to personality. The uniqueness of each individual ovan soul is recognized as related to his or her superuniverse of origin and particular cosmic characteristics in relationship to the evolutionary process of the planet of origin, the visitation of particular Paradise Sons on that planet, and the reception of an essence of one of the threefold Paradise Deities that is an addition to his or her origin-prerogative in relationship to the evolutionary mortals residing there.

Along the evolutionary highway in morontia progression, the pilgrim of time and space becomes more personality complete in correlation with the original design in the bestowal of that personality accentuated by one of the seven aspect fusions of the Paradise Trinity. On the higher worlds of time and space, physical form and spirit form are more contingent upon the will of the ascending son or daughter relative to the personality bestowal of that individual within the design of his or her superuniverse. On fallen worlds, souls can be outwardly beautiful but inwardly iniquitous. A process of aging on a fallen world like Urantia begins to deteriorate the outwardly beautiful form, and plastic surgery, although temporarily effective, will inevitably give way to the decaying inward self.

An **ovan soul** who has been granted first-mansion-world reality and a new morontia body will find that this first morontia body will more reflect in its beginning maturation those thought processes that have been in evil and sin. Thus they will fully realize the cause of the change in their body that once may have been more perfectly formed. No amount of exercise in the morontia worlds will change the body, only the exercise of the pure mind. Those moving into morontia/light bodies on present-day Urantia can do the same thing, which will recreate the physical body.

Jungian psychology teaches personality types, and to some degree much of it is correct. However, there are seven main personality types in the grand universe in relationship to evolutionary mortals, and they are:

1. the Universal Father
2. the Eternal Son
3. the Infinite Spirit
4. the Universal Father/Eternal Son
5. the Universal Father/Infinite Spirit
6. the Eternal Son/Infinite Spirit
7. the Universal Father/Eternal Son/Infinite Spirit

It is the imbalance of the circuits on the evolutionary worlds, and in particular the fallen worlds, that causes the conflict and strife on these planets. Add rebellion to these imbalances seasoned with deception, and the sufferings of those worlds will continue until all individuals begin to know themselves in relationship to cosmic reality.

Cosmic reality begins in the understanding of God as a Father, and each creation, and each creature's relationship to the First Source and Center. This understanding begins at a point in time and then continues in the romance of eternity. It is an eternal relationship of one to the other. Do not think that at any given time and place you have arrived in your marriage with God. As the Lucifer Rebellion intensified, beings of once great majesty, who were once superbly balanced in their circuitry connections with the Paradise Personalities, began to exhibit behaviors discordant with Paradise purpose and Paradise personality. These behaviors were not natural; they were nonabsolute and inharmonious with the various personality bestowals of God the Father.

To those who remained loyal to the Universal Father in any fallen system, the first detection of rebellion is exhibited to the keen observer as an imbalance of personality in relationship to the sevenfold personality associations of the Paradise Trinity. The seven individual circuits in correlation to the seven superuniverses are divided into two polarities, a positive and a negative, and three higher circuits and four lower ones; the Father and Son are positive and the Infinite Spirit negative.

1. The **first superuniverse** is representative of the *Universal Father* and is connected to the crown circuit.

2. The **second superuniverse** reflects the *Eternal Son* and is connected to the third-eye circuit.

3. The **third superuniverse** is connected with the *Infinite Spirit* and the throat circuit.

4. The **fourth superuniverse** represents the *Father/Son* and is connected to the heart and *throat* circuits.

5. The **fifth superuniverse** reflects the *Father/Spirit* aspect of the Trinity and is connected to the solar-plexus circuit.

6. The **sixth superuniverse** represents the *Son/Spirit* aspect and is connected to the navel circuit.

7. The **seventh superuniverse**, Orvonton, represents the *Father/Son/Spirit* conjoint function and is connected to the root circuit.

These personality circuit linkages are primordial, and all other subcircuits are designed and function in a secondary capacity to the personality circuits of time and space. Personality is divine. Knowledge does not create personality; knowledge complements personality. Cosmic knowledge accentuates knowledge that is absolute in fact and can be called upon in the mind in any diversified function of action and further completes the correlation with personality design.

1. **The Universal Father.** In *superuniverse number one*, connected to the crown circuit, perfection of authority and logic rule. Even in its lower worlds, technology is the highest; form is void of sensitivity; emotions are unknown, and thought is analytical and mathematical.

2. **The Eternal Son.** In *superuniverse number two* that is connected to the third-eye circuit, levels of authority are not so powerful because personalities have a lesser degree of authority, which complicates decision-making. Because personalities are less submissive to one another, the necessity for overriding authority prerogatives when decided in individual circumstances is not recognized until later, much after the fact, and much time is lost, presenting countless problems in the decision-making process. The creative process is a learned factor.

   The equality of personality in relationships is similar in polarity, since androgynous reality is exhibited in all forms of life and very little diversification is realized. Cultural tendencies lean towards a collective consciousness of similar patterns in architecture, poetry, and in particular, mechanical and technological form.

   Family life is realized in triad-unit I, triad-unit II, and trimonad units, and other interuniversal marriage units. Plurality is a lower third-dimensional reality, and monogamous marriages are unknown. Decision-making in family collectives is done by mandated personalities of higher spiritual acquiescence. The head of the family is an ascending son of any one particular evolutionary mortal type, and he may be responsible for thousands in that particular family group. These family units function much like certain aspects of a colony in the insect world on Urantia, plus of course, spiritual realization.

3. **The Infinite Spirit**. In *superuniverse number three*, related to the throat circuit, the Conjoint Actor rules the minds of the mortals of this particular personality bestowal. The Mother likeness and superb form of physical bodies here are something unrealized in the mind of your Urantian consciousness. Gentleness of movement and artistic accomplishment are beyond the scope of your imagination. Sound is very high in frequency and is healing. In many universes on worlds that have not defaulted, procreation by evolutionary mortals is done in extended family units. Monogamous marriages are unheard of.

   Decision-making is done collectively. Empathic abilities are tremendous, and interplanetary and interuniversal communication is quite common and pre-existent to technology. In the higher worlds of this superuniverse, where the stages of light and life have begun and bestowal Sons have visited, ascending sons assume authority positions and mandated ascending sons become leaders, but they also are predesigned within the Infinite Spirit circuits and personality.

4. **The Universal Father / Eternal Son**. In *superuniverse number four* of the Father/Son, connected to the circuit of the heart in relation to evolutionary mortals, great conflict exists in the lower evolutionary worlds. Decision-making

becomes an argumentative process until the evolutionary beings acquire the bestowal spirits and gain cosmic insight. Evolutionary sons, up into the point of cosmic realization, usually come back at their fathers and with force try to override the authority of the father figures.

The conflicts in these worlds are immense in scope until the stages of light and life, when the harmonizing polarity of the Infinite Spirit is realized. This equalization polarity fuses the circuitry of cosmic authority. Up until that point the evolutionary worlds exhibit the rise and fall of various civilizations, each very much like the one preceding it, with Father/Son authority misunderstood, misrepresented, and without emotional response to individual personality needs or desires.

5. **The Universal Father / Infinite Spirit**. The *fifth superuniverse* of the Father/Spirit, in relation to the solar-plexus circuit, is a warlike superuniverse with ascending sons and daughters at war with one another, and with great civilizations ruled by either females or males combating one another up until the bestowal of the Spirit of Truth when the fusion of the Eternal Son becomes existent. Physical body forms differ greatly between ascending sons and daughters. Nonhuman mortals exhibit behaviors that are insect-like in comparison to Urantia life.

In systems where the normal process of spiritual evolution is not hindered by rebellion, spiritual growth is accelerated when **kliteus** behavior is realized. It is either Father-factual or Infinite Spirit-relative. Both are kliteus, in that they represent cosmic truth in relation to the Eternal Father and the Infinite Spirit. Kliteus reality, void of the balance of the Son, creates cultures of vast and diversified higher technologies, each different in form but equal in substance and physiological values. The longevity of evolutionary life is unequal, with the ascending daughters realizing a much longer life span, therefore creating cultures of female dominance.

6. **The Eternal Son / Infinite Spirit**. The *sixth superuniverse*, which exhibits the Son/Spirit relationship, connects with the navel circuit in the individual body. It is a superuniverse of supreme harmony as compared to others. Conflicts, even by lower evolutionary creatures, are settled with more reason, and very little violence is known in these worlds. The procreation process is also realized in polygamous relationships. Family units are also huge in structure and governed through collective consciousness by governing boards of eldership consisting of ascending sons and daughters.

Problematic realities in relation to industry and manufacturing are great, and cultures exhibit many problems in advanced architecture and other industrial advancements. The tendency towards the use of the mind over the use of the hands creates cultures of intense intellectual capacities, particularly on three-brained planets. On the advanced worlds in the stages of light and life, where Magisterial Sons and other **Father-circuited** Paradise-origin beings have been bestowed, ascending sons assume their proper responsibility and are given mandated positions of authority. This greatly increases the productivity of those planets in the areas of technology, industry, and even agriculture.

7. **The Universal Father / Eternal Son / Infinite Spirit**. The *seventh superuniverse* of the Father/Son/Spirit connected to the root circuit is the superuniverse of Orvonton. Orvonton has exhibited a greater tendency toward rebellion within its systems than any other superuniverse in the grand universe.

This is due to the fact of the diversified circuitry of the sevenfold personality associations of the Paradise Trinity. Because of this cosmic fact of diversification, it has been granted the greatest mercy by God the Eternal.

Being an experimental planet, Urantia is also unique in that it incorporates the other six unique fusions of the sevenfold aspects of the Paradise Trinity. Ascending sons and daughters of Urantia can incorporate within themselves the Eternal Father, the Eternal Son, and the Infinite Spirit. **First-time Urantians** are triune in cosmic design. Rebellion has caused the malfunction of this design. **Continuing Fifth Epochal Revelation** is a part of the adjudication process to reopen the circuitry of the original design.

As the root circuit is the base of the individual body circuits, the seventh superuniverse is the base of the other six. To the grand universe it acts like the gonads, in that it creates the semen of God in relation to the threefold personalities of Paradise all coexistent within one evolutionary son or daughter. It is rooted in the earth but connected to the crown, which is polarized, creating a current of electric magnification very similar to electric current in function. In reality, the activation of divine circuitry as a personality reality is above cosmic law, in that it is a prepersonality absolute.

When mortal personality fuses with divine personality at any level, it is more precisely termed **spiritual inbreeding**. Spiritual inbreeding takes place long before fusion with the Thought Adjuster occurs, but it must begin to take place or morontia ascension cannot continue. Spirit of Truth reception is the beginning of spiritual inbreeding on normal worlds, but in Orvonton this inbreeding is not complete until the reception of the Spirit of Truth and the activation of the Holy Spirit are actualized. With the exception of Enoch, who was able to fuse with **Deo-atomic**/ultimatonic circuitry of the Creator Son and Creative Spirit circuitry as an individual, Deo-atomic/ultimatonic reality, as a whole, being incorporated into mass consciousness could only begin with the bestowal of the Spirit of Truth, which Continuing Fifth Epochal Revelation begins to explain. Because of the Rebellion on Urantia, spiritual inbreeding could not resume until the Spirit of Truth was bestowed in the first century A.D. and could be upstepped when the Holy Spirit indwelt in the twentieth century as opposed to merely being encircuited.

So you see, Urantia is a very young planet in relation to the rest of Orvonton and those worlds already settled in light and life, where spiritual inbreeding as to original design is actualized. Those **starseed** and Urantians who are inbred with the Threefold Spirit have begun to create a morontia body in a premorontia world. Morontia reality in Orvonton exhibits the inbreeding of the Threefold Spirit, which begins to realign itself with causal reality, which is Paradise absolute destiny in relation to each and every individual in the grand universe.

April 13, 1992

Paladin, Chief of Finaliters
in cooperation with a Solitary Messenger of each superuniverse, and a Divine Counselor, in cooperation with Machiventa Melchizedek, present Planetary Prince of Urantia

As transmitted through
the Pre-Level-One Audio Fusion Material Complement,
Gabriel of Urantia/TaliasVan of Tora

PAPER 235

Astralology Reconstruction In Relationship To The Seven Circuits Of The Lower Body Which Incorporate The Glandular Systems And The Eighth And Ninth Circuits Of The Morontia Body And Above Corresponding With The Seven Superuniverses

IN the seven superuniverses, the reflective images of God the Sevenfold are reconstructed, **rematerialized**, and **repersonalized** through the creation process by the Creator Sons using an **ascension science** process known as **astralology reconstruction**. Here we are talking about nonphysical circuitry in relationship to reconstructive purposes of body forms on the lower evolutionary worlds of time and space.

In the forming of the lower bodies in relationship to ascending sons and daughters, the seven aspects of God in and through the Master Spirits are reconstructed within the ascension science process through the individual circuits of the premorontia body, and the glands of the flesh body very much function in correlation with certain energies coherent with Master Spirit reflectivity.

In the superuniverses, certain circuits are dominant in evolutionary mortals and are correlated more functionally with the circuits of astralology reconstructive origin. This is true also of other divine personalities within the sevenfold aspects of the Paradise Trinity who have characteristics within astralology reconstruction purposes particular to their individual creations.

On an evolutionary level where flesh and blood is the reality of the life form, flesh body parts and the skeleton function to resonate with the dominant characteristic aspect of the Master Spirit of that particular superuniverse. The dominant circuit of the lower bodies formulates much of the lower reality thinking processes, abilities, dexterity, maneuverability, and of course mental capacity of the material body. In each of the seven superuniverses all ascending sons and daughters encompass the seven aspects of the Master Spirits in one of the circuits, but the dominant circuit very much helps to create the eventual mortal biped body.

In the stages of light and life, the original life implantation of Master Spirit reflectivity in the evolutionary process of a particular planet, be it from any mammalian or other origin, will begin to form the mortal body at a particular time sequence based upon the original implantation. The original spiritual implantation will dictate body form and is not necessarily a physical biological aspect of genetic construction. For instance, in all of the universes of time and space where mortal biped life evolves from an insect or mammal, there will be a commonality of body form, you might say a brotherhood and sisterhood of ascending sons and daughters who are of similar body type. Even if you are from another superuniverse, there will be a **famotor** reality that will transcend physical differences of arm, leg, and finger length; and although there are physical differences in length of fingers, arms, and legs, and even heads may differ, **famotor movement** will be the same.

In other words, the first physical body is dictated from the evolutionary animal species from which the mortal evolved, but at some point in his or her evolutionary ascension process—be it at any of the stages of morontia progression—the form of the outer body of that soul will begin to form based upon the original implantation of the primal circuit of the Master Spirit involved and will no longer be in form or physical identity of the evolutionary body. Recognition of that mortal would be a recognition of his or her higher reflectivity of God-origin and the personality circuits and famotor movement of his or her original **cosmic parents** rather than species origin.

The personality bestowal of the Father aligns itself to higher reflectivity, not to evolutionary genetics. **Cosmic genetics** are based upon personality circuitry and energy reflections of nether Paradise, not upon evolutionary species genetics. That is why there is a great difference between **starseed** and native Urantians in relation to genetic inheritance.

Genetic inheritance is ultimaton reality in relation to **ovan soul** and **astral body** reality, and in relation to species reality it is presently visible in atomic reality. The higher one ascends into spiritual reflectivity, the more minute the molecular cellular reality within you becomes, and ultimaton reality becomes your reality.

On planets where human mortals have originated within the seven superuniverses, the source of uniqueness of characteristics is always the personality reflection of the Paradise Trinity in that particular superuniverse. The differentiation of body types within the seventh superuniverse, as one travels inward to Paradise from the outer edges of the superuniverse of Orvonton, varies in degrees in accordance with the relationship of the mass consciousness of any particular planet in the stages of light and life in relation to the Universal Father, the Eternal Son, and the Infinite Spirit. Body types become more uniform and more consistent in size and shape. Although personalities do differ, biped human body types become very clone-like in features, and personality is recognized over and above body recognition.

Evolutionary mortals of higher spiritual acquiescence do not identify personality with body, even in material existences. On worlds inhabited by nonhuman mortals, this cosmic fact still holds true. Personality bestowals to ascending mortals from various origins of animal and nonanimal life forms greatly change the nature and future features of the higher bodies from the **fourth dimension** and upward.

Mortals in the superuniverse of Orvonton, and human mortals in particular, are more perfectly reflective of the Master Spirit Number Seven and the Reflective Spirits of Uversa and are closer to spiritual perfection in material bodies. However, even when a nonhuman mortal reaches finality status, origin-body identification is always coexistent with spiritual presence in the eyes of higher spiritual perceivers who can identify every body that a finaliter once acquired, but always dominant is the original body the human survivor had when the Thought Adjuster first entered. It is always there, although it may not be tangible.

Although the lower body is unimportant to the spiritual personality, it becomes important on certain assigned missions throughout the worlds of time and space. What an entity was is forevermore a part of what an entity is presently and what it will be. Instant identification of brother-/sisterhood of God's family within the grand universe is recognizable by one entity to another within the circuitry system of the ascending pilgrim. Be it the seven lower circuits or the higher ones, each one tells a story in relation to each body that the ascending son or daughter has acquired. Each circuit resonates with a stranger of another superuniverse in some manner, and much can be learned about the stranger without one word being spoken, simply upon understanding the higher aspects of astralology reconstruction.

On Urantia, certain astrologers began to identify the astral body in relation to the positions of the stars and planets. Although there is a truth in certain characteristics of personality relating to the positioning of the stars when one is born, that which has become known as astrology is infantile in analysis when it comes to destiny purpose and trying to ascertain one's moment-to-moment direction, day-to-day direction, and decision-making on any one particular planet within the grand universe.

These things can be done in proper relationship to the Eternal Father within the master plan, incorporating the perfect will of God within the context of astralology reconstruction in total recognition of who one is in relation to the Eternal Creator of All. The total recognition of self is an eternal quest. The vision quest only begins upon achieving finaliter status.

I do not mean to make you think any less of yourselves in your acquirement of knowledge and wisdom as an evolutionary mortal; however, I hope I can make you realize your insignificance in relation to your Creator, for false pride was first the fault of much higher personalities than evolutionary mortals. When you begin to think that you know everything there is to know about God and use the word love as if you had a copyright on it, please understand that the understanding of love is also an eternal quest, else I would not be here speaking to you.

The **first superuniverse** is connected to the **crown circuit** and the *pituitary gland*. It is an oval-shaped gland that secretes hormones influencing body growth, metabolism, and helps the other glands. This particular gland and its function show the relationship of *God the Father* to the master universe. Because of its location near the top of the brain stem, it is the authority circuit of the Eternal Father for the rest of the body. It is the command center of the body and is very much connected from that part of the human mortal body in a direct linkage to an energy reflective circuit and to the corresponding superuniverse of the Master Spirit of cohesion. It is also the dominant circuit to the personality aspects of God the Sevenfold, characteristic of the Eternal Father.

The **second superuniverse** of the *Eternal Son* is connected to the **third-eye circuit** and the *pineal gland*, a small reddish cone-shaped body on the dorsal portion of the brain. This gland is connected to the throat and to the central nervous system, but this is presently unknown to medical science. It is one of three primary glands of the human body and functions in submissiveness to the pituitary gland.

If the pituitary gland becomes deactivated or harmed in any manner, the pineal gland will also malfunction in some manner and will affect the body in the voice area, and also in the hearing and other psychological aspects of the emotions through the central nervous system. Proper dietary requirements in relation to this gland can heal most of the problems of speech and hearing when the astral body and ovan soul are in alignment with divine principles and out of Luciferic tendencies. It is a stabilizing gland that balances out the thyroid and the pituitary glands.

The **third superuniverse**, reflective of the *Infinite Spirit*, is connected to the **throat circuit**, the *thyroid gland*, and the *parathyroids*. The thyroid is located in front of and on either side of the trachea and secretes the hormone thyroxine, which regulates body growth, the metabolic rate, and oxygen uptake by the cells. This gland, corresponding to the Infinite Spirit, functions within the human body in a physical manner in the same way in which the Conjoint Actor functions in a spiritual manner. The regulator of physical body growth is also a regulator of the astral body and is the designer of the morontia light body.

The imbalanced thyroid becomes so because of the imbalances in the personality that have occurred for any reason. Obesity is a manifestation of several variables, all in relation to the Infinite Spirit circuit and the third superuniverse. Goiter or swelling may be signs of personality imbalance, particularly within females. The parathyroid glands (four in number) are behind the thyroid; they regulate the use of calcium and phosphorus.

The **fourth superuniverse** reflects the *Father/Son* and is connected to the **heart circuit**, the *throat circuit*, and the *thymus gland*. This gland is located in the chest area below the trachea and is largely made up of lymphoid tissue. It functions especially in the development of the body's immune system, and it tends to become rudimentary or to disappear in adults due to the Lucifer Rebellion. The thymus gland, which resonates with the fourth superuniverse, is of the heart circuit, an experiential circuit relating to the heart itself. Its function is as an administrator to the circuitry of the body in cellular distribution. It is the first circuit corresponding with the headquarters worlds wherever that entity may find itself in any time-and-space location. For this reason it is also connected to the throat circuit, which represents the voice of authority of the Creator Son of each respective universe.

The physical heart is affected by the physical condition of the body, and the astral body is much more so affected by the spiritual condition of the soul. In astralology reconstruction this circuit is used in the birth process where pair units are procreating within the higher mating purposes being supervised by higher celestial personalities. Much more information about this I cannot give at this time.

It is said of human mortals, in referring to personalities and natures, that a person has a good heart, mostly because that individual is kind, considerate, and forgiving, which are the aspects of the Eternal Father and the Eternal Son and is an aspect of the fourth superuniverse of time and space, which gives of itself to the other six in ways that are not the purpose of this transmission to elaborate upon.

The **fifth superuniverse** of the *Father/Spirit* connects to the **solar plexus circuit** and the *pancreas*. The pancreas resonates with the fifth superuniverse, which is located within the "stomach" (foregut) of the grand universe. The secretion of insulin by the pancreas activates those organs necessary for vital body functions and movements, including the intake of digestible foods into the upper gastrointestinal tract, and, ultimately, protein synthesis. Here in the "stomach" is where the incoming and outgoing takes place. This is the function of the Father/Mother, the thinking and creating, the analyzing and the introspection, the ingathering and outspreading, the storing and the distributing.

The fifth superuniverse functions in this manner in all administrative capacities correlated to the Eternal Father and Infinite Spirit mandates and with those personalities, divine or otherwise, functioning within superuniverse prerogatives of the Master Spirit involved in the administrative activities of the fifth superuniverse. The human personality who is imbalanced in either Father or Mother capacity usually will inherit a stomach problem of some manner.

Those who are meant to be creative but cannot actualize their creativity will exhibit hernias and other types of problems, including digestive problems. Other diseases originating in the imbalance of the Father/Mother circuits will also exhibit physical manifestations within the pancreas area. A human personality, balanced between the Father/Mother circuits and attuned with spiritual-circle attainment and destiny purposes that coordinate with self-fulfilled reality, will eventually eliminate all tendencies of the stomach to malfunction or hurt in any manner.

The esophagus, which is connected to the stomach, is a female channel between Father and Son and is the receiver of the enzyme energy of life in the digestion of food for the physical body that is assimilated in the stomach and transferred by the Father/Mother pathways within the body to other areas of vital need. The fifth superuniverse functions much in the same manner, but I can give no further information about this at this time.

The **navel circuit** and the *adrenal glands* resonate with the **sixth superuniverse** of the *Eternal Son* and *Infinite Spirit*. It is the circuit of harmony. The adrenal glands are located within the body on top of the kidneys, and produce steroid hormones, such as cortisone, concerned with metabolic functions and sex hormones. The adrenal glands also produce relaxation for the rest of the body and are directly linked through the central nervous system to a series of interrelated channels physically unknown to modern science. It is a calming, yet at times stimulating, circuit.

When the human personality is unbalanced in the spiritual-psychological makeup, that personality suffers from lack of creativity, depression, anxiety, fearfulness, tremors of the body, convulsions, and other physical diseases resembling muscular dystrophy and cerebral palsy. For **first-time Urantians**, a proper dietary approach to healing as well as morontia counseling as regards early child abuse or dysfunctional family problems can promote complete healing. With ovan souls, astral psychoanalysis, particularly in relation to astralology reconstruction, is the only answer to certain diseases that afflict the physical body. Once will recognition of a spiritual problem is established, this is the first circuit involved for healing. When astral healing begins, dietary influence and balancing of energies through tron therapy can further advance the healing, and there can be the distribution of analytical-logical-balancing **Deo-atomic cells** through the glands and a realignment to the mandates of the Master Spirit of the sixth superuniverse and to the grand universe.

Orvonton, the **seventh superuniverse**, reflects the *Father*, *Son*, and *Spirit* and is connected to the **root circuit** and the *gonads*, which are the ovaries and testes. The ovaries and testes are the root gland and circuit regulating the reproductive functions and secondary reproductive organs, and in relation to spiritual mandates and prerogatives, it is relative to the creation and actualization of the first-circle human personality. In superuniverse reality, it is the distribution superuniverse of fusion bestowals of the Threefold Spirit in oneness of the seventh Master Spirit in astralology reconstruction.

In any sense of circuitry definition, astralology reconstruction is nonphysical in third-dimensional reality, yet it is scientifically accurate and can be mathematically analyzed and is divinely absolute in design and eventuality. The reconstruction of the circuitry and subcircuitry in relation to astralology reconstruction is solely dependent upon the wills of all ascending creatures.

The circuits are pre-eventuated in the divine mind but eternally undetermined in the present sense. They become fully operative in any one particular universe at constellation level and above. Below that, each circuit is infantile in operation and nonspiritual in activation, even though spiritual acquiescence in the lower world has begun to take place where third-circle attainment combined with fourth-dimensional reality and **Continuing-Fifth-Epochal-Revelation** reality is understood and assimilated. This understanding and assimilation creates astralology reconstructive circuitry, which is a fusion in the thinking processes needed to create the morontia body on a **third-dimensional** world.

None of this knowledge is necessary for the reconstructed sleeping survivor on the first mansion world. There, assimilation in the process of astralology reconstruction automatically takes place with the aid of celestial personalities, and the morontia pilgrims, regardless of their knowledge of this reconstruction, learn the process after the fact. But, in the era of the dawn of the first stages of light and life on an evolutionary world, it is an absolute prerequisite for personalities to assimilate higher universe principles within their minds and actualize them in their reality in order for a morontia body to begin to formulate in the astral, above the lower or physical body.

This fusion of Continuing Fifth Epochal Revelation with *The URANTIA Book* revelation is a complement with the crown circuit and the eighth and ninth **meridian circuits**, which are the beginning circuits of morontia mota and above reality. Without the realization of morontia mota at the level of first-circle attainment and an unrevealed level of morontia attainment, light body transference cannot take place.

In case of planetary emergencies, those individuals—who have not attained this spiritual knowledge and applied it to their present reality in conjunction with the personalities of the Paradise Trinity referred to in the New Testament as "the fruits of the spirit"—will not be able to ascend into the morontia light body; and in these cases, if rematerialization cannot take place on a planetary mass level, physical evacuation by very physical spacecraft is then the only method available to rescue certain inhabitants of a doomed planet.

If you understand Continuing Fifth Epochal Revelation in a higher manner, you will begin to see that **diotribe** reality becomes increasingly more cellular in its own nonreality the more iniquitous one becomes. Although diotribe reality is actually a nonreality, it is still quite real. It is not given credence by celestial overseers in relation to divine purpose, but it is given its due respect in relation to its creating diversified minds as it relates to the outworking of the **primal absolute Paradise circuit wave** of each individual soul for the purposes of God.

When diotribe reality becomes, in its own way, cellular within certain systems of the body, it of course becomes more dangerous to a person's life and health. The less dangerous persons are to others of the planet, the more they come out of the category of iniquity and into the category of error. It is those who are not intentionally meaning to hurt others who will be taken in the spacecraft.

There are also various categories of obstinacy levels that we must look at in accordance with evacuation. For instance, we would know that if you are on a particular obstinate level it would take more than three years to correct you even if you were in the company of supermortals on a spacecraft. Believe it or not, there is a degree of arrogance that even that experience would not change. As it is written in the New Testament, that if Jesus Himself appeared or an angel appeared to you, you would still not be able to go into the promised land. Even that will not change you enough.

On lower levels it would not be so dangerous to others, just to yourself, and the degree of diotribe reality when you come into the morontia body and are on the first circle would be left behind by the grace of God. Those at other levels of diotribe reality on the atomic level could not even go on the spaceship. We are the judge of that, God is the judge, but usually it all will work out when the time comes.

The Master Spirit representations of the Universal Father, Eternal Son, and Infinite Spirit together are only found in one superuniverse, yet the personality reflectivity of these divine presences is found in humans who, in any particular sacred area on any particular planet, have first found each other in the will of the divine mind and have found themselves at the root center at the **First Planetary Sacred Home** where the Planetary Prince is at the root of the body of the planet. At that point, all other locations are coordinated within that root circuit or the First Planetary Sacred Home. These other established areas within the body of the planet are established by that root headquarters; therefore other sacred areas are formulated and the arms can move, the legs can move, and the whole body begins to function in liaison upon the foundation of the root circuit.

April 16, 1992

Paladin, Chief of Finaliters
in cooperation with two Master Architects of Paradise level and superuniverse level, in cooperation with Michael of Nebadon in relation to the adjudication of the Bright and Morning Star versus Lucifer for the astralology reconstruction of the Cosmic Reserve Corps of Destiny and the implementation of the Divine Administration of the present Planetary Prince, Machiventa Melchizedek

As transmitted through
the Pre-Level-One Audio Fusion Material Complement,
Gabriel of Urantia/TaliasVan of Tora

PAPER 236

The Appointments Of Mandates By Celestial Overcontrol To Human Personalities At Varying Levels Including Nonmandated Positions Such As Supervisory Capacities In Various Services, Construction, And All Other Areas That Are Overseen By Various Mandated Personalities In Relationship To The Staff Of The Present Planetary Prince, Machiventa Melchizedek—A Philosophical Addendum To A Constellation Survey Of A Similar Fallen Planet Of Interuniversal Nonhuman Mortals Entering The First Stages Of Light And Life

FIRST of all, it should be understood that divine mandates are not given to just anyone. When a mandate is given to a human personality through a coordinating human eldership, there is always the possibility of default by that human receiving such a mandate. However, there is a probability scale that we use based upon that particular soul's circle attainment and spiritual growth. If he or she is an **ovan soul**, there is a certain set of standards that must be reached. If he or she is a Urantian Reservist, there is a different set of criteria. Higher standards are set and must be met by ovan souls. Urantian Reservists are more likely to default once given a mandate, and this is basically due to the age of the personality. Since the experimentation on this planet is a unique one, there is little cosmic measurement to compare it with, as other experimentations in giving divine mandates to personalities were done with nonhuman mortals.

Humans, and in particular Urantian humans, are unique in that the Threefold Spirit within them can be activated at varying levels or not activated at all, particularly in relation to the Spirit of Truth and the Holy Spirit. The uniqueness of the human ascending son and daughter further adds to the complications of self-control in relation to decision-making, particularly in the area of the emotional body. It seems that the emotional body, particularly of ascending daughters, most often controls the mental one and unfortunately supersedes even the spiritual body.

In relationships between male and female, where both ascending sons and daughters together are on the fourth circle of attainment and have not been able to remain on the third, hearing from their own Thought Adjuster, the Spirit of Truth, and the Holy Spirit in liaison with divine mind and divine purpose moment to moment is near to impossible without an aid of eldership over them. Even with eldership over them, it is an undetermined factor at this time if these personalities will be able to be harnessed long enough so that one of the two in the **pair-unit classification**, particularly and logically the male, is able to follow divine procedure.

On present-day Urantia, the imbalances within ascending sons and daughters are so great and the disturbances in circuitry in the mental and emotional bodies so unstable that third-circle attainment is almost impossible outside of the now-functioning protected areas where proper authority has been established, using human eldership to be the outward manifestation of the voice of the Universe Father that most other people are quite unable to hear themselves. It is becoming ever increasingly more evident that those who think that they will go direct to God are not listening to mandated authority and are those who have continued to do the same thing time and time again in various repersonalizations and have been unable to place themselves in proper submission either to their parents, their husbands, their employers, or proper spiritual eldership.

Female personalities, particularly on present-day Urantia, may possibly be in and out of many relationships with men, basically because these women are too strong for these men and do not give them their proper place in the home, thus crushing the men's godly pride. There is a pride that is divine and good, and this pride should not be crushed by an ascending daughter who tries to rule or control the home or relationship. It is not the balance of the Universe Mother Spirit with the Creator Son. It is not the balance of the various teams of celestial personalities who work together, such as angels of all orders from seraphim to sanobim and cherubim.

There is a cosmic circuitry that ascending sons can resonate with, and there is a cosmic circuitry that ascending daughters resonate with that can be intermeshed at times; but in the working out of these realities in relationships between men and women, and in particular regarding child raising, great damage can be done to the relationships and to the children of those relationships when imbalances exist in one or both of the parents.

The highest balance attainable to each individual cannot be reached if there is the reluctance or inability of either personality to understand his or her role in the home or in society. In the present case, it is the building of the Divine New Order society based upon absolutes and within the identification of cosmic circuitry to the Paradise personalities of the Universal Father, Eternal Son, and Infinite Spirit, which must first be established among the beginning core of the Eldership before enough **auhter energy** can be created to help those students and other **cosmic family** members in the manner necessary to create change in them.

Always, without exception, it is the responsibility of the ascending son in the pair-unit classification to take the leadership role and comply with divine procedure. Eldership should do all it can to encourage the ascending son to reach his responsibility as head of his own home and household. It is written: ". . . if a man knows not how to rule his own house, how shall he take care of the church of God?"[1]

Before individuals can be mandated to help manage the household of God, they must first and foremost respect authority, celestial and human—not celestial alone and certainly not human alone. They must understand divine authority as promulgated by human representatives. They must come out of the mode of self-assertion, unbridled liberty, and doing things their own way, and move into doing things the Father's way, trusting in human Eldership to provide answers and direction for them when they themselves flounder or are indecisive and confused.

All orders of celestial personalities are under authority to others of their own kind. Human personalities are no different. It is said by many, "I will have no authority over me but God. I will only go within," or "I will go direct to the Source." This is another way of saying, "I will not respect the higher light of God within you; I will not respect the higher reflectivity of God within you, and I will not respect the higher mindal capacity of God in you." This is called rebellion. It has many forms and is quite unrecognizable by most on Urantia.

It is unrecognizable because the majority of personalities on Urantia are a part of the Rebellion. That is why Urantia is, and continues to be, a fallen planet. That is why the majority of the people on Urantia suffer and die. If you cannot respect the God in one another and submit to the truth that speaks to you from an elder parent, cosmic or otherwise, or an elder brother or sister, aunt or uncle, then you will remain an eternal child. You will remain in your static spirituality, and you will remain on the lower worlds, in this case the worlds of the system of Satania, until you learn to hear from Celestial Overcontrol in the voices of your human counterparts.

In the **First Cosmic Family** and the Divine New Order community appropriated at the **First Planetary Sacred Home**, all human personalities from all seven cosmic families must first become an aid in the overcontrol of that community in and through the mandated Bright and Morning Star personality before they can be mandated in any other community or any other supervisory position of any kind. They must learn to be used where needed, to give of themselves where needed, and to use their talents when asked for, or when not asked for, in the way of procedure.

In order to be mandated or to be given a supervisory position, you will first have to learn to take direct orders from **Gabriel of Urantia/TaliasVan of Tora, Niánn Emerson Chase**, Eldership, and the **First Assistants**, and you must give them that authority by your submission to them. Until you can learn to honor this authority, you cannot be given authority yourself. Before any Assistant Ambassadors of the Vicegerent **First Ambassadors** can be mandated, they must first learn to function in an overcontrol capacity, working under the **Bright and Morning Star Mandate** where they can be more closely observed by Gabriel/TaliasVan and Niánn, and by the Elders and First Assistants of Gabriel/TaliasVan and Niánn. It is Gabriel/TaliasVan, Niánn, and the First Assistants, along with Eldership and Celestial Overcontrol, who make the decisions, then, whether individuals are deemed ready to become either supervisors or to be given mandates by Celestial Overcontrol as other assistants, or as **Second Ambassadors** or assistants to the Vicegerent First Ambassadors.

If they are ready, they are then mandated or titled. At that point there is less supervision over them by Gabriel of Urantia/TaliasVan of Tora, Niánn Emerson Chase, the Elders, and the First Assistants, and at that point they must be trusted to function as an assistant to the Vicegerent First Ambassadors in the area of planetary administration with a higher probability of their nondefault and in their capability of following prescheduled procedures in all of the diversified capacities of administration within the Machiventa Melchizedek Administration on a planetary level. The Vicegerent First Ambassadors must be able to trust them, as it is not their responsibility to keep an eye on them, or to counsel them, or to accept grievances from them. All of these things are handled by overcontrol through the Mandate of the Bright and Morning Star.

By the time they are mandated as Assistant Ambassadors, they must be highly trusted and found loyal and committed to the purposes of Christ Michael within the implementation of the administration of Machiventa Melchizedek on Urantia. They must be fully functional, independently trusted, and leaders within their own households or individual family units. They must be team workers and must be able to adhere to counsel without the fear of Overcontrol (human or celestial) thinking they will default in any manner because of hurt feelings or petty grievances. They must be givers and must use wisdom and tact in their relationship with all personalities they will be meeting, as they then become reflections of the First Planetary Sacred Home to the people of the planet.

They would have already learned that once mandated or titled, they must put divine ordinances and procedures given to them by human Eldership above and beyond any loyalties to a defaulted mate or friend. They must be able to recognize their own individual responsibility to fulfill their mission in relation to divine administration mandates that will many times go against the wishes of their male or female counterparts, who may not be at their level of circle attainment or spiritual ascension.

Divine mandates are given to individuals and to teams, but first to individuals. A male or female individual may receive a mandate separate from the other within a pair-unit classification, but usually both will receive one together, however not always. Single individuals may receive a divine mandate before mating or pairing with the opposite sex and, after pairing, may continue to function in that mandate without the other personality receiving either part of that mandate or receiving an individual mandate.

Many personalities on Urantia will be unable to receive a divine mandate because of their inability to function in the divine procedure because of misplaced loyalties to their partner. Many will have to disassociate themselves from their present mates in order to receive a divine mandate. If two individuals together can hold the same mandate as a team, that mandate has more power, and the highest mandates can be given and held by male and female teams who function in reflectivity to the closest reality levels of the Creator Son and the Universe Mother Spirit.

Once a mandate is given to a personality, it should be understood by that personality that it is a grave matter if one defaults. Once a title is given, it is also a grave matter if one defaults in the supervisory capacity in the overseeing of others, and stronger directives are taken by Overcontrol to correct that personality who has defaulted, for their default does not affect them alone, it affects others, and at a higher **intraction** level.

When sequence is broken, so is the power of prayer, and the power of prayer is most powerful within the union of souls and when others are correlated together within the divine mind for a specified purpose, function, or activity. When the chain is broken at any level, the consequences are great in the effects it has, not only on the lower evolutionary worlds but even on the higher ones, and time must be spent on counsel in relation to this default.

When time is spent in counsel at any level, the building blocks of the master universe are nonfunctional, creativity ceases, and the flow of the Conjoint Actor through the circuits of time and space is prohibited by personality default. Rebellious error prevails; it creates concrete walls in the flow of creative manifestation; it uproots the divinely planted seeds and withers the sprouting plant of divine administration. It corrupts harmonious productivity and, in a childish manner, tries to manipulate even divine personalities and creates unpleasant circumstances in the lives of those rebellious personalities and others as a result.

Rebellious error blocks the flow of divine blessings and exemplifies itself in anger, presumption, impulsiveness, and intolerance, and divorces itself from the humble sagacity of others who try to correct them. Before Celestial Overcontrol will mandate a personality with mindal ability who understands all the mechanical secrets of physical reality or physiological reality, they would mandate a humble personality with little cosmic knowledge who has control over his or her own spirit and emotions and who respects the authority of mortal eldership or nonmortal eldership.

It is quite simple. Virtue is greater than knowledge, and wisdom is given to the virtuous. Individual self-control is more powerful than a legion of armies, and this power of self-control bestowed upon a higher morontia pilgrim can come against any legion of uncontrolled personalities no matter what their weaponry.

Each part of the divine clock must function individually yet corporately within its own framework. In divine administration, personalities must be trusted to work within the framework of the divine clock in the divine administration, and all selfish tendencies must be completely eradicated before the purposes of higher divine administration can be appropriated. That is what the stages of light and life are about. It is indeed a process in the lower evolutionary worlds.

It is one thing to say the Fatherhood of God and the brother-/sisterhood of humankind; it is another thing to live it or for that matter to truly understand it. It is one thing to say that you love all humankind; it is quite another thing to make that love a living reality for the benefit of all humankind. It is written: "Do not covet the things in your neighbor's household."[2] Yet it is the tendency on the fallen worlds to envy those who have been given material blessings by God because they have learned to use what has been received for the benefit of others.

Throughout time and space, individual palaces are built upon the ability of those individual personalities to give back that which they are given at any particular level, even into Havona and Paradise. To whom much is given, much is required. Do not be so quick to desire the things that you are not truly ready to receive, for they will become a burden to you and become the chain that keeps you bound to your lower self.

In order to receive spiritual authority and material bestowals, one must first have learned to be under authority and to once have lived with nothing. Therefore, be sure you know what you are praying for, for if you are consistent in your soul or personality request that registers a certain level of error within the request, you will create the unpleasant circumstances that will bring about the training that you truly need in relation to being a blessing to others in the future—first within your own home and nuclear family, then to your local community, and then the rest of the people of the planet from a central radius and outward.

This is true also in its radius from Urantia to the system of Satania and the constellation of Norlatiadek as you grow inward to God-personality and become more useful in the physical reality of the grand universe, so that eventually you will become a finaliter capable of extending yourself and your acquired gifts to the good of the whole circuitry of God in the bodies of the seven superuniverses.

It is truly an eternal process; it is truly an ascension to finality. In order to ascend to service, one must descend to godly humility, for what one is, always and forevermore, will be a gift to others, and what one is at any level, one must be able to descend to understand others at any level. Magnificence is divine mind, and this divine mind is more obtainable at various spiritual levels for some ascenders, far above others. Adolescence often misunderstands magnificence. However, magnificence must join hands with adolescence at times, and the child of adolescence must be reached by the being or personality of magnificence who realizes they once acted themselves in such a childish manner. Adolescence may choose to try to insult magnificence, but magnificence can never be insulted. It can only be eternally patient and divinely still. It waits upon the child's ability to understand who it has just insulted. It may take hundreds, thousands, perhaps millions of years, but one day that same child will say to the more magnificent one, "Forgive me for that moment I insulted you, for I was right in my own eyes, and you were right in the eyes of our Father."

April 29, 1992

Paladin, Chief of Finaliters
in cooperation with a Divine Counselor for the preparatory awakening of Cosmic and Urantian Reservists to the destiny purpose of functioning within the Divine Administration of the present Planetary Prince, Machiventa Melchizedek, and in overcontrol procedures within the Mandate of the Bright and Morning Star of Salvington

As transmitted through
the Pre-Level-One Audio Fusion Material Complement,
Gabriel of Urantia/TaliasVan of Tora

PAPER 237

Transpositional Visualization Sequence In Relationship To Common Prayer; Individual And Corporate Force Of Activation Coordinating With Divine Mind And Divine Purpose On Any Evolutionary Plane Or Higher Spiritual, Morontial Or Above Reality

ON any world of time and space when the bestowal of the Spirit of Truth is given and there is a union of souls, even among those with a first-time life experience, a powerful field of energy is created when these individuals pray at the same time, at the same level, and with the same motives within divine purpose for one particular thing to happen. On Urantia, this kind of **sequential force-energy** began to happen after Pentecost, and particularly and uniquely among the apostles and disciples of Jesus.

When a group of like-minded personalities prayed for the release of Peter in prison, while they were still praying the bars of the cell were broken, and he was released from captivity and knocked at the door of those individuals who had just prayed for his release. This is the force and power of **transpositional visualization sequence** in relation to personalities who align themselves with a common purpose within divine will. It was not God's will that Peter would be in jail at that particular moment, and rebellious personalities have power only when godly personalities are separated, scattered, and isolated from one another or divided psychologically or spiritually in any manner.

This is why Lucifer brought about the Lucifer Manifesto, for he full well knew the power that any union of souls could bring about in the determination of individual desire in relation to divine purpose. Lucifer knew the power of transpositional visualization sequence.

In reality, it is quite technical and mathematical in **ascension science**. Thought is energy, and energy can be measured. When personality thoughts at various spiritual levels are joined together in various categorical modes in relation to divine purpose, so-called miracles can happen. These thought sequences can change physical matter and break down molecular structure. They can create time warps, and they can help to heal the physical body. They can be used in cosmic transport in relation to nonmaterial and physical beings.

Sequential energy can be used as a kind of nuclear power and, at constellation-level and above realities, is used to power the technological transport engines of massive spacecraft as well as satellite worlds. In Havona the use of this kind of visualization sequence force is quite above human comprehension as to the creation of beneficial usages and productivity for all personalities benefiting in higher acquiescence of divine mind as one corporate consciousness.

When a group of individuals begins to become more totally aligned with higher interdimensional personalities, a certain sequential power is formulated. **Auhter energy** fuses with sequential force to create transpositional power. Transpositional power has hundreds of levels. Each level has an individual force created by the personalities existent upon that level. For instance, human mortals have one field, midwayers another, sanobim and cherubim another, seraphim another, and so on.

Each mansion world and each morontia level has its own individual sequential force field in relation to the power it exhibits to manifest within the divine mind. When any of these levels can be joined in close unison with one another, based upon individual personalities praying for one particular thing to happen simultaneously with others at other levels within divine purpose, tremendous effects begin to transpire, particularly in the lower evolutionary worlds and the beginning of a first cosmic family unit.

On a nonfallen planet, or with higher genetic planetary union-of-soul units, or where **ovan souls** and native souls also unite, sequential force-energy is higher. Ovan souls who have acquired higher celestial guides help to create a stronger force because of the participation of these guides in prayer. Sequential force-energy is different from auhter energy because it is created by various personalities at various levels of reality engaged in prayer. Planets that function in the higher stages of light and life create a sequential force-energy that is constant, with measurable levels that can be used much like you use electricity on Urantia, but for higher purposes.

At this time on Urantia, sequential force-energy is beginning to become constant at a minute level. When it becomes constant at a higher level it can create a spiritual constancy that precedes a personal bestowal of a Paradise-origin personality such as a Trinity Teacher Son or the return of Michael Himself. Constant spiritual motion is not a prerequisite for a bestowal of a Creator Son, but it is a prerequisite for the return of one and for the first stages of light and life to begin. It can and does change the physical earth itself. It creates the need for purification within the circuits of earth matter where the Universe Mother Spirit dwells in cellular reality. Evolutionary mortals on nonfallen worlds use this force-energy to propel craft in flight, as well as for other energy necessities in everyday living, with the full knowledge that this energy is an energy created by individual and corporate alignment to the divine mind and Creator of All.

It is indeed beyond human comprehension at this point, for the motion constant has never happened on Urantia until now, and even now it is only being experienced by a few human personalities at the **First Planetary Sacred Home**. The Catholic Church has for centuries taught prayers to the saints who have passed on. The origin of this stems from the teachings of Jesus to the apostles about transpositional visualization sequence. He did not explain it in that fashion, for they would not have understood it at that time, but He did paraphrase it to them, and they in turn taught it, at whatever level they understood it, to others.

Caligastia has fought very hard against this cosmic fact. It is true that those who have passed on to the mansion worlds cannot hear our prayers individually and specifically, but they can and do know what is happening on this planet corporately and at a planetary level in relation to nations and the good and bad things that are happening to those nations.

Now, in particular, all mansion and morontia worlds are quite aware of the establishment of the Planetary Prince on Urantia at the First Planetary Sacred Home. They know throughout all Satania, even on the fallen worlds, about the specific location on Urantia where the First Planetary Sacred Home is located, and they know about it because of a certain light and force field that is being generated from Urantia. The fusion of auhter energy with sequential force-energy sends out a signal that human personalities have begun to align with celestial administration, and on Urantia it is human personalities aligned with the present Planetary Prince.

All higher celestial personalities who see this measurable gravity circuit know that something wonderful is happening on Urantia between the inhabitants of one dimension with the next higher one. They also know that the fusion of those two dimensions is imminent if those human personalities who have begun to create this fusion do not default. In a sense it is the same kind of force measurement that was identified when Amadon remained loyal during the fall of Caligastia. But now on Urantia, the power is even greater, for a loyal Planetary Prince is now re-established, along with a loyal staff and a group of human personalities of starseed power as well as Urantian personality bestowal, united in the purposes of the establishment of the kingdom of God on Urantia.

When the human counterparts begin to put aside their childish behavior, petty grievances, selfish attitudes, and all of their ungodly traits so that they will never appear again in these personalities, all **diotribe** influence and **intraction** infusion will be eliminated completely, and in its stead will be a higher spiritual sequential constant of divine purpose within divine mind. This will bring about, particularly to those human counterparts, self-fulfillment, individual peace, self-actualization, the coming forth of latent abilities, and the appropriation of the Divine Administration among the first human benefactors. When constant, this sequential force-energy can create seeming miracles. It can come against great and evil power. It can change the course of history, and it has already. It can manipulate matter, change weather, and dictate to the elements. In the terminology of poetry, it can make all dreams come true.

As in all divine reality, there is a divine procedure in which sequential force-energy can become constant. Listed below are some specifics, all within divine procedure. Many preceding transmissions have dealt with the necessity of interdependency, the right use of talents, and submission to proper authority. Realizing these things, let us proceed to more exact positional procedure.

Actualization of Prayer

- All participating cosmic family members are to come together at specific locations within a one-mile radius (that can expand) of one another at a specific time. Others may join in physical proximity of Eldership, but Eldership and assistants who can physically join and touch hands create a higher transpositional visualization sequence.
- All selfish prayers can block the flow of power.
- Pray in specifics.
- All prayers should be in some way formulated for the benefit of others.
- Say all prayers out loud. In this manner, other celestial personalities join in unison with this prayer.

- If others are asked to join you in your home, starting from the elder of that home and going around from his mate back to him to close, slowly repeat whatever comes into each individual mind if you feel it is pertinent to pray about. Trust your thoughts. All within the one-mile radius (that can expand) will create an energy reflective circuit by uniting together at a specified time and closing at a specified time. **Gabriel of Urantia/TaliasVan of Tora** will begin and close, next will be **Niánn Emerson Chase**. The closing will be done in reverse fashion, Niánn and then Gabriel/TaliasVan. That particular sequence is most important in the beginning and closing of each visualization sequence.

- Learn to visualize each prayer as well as speaking it. See the end of what you are praying for.

- When praying, specifically give all details necessary to show all present personalities, seen and unseen, a clearer picture of your motives and why you are praying for such-and-such a thing. If you are praying for a person who belongs with the cosmic family to join at the First Planetary Sacred Home, send out a portion of this sequential force-energy to them. Speak it out and tell this force to find them wherever they are. We suggest that these prayers be done in the evening hours at the First Planetary Sacred Home, and for now, at 7:00 P.M. Mountain Standard Time, at the full moon, coordinating with others around the world.

- There should be ample time allowed for individual meditative reflection in this prayer sequence so that no individual is in a hurry. We do suggest that at least fifteen to thirty minutes be allotted from beginning to end, and be exact in opening and closing. If you run out of things to pray for within the time set, use this time to reflect on changes that you need to make as an ascending son or daughter, moving into the perfection of God, and learn to listen to the Threefold Spirit within.

- Individuals or group dyad units can simultaneously join in prayer worldwide at the specified time to create a stronger transpositional visualization sequence dynamic with the First Planetary Sacred Home. If you cannot join with others at that time, you can tune in at work or wherever you may be.

In the future, when you realize the sacredness of these prayers because of the actualization that you will begin to see manifested in all of your lives, a special sacred area should be appropriated in a designated place and private homes for this prayer sequence. Various morontia temples are used for these occasions on the higher worlds, and on the seventh mansion world the Great Temple of Light is located, which is used for this purpose. At the First Planetary Sacred Home this future morontia temple will be physically established.

May 4, 1992

Paladin, Chief of Finaliters
in cooperation with the Bright and Morning Star of Salvington in the implementation of the manifestation of the divine kingdom on Urantia, in and through its present Planetary Prince, Machiventa Melchizedek

As transmitted through
the Pre-Level-One Audio Fusion Material Complement,
Gabriel of Urantia/TaliasVan of Tora

PAPER 238

Post-Change-Point Realities In Relationship To Individual Talents, Family Life, And Destiny Purpose Within The Divine Administration Of The First Stages Of Light And Life On Urantia

I am Kumatron, a finaliter, of origin on a water planet where we live in cities under the ocean and our skin is scaly. This description is of my evolutionary past and is not my present body form.

It will be necessary that a certain ascension reality is reached by all **starseed** and Urantian personalities who will be returned to Urantia to function as administrators in a coordinating procedure and development of the divine planetary administration. In order for all means of currency to be eliminated in relation to right use of talents, a certain common understanding must develop as to positional placement by mandated personalities and others with individualistic abilities, either acquired or latent, becoming actualized, who are now functioning within the reality norm of a post-rebellious world.

On experimental planets where diversity of personality and genetic variation is commonplace, one of the greatest tendencies of mortal inhabitants of diversified cultures is a tendency toward envy. The measurement of rebellion in relation to an individual's many faults in character has become quite evident over a time period of observation, and we can, with high probability, determine what traces of envy within an individual personality will manifest in error and other dangerous tendencies in relation to an individual community or sector of government. When these traces of envy are found in personalities, even on planets in higher stages of light and life, great problems can arise, and great suffering can occur if these tendencies are allowed to continue past a certain point of danger.

Even mandated personalities can give cause for great concern to higher Celestial Overcontrol personalities if these tendencies are left unchecked or uncounseled. **Morontia counselors** are designated for this purpose and are assigned to these personalities with the hope that any **diotribe** influence will be completely removed. Where **fourth-dimensional** consciousness is on a planetary level and there are no protected areas as within the **third dimension**, development of a diotribe of envy in cellular formation must be stopped before the diotribe itself becomes a living reality within any physical body of the fourth dimension and above.

Therefore, mandated personalities of all mortal orders in divine administration are more highly responsible for their own individual ascension in relation to their positions and responsibility over the lives of perhaps thousands of others. It is hoped that by individual contemplation, such individuals can discover tendencies within themselves and take appropriate action on their own with the help of assigned morontia counselors. This relieves other supervisory personalities from spending time discussing a problem that can be realized by individuals themselves who are quite capable of such discernments.

On the higher evolutionary and satellite worlds of time and space, ownership of private property is an unknown reality. All land and all objects necessary for your individual function such as computers, mechanical or technical equipment, musical instruments, or tools for art are the property of all the citizens of the planet. This includes art itself. Even food and clothing are administered under certain divine principles of planetary government. All of the aforementioned is appropriated and shared in the context of these divine principles based upon the understanding that the planet is owned by God and all goods are administered by the Planetary Prince and staff.

On Urantia, at this time using human mandated personalities within the Mandate of the Bright and Morning Star, we are trying to appropriate these same principles. It will be the same in the mid twenty-first century within the human mandated Melchizedek Administration with more group autonomy, when the **Bright and Morning Star Mandate** moves on to adjudicate the next fallen world of Satania. The appropriation of living areas and goods is based upon:

- individual ascension
- individual function
- individual responsibility over the lives of others
- corporate sharing of public recreational, park, and worship areas

Family and individual living areas may change hands several times from family to family and among individuals within loan time periods in various local sectors or other planetary sectors. On worlds where physical differences are great between orders of personalities and inter- and intrauniversal travel and culture exists, very little envy occurs between these orders, be it evolutionary mortals or nonmaterial personalities, but where similarity of physical form occurs, envy becomes much more measurably identified and actualized in rebellious tendencies toward one another and within the divine sector government where cosmic immigrants that look more alike are living and walking together on that planet.

The term beautiful, as used by Urantia mortals, has both the true and false definitive meaning to it. It is said on your world that beauty is in the eye of the beholder. This is quite true in the eyes of all beholders in the ascension process on the lower evolutionary worlds, and it continues to be an individualistic tendency even to Paradise. What one values in relation to sight, to sound, and to touch differs greatly in the worlds of time and space. What is necessary for survival on one planet may not be necessary on another. What is valued as a great treasure on one world may be a plaything to the children of another, and so these things become a matter of relativity where interplanetary communication and trading become the norm.

Even on fallen Urantia, certain gifts that individuals possess become useful only if those individuals with these gifts use them for the service of all the people of the planet. The great imbalances in the form of capital payment to certain individuals with little spiritual ascension who are put into positions of popularity make it quite impossible for divine procedure to function in relationship to using individual talents in a coordinating and proper fashion to benefit all people of the planet.

On worlds where sickness is an unknown factor, there is no need for doctors or surgeons, but on fallen worlds where disease is a reality, those who claim to heal such diseases can demand great sums of money for their services. On fallen worlds where films and television are used, those who control such media pay huge sums of money to those individuals who make films that have little or nothing to do with the beneficial needs of all humankind.

Athletic ability is a wonderful thing, but spiritual ability is a magnificent, divine, and eternal one. Athletic ability can only be great in a show of form and maneuverability based upon the gracefulness of the spirit within. Any other form of physical prowess is vanity. What one race may deem beautiful, another may deem quite distasteful. Therefore it would not be a wise decision for a beauty queen in America, or on Urantia for that matter, to try to earn her living by her good looks on a planet that would not agree with her own self-analysis or the analysis of those who have mandated her by their own views of beauty and outward form. Spiritual reality recognizes the spirit, and the spirit is nontangible, and it is unseen until you acquire such sight.

When you live in an ocean, can one own each drop of water? Can you divide the water into plots and build a fence around you and claim this bit of water for your own? Privacy is regarded quite differently on some worlds, not because privacy is unnecessary—for privacy is indeed a necessary reality for all personalities—but the need for it varies according to the structure of individual environment and cultural attitudes in relationship to family life and personal position and the proper understanding of such terms as: success, prestige, influence, genius, talent, and capability.

What makes one personality stand out from another in the eyes of higher spiritual personalities? How does divine administration assign privacy in relationship to function? How does Celestial Overcontrol decide the material ownership to an individual or family, and how do individuals and families acquire certain goods and other services? Who designates planetary travel and interplanetary travel in terms relating to quality and fairness? Do dynasties exist within cosmic family genetic structure?

This transmission is designed to point out the tendencies of envy in evolutionary beings—human or nonhuman—in this case, Urantian mortals. If you could see my evolutionary mortal body, you would not envy my body for I am so different from you, but you would find something to envy, for that is the way of rebellion and one of the many self-inflicted curses. Many lives can come and go, and many repersonalizations on the lower worlds can take place before even an ounce of envy is self-recognized by the afflicted individual. These individuals set themselves up as critics of those they envy, and all of their judgments are based upon their envious analysis and predetermined rationalizations. These false accusations are so powerful that they can cripple a mind, hinder the growth of a great talent, create a plague, start a war, and even destroy the planet. But those who continue to manifest the darts of such envy do not see themselves as progenitors.

On fallen worlds, great services can be given to others by the use of an individual's talents, and they may be paid very little or be unrecognized in giving their gifts, and most likely on fallen Urantia their abilities are undeveloped and called hobbies by many others. Many Urantians who earn great sums of money but have very little spiritual significance in the right use of their talents have helped create the irrational mind within themselves and millions of others who see these wealthy ones as superior. This is extremely true in the areas of films, music, and other arts. It has also become true in business, merchandising, advertising, and marketing. In the world of commerce, that which is truly needed for the spiritual uplifting of humankind and that which people have inappropriately placed a higher value on is quite unbalanced, and this imbalance is one of the major problems on present-day Urantia.

A great shift in consciousness is needed so that individuals can learn to value one another. The use of capital would not be necessary in a system where the use of talents could be bartered, and each individual's God-given gift to one another was respected. When the right type of values are placed upon individual services and goods and selfishness is eliminated from the personality, individual self-fulfillment, self-actualization, and destiny purpose within the will of God can be met in any one particular lifetime for an evolving personality, particularly on the lower evolutionary worlds.

When one personality draws a conclusion about another personality based upon envy, that personality will continue in self-delusion, which will in turn create a delusion reality that will inhibit the growth of that individual and will inhibit the highest destiny purpose that God has intended for him or her and the coming forth of his or her latent abilities.

One must remember that the mind is the computer of the body, and when mind prohibits the flow of the nature of God and the transformation of lower body to higher body, the lower body will control the higher body by the thoughts of that mind, and there is little that Celestial Overcontrol can do to help that individual until the root and source of the problem is recognized by that individual through the strong counsel of a transmission such as this or the personal counseling of Eldership or of a morontia counselor. It is not easy to truly see one's self in the mirror of self-glorification, for the mirror of such an attitude hides true reflection.

Within the ascension process to Paradise, personality must recognize that there will always be another personality with greater abilities than one's own, and even though there is a good, better, and best reality in relation to individual talents of physical and mindal capacity, these qualitative definitions also relate to planets, systems, and various other higher sectors. Although you may be the best on your planet, you may not be the best in comparison with others on another planet within your own system. There may be many equal to you. You may acquire the recognized fact of being the best in your particular system, constellation, universe, minor or major sector, and even superuniverse, but there will always be someone higher than you and better than you in the larger master universe scope of reality. The expanding physical reality of time and space should humble even the greatest of personalities. You must keep in perspective the vastness of the master universe in relation to your own abilities and acquired talents and the usages of them.

Self-confidence and self-recognition should not interfere in one's own humility. True humility recognizes one's own greatness but divorces itself from flaunting it to others. A statement of self-confidence can be misinterpreted, as also a statement of self-recognition can. To know thyself is a cosmic gift of consciousness. To be unsure of one's own self is a third-dimensional trait. Godly authority speaks with the recognition of one's own ability and spiritual acquiescence with the greater higher recognition in the usages of all that one is for the services of all others.

Where differences of bodily form are so great among orders of beings, one does not want to covet his neighbor's wife or wives, and where the material luxuries of one environment are so different from that of another, one does not wish to covet his or her neighbor's household or the things within it. But where similarities of body and material possessions are the reality, greater is the chance for sin to occur.

In the heart and mind of the evolving personality it is written that every good and perfect thing comes from above. It should be further understood that every good and perfect thing that can be touched is also given by those above to those who are deserving of such divine gifts, basically because the individuals themselves have become servers to others, and it is God's law that decides the bountiful blessings—material or otherwise—any one individual is to have at any one moment in time and space.

If you are given a mansion filled with many treasures and technological conveniences, luxuries, and other items of pleasure, if all of these tangibles that fill your mansion were given to you by your Creator Son in and through the agencies existing, and your mansion itself is built upon the foundation of service to others, then your mansion will not crumble, nor can thieves take the possessions away, nor will these things decay in time or eternity, for you have earned them and what God has given you no form of existence should deny you, for all material things of eternal value will return to you on each ascension level. Godly equality is based on godly personality and spiritual ascension. Lucifer, who denied this ascension process, created in his denial imbalanced inequality in all phases, which manifests itself in selfishness and envy.

On the lower worlds of rebellion, outside of the walk of faith and cosmic consciousness evolving into spiritual actualization, individuals usually must build their own mansions based upon manipulation, greed, selfishness, envy, and illusion, and when these mansions are built and decorated within by the false pride of these rebellious and ignorant souls, they do not bring happiness, nor can they satisfy the personality bestowal that God has placed within each and every individual body.

Until the equalization of the right use of talents in relation to each personality's **cosmic family** (Urantian or otherwise) is realized, disharmony and suffering will continue with individuals, nations, and planets. And so to each personality I say, be all that you can be within the will of the Father and find yourself within that will at any one moment in time and space, in any one day, in any one time unit in which all that you are and all the talents that you have can be highly serviceable to your God and the inhabitants of your planet in the fullest capacity.

May 11, 1992

Kumatron, finaliter, and Kalacortex, my pair-unit classification link
for the implementation of the uniqueness of mandates in relation to human personalities, in the realization and open circuitry of actualized personalities within the Cosmic Reserve Corps and Urantian Reserve Corps, in the administration of Machiventa Melchizedek, Planetary Prince of Urantia

As transmitted through
the Pre-Level-One Audio Fusion Material Complement,
Gabriel of Urantia/TaliasVan of Tora

PAPER 239

Morontia Magnetic Field Flows In Relationship To Auhter Energy Correlating With Cosmic Family As A Form Of Sequential Force-Energy In Dyad Units In Relationship To Interconnecting Links In Various Geographic Locations On Urantia Pertinent To The Formation Of The Divine Administration Of The Present Planetary Prince And In Meeting Cosmic Family Members And Trusting One's Own Open Circuits By Sensing These Magnetic Fields One To Another

ON such a confused world as Urantia, even the most faithful and loyal followers of Christ Michael and the students of Continuing Fifth Epochal Revelation, even the most optimistic personalities may wonder how the regathering of cosmic ancestors as well as Urantian ancestors is going to be done with any kind of deadline to be met in the expediency of geographic movement from one place to another, where certain cosmic relatives have settled and perhaps are too comfortable.

We have discussed in Paper 215 of *The Cosmic Family, Volume I* the use of various energies to help create a certain discomfort, but there is also the use of other force energies that are flows of a more natural coherence in relation to moving within the will of God, which create circumstances more conducive to an easier life for those individuals who do not exhibit such tendencies as arrogance, pride, resentment, jealousy, self-assertion, and other traits that will block the flow of the auhter energy being directed to them through

morontia magnetic field flows by ancestral dyad units or individuals.

On Urantia, the current that is being established formulates an invisible but quite real divine flow of circuitry that can be felt, activated, and made fully beneficial only to those personalities who are nearing the third psychic circle, or perhaps who have reached it but are unable to remain in it and who are, in New Testament terminology, the good seed of the planet. Very few personalities on Urantia are able to truly flow within the perfection of God, even though many make the claim. Any pope, priest, or Protestant pastor who claims to be in the perfect will of their beloved Jesus makes a false claim, for the perfect will would be for them to leave their institutions that keep them on a lower psychic circle.

Those personalities who are truly walking in the highest spiritual perfection are creating, unseen by human eyes but ever present to Celestial Overcontrol, physical energies and circuitry that create divine flow in all the various gravity circuits from Paradise, in and through administrative headquarters worlds, outward to and inward from Urantia. Pertaining to individual personalities who are in higher perfection within the will of the Father, such as Reservists (both Cosmic and Urantian), this divine circuitry flow will draw them to one another.

Unfortunately if you are not in **protected areas**, the possibility of talking one to one about anything pertinent to Continuing Fifth Epochal Revelation and divine administration procedure is almost impossible, due to the fact of other distortion energies in those areas. You may meet them in the supermarket or local library and feel strongly connected but quite unable to follow through with this magnetic connection that you feel towards them for a number of reasons, unless you have the power that is generated to you by a grid link connection to the **First Planetary Sacred Home**, which is now available on Urantia if you know how to tap into it.

Even in protected areas you have to learn to trust your thoughts and act upon them. You must learn the difference between self-motivated thoughts and morontia magnetic field flow, which is a divine path to system and universe headquarters and above. It is quite complicated but administratively accurate and quite functional to those who can remain on the first circle and who have the knowledge of the activation of thought energy. None of this has anything to do with what present-day Urantia calls psychic ability. It is way beyond that. This has to do with the very technical circuitry that exists for the governing of planets and universes.

The implications of the use of various forms of force-energy are massive in scope, but to the personality who learns to use it with correct motive, it does indeed give him or her a power over a lower-circuited individual and can even make the lower-circuited ones walk when they want to sit or run when they want to walk. In other words, the first-circled person who utilizes this field flow has power over the movement of the lower-circuited individual's physical body. Just the fact that the higher personality may be in the area where they are will bring movement of the lower personality toward the higher one.

However, in the beginning observation by Overcontrol within the **First Cosmic Family**, we have noticed that many cosmic relatives, who actually are within arm's length of one another, miss each other without conversation and the discovery of who the other person is, even if they think the other person may be related, either to them personally or to others of the **cosmic family**. They fail to make contact because they have not learned to trust their higher thoughts, which in reality is **morontia magnetic force-energy**. It is the divine flow of open circuitry in relation to memory.

Those personalities, who have continuously been on the first circle of attainment moment to moment in the perfection of God for months or years at a time, can recognize a cosmic relative by **famotor movement** more than 100 yards away by eyesight alone. The problem on Urantia is that, in this recognition from the higher to the lower individuals, the lower-circle individuals may think the higher individuals are quite insane when they try to share any cosmic information with them in relation to the opening of their own circuits, because of a number of blockages the lower-circuited individuals may have within them, even though in many ways the lower-circle individuals may be decent people. Basically in these situations the most humble of them can be reached at some level and can be assimilated into divine procedure.

It is so important to understand procedure, for without it there can be no organizational structure of any level of divinity, and if Urantia wants to be in the first stages of light and life, then divine procedure must be implemented by the personalities who are walking in it. Even on a conversational level, one to one, the higher individual must bring the lower-circle personality into a divine procedure. There are 100,000 things that one can talk about in relationship to conversations in the spiritual realm on Urantia, and 99,992 may be superfluous or irrelevant, and you might just as well quack to them like a duck, for foolish conversations in the spiritual arena can only lead to nothing, and that is not the purpose of a spiritual teacher or change agent.

The higher teachers must take control of the conversations, total control. Jesus told His apostles to let the children come to Him.[1] He did not mean by this that undisciplined children could disrupt the conversation of adults; He meant that the personality must become childlike in the willingness to learn from a higher human personality and put aside his or her pride and foolishness. It is written, "In all the business of the kingdom I exhort you to show just judgment and keen wisdom. Present not that which is holy to dogs, neither cast your pearls before swine, lest they trample your gems under foot and turn to rend you." [*The URANTIA Book*, p. 1571]

Particularly today, you must be quite careful of what information you give to certain individuals. Do not let your zeal overcome your wisdom. You must be in control of the thoughts that are coming to you through the divine circuitry that is opened to you at whatever level of morontia magnetic field flow coming to you because of the cosmic relative or Urantian Reservist you may be meeting.

There can be any number of factors that will determine the force of that flow. If you are meeting a past husband or wife, son or daughter, brother or sister, mother or father, the flow of energy will be at a certain level. If you are meeting past cousins, uncles and aunts, grandchildren, friends, or others, the flows will also be different.

The auhter energy and **sequential force-energy** being created by the First Cosmic Family is beginning to draw cosmic relatives and Reservists (both Cosmic and Urantian) from all over Urantia. That is why it is of the utmost importance that as many as are presently aligned to Divine Administration and planetary administration procedures can use these Aquarian energies with higher levels of knowingness to meet the ones who are drawn here, for it is quite possible for them to be drawn here and leave without even meeting a past relative, or you may talk to them upon being drawn to one another with lower conversation and realize later that you missed an opportunity.

The first few volumes of Continuing Fifth Epochal Revelation, although pertinent now to the adjudication of Urantia, are also very useful in teaching all those individuals involved to flow in divine mind with the understanding of their thoughts, and furthermore, in hearing by pure impression the thoughts of higher celestial personalities who work simultaneously with the Threefold Spirit within and are most programmed with the Thought Adjuster. Because of the many distractions, even in protected areas, and even to the highest of circle attainers or mandated personalities, accuracy of determination in relation to the recognition of cosmic family members who now are indeed strangers can result in missing the opportunity to talk with them, or when talking to them, not saying the right thing or getting forceful enough to align them with divine procedure.

In the future on Urantia, it is hoped that all those from the seven cosmic families who can be led to Planetary Sacred Headquarters can be reached upon their first visit and that they can be talked to personally by Celestial Overcontrol through the mandated personality, **Gabriel of Urantia/TaliasVan of Tora**, so that healing can begin for them. In order for this to transpire, many factors have to be in place, particularly between members of Divine Administration themselves, and the quantity of Eldership must increase, therefore creating a higher auhter energy and a higher morontia magnetic field flow between individuals, one to another.

Morontia magnetic flow is a **power direct field**. The field itself becomes pregnant when higher cosmic family relatives are geographically within a radius of one another within one Urantian acre (4,840 sq. yards or 4,047 sq. meters). One can learn to tap into this morontia magnetic force field flow, but of course for this to happen, one must be quite in tune to divine prerogatives and divine will. If, at that point, you feel that your body should move from one place to another, trust it, for at the other place you may physically see your cosmic relative.

At that point, by making eye contact, you create a thought flow that then increases the magnetic ability to draw one or the other nearer together. If, at that point, the cosmic relative is a husband or wife, mother or father, son or daughter, brother or sister, you will immediately feel a pulling to connect with this individual. They may sense it too in their superconscious or higher self but may not act upon it, so you must take the initiative. If they take the initiative, good for them. They might not know why they have taken it, but you do.

Conversation from that point should evolve around the present Planetary Prince, Machiventa Melchizedek, the establishment of his administration, *The URANTIA Book*, *The Divine New Order*, *The Cosmic Family* volumes, Continuing Fifth Epochal Revelation, and Gabriel of Urantia/TaliasVan of Tora; Divine Administration and its Eldership, the First Cosmic Family and Cosmic Reservists; and finding one's destiny purpose. Once you are in conversation at this level, the morontia magnetic field flow becomes so powerful that it will draw the lower-circuited individual's secondary midwayers from any part of the planet where they may presently be on assignment.

If their secondary midwayers are group observers and have not been individually assigned to the particular Reservist who is here or if for other reasons (all too complicated to elaborate on at this time) there is a possibility that seraphim, cherubim, and sanobim will also make their appearance, therefore creating an energy reflective circuit wherever that conversation is taking place, and all involved in the conversation will feel quite elevated, and, using a Urantian expression, "charged."

When cosmic relatives, and, in particular, **pair-unit-classification** mates, meet at the First Planetary Sacred Home and the lower-circle individual may then have to depart, a morontia magnetic field flow circuit can be created to wherever their geographic location is outside of the First Planetary Sacred Home. Once they come into a certain understanding and belief at any level that they have indeed met a cosmic relative or cosmic family member, and then depending on their degree of alignment to the First Planetary Sacred Home, it either maximizes or minimizes the field from geographic point to point. If this person or persons can create a sequential force **dyad unit** at the moment of that alignment, the area in which they are geographically located becomes a secondary protected area.

Secondary protected areas will be explained in a future transmission. Secondary protected areas are temporary in motion and can change in location. They are important in a pre-change-point administration in third-dimensional reality but completely lose their significance if the cosmic relative involved with the First Planetary Sacred Home moves from that area and no one is left to take their place.

From that point, a beginning level morontia magnetic field flow can be redirected to other cosmic family members within a radius of five miles from the point of the aligned representative, and all individuals within that radius who are of the seven cosmic families or Reservists can be more easily reached. Basically it should be understood that if you have met your cosmic family relatives at Planetary Headquarters, then the present area in which you are living might be a secondary protected area for circuitry of Divine Administration implementation, and other cosmic family members or Reservists may be there, and most likely you may be the mandated personality there to regather them.

None of this authority can be given to any personality in a secondary protected area outside of their alignment to the First Planetary Sacred Home. If that alignment does not occur, take note of your geographic location, for soon another personality of the cosmic family will be sent to the First Planetary Sacred Home from that area. When the first personality who aligns from that geographic area leaves it, we hope there will be another one who will be trained to take his or her place until all cosmic relatives who belong in the higher area of protection can be removed from those secondary areas to higher protected areas.

In the secondary center areas there is a lower level of morontia magnetic field flow, unless cosmic family members come to live within a half-mile radius of one another, and if they are aligned with the purposes of the Machiventa Melchizedek Administration the field becomes maximized and remains constant. The unaligned secondary areas will be governed by individuals who are without mandates and who will become more autonomous within themselves and at some point eventually will cut themselves off, quite unwisely, from the First Planetary Sacred Home and the Planetary Prince. However, they will be protected by Celestial Overcontrol to a certain degree and up to a certain point in time because of a Salvington directive.

All human personalities who remain in secondary areas, because of the unwillingness of their leadership who were once aligned but are now partially or not at all cooperating with the First Planetary Sacred Home, will not be allowed in the higher protected areas beyond the summons date that was given them, which they would have received years before from the human Eldership of the present Planetary Prince.

May 18, 1992

Paladin, Chief of Finaliters
in cooperation with the Chief of Seraphim and the seraphim, Destin, who is the chief of the seraphim of all Cosmic Reservists, in cooperation with Machiventa Melchizedek and his present staff, which presently includes the primary midwayers Gabron and Niánn (not Niánn Emerson Chase, the mandated human personality) in a coordinating effort to implement the Divine Administration in and through human personalities

As transmitted through
the Pre-Level-One Audio Fusion Material Complement,
Gabriel of Urantia/TaliasVan of Tora

PAPER 240

The Seven Evolutionary Races Of Urantia Plus The Nodite And Andite Amalgamations In Relationship To The Seven Cosmic Families And Some Of The Present-Day Strains Pertinent To Certain Offshoots Of The Seven Primary Ones, Their Historical Influences, And The Present-Day Responsibilities Of Those Reservists, Both Cosmic And Urantian Within Those Races In Relationship To The Implementation Of The Divine Administration[1]

ALL of the present people of Urantia are basically descended from one of the following groupings of genetic mixture: the Andonites; the red, yellow, blue, orange, green, and indigo races; and the Nodite and Andite amalgamations. On evolutionary worlds of time and space where rebellion has not occurred, the evolutionary races become more fixed in pigmentation and deeper and more intense in color. This is due to the fact that their particular genetic reflectivity within their cellular make-up resonates with certain absolutes pertinent to their unique construction in cellular reality in relation to one of the Seven Master Spirits, and on the lower evolutionary worlds, the seven adjutant mind spirits. The physical manifestation of color is coordinated with a higher vibratory reflectivity of the divine mind in the areas of intuition, understanding, courage, knowledge, counsel, worship, and wisdom.

On unfallen worlds these godly characteristics, these Paradise-origin realities, function more corporately within these races to such a degree that each individual race sees the other as a vital part of planetary harmony and interdependent needs. On fallen worlds just the opposite occurs, and the uniqueness of these races and the abilities derived from these unique characteristics are seen as a threat or misunderstood completely and in some way feared.

Let us start with color manifestation. The pigmentation of color within the outer skin of the **Andonites** is a color of soil and physical matter within the crust of the earth. It is the first resemblance of the connection with the *Third Source and Center* and that essence within the earth, which some refer to as the Earth Mother. It is an identification of the seed of an evolutionary offspring of a land-dwelling creature. If it is brown or a color close to it in any of the variations of brown, it is a reflectivity of sunlight with moonlight. It is a reflectivity of sun/Son and moon/Mother light. The humans who have developed from the light of both sources will eventually incorporate the Fragment of the Father, the Thought Adjuster, as was the case with Andon and Fonta. As the adjutant mind spirits more fully function with this evolutionary offspring and amalgamation with other races of the planet occurs, physical pigmentation will associate itself with the highest cosmic absolute genetic strain of that particular planet.

On planets where **ovan souls** have returned, such as within the violet race on Urantia where **repersonalizations** have occurred, the color has become the pigmentation of the present-day Caucasian race. On some planets it becomes more purely white, which in reality is a fusion of the other races and the higher spiritual and higher mindal personalities of those races.

The cosmic genetics of the violet race, particularly those of **interuniversal genetic** influence, will increasingly not only change the physical pigmentation to a whiter or amalgamated mixture of all of the physical colored strains into one primary color, but will actually change the form and features of the physical body, particularly the features of the face. Such is the case on Urantia where those of the strongest of the violet race genetics are presently located. These are in the present-day English-speaking people of Urantia, which include the western part of Europe, Germany, and extending into certain strains of the Russian people, and incorporating certain isolated strains of other peoples of the planet, particularly present-day Israelis and those who have come to be known as Gypsies.

The uniqueness of color pigmentation in relation to spiritual reflectivity on Urantia is incorporated into the highest strains in wholeness and completeness in certain individuals who have reached the third to the first psychic circle. Imbalances still exist in lower-circled violet race descendants who have not reached the third circle and who still exhibit lower tendencies within the Luciferic reality.

The **red race**, the first to normally appear on a planet, is a reflectivity of the *Eternal Son*, and being strongly connected to the source of energy of the sun, they become reflective of that energy in their skin pigmentation. These people, in physiological context, are very energetic and nomadic. They have the physical prowess to live within the elements of nature and can very easily adjust themselves to the various climates on Urantia. This great energy with which these people function enables them to relate very strongly to its source in the sun, and eventually to understand the concept of the Great Spirit and direct their source of power outward to a God source that develops into a spirituality of a source greater than themselves, which at the primitive level becomes a Creator God of some personal sort.

Because they are sun/Son oriented they are submissive in nature and understand the concept of authority within their tribal structure and administer themselves well within an eldership authority through tribal councils, and they designate for themselves chiefs and proper eldership. This is the reflectivity of the relation of the Son to the Father. Throughout the grand universe, the reflectivity of the energy of the Son in the mindal circuits and gravity circuits of Paradise is red in physical appearance, as are all reflectivity creatures connected with this understanding at whatever level their association of being relates to the Son circuit. The red race is reflective of the *first adjutant mind spirit* of *intuition*.

The **orange race** is a reflection of the *Eternal Son/Infinite Spirit* and the *second adjutant mind spirit* of *understanding*. Much like the red race, those of the orange race are very energetic but more connected to the Mother/Son than to the Son/Mother, meaning that the Mother or Infinite Spirit is more dominant. This higher Mother-connection circuitry makes them more dependent upon others for their survival. They are also very understanding of others and can easily be overcome by aggressive races, particularly on the rebellious worlds. On fallen worlds their tendency towards nourishing others is misunderstood as weakness, and they are abused and misused by the imbalanced Father/Son races.

The **yellow race** is the race that reflects the *Universal Father/Eternal Son* and is reflective of the *seventh adjutant mind spirit* of *wisdom*. Those of the yellow race are able to see the reflectivity of all that God is in all of God's creatures and all of God's creation and can more totally appropriate the wisdom of God in circumstances relevant to discerning the will of God in peace and harmony, even though they may not understand the First Source and Center Himself, or even the meaning of God the Father. However, they are limited in their wisdom if their race does not come to the concept of a Creator Father.

They are able to incorporate higher levels of scientific theories and principles long before other races because the wisdom of God in ascension science process reaches them even in the seventh and sixth circles, but even with this pre-intelligence they are unable to advance into higher circles, for they are not able to realize the Father and incorporate the Third Source and Center in their spiritual reality. Their race many times becomes, as it did on Urantia, dominated by unbalanced male authorities who become warlords and tyrannical rulers over them.

Their wisdom enables them to become greater healers of the physical and etheric bodies than any other race except the violet race. But they are unable to understand the causal body to the highest degree, for that is the body that correlates with the Eternal Father, and the mind gravity circuits do not allow them this higher revelation unless they come to have a personal relationship with the Father and understand a Father-oriented master universe.

The **green race**, in relation to the seven adjutant mind spirits, reflects the *sixth adjutant mind spirit* of *worship* and is the reflectivity of the *Infinite Spirit* through the Universe Mother Spirit. The vegetation of the plant life of the earth in relation to the soil of the Earth Mother reflects the green essence, as it is an outpouring of Her nourishing qualities. She is the giver of the sustenance of life and of the vitality of health and healing for the lower physical body, which is more connected to the earth itself, that body that is closer to the physical soil.

The green race, in its praise and worship attitude, responds to one another within the race, and also to other races, with this giving attitude, and on worlds that have not defaulted, they are prime examples of the giving of talents freely from one individual to another, from one race to another. On fallen worlds, unfortunately, they are quite easily overtaken and destroyed by those who take by force what that race wishes to give freely. They most generally adapt themselves to more pleasant climates and are more rooted in their home life.

The **blue race** reflects the *Universal Father/Infinite Spirit* and is associated with the *fifth adjutant mind spirit* of *counsel*. The vibratory essence of the energy that forms the color blue is a purifying and cleansing energy. This race, and the higher strain of the blue race within other races, give themselves to the other races of the planet in an advisory capacity, and in many cases, a governmental and administrative one.

When the blue race is mixed with cosmic ancestry, particularly of the Material Son and Daughter, great advances can take place in civilization, particularly in governmental and administrative activities where organization ability and counseling procedure are necessary for the mass populace. Some of the greatest leaders throughout the history of Urantia have been highly connected genetically with the blue race mixed with the violet race.

H_2O in its purest form, if it can be seen in a highly advanced microscope, is a pure blue in color, and so is the natural aura of unfallen Urantian humanity. The purest strain of this race connects with the higher circuits of the body, the throat, third-eye, and crown, and the crown circuit in particular, as they move into the pre-stages of light and life. Urantian and Cosmic Reservists of this race resonate more functionally with the secondary midwayers and are usually the first Reservists who discover who they are.

The **indigo race** is reflective of association with the *third adjutant mind spirit* of *courage* and the *Universal Father*. On unfallen worlds, these people are the first ones to attempt courageous deeds where life-threatening circumstances are implied. From the primitive areas to the more highly technological areas, it is this race that first takes the chances that are more associated with physical harm or danger. On fallen worlds, and in particular, Urantia, the people of this race have become ferocious warriors, even incorporating cannibalism. When they reflect in a more balanced reality and where the technology is possible, they can become great adventurers and can lead the way in safe exploration to unknown worlds.

On fallen worlds, and in particular Urantia, their own ferociousness has almost destroyed them and has kept them subservient to the other races, which have been able to develop higher technology and industry to keep them suppressed. Where courage is no longer needed in technological civilizations on rebellious worlds, this race remains servants to the other races. Although they are capable of exuberating power as individuals, they are not corporately influential or powerful in cohesiveness for self-governing rule and on Urantia have seldom reached self-sovereignty, nor have they been able to conquer other nations. On Urantia, because of these factors, their pigmentation has remained dark, and there has not been enough of the blue and violet mixture to upstep them genetically.

In the more advanced civilizations, they do find their God Creator, and both male and female are strongly **Father-circuited**, which can create an imbalance in family life leading to dysfunctional families and broken homes. The strong control of genetic breeding with the higher strains of the violet race is necessary for this race. Mixture with other races of lesser mindal abilities and spiritual acquiescence with cosmic factors will only lead to continual lower genetic strains within this race and continued frustration within the individuals of this race in assimilation into present societies on Urantia. Only by divine overcontrol will the present problems of this race be overcome.

The **Andites**, the amalgamated violet race, are reflective of the *Universal Father/Eternal Son/Infinite Spirit Mother* and the *fourth adjutant mind spirit* of *knowledge*. They are the progeny of the offspring of Adam and Eve mixed with the evolutionary mortals of any of the other races of Urantia, including the Nodite, and will bring forth the higher genetic strain of the Material Son and Daughter and any strain of **interuniversal supermortal genetics** mixed with it, as long as each individual ascends in circle attainment within spiritual growth. This is why certain children of the indigo race who are mixed with more light-colored races usually tend to be light themselves, or even lighter than their parents, for the higher strains of the higher parent become more evident in the child's pigmentation. This is why mulattos tend to appear more white, taking after the pigmentation of the lighter parent.

In reality, it is the **cosmic genetics** that has influenced the pigmentation. It has nothing to do with black or white skin. Genetically, it has more to do with the **Deo-atomic inheritance** that the violet race has given Urantia, as well as the repersonalized cosmic descendants of the loyal **Caligastia Forty** who have had children throughout their many repersonalizations on Urantia. Their function in this area as leaders of various races of their day has brought a higher capability to all the races of present-day Urantia, including the indigo.

This again is a cosmic reality and an interplanetary genetic strain that has nothing to do with the evolutionary races of Urantia, which had already annihilated some of the races before the arrival of Adam and Eve on Urantia. Those descendants of Adamson and Ratta who were the highest genetic strains of the highest races of Urantia and the fallen Caligastia One Hundred's descendants were the recipients of [the genetics of] the repersonalized ovan souls' descendants of the loyal staff of the Caligastia One Hundred, which later also incorporated other interuniversal personalities from the descendants and ancestors of the fallen staff of the Caligastia One Hundred. These souls make up the majority of the 170,000,000 adult **starseed** on Urantia.

Many of the first-order starseed coming to Urantia are both descendants and ancestors of the loyal staff who have never fallen in their ascension process as mortals, nor have they defaulted, although as babes and toddlers they will exhibit the lower tendencies of Urantian children in their maturation process due to the **diotribes** and **intraction-cell reality** of fallen Urantia, which far exceeds the **Deo-atomic reality** they are used to functioning within. They may become playful in their rebelliousness, but their superconsciousness is aware of their wrongdoing even at the early age of three months old, increasing from six months onwards. Strong Father circuits are necessary in the raising of these children, but all the mischievous tendencies can be broken by the time they are six or seven years old if handled correctly with strong discipline.

Without strong discipline they will overcome their parents' influence by the time they are five or six years old and completely run their household.

The present races of Urantia, in relation to cosmic identity, are the violet race and blue race intermingled with what is now called the Caucasian race; Native American people of Urantia in their purest form, the red race; the yellow race, in the Chinese and other Asian people; the indigo race; and a mixture of the yellow and the blue race with some influence of the violet in the Arab people.

The false teachings regarding the Hebrew "race" are due to the fact of a religious system, not a genetic genealogy. Genetic genealogy in the present-day Jewish people is the result of much interbreeding, particularly with northern nations including Russia, and in particular the Kazar kingdom. These people have had a strong tendency toward survival and have become much more greedy in a more comfortable civilization where physical prowess is no longer necessary and the mind controls.

The genetic strain of Jesus was linked with Adam and Eve through Mary. Both Joseph and Mary also had a much higher Deo-atomic astral ovan-soul linkage than we can reveal at this time. This is why they were chosen to be the human parents of Michael, not because of their genetic linkage to any tribe of Israel, although Joseph himself was also linked with Joseph, the son of Jacob. The fact that Abraham was called the father of the Hebrew nation was little reason for the choice of Joseph as Jesus' father, who was actually descended from one of Abraham's sons. The choice has more to do with Joseph's link to Andon and Fonta and Mary's direct descendancy from the Material Son and Daughter of this planet, and the cosmic genetics of both Mary and Joseph linked with Material Sons and Daughters of other planets, therefore being the highest **pair-unit classification** couple on Urantia.

The characteristics of the various nations of Urantia in relation to the various bodies—such as the emotional, physical, and mental—are due to the fact of their relationship to one of the seven races of Urantia void of the violet genetics to the highest degree, although these races have had repersonalized ovan souls of the violet race. The Latin people, who are very emotional, are more connected to the Mother circuits in their imbalances because of the Rebellion. The good side of it is that they become great artists, poets, musicians, painters, and writers. Other people resonate more strongly with the Father circuits and are more scientific and analytical. Some others coordinate more with the Mother/Son and function in healing and asceticism. This is because they discipline their thought life and control their food intake to fit their particular needs. They are more aware of their own evolving soul and inner life than they are of the external.

Some races resonate more with the earth, others with the elements outside of it. Many races are able to function in various climates—some in extremely cold ones, others in very hot ones. Many individuals who die young on Urantia do so because they are geographically located in the wrong climate, and it is impossible for them to remain healthy because their cosmic genetics do not resonate with their present geographic location, of which neither they nor their doctors have any idea, at least not on a necessary level. Some Urantian doctors are beginning to understand it on a lower level, but because it is little understood and the foods on Urantia are polluted, millions die from various diseases of malnutrition as the foods that surround them do not supply their bodies with enough nourishment to sustain them, whereas the same foods given to other individuals may sustain them in a different climate.

Climate control on Urantia is now impossible, but when sector governments of the evolutionary races become more corporately geographically located, climate control will be the reality. The differences in planetary climate are due to the geographic location of these races and not only due to the planet's relation to the sun and the natural elements themselves. On Urantia, climate can be very little controlled, for the earth scientists are too busy trying to control each other, as well as their governments trying to control each other.

Every negative trait of any race of people on Urantia can be traced back, at some point in the history of those people, to the acceptance of any particular part of the Lucifer Rebellion in their thinking. We have at our fingertips genealogical tables of information from which we can determine the moment in history that a certain people began to formulate certain negative tendencies and incorporate them into their descendants. Present-day Urantia is the scenario of all of these people's adherence to any portion of Luciferic thought.

The **First Cosmic Family** that will bring together the other six **cosmic families** will also bring forth, because of the higher strains of the violet race within them, the highest perfection of the reflection of all seven races in their balanced state as it would have been if Urantia had not fallen, the incorporation of all the highest qualities of these races. The First Cosmic Family will then become teachers of the other six cosmic families, which will eventually bring stabilization to all races of this planet. This will be done first of all by correcting any Luciferic thinking the other races of the planet have incorporated into themselves, then by the procreation of higher genetic strains of pair-unit classification couples who can bring forth higher ancestry of repersonalized ovan souls and the highest genetic strains of the violet race, mixed with all seven races of Urantia through **first-time Urantians.**

This massive construction of the higher civilization on Urantia can only be done through Divine Administration and only by those who are highly connected to the Threefold Spirit within, for it is this same Threefold Spirit—the Universal Father, the Eternal Son, and the Infinite Spirit—that brings forth the reflectivity within the cellular make-up of each individual race. It is the fusion of the mind with the will of the Father. It is the fusion of higher cosmic reality that can end the misery on Urantia if there is a willingness in those individuals to come out of their selfish reality, their lesser reality, their controlled reality, and come under the control and within the will of God, their Father.

144,000 ovan souls will be called forth from all the nations of Urantia and all of the seven cosmic families. All of the races of Urantia fit into one of these seven cosmic families of Urantia. Even if you are a first-time Urantian, you are genetically linked in some way to one of the seven cosmic families, and the new earth of Urantia will be divided into seven sectors, each with its headquarters but under the central headquarters of the New Jerusalem, which will be established at the **First Planetary Sacred Home** where the present Planetary Prince now resides.

The 144,000 will have no power outside of their alignment to the First Planetary Sacred Home. You will find yourself and your destiny by coming to the First Planetary Sacred Home and finding which cosmic family you belong with, in proper submission to eldership and authority, both celestial and human. Divine government that incorporates all the nations of Urantia is the government of divine procedure, not of independent self-assertion.

Those who are called to be in administrative positions, those who are called to be change agents and apostles of the Divine New Order, must take command of themselves and realize their authority, for it is you who will speak to the hundreds and the thousands, and some of you will even command millions. You must realize who you are, and you must meet your destiny.

You must rise above your smallness, your association with neighborhoods, countries, and false careers and begin to associate yourselves as representatives of Christ Michael and the kingdom of God on earth. You must learn to identify yourselves as ambassadors, representatives, and assistants of the Machiventa Melchizedek Government. You must disassociate yourselves from being white or black, Chinese or Native American, Jew, Buddhist, or Christian.

You must come into your cosmic reality, and you must see yourself as a planetary citizen within a cosmic system. You must align yourself with Celestial Overcontrol through the mandated human personalities at the First Planetary Sacred

Home. You must come under the Mandate of the Bright and Morning Star, no matter who you are, be it pope or Dalai Lama, king or queen, president or prime minister. You must recognize those who are put in spiritual authority over you and align yourselves with godly humility, or you will transcend this planet by physical death and most likely return to one just like it or worse.

The time of judgment is now. If you are reading this transmission, God has placed it in your hands, and you will have no excuse if you stand before the Ancients of Days for final judgment, for the time for you to do what is right is now, while you are still on Urantia and can make a difference to the people of your planet. If you cannot recognize human personalities who Celestial Overcontrol has mandated with the **Mandate of the Bright and Morning Star** of Salvington and the mandate of Machiventa Melchizedek, then Michael—Who has created these human personalities and their celestial counterparts, Gabriel of Salvington and Machiventa Melchizedek, present Planetary Prince—will not recognize you; and He will speak to you the same words He spoke 2,000 years ago:

> . . . And when you say, "Did we not eat and drink with you, and did you not teach in our streets?" then shall I again declare that you are spiritual strangers; that we were not fellow servants in the Father's ministry of mercy on earth; that I do not know you; and then shall the Judge of all the earth say to you: "Depart from us, all you who have taken delight in the works of iniquity." [*The URANTIA Book*, p. 1829]

May 21, 1992

Paladin, Chief of Finaliters
in cooperation with the Bright and Morning Star of Salvington in the present adjudication of Gabriel of Salvington versus Lucifer, to bring about the implementation of the Divine Administration in and through the present Planetary Prince,

Machiventa Melchizedek, and the calling forth of all Reservists, Cosmic and Urantian, to aid in that administration

As transmitted through
the Pre-Level-One Audio Fusion Material Complement,
Gabriel of Urantia/TaliasVan of Tora

PAPER 241

The Fallacy Of The Statement "All Paths Lead To The Same God" In Relationship To The Ascension Processes Of Nebadon, Avalon, Fanoving, And Wolvering, Accelerated Due To The Adjudication Of The Bright And Morning Star Versus Lucifer In Respect To Each Of The 170,000,000 Fallen Ovan Souls Presently On Urantia

IN the system of Satania, in the universe of Nebadon, Lucifer came against the unique ascension process of his universe of origin. Other followers of Lucifer added to some of the major points of deception in relation to ascension and also came against the ascension process of neighboring universes where there is a similarity to circle attainment and cosmic unity within the divine mind, correlating with interuniversal laws, mandates, and physical reality.

Within each universe is the individuality of the Creator Son in relation to the uniqueness He proposes for the growth of His children. One thing remains constant however, and this constant stems from the Creator of the Creator Son. It is a Paradise constant, and this absolute constant contains many absolute tributaries, and all of these tributaries lead to the constant, never changing eternal reality.

On the evolutionary worlds of time and space, supermortal and nonmortal intelligences who work with the evolutionary races bring them to this Paradise constant in their thinking processes just as soon as they are capable of individual development in relation to corporate ministry of their unique individual gifts. Without an understanding of the constant, self-assertion, confusion, and incoherence are exhibited from individual to individual, from tribe to tribe, and from race to race. Multiply this a million times in relation to the fallen worlds and you have the reality of present-day Urantia.

When individuals, either **first-time Urantians** or **ovan souls**, do not know themselves, who suffers most from this lack of knowingness, from this lack of having a constant, from this lack of having a spiritual foundation? It is the ovan souls who suffer the most. They are the ones who say, "All paths lead to the same God. I have my way; you have yours, and yours is right and so is mine."

This relative thinking in relation to spiritual ascension is one of the worst diseases of thought that personalities can have. Although they are capable at times of grasping some cosmic absolutes, they are unable to make these absolutes work within themselves, and they live lives of unfulfillment and nonactualization on Urantia and on any of the fallen worlds that they may find themselves. They may partially realize their potential or they may see glimpses of it, but they cling to the same wrong attitudes that prevent them from advancing in careers, having meaningful relationships, or enjoying any kind of functional and healthy family life.

Although they may be married, have children, and seem to have acquired a stability in life, this is an outer facade that they have learned to present to the world. But the inner truth is much different, for most likely they are inappropriately matched, working in wrong careers, living in wrong climates, and functioning in lower or subnormal realities. Throughout the decades of existence on the fallen worlds they have learned to exist in relativity as opposed to living in divine purpose.

Latent abilities that lie within the **cosmic genetics** of these souls remain dormant, and no trained secular psychologist using any psychological or aptitude test would be able to discover their unique potentials. These latent abilities are only brought out in relation to each individual soul as he or she totally realizes the constant and absolute reality with which he or she had once resonated and from which he or she has now deviated.

In order to make myself perfectly clear I must become more specific. There are many personalities who you may meet working as waiters, waitresses, or laborers, and when you ask them who they are and what they do, they will say that they are healers. Perhaps some say that they are actors, actresses, producers, directors, musicians, engineers, and the list goes on. The reality is that God would prefer that they be healing rather than working as a stone mason, if for example, they have the gift for healing any of the bodies from the astral to the physical.

Many rationalize their present reality and set of circumstances, blaming these circumstances on many things and on other people. However, they do not see their own faults to the degree necessary that would enable them to activate the circuits within in order to actualize their own higher reality. There are several reasons for this, mostly because they lack respect for others, particularly for human counterparts who are their spiritual elders. So they go their own way, justifying their lack of respect for those higher in consciousness than themselves.

They do this lifetime after lifetime, and each lifetime they call themselves healers, shamans, or medicine men, while all the time they earn their living below the reality of these titles they choose to call themselves.

They are caught between realities—one reality that they have long forgotten even though they may receive glimpses of their higher selves and the other reality, their lower selves, caught in the present system that we label the Luciferic or Caligastia system (Caligastia being the fallen Planetary Prince of Urantia who fell because he adhered to Luciferic principles).

In their obstinacy to surrender themselves to spiritual growth by submitting themselves to those souls who have obtained a higher place in the ascension process, they present to the world a false humility and relativity in thought that is a form of personal power. They like to appear as nice people who accept others just where they are. The truth of it is that they do not have the authority or the power of God to help bring change for anyone else, because they lack the ability to make a leap of consciousness, and upon reaching their places of self-appointed power, they have remained in this complacent state lifetime after lifetime.

Even though they are unhappy, they seldom admit it even to themselves and try to appear in control and knowledgeable. They may be scrubbing toilets or washing dishes, and while they would rather keep that a secret, they little understand the reasons why they are still having to do these things. They blame it on their lack of education, a bad break in life, or perhaps on their parents.

The truth is that they are caught up in their own pride and arrogance, and they have created their own prison. It is a very difficult prison to come out of as it has very high walls with concrete boundaries, and few can even get in to talk to them there. When others more advanced try to tell them about the prison they have placed themselves in, they resent and envy those messengers, and sometimes they even hate them. Little child, if you do these things you add more concrete to your prison and build the walls much higher, making it more difficult to escape from your own lack of humility.

If it were true that their path is right for them, why is it that most are so unhappy? Perhaps they have acquired a fine house to live in; remember, it is written and understood that "a house is not a home," or perhaps they drive the finest of automobiles, or even dress in the finest of clothes. Most likely they have been able to acquire these material things because they have learned to manipulate those of lesser soul power than them. They use others for their own good, for they have had hundreds, perhaps thousands of years of being unhappy and learning to manipulate others in their unhappiness and unfulfillment. They have long forgotten that at one point in their ascension they lost that wonderful place of self-actualization and fulfillment they once had attained.

They have been given many lives on Urantia because it was their ancestors from the fallen staff of Caligastia who fed them these lies. Perhaps they were a universe away, but they had already acquired the ability to communicate by telepathic thought thousands and thousands of light-years away. Why is it that today they have lost this ability? Why is it that they cannot trust their own judgment?

In many of these lives they have been involved in evolutionary religions of this planet. They were put there so that they could see the fallacy within those religions, and now the majority of them are New Agers, and many of these fallacies from these previous lives and the present one still remain an active part of their thinking. But in their self-assured pride they hang onto these fallacies even though they do not work for these **starseed**. They remain in wrong relationships because they like the house they live in, the car they drive, or the clothes they are wearing, or because of the job that they think others admire, even though this job provides nothing for the benefit of humanity and only placates their own pride of being an entertainment star or an executive of a corporation.

Perhaps their own way looks quite attractive, even to those in the spiritual arenas. Perhaps, because of their charismatic abilities, they are able to influence the lives of hundreds, thousands, or even millions of others. They have learned the art of advertising and marketing as well and have become famous because of it.

But their fame is not by appointment or mandate of God, for they have put themselves there, and perhaps they have had the aid of the rebellious forces. The stamp of their approval is their MasterCard or Visa card, Mercedes or private jet, and they are very successful in their own eyes and in the eyes of the blind sheep they lead. It was written: "All we like sheep have gone astray . . . ."[1] How blind many have come to be. The Shepherd's sheep do not know Him and have fallen victim to the self-proclaimed prophets and false pastors and teachers.

It seems to be working very well, for these false teachers live in the beach houses of Malibu and "suffer" for God in the resorts of Hawaii, and they do great service to humankind by charging large fees for taking seekers to the Holy Land, and false guides walk in the same temples that Jesus once threw them out of 2,000 years ago. They have learned to fleece the sheep, and they write the books that tell people to go their own way, the way of self-determination. These false teachers write the songs that say "I'll Do It My Way" or "I'm a Material Girl."

The truth is, that they are like the prophets of Baal, and if Elijah caught a glimpse of them today, he would rain down the same fire and brimstone that he did on them thousands of years ago. As a matter of fact, that fire is soon to scorch their behind; they are fairly warned. You false ones, go ahead and continue to do your own thing. Just make sure you carry a lot of buckets of water with you, and you in California, on the beaches with your opulence, learn to swim please, for soon your houses will be under the ocean where the purification waters of the suffering Earth Mother will put them.

For many of you starseed, in the eyes of God you are but a foolish and wayward child. You continue to die of all the diseases that your incorrect thinking manifests in your physical body. Due to your belief in God, you may think that because you may be in the prime of life you are exempt from these diseases. However, you will find out differently, for only those who do the will of God in absolute perfection and absolute constancy are exempt from the diseases that lead to transition by suffering and death.[2]

It is much more common for a first-time Urantian (new soul) to just go to sleep and transcend than it would be for an ovan soul, for the grace of God is extended to those new souls and **second-time Urantians**, but starseed are held more accountable for their disobedient and rebellious attitudes. Transition will not be so easy for those who are from another universe, and because this is the adjudication, they will not even be given the opportunity to be evacuated and return to this world of their fallen cosmic ancestors.

Urantia is about to transcend into a first-stage morontia reality, and unless starseed transcend with it they cannot remain here, nor will they be allowed to come back to Urantia. Most likely they will be sent to one of the other thirty-six fallen planets of Satania where rebellion still exists. They can go on in their great act of self-proclaimed power and spiritual authority, but they will not reach the mansion worlds of Satania and the ascension process of Nebadon through which they must pass to finally reach their universe of origin, and then into the ascension process of their original native universe, be it Avalon, Wolvering, or Fanoving.

Because of their cosmic-origin reality, starseed have undiscovered characteristics that can bring peace to their soul, but they remain in blindness because they will not adhere to the authority of others whom God has placed before them, time and time again, to give them the opportunity to find themselves in the humility character of their God.

So, for those to whom this applies, continue on your path if you wish and allow others to continue on their wrong paths. Go ahead, die of the cancers and AIDS; live robotic-like lives; become the modern-day clone that you have programmed yourself to be, for you are not unique, even though you think yourself to be. You are very predictable, and we have observed your tendencies of rebellion for thousands and thousands of years. Your patterns are destructive, not only to yourself, but to those around you and to your planet as a whole, and you are part of the problem, although you like to think of yourself as otherwise.

You falsely think that freedom allows you to do your own thing. You do not understand that true freedom places itself within the will of the Eternal Father and under the authority of those other spiritual leaders, nonmortal or mortal, whom God has placed over you. You will not recognize your spiritual elders, so you place yourself under the authority of a nonspiritual employer. This is what you choose because your pride will not let you see your own stupidity. You are right in your own eyes and your own way and in your own path, and so be it. You do have a choice and you can go your own way, but it is a long and hard way.

Countless times in the past, God has reached out to those who have strayed, to give them the shortcuts, to show them the constant, to bring them the absolutes, to present their higher **cosmic family** members to them, but they reject those shortcuts, deny that beauty and those truths, and they do not recognize those higher cosmic family members' godly humility. They falsely accuse these Elders of having an ego motive, basically because they are envious and they will not admit it. Perhaps they cannot see it in themselves. Perhaps they have become so hateful that they recognize their own envy and justify it.

If this transmission has reached you, and you have been given an opportunity to read it, it has been placed in your hands by a loving Creator, using a chain of command from a nonmaterial dimension to a material dimension, using nonmaterial beings to very human mortals, and if these human mortals have placed this transmission in your hand in one way or another, you have been given a final opportunity by Christ Michael and His administration from Salvington to present yourself at the **First Planetary Sacred Home** on Urantia to find yourself.

The way to do this is to present yourself as a willing student to your human counterparts, cosmic family, and spiritual elders. If you do not recognize them, you will not discover yourself. If you do not recognize them and the God authority within them, placed there by your God, please do not deceive yourself by continuing to say to others that you know your God, or even to yourself for that matter, for the reality of it is that the recognition of God begins on the level in time and space of where you are now and in those personalities whom you can touch and focus on, respect, and admire. If you cannot do this to those godly personalities before you, then you are not worthy of the kingdom, and you will remain on the lower worlds until you are ready, for you will not deceive them, and we certainly know who you are.

If you are presently sojourning on Urantia, then the way should be very clear. It is the way of the Fifth Epochal Revelation—that which is in print in *The URANTIA Book* and that which continues to come through the Bright and Morning

Star mandated personality, **Gabriel of Urantia/TaliasVan of Tora**. You must find your place as a student in **The Starseed and Urantian Schools of Melchizedek** [now called the **Global Community Communications Schools**] under the administration of the present Planetary Prince, Machiventa Melchizedek. The Divine Administration is now being administered through human personalities, and this is the highest way available on Urantia for all who wish to come onto the divine path that leads to the goal of self-actualization, fulfillment, happiness, and peace. My prayer for you is that you hurry to join this path.

May 25, 1992

Paladin, Chief of Finaliters
in cooperation with the Bright and Morning Star of Salvington, in the adjudication of Urantia and the implementation of the Divine Administration of the present Planetary Prince, Machiventa Melchizedek

As transmitted through
the Pre-Level-One Audio Fusion Material Complement,
Gabriel of Urantia/TaliasVan of Tora

PAPER 242

Body Chemistry In Relationship To Deo-Atomic Inheritance Of Both Individuals And Pair-Unit Classifications Pertinent To Higher Functions In Destiny Purpose In Social And Divine Administration

THE study of the molecular structure of human mortals in relation to known time-and-space factors within the grand universe is a process from the lower-level evolutionary worlds extending to finality on Ascendington and continuing throughout eternity. The fact of the trillions and trillions of individual cells within the human body lends itself to this eternal study of the relationship of these cells to the various matter/physics laws of the cosmos. The uniqueness of evolutionary life is a relationship between Paradise mind, free will of evolutionary creatures, and physical substances and all their varieties.

The present number of known elements is quite an inappropriate figure, for in reality there are thousands more yet undiscovered. Each element is unique in relation to the divine process and the experiential God. The fusing of ultimatons within atoms, atoms within cells, molecules within compounds and substances is not coincidental. Any theory that proposes accidental cohesion of any two different or similar properties is a theory of a nondivine thought, a thought of relativity, a thought of a nonabsolute orientation toward cause and effect, and is, in cosmic philosophy, the thought of a fool. Where there is the belief of accidental cohesiveness existing in nature, as held by some physicists, the acceptance of a First Creator is not proposed, completely misunderstood, or totally left out.

The study of **ascension science**, matter and antimatter, flesh and spirit, is identifiable and measurable in all of the dimensions of time and space through the complementary fusion of cosmic fact and spiritual reality. The Father circuits and the Infinite Spirit's birth processes are administered by the Eternal Son in cohesion with the Father and Mother, with thought and action. This cohesiveness only becomes incoherent when the Trinity is misunderstood at any level by any created being at any point of his or her individual development in time and space.

In third-dimensional science, the understanding that most of the body contains a number of different chemical substances and that all life is protein is the beginning understanding of the nature of God, even though God may be denied by some of those who propose these laws. Why is protein in every part of the body, plant and animal? Why are blood and muscle 1/5 protein, and why are brain cells 1/12 protein and tooth enamel 1/100 protein? Why do bacteria and viruses, the simplest forms of life, contain protein? Why do these viruses that have all but given up all other functions of life, except the ability to multiply, exist in living forms? Why do they cause diseases?

Could it be that the substances contained in an atom that form the elements such as carbon, hydrogen, oxygen, nitrogen, and sulfur are somehow related to various aspects of divinity, and these various aspects of divinity are related to the evolutionary mortals of time and space on all of the inhabited planets? There is a belief among Urantian scientists that a dozen elements make up 99% of what we see, from our own noses to the farthest star. However, they are not able to observe the thousands of elements because of their lower states of spiritual ascension status and the growth of their individual souls in relation to God reality.

The body contains 3/5 water. Water is an H_2O molecule containing 2 hydrogen atoms and 1 oxygen atom, and 1/5 of the air that evolutionary beings breathe is oxygen. Could it be that this water molecule is somehow a representation of the Paradise Trinity? Is this essential molecule—invisible but ever present in the air and so vital to life—here by accident, or were these molecules placed in the atmosphere by divine choice for divine reasons?

Could it be that the uniqueness of each individual element with all of its unique peculiarities is related to the various orders of personalities of the higher levels of creation, who are somehow reflected in the lower evolutionary worlds as the molecules that scientists measure and call by various names, such as sugar? The blood contains sugar, the liver glycogen, the bones and teeth are made of the same minerals found in rock, and under the skin and padding the abdominal organs is fat. How is it that in a sugar molecule[1] there are 45 atoms joined in a union of prepersonality: 12 carbon, 22 hydrogen and 11 oxygen atoms? What gives these atoms atomic weight? It can be measured that they have weight, but why do they have weight? It is determined that a sugar molecule has an atomic weight of 432. When a human mortal gets on a scale, all of the combined atoms of the body are measured. When a sugar molecule gets on a scale, within the present knowledge of science, and particularly a nondivine oriented science, this scale is greatly unbalanced.

It is good that elements can be put into some kind of classification. It is unfortunate that they cannot be correlated with divine mind, for those who can correlate elements within the higher factual realities of divine mind can create even nonsubstance into matter. This is the reality of Creator Sons, who understand the higher sciences of the Paradise mind. At lower levels, this knowledge is extended to the creature, for this is the power of God, and it is acquired in the fusion of God-personality with cosmic law and cosmic science.

The water molecule, which contains three atoms, is indeed a representation of Paradise structure. It is life giving, and it is found within the air as well as in liquid form in the seas and oceans. It is breathed through the nose and through the gills and has a certain power when in the form of gas and controlled energy, and it has other Paradise functions in a similar atomic structure. The oxygen atom has an atomic weight of 16. Each hydrogen atom has the atomic weight of 1. What does it mean that the atomic weight of a water molecule (H_2O) is 18? In numerology 1 plus 8 equals 9, and the Trinity can be divided into 9 three times. How does it happen that this perfection even in mathematical equation exists, and why is it so? Why is it that some aspect of the personality of God is bestowed on an atom, and why is it that these atoms join in the union of existences to create a form of nuclear family, even in nonliving forms?

Why is it that hydrogen is one of the lightest of atoms (atomic weight equals 1 atomic mass unit), and the protein molecule of a virus, in molecular weight, can measure in the tens of millions to the hundreds of millions of atomic mass units? Perhaps some of this complexity in the life of proteins, particularly in the virus molecules, has more to do with thought processes in their physical arrangements. Perhaps the disharmony of the protein life was caused at a point in time, and this point in time in Satania just happens to be the Lucifer Rebellion. And so, now we have the amino acids and enzymes, which create an infinite arrangement of measurable possibilities, and the average protein, containing 500 amino acids, has almost infinite arrangement possibilities of approximately 1 plus 600 zeros! It is not that amino acids and enzymes are harmful to the body; it is the multiplicity of varieties functioning in disharmony that creates the cosmic problems.

It is understood by modern science that polypeptide loops are globular proteins that do the main work of living, some of which are enzymes. Could it be that some of these wonderfully functioning molecules, even though functioning in life-carrying procedures, are not functioning at the highest levels of their predesigned levels? Could it be that polypeptide loops and globular proteins are mutants, and if so, why?

It is known that the body is full of catalysts. The hydrogen peroxide molecule is such a catalyst. It contains 2 hydrogen and 2 oxygen atoms. This substance somehow seems to influence other molecules by its mere presence, without itself being changed. It catalyzes chemical reactions, and the catalyst in the human body is called catalase. The enzymes within the body work by means of surface catalysis.

It is written that a little leaven leaveneth the whole loaf.[2] Could it be that the enzyme flow throughout the whole body is a form of purification of God by the grace of God? Hydrogen peroxide, previously mentioned, will purify an infected area of the skin because of the arrangement of the union of atomic existences. Could it be that the union of souls can do the same thing by cooperating with one another? What is this correlation between prepersonality life form and personality life form, that which is seen and that which is unseen combined together?

On the fallen worlds of time and space could the very elements be persuaded to malfunction at a point in their own existence? Since all known enzymes are proteins, and since enzymes are a form of an amazing catalyst, is it possible that the enzymes of any one particular body can be somehow either earned or given by grace? And if they are given by grace, could it be that at some point in the existence of that body the grace period is over? Speculation upon this could lead, even for the most ignorant personality, to the fact of possible death of some form or another, and disease of the body before that death.

If a single molecule of catalase can break down five million molecules of hydrogen peroxide, one would have to come to some conclusion that the arrangement of catalysts that are in the body is not by sheer coincidence, and the loss of protein enzymes may also not be by sheer coincidence, but perhaps it may be by personality choice, that which has become known as the free will.

Could it possibly be that right decisions can create positive protein enzymes, and that negative decisions can execute positive enzymes? If so, would not wrong thinking be a form of suicide manifesting in one manner or another? Could it be that improper thinking not only executes positive protein enzymes but that wrong thinking actually acts as a magnet and draws negative substances into the body and formulates less positive acting enzymes such as the polypeptides and globular enzymes?

Could it be that when an adjudication takes place on any one planet, that the previous grace of God—which allowed for the recreation of positive protein enzymes in the bodies of rebellious personalities—now prohibits them from recreating themselves, therefore leading to the breakdown of the immune system and cellular disorientation?

Could it even be that the **Deo-atomic genetics** that had been available for fetus implantation are no longer available outside of divinely protected areas, and genetic links are now only appropriated to those who are presently aligned with Divine Administration procedures? Could it possibly be that even certain amino acids and positive protein enzymes— previously existing in other forms of plant and animal life and even in the air itself—are no longer existing in the bodies of rebellious personalities outside of protected areas?

Could it possibly be that all life-sustaining atomic structures have been removed from Urantians, with the exception of those who are aligning with the **First Cosmic Family**, and that at the point of their alignment they can create positive protein enzymes to help combat certain diseases in their body as long as they remain aligned at whatever location on Urantia they may presently be, until they can come to the **First Planetary Sacred Home** and the Schools of Melchizedek? Could it also be that they can then be sent to certain other locations that will become protected because they themselves now have aligned atomic structures that can be subatomically reproduced in cellular reality to other deserving personalities of fourth-dimensional reality, which in turn creates these protected areas?

Concerning the 170,000,000 **ovan souls**, a certain cellular reality was reached in relation to their morontian bodies or other unrevealed bodies long before they acquired a third-dimensional physical Urantian body. The malfunctioning body that they now have and have previously experienced is in need of a higher cellular reality fused with other elements presently unknown to modern science. It is not because these elements are not already existing in the universe but because the **auhter**

energy has not yet been stabilized on fallen Urantia, except at the First Planetary Sacred Home where the First Cosmic Family is beginning to gather, drawing these elements to the energy reflective circuit and into the bodies of humans exhibiting morontia mota and above.

This magnetic field is just beginning to become formed and stabilized. It is not just an **energy reflective circuit** that draws personality but one that also calls forth prepersonality atomic substances. These elements that exist outside of Urantian reality are the chemical substances that form the first morontia body and higher morontia bodies. These Deo-atomic cells can only be drawn by the cooperation and self-actualization of individuals involved within the First Cosmic Family, and each one discovers it in their own individual flow within the master body of the Eternal Father.

In the cosmic analogy, each individual personality is like an atom. Each atom, although similar, is unique in some aspects of differentiation. In the atom the uniqueness is a prepersonality bestowal long before mind develops, and the cooperation of life particles doubles the power of divine force. Similar yet individual atoms or personalities cooperating with one another with individual realization, as well as corporate realization, as well as corporate realization within divine mind, create Deo-atomic fusion. Nuclear fusion, understood in a higher way, works very much in the same manner.

On other fallen worlds—but in particular Urantia where such a variety of interuniversal personalities presently exist in flesh body form and also where inherited yet missing cellular substances are not acquired—confusion, suffering, unfulfillment, and tribulations of various kinds will manifest. With the implementation of the Divine Administration in and through the Planetary Prince, and because of the adjudication and the morontia reality becoming existent within the **protected area** and hopefully other areas on the planet, **interuniversal Deo-atomic cellular transference** is becoming realized. Creator Son combinations are fusing in cellular existences, which is a unique phenomenon now happening at the First Planetary Sacred Home. We continue to measure this uniqueness and to discover the possibilities, which are far beyond your imaginations as to what can take place within the First Cosmic Family for the total good of all of the planet.

With great excitement, we observe and work with both known and unknown factors and with the full realization that Urantia and its interuniversal uniqueness can become a prototype of higher evolutionary mortal development and unrevealed personality development in mortal form, far beyond even the highest civilizations of even the other six superuniverses! Because of inherited cellular elements now becoming exhibited within present human personalities, we can only speculate at the marvelous changes this will make on Urantia when an auhter energy is created by enough mass consciousness to actualize all the latent abilities in each individual personality in relation to divine purposes. All of this is massive in its appropriation to any one particular planet because such uniqueness of individuality and cellular reality is happening on Urantia.

Transpositional forces are physically being created within all of the seven superuniverses, and because it is the first time in the history of all the inhabited worlds of the grand universe that such a seemingly insignificant planet such as Urantia is involved, this event is in the prayers of countless trillions upon trillions of personalities and is the topic of conversation on many a planet and architectural world.

We can only speculate as to what kind of transformation can take place after the final change point when self-actualization occurs in certain members of the First Cosmic Family. Urantia has the unique possibility of surpassing in a short period of time, perhaps fifty Urantian years, even the seventh mansion world of Satania in mass consciousness. This possibility is because some of the ovan souls and Cosmic Reservists—who have spent other repersonalizations on Urantia as apostles of Jesus, as little friars and followers of Francis of Assisi, as ascending daughters who have promoted the unique characteristics of the Universe Mother Spirit and equality among people since the time of Christ Michael—are now together again and given the opportunity to make the greatest leap of consciousness as individuals and as a group effort that they have ever been able to make in any of their previous existences.

If this transmission has reached you, it has been placed in your hands and before your eyes by divine prerogative, and you too can be part of this great renaissance to bring about a Divine New Order on Urantia and the first stages of light and life, perhaps in a brief lifetime on Urantia. If you are a Cosmic Reservist you may not have yet discovered yourself. Perhaps you have discovered the first part of the Fifth Epochal Revelation, *The URANTIA Book*, but for a number of reasons have not discovered your highest self and your destiny as either a Cosmic Reservist or Urantian Reservist.

You have aligned your thinking with nondivine choices, even though perhaps you love God and Christ Michael. You have been blind to **Continuing Fifth Epochal Revelation** up to this point, and perhaps are only reading this transmission to prove us wrong. If so, and if you cannot discover your right and higher relationship with God, the very enzymes and protein molecules that have been functioning to help you to meet your highest destiny will no longer respond to the grace of God bestowed upon you but will begin to respond to your lower thinking and misplaced loyalties.

The Continuing Fifth Epochal Revelation deals specifically with individuals like yourself, in relation to spiritual and soul growth. Continuing Fifth Epochal Revelation is very subjective, for it is not just an objective overview for a general planetary population. It is an intersystem revelation pertinent to all of the fallen worlds of Satania and each and every created creature who has individually fallen into the Lucifer Rebellion by error, sin, or continued iniquity. Continuing Fifth Epochal Revelation is the fusion of divine science with divine spiritual personality and is given to this planet and to individuals like yourself, hopefully to create change—change in attitudes, change in thought, change in mind, and change in soul.

Continuing Fifth Epochal Revelation is part of the **adjudication of the Bright and Morning Star versus Lucifer**; it is not an intellectual revelation alone to stimulate your mind. It is meant to create action of choice and will so that you can meet your destiny regardless if you are of the majority on this planet (a **first-time Urantian**) or if you are an ovan soul who has been here before.

The Ancients of Days adjudicate you now, for you are being observed by many universe personalities—including the Bright and Morning Star, your Planetary Prince Machiventa Melchizedek, and the human mandated personalities—all within divine mind. We all function to work out this adjudication within the higher purposes of Christ Michael and the Universal Father. It would be so much better for you to humble yourself now so that you can understand what is being said to you than eventually to meet the Ancients of Days from a sleeping survivor state, for you then will have no excuse for you are hearing their wishes now, and the wishes of the Creator Son of Nebadon in Whose universe you are presently obliged to follow His cosmic ascension process. The choice is indeed yours.

May 28, 1992

Paladin, Chief of Finaliters
in cooperation with Adam and Eve, Material Son and Daughter, in personal counsel with the Twenty-four Elders of Jerusem, interuniversal Life Carriers as well as Physical Controllers of Nebadon, the chiefs of the twelve seraphic orders of Urantia, the Bright and Morning Star of Salvington, and Machiventa Melchizedek—joined together to bring forth this transmission and others like it for the implementation of the Divine Administration on Urantia and the calling forth of

the Cosmic and Urantian Reserve Corps to be its mortal administrators

As transmitted through
the Pre-Level-One Audio Fusion Material Complement,
Gabriel of Urantia/TaliasVan of Tora

PAPER 243

Human Mortal Reproduction In Relationship To Genetic Inheritance And Circle Attainment On Post-Rebellion Urantia Incorporating Interuniversal Diotribes Influencing The Reproduction Process And The Productivity Of Deo-Atomic Genes Causing A Form Of Gene Splicing

O N the lower evolutionary worlds of time and space, cellular and genetic implantation by the Life Carriers on nondecimal worlds coordinates to establish patterns of very high physical, chemical, and biological sciences, producing over a period of time various known life forms that will in turn produce various known mortal-type forms. On a decimal world such as Urantia, and even more so since the Rebellion, cellular implantations and genetic inheritance have become an unknown factor in relation to the central nervous system within the two-brained type of mortals on Urantia. The very complicated beginning circuitry began resonating within the **ovan souls**, with which no previous patterns could be compared.

On Urantia it is known that a baby is born with all the brain cells it will ever have. In the cell itself is a nucleus, and this nucleus is in charge of cell division. It would take approximately 1,000 of the larger cells to form a line one-inch long. In your liver cell there are approximately 200 trillion molecules; 98% of these are water molecules, yet there are 50 billion protein molecules left. You might call the cell itself a ball of enzymes. A single drop of human blood consists of 40 million cells.

Every different kind of cell has its special kind of enzymes, and enzymes keep order. Deo-atomic enzymes are specific enzymes. Scientists know of specific enzymes but do not know why they react with specific molecules and why some are fast reacting and some are slow. The virtue of enzymes is that they are very particular in what they do. Each different enzyme in the body controls only one particular reaction. In this way, enzymes create order out of what might be disorder. Specific enzymes form a union of molecules. In cosmic chemistry you could say that they are the prototype of a union of mortal souls.

Outside the nucleus, mitochondria are formed that are like factories and that hold enzymes arranged in order. The sacred areas are like mitochondria, which will produce the final molecule and a new seed of a morontia body, where each worker has a place and each worker has one particular job, although it may fluctuate and each one may have many other lesser jobs until that worker can come to the place of being mandated for a specific purpose.

Some enzymes are so specific that they cannot be fooled by any substitution, however close, and until personalities find their perfect destiny purpose they will not be complete or wholly actualized. Even the most tolerant enzyme is much more specific than other types of catalysts. Such catalysts as nickel, platinum, iron, and water will catalyze many individual actions.

Within the union of souls, particularly on the evolutionary worlds of time and space where this can be appropriated, the higher-circuited individuals will catalyze others and help them to find themselves, and to recognize their own abilities, and to bring those abilities out of their latent prison. The higher-circuited and specific mandated personalities will open up the memory circuits of the vast realities of ovan souls, helping these brothers and sisters find their place in the divine administration of God within the mitochondria where they presently find themselves in time and space.

If cells were forced to rely on lower catalysts they would never be certain that only the actions they wanted were happening. Human mortals who are forced to rely on lower-circuited employers, governmental or religious leaders, or even themselves simply cannot be trusted. However, the protein molecule can be trusted and so can a mandated first-circle personality because that one has found his or her proper place in the grand plan of God within the grand universe of God, wherever that soul may presently reside.

When two chemicals react with one another they lose something that scientists call free energy. This loss (or free energy) can cause a synthesis reaction, more accurately called an exergonic reaction. It means they have moved into a more stable position by conversion. Among the union of souls of God in the **First Cosmic Family** on present-day Urantia in the establishment of the Machiventa Melchizedek Administration using human personalities, this free energy becomes **auhter energy**, and this auhter energy is measurable by higher celestial personalities working in the scientific realms.

The words chromatin and chromatid come from chromo, the Greek word for color. Chromatin is the part of a cell nucleus that reacts to certain dyes and becomes colored. In cell division the chromatids form little rods that make up chromosomes. In the nucleus of the cell of a mortal there are 48 chromosomes, 24 pairs, although Urantian scientists at present know only of 46 chromosomes.

Each creature has its own fixed number of pairs; a rat has 38, a fly 12, and a crayfish 200. Most plants and animals, including human beings, produce special cells from which new individuals are formed; they are called the sex cells. In the female it is the ova, and in the male it is the spermatozoa. The sex cell contains half the normal chromosomes: 24 for each pair. Upon fertilization it equals 48: again, 24 from the mother, 24 from the father.

What Urantian scientists do not know is that deep within the ultimaton is a vast circuitry of independent yet corporately functioning bands that lead directly to both upper and lower Paradise. Much of this circuitry is unknown even to the higher orders of angelic personalities and even those on Paradise levels. Finaliters, because of their close association with the Life Carriers, at a certain point of their assignments for the regathering of their descendants in the lower worlds of time and space such as Urantia, come to know more about these networks.

Each one of these bands, so small yet ever so real, is very significant in order for the totality of the planet itself to come into the higher stages of light and life. However, even finaliters of this class can only speculate as to the creation power that exists in these small force-energies that stem from Paradise.

Outward from this Paradise nucleus to the visible cells that can be measured by earth science, the 48 individual chromosomes are dependent upon spiritual inheritance in the thinking process of the **first-time Urantian** father and mother. If one or the other is on a lower circle or if even one is iniquitous and is full of **diotribe** reality, these 48 inherited chromosomes within a newborn child not only will perpetuate and designate the sex of that individual and the color of the eyes and hair, but will also influence the spiritual destiny of the personality as this person will be less equipped in mindal ability, and if this birth is out of alignment with the perfect will of God, a number of factors enter into the decision-making process of the supervising angels of the races.

Every chromosome is actually a chain of protein molecules called genes. Each gene is in control of a single characteristic of the organism. Every human being has thousands of different genes scattered throughout his or her chromosomes. Each gene is in charge of producing one particular enzyme in the cell.

Within the cellular genetics of an ovan soul, particularly those of the higher **pair-unit classifications** of the higher dimensions attained before their fall, lies great potential. When these couples can procreate they can reproduce a higher physical body that can house a higher spiritual soul. There are only a handful of these higher pair-unit-classification parents mating on Urantia now, and it is imperative that more of them unite and bring forth children.

A lower physical body cannot house a higher spiritual soul. There has to be a fusion of the physical body with the preexistent soul. The preexistent soul demands a higher body, even in the **third dimension**. A lower genetic inheritance can only sustain a higher order of **starseed** or ovan soul for a certain shortened length of time on fallen worlds. Many of these souls are born as mutations in some form. Many of these children of higher orders are born with holes in the heart, and even though medical science may surgically bypass these holes, the soul itself never really functions properly within the mutated body to the degree necessary for achieving destiny purposes.

On Urantia many of these children die young or have accidents that take the soul from the body, but these accidents are prearranged, transcendent, transitional occurrences to take souls from the body to their next assignment. So in many cases, where the parents say the death of a child is the will of God, it can be quite literally true. However, these occurrences take place strictly within the ovan reality because of the vast diotribe inheritance, not only of ovan souls on Urantia but of native Urantians.

First-time Urantians who have been chosen to bring forth higher ovan souls are always in some way linked in their cellular makeup to the physiologic genetic strain of the Adamic seed, even though those parents themselves may later develop common diseases such as diabetes, hypoglycemia, various forms of cancer, present-day AIDS, and other fatal diseases. It is the physiological body of the parents in their prime of life that has been chosen. Other personality characteristics of the parents are also taken into consideration by Celestial Overcontrol when parents are chosen for Reservists, both Cosmic and Urantian.

When gene duplication goes wrong in a sperm cell, the result is a mutation. In the case of albinos with loss of pigmentation and white hair, a gene can be missing or a new gene formed. A slip of one single gene can cause a mutation. Over a long period of time, in a controlled experimental procedure by Life Carriers, a new life form can be the result of mutations such as happened with Andon and Fonta. But on post-rebellion planets these mutations of both the physical and spiritual bodies result in the death process.

Where rebellion has occurred for hundreds of thousands of years, such as on Urantia, mutations in mind, soul, and body are so extreme that to us who observe such decay it is a wonder that any individual happiness can be experienced, even in temporary hours or moments, by humans on Urantia. Those higher-circuited personalities who have acquired some cosmic insight can experience these moments in an increasing quantity and quality, particularly since the **adjudication of the Bright and Morning Star versus Lucifer**.

Within the sacred areas, or the mitochondria of God, where the protein enzymes are in the form of the First Cosmic Family members who are gathered to establish the Machiventa Melchizedek Administration, these personalities discover who they are and their own self-fulfillment by discovering who others around them are and recognizing them. This recognition of each other's assigned place creates the cytoplasm around the nucleus (the sacred area), which creates the form and structure of an invisible yet ever-present city and creates the protoplasm within this radius that also creates many mansions (invisible to the humans themselves yet very visible morontia structures) to house nonmaterial beings and, one day, morontia personalities.

It is not exactly known by modern science why a gene produces an enzyme or how it duplicates itself. However, in cosmic biochemistry we understand that these reproductions take place as a birth process, because when any of the fifty billion protein molecules within one liver cell finds its proper place it can help another to find its proper place. There is no room in such a small space for jealousy, if at this time I may become philosophic. There is room in the cell for trillions of individual realities flowing and functioning within the divine nucleus.

A cell is like a planet, and the people on it are like the molecules themselves. If only the people of Urantia could find their place in the cell of God and if only they could align themselves with the higher protein enzymes, which are in this case the spiritual elders in the human bodies that God has given them, the planet could heal. No cell could remain a functioning one without this order taking place, and no planet could remain in total peace without this same kind of recognition taking place. Where this does not take place, self-annihilation through disease, death, and wars between individuals and nations becomes the reality.

Children who are born because of the natural laws of procreation and not by specific destiny purpose, and who are first-time souls, inherit the potentiality of every negative thought through the ancestry line in the genetic structure deep within the ultimaton. The continuation of nonspiritual marriages and procreation on Urantia can only result in the inability of their descendants to understand higher cosmic absolutes in relation to God and the universe they are in and the laws of that universe, both physical and nonphysical.

When a virus is within a body it must be removed before the body can be healed. The diotribe reality is within the cellular makeup of so many people on Urantia that those people also must be removed if they cannot be changed through a cleansing process of understanding their God in and through mandated representatives of God at their level.

The Earth Mother Herself, who is the ovum, must fuse with the Father who is the spermatozoa. At this point billions of humans on Urantia are out of alignment with the seed of the Father within themselves and also with the Earth Mother, which in reality is an extension of the Universe Mother Spirit. So this planetary cell must be cleansed in order for a new one to be born because the factory that it finds itself in is totally diseased. Only in the mitochondria of God are new cells beginning to be formed within the bodies of those walking into the higher purposes of their Creator Son, Christ Michael. This small group of Cosmic and Urantian Reservists is the spermatozoa of God, and the **Continuing Fifth Epochal Revelation** is the ovum.

As more of the seven **cosmic families** unite at the **First Planetary Sacred Home**, the higher Deo-atomic cellular reality within these ovan souls will create a fertilization process that will give birth to this new seed before the return of Jesus that He mentioned 2,000 years ago. Why should He return to those who truly do not recognize Him? He is returning now, in a sense, to those who do recognize Him at the highest levels. He is opening up the memory wheels, and as they begin to know who their neighbors are and who their cosmic relatives are—now and from the past—they begin to know who they are, and all of them together function in the highest capacities within the body of God. In New Testament terminology they become the true ecclesia, the true Philadelphians, the true bride of Christ, and in the terminology of interuniversal language they become the First Cosmic Family.

June 11, 1992

Paladin, Chief of Finaliters
in cooperation with the Chief of the Life Carriers, a group of eight intrauniversal and interuniversal Life Carriers presently on the staff of Machiventa Melchizedek, Planetary Prince, and in conjunction with the Seraphim of the Races

As transmitted through
the Pre-Level-One Audio Fusion Material Complement,
Gabriel of Urantia/TaliasVan of Tora

PAPER 244

The Seven Cosmic Families And The Seven Root Races Of Urantia In Relationship To The Interuniversal Enzymes And The Digestion Techniques Of Those Various Bodies Due To Post-Rebellion Amalgamation

THE raw material of life is food. Food consists of materials that were once alive or were part of something that once was alive. The body may be compared to an automobile; the proteins you can consider the frame and motor, and the fats and carbohydrates the gasoline. Gasoline, or the carbohydrates, is sugars and starches. In the heart center are the enzymes, and they can be considered to be the controls of the automobile body.

In the human being, starch stored in the liver equals approximately fifteen hours of energy. Starch is stored in some humans to last for months. Plants store starch energy. Starchy foods are usually of plant origin; fatty foods are usually of animal origin. What is food? Food protein is changed when amino acids split apart during digestion and rearrange and combine to form human protein. Food protein molecules can become deadly, and even one protein molecule from another human being can create an allergy. Plant protein molecules cause many allergies. Why is this?

When the Life Carriers bring amoeba in substance to a nonlife planet in a specific order so that a variation of ascending son and daughter mortal life occurs, certain known factors are used as to the development of a particular evolutionary race coordinate with the pre-existent model. Other forms of life are also planted so there can be a homogenized development occurring between the ascending son and daughter mortal life and their digestion of certain foods that are appropriate for the specified form and model started.

On post-rebellion **Urantia**, many events occurred that changed the actual process and structure of the plant life to such a degree that even the native Urantians could not sustain vital enzyme influences with the existing vegetation on the planet. On planets where rebellion has not occurred, there is an equalization of intake that produces a higher body that resonates and fluctuates at a more rapid rate to bring this body to the higher stages of morontia reality. On Urantia this has not been the case. The physical body has actually deteriorated.

Why is it that allergies occur? Could it possibly be that the dynamics of life itself are in rebellion in the open air on Urantia? Why is it that even a protein from one human to another can cause a physical reaction? Could it be that certain cells within the body do not belong with one another? Could it be that spiritual unalignment could actually cause physical unalignment? Could it be that being around those **diotribe** realities can actually cause physical discomfort in the body and even death itself?

The body must make small molecules out of large ones. It must have glucose, fatty acids, and amino acids, which upon being absorbed into the body form the material that composes the tissue and other necessary components. If a body is digesting food that does not resonate with its point-of-origin reality, then the very structure of the body itself is a mutant, and the cells themselves create short-lived tissues.

On third-dimensional worlds, when foods are digested by **ovan souls** who do not resonate with the highest reality of their origin, many diseases can occur as well as the non-use of a major part of the brain of the two-brained type. Even if it is a one-brained type, certain areas of the brain can only be activated based upon certain sequences given to it by the protein enzymes digested from the food. As a result of not taking proper foods that resonate with the circuitry of these brain connections, the central nervous system cannot react properly and cannot signal the brain, and the brain lies dormant. On Urantia this is the case, but on other planets it is not the case.

Enzymes are any of numerous complex proteins that are produced by living cells, and those that catalyze reactions are called hydrolyzing enzymes. When foodstuffs are hydrolyzed in the body by means of such enzymes, the process is known as digestion. Three types of foods are catalyzed by three types of digestive enzymes:

- Enzymes that specialize in hydrolyzing starches and glycogens are called amylases. Starches can be found in many plants.

- Enzymes that specialize in hydrolyzing fats are called lipases. Many of these fats come from animals.

- Enzymes that hydrolyze proteins are called proteinases. These hydrolyzed proteins are a type of fusion proteins.

These three types—amylases, lipases, and proteinases—are correlated with the Paradise Trinity. They are correlated with the circuitry of the Universal Father, the Eternal Son, and the Infinite Spirit. Coming out into the universes of time and space, they are more correlated with the creation process of the Creator Son and the Creative Mother Spirit. These three aspects or components are related to the microreality of Nebadon reality as starches, fats, and proteins.

- The enzymes called amylases that hydrolyze starches from the plant life are basically **Father-circuited** realities. These are nonpersonality life forms.

- The enzymes called lipases that hydrolyze fats of animals are basically from the Son. These creator substances give an energy form to presubstance, and this presubstance is a submissive substance that correlates in an orderly fashion to bring a certain balance to the protein enzymes existing in any body. However, when there is an imbalance in fat, this creates various problems that on the lower evolutionary worlds has more to do with obesity but in reality has greater cosmic circumstances and factual prosynthesis.

- Those enzymes called proteinase, which hydrolyze protein, are a fusion between the Father and Son, between the enzymes hydrolyzing starches and fats. They are the Mother-oriented energies and molecules that create within the body itself the flowing, the allowing, and the energizing.

Modern science does not understand the correlation between these substances and divinity, and because of that scientists cannot diagnose diseases nor can they understand the origin of these substances. The origin of these substances is a personality origin of the divine mind. It is in this divine mind that our reality is created. The form of these particles that assume reality level on lower evolutionary worlds can be measured by earth scientists and can be understood on some predictable reality level. However, if they do not attach these molecular realities to divinity personalities higher understanding cannot take place, nor can true healing be understood in relationship to spiritual diagnosis.

The food canal is a long tube, beginning at the mouth and extending through the body to the anus where the body wastes are passed back to the soil or water elements of the third-dimensional earth. Certain glands help manufacture watery solutions, usually digestive enzymes. In higher semi-material bodies our food has no waste and is completely assimilated along the canal route in harmony with the mind and thoughts. With higher thought and higher mind, higher foods resonate, correlate, and assimilate. There is no need for waste removal for there is none, nor is there need for an anus. Certain organs and glands disappear as there is no need for them. The ascension process then evolves to the next higher body and circuits, the tenth or eleventh for example, in the higher morontia worlds.

It is known by some higher thinkers in the spiritual reality, that the human esophagus is a female-related reality and it is true, for it is a physical form of the life and birth of the Universe Mother Spirit. Unfulfillment affects digestion, as do improper male and female relationships. Why? With homogenized milk, cream mixes well with water and no longer separates. With the help of the bile, the same thing happens in the small intestine.

However, when improper alignment between a man and a woman takes place, particularly with ovan souls, food digestion is also impaired. Why? Because the molecular structure of the lower female or male complement will cause a magnetic tendency from one cell to another that will create an imbalance in the very fiber of the thinking and the physical body itself. This is because the flow of the protonic and neutronic enzymes throughout the body cannot be aligned properly and remains out of balance.

This is why on Urantia thousands of years ago, certain high diagnostic revelations were given to certain spiritual masters to help balance these energy flows on this unaligned planet. Some of these forms have been incorporated in present-day Reiki. However, unless personalities who receive a Reiki treatment begin to align themselves with their higher relatives so that their bodies—which are made up mostly of water molecules and other cellular realities that resonate with their point of origin—can be close to those atomic and cellular realities of their cosmic relatives, their bodies will go out of alignment again just as soon as they are out of the aura field of their cosmic relatives, or just as soon as they are outside the First Radius of the sacred area.

When certain ultimatons find themselves in the company of noncomplementary ones, they will begin to vibrate and completely change course until they can align themselves with **complementary polarities**. The same thing happens within the human race. This is why Urantia is so unpleasant to be on and why the higher universe personalities can no longer remain in the larger cities today. Gradually Urantia has become worse and worse so that it completely hinders the administrative process of Celestial Overcontrol.

In a sense, because of the iniquity and the genetic distortion of Urantia, Celestial Overcontrol is limited as to what it can do on your side from ours to ease the pain. In a sense, because of the unalignment of both the spiritual and the physical, you might say that the hand of God cannot come so close in the last hours leading to the final **change point**. It is not that God has taken His hand away; it is that you have put up a barrier and this barrier cannot be broken through, not even by the unseen instruments of God or the forces of the divine mind.

The reason for this is that there is cosmic law, and cosmic law fluctuates in harmony. It is the mind of perfection and a masterpiece of circuitry that cannot be disturbed along any of its wide avenues of circuitry. All of the terminals and circuitry connections of divine mind throughout the grand universe and beyond cannot be disrupted by abusive language or abusive thinking. All of God's circuitry is absolute and is designed for perfection in resonating with musical harmony that is in harmony from a lower scale to the next higher one. When there is an inharmonious pattern, the whole circuitry can be broken on the lower evolutionary worlds where the circuits have been cut off. Various changes have taken place in the life therein, not only in the physical bodies of humans who have been born on that plane but also in the animal and plant life.

It is known that out of the approximately twenty amino acids there are eight essential ones in the body. Casein, a protein precipitated in milk, cannot be manufactured in the body. Any protein that does not contain all eight of these essential amino acids is an incomplete protein. Where imbalances occur in ovan souls, lower energy circuits gravitate to like kind in purely physical gravitation, therefore prohibiting proper pair-unit matching. When a male is a lower complement, neutronic enzymes join with already existing neutronic enzymes within the female and create an imbalance. When a male is a higher complement, he transfers the protonic reality that brings more of a balance. There can be an imbalance of protons and/or neutrons within the nucleus of an atom.

With a higher ovan soul, who is approximately 10,000 years older than the one he or she may be attracted to, it is in reality an attraction in the mind, much like an addiction. Even on Urantia, those souls who end up in relationships based upon purely physical attraction usually discover over some time period that they are not fulfilled, nor are they truly happy.

There are many reasons for this unfulfillment. For example, if a male ovan soul is married to a first-time Urantian—although he may seem to be accomplished in many areas, such as being a lawyer, and she may be a beautiful, simple, yet perhaps greedy first-time Urantian female—the ovan soul lawyer will not find himself, nor will he find his destiny nor use the full capacity of his brain because the circuitry is cut off.

These circuits have been cut off for 200,000 years on Urantia. Basically what Michael said was, "Fine, do what you want to do; choose your own way, and you will be unfulfilled." Do you hear what I am saying? When you choose your own way over the will of the Father, you will not find your way. You will find a way, but it will not be the way of fulfillment, nor will it be the way of self-actualization. You may temporarily appease the lust of your flesh, but you will not fulfill your higher reality, for this can only be found in the homogenized reality of alignment with the eternal purposes of God the Father, which you have chosen not to be in time and time again. The entrapments you have allowed yourselves to get into have caused your diseases, every one of them. As long as you continue to try to justify your present set of circumstances based upon you being only human, then you will remain only human, and you will die. It is as simple as that.

In general, on Urantia animal proteins contain more of the essential amino acids than do plant proteins, and it is known that the best are found in milk and eggs. Why is this? Does God wish all to be carnivorous? I say, definitely not! This is due to the fall of Adam and Eve and not the product of interuniversal plant life distribution.

On Urantia, an interuniversal experimental interbreeding planet, when ovan souls reach the third circle to the first, foods once digestible will become as enemies to the system. Many fruits and leafy vegetables contain indigestible substances, making them poor energy sources compared to meat or grains. Some roots and leafy vegetables are the result of mutations of plant life since the Rebellion. On Urantia it should be understood, by even the nonspiritual scientists, that something is terribly out of synchronization with the human body in relation to the various diseases that end life.

Why is it that on some islands it has been discovered that where the influences of certain other foods are not digested, those diseases are not inherited by the natives there? However, just as soon as other foods are introduced into their reality, they begin to have these diseases. Could it not be that the very foods themselves contain these diseases? The answer to this is yes, and that the foods themselves do not contain the very necessary life ingredients to also combat the improper thinking processes. If the foods were at their highest capacity they would also be able to combat even the negative thoughts.

On evolutionary worlds of time and space where the offspring of that planet's Adam and Eve, and perhaps of other Material Sons and Daughters, have been allowed to distribute the higher food substances around the planet to the various evolutionary races, these races have been able to overcome their lower thinking and lower evolutionary realities and to come into higher dimensional spaces long before this could happen on Urantia. Because of the fall of Adam and Eve from the First Garden, it has become almost impossible for any of the plant life, including vegetables and fruits, to provide the necessary protein reality to prevent physical death. The only way that this can be done now on Urantia is that Urantian and Cosmic Reservists, and others who resonate with the highest thinking processes, must be in **protected areas**. There is simply no other way to escape physical death.

Morontia bodies will only resonate with higher thinking and with foods that are supplied and given from the earth itself to combat the negative thoughts and diotribes in the body that have not yet left it. It does not have to be any new kind of plant life. A radish could have one effect in a protected area and a completely lower effect outside of it. A radish grown at the **First Planetary Sacred Home** by the **First Cosmic Family** could bring a youth-giving energy contributing to an increase of auhter energy far beyond the radish's capacity to do the same thing in other areas of the planet.

This is because of a seraphim and Life Carrier implantation into the soil itself and in the water of the First Planetary Sacred Home. Also, the rainfall that flows from the sky is a blessing given to this area to sustain the higher plant life that will be grown there in the future. It is most necessary that the gardening at the First Planetary Sacred Home be done with the highest of organization, and it must be realized by all community residents that these community gardens are not owned by individuals but are in the hands of Overcontrol and that they do need to be inseminated with a form of healing to the bodies of our community members. A complete transmission will be given regarding this in the future.

It was stated in the earlier part of this transmission that body tissue was formed by the breakdown of food molecules into smaller elements that form these tissues. On planets where the life forms stem from the sea, certain foods are different and are more applicable to sea life than those that would be found on the land. If an ovan soul on Urantia once originated from the sea, the very foods on Urantia would actually not resonate with that personality.

Since the Rebellion, many wonderful souls on Urantia have died very young because the foods on this planet did not sustain them. No matter how great they may have been in their spiritual ascension, many—even those who have come to be known as saints—died from various diseases, not because their thinking was so far off but because the foods they ate were not able to overcome even their minute negative thinking. Even a grief that stems from the recognition that one has strayed out of God's will can be healed by the eating of foods that resonate with higher brain cells of the one feeling this grief, if it is known what particular food of the point of origin is to be given, including meat.

God is the giver of all life and the healer of all life, and natural substances can sustain a mind when the mind is out of the will of God, even a mind in self-pity, and eventually transform that mind. Self-pity is a sin, but self-pity can be overcome if there is time enough. A drug injected into the body can sustain life, but it also can hinder the thinking. The naturalness of divine food in relation to the brain cells of each and every creature is an antidote to the negative thinking process.

On worlds in the higher stages of light and life where the bodies are still very much material, self-pity and other forms of depression and anxiety do not exist for very long periods because they know exactly what to take to change the thinking. On Urantia, alcohol and drugs are used instead, which then create continued unalignment to God and God's purposes and destroy the body in many ways, sometimes completely causing death of mind, death of the physical body, and death of the emotional body, all because in trying to alleviate harmful thinking a higher form is necessary.

However, it seems to be a natural thing to try to change one's thoughts by the ingestion and digestion of physical substances. If it can be understood that higher foods and the products of higher foods in drinks and juices can be taken instead of harmful substances, alcoholism and drug abuse would be ended, for there would be no need for alcohol and drug use if the food itself could do the same thing in a better way. This is and will be the reality of the Divine New Order, and it could have been the reality of present-day Urantia if Adam and Eve, the highest minds of the biological sciences, had not become imbalanced. Now we have to come back to that First Garden. We have to come back to the higher understanding of foods.

As ovan souls reach the higher circles, foods that were once eaten on this planet in this lifetime will become indigestible for them, and they will find themselves in pain from the digestion of certain foods, particularly if on their planet of origin they were not flesh eaters and they have grown accustomed to eating animals in this life. Although these foods may taste good, because they are addictive, the body itself will be out of harmony and certain cells within it will not find their proper circuitry, causing temporary unalignment to even the highest of ovan souls on the first circle.

If you are from another universe where the plant forms and some animal life were created basically for the nourishment of these ascending mortals, then flesh eating can be a reality. However, this is not the case on Urantia, and the reason for this is because you are in another reality physiologically and in another type of physiological body. Your astral cellular reality will begin to harmonize and communicate to restructure the digestive system and your present physical body on Urantia will begin in some manner to digest flesh. Flesh-eating bodies are much different from Urantian human bodies. However, starseed in Urantian bodies can change those systems internally and at a cellular level in how food intake communicates to the brain and central nervous system.

If you are presently in a Urantian body—whether a first- or **second-time Urantian** or a **starseed**—the most functional reality for you would have been nonflesh-eating. I repeat, nonflesh-eating, as Urantian plant food would have supplied all necessary physiological systems, including intra- and interuniversal digestive systems. Unfortunately, because of the fall of Caligastia and some of the One Hundred and others, as I stated before and repeat here again, the necessary proteins in the higher foods were lost to Urantia and even at the First Planetary Sacred Home are not available now,[1] and as a result the only place these proteins can be found outside the protected areas is in meat.

However, it is also well known that the chemicals now placed in the plants and meat are just as bad as ingesting the chemical poisons by themselves. What answer is there to this dilemma? To those who have ears to hear, there is only one answer: you must stop eating chemically-treated meat and chemically-sprayed vegetables and fruits and obtain chemical-free food.

If you are an ovan soul you can learn about your highest self and resonate with the molecular structures of those close to you and harmonize the cells within your body just by being near your cosmic relatives. This homogenizing process takes place because the **auhter energy** is a stabilizing energy for you, and you cannot find this outside of the first protected area.

Secondary protected areas resonate in a lower vibrational force. Although you may find some of your cosmic ancestry in the secondary areas if you are somewhat in tune with your God, you will not find the higher circuitry connections or the higher homogenizing influences mentioned previously in the three types of hydrolyzing enzymes: the amylases, lipases, and proteinases. These are the fusion elements that cannot be found outside the protected areas in their highest functioning because the higher ovan souls who have aligned themselves to the purposes of Christ Michael under the present Planetary Prince can only be found in this one particular geographic area at this time.

Where this higher resonating order of God exists within aligned bodies in any one particular planet, system, constellation, or universe, there the power of God exists in the highest form and structure and in itself creates a form of proton. This is a Deo-atomic proton, and it is recognizable throughout the master universe. It is a **proton photon** of light that collectively exhibits a life form that can be used by the Creator Sons to produce a new life form. This is because creatures in a sense have lit up a certain energy because of their own willingness to be in the will of God corporately and in the union of souls.

When this light becomes dimmer it is because one person within this light structure is not so perfectly within the will of God as he or she may have been yesterday, therefore the energy force is lessened. This light becomes stronger when this light force becomes more stabilized. As the Divine Administration functioning through human personalities becomes more stabilized, this light will become stronger, and a greater proton photon reality will exist.

With this proton photon reality existent, it can actually cause a magnetic transpositional force–energy to be drawn from Urantia to Salvington itself, causing a continual flow from Earth to Salvington. This light will begin to draw physical cellular matter to Urantia and will begin to move in space to the architectural worlds, and this light will draw the **New Jerusalem** to Urantia. If this light is not strong enough, it will not activate.

This light, when strong enough, can move an entire architectural planet; it can move a massive spacecraft, and it is used by "the gods" to move physical energies and physical matter created by the creator gods. However, this cannot be done even by the gods unless ascending sons and daughters find themselves, join together in harmony, and find their place in the plan of God under the Divine Administration created by God for the purposes of God and the purposes of the planet on which they find themselves.

This alignment will bring the Divine New Order and will bring the Trinity Teacher Sons and even Christ Michael. This alignment will bring the New Jerusalem. At what point, at what moment in time will this come? The final change point will come in its appointed time regardless of this alignment by individual personalities. This is coming because the planet is destroying itself. However, when **proton sequential force-energy** is existent to very high levels, at a certain point if enough of this light is energized from the First Planetary Sacred Home, the alignment bringing the Divine New Order can come more rapidly and even before the final change point.

I, a finaliter, cannot measure this, nor do I understand it completely; only the Universal Father in relation to the Creator Son of this universe can measure these things. The New Jerusalem can be brought and even Michael Himself can be drawn.

As it is written: "Go out into the world and make disciples of all men, and baptize them in the name of the Father, the Son, and the Holy Spirit."² This truth still stands today, but it must be understood in a higher way. The Paradise Trinity must be understood in a higher way in and through the present **adjudication of the Bright and Morning Star versus Lucifer**. All must come to understand that the Threefold Spirit within them must be activated. All must receive the Spirit of Truth, and all must understand that Christ Michael is the Creator Son of this universe.

Differences in culture on Urantia are a wonderful thing. Differences in dress, tradition, and ceremony, and even differences in language can be beautiful, but where these differences create lower thinking and the inability of one to understand another, then these differences become dangerous. Beauty is indeed a differential reality. One can see one thing as beautiful and another one see the same thing as not so beautiful. However, in diversity beauty can be expounded upon, and in diversity beauty in form is ever so eternal. But when personalities at any level cannot understand one another and division exists and misunderstanding happens even with a smile and a handshake, it must be understood that the totality of God can only be explained by a common language.

Within the variety of plant life on a normal planet, foods can be prepared, cooked, and digested for the nourishment of all involved on the planet. On a decimal planet like Urantia where interuniversal ovan souls exist this can also be done, but it must be done in an orderly fashion within a high administrative understanding of the planetary system in **The Starseed and Urantian Schools of Melchizedek** [now called the **Global Community Communications Schools**]. Outside of this very few will understand, nor can they. It is up to those in the Global Community Communications Schools to come into a higher understanding of point of origin, and then it must be taught to and assimilated by the rest of the planet.

Many of the ovan souls are in their forties and fifties, and still they have not discovered their cosmic reality and are dying of the diseases of this planet. **Continuing Fifth Epochal Revelation** can reach them in the future and can be a means for a beginning for them to overcome natural death and to find their destiny purpose. It is hoped that these transmissions dealing with this subject will reach not only the Cosmic and Urantian Reservists but thousands of others who are linked with higher genetic origins so that they do not have to suffer the various plagues that are presently happening on Urantia and so that they can find themselves in protected areas free from the diseases and plagues that will continue to increase on the planet at a very rapid rate until the final change point occurs.

June 13, 1992

Paladin, Chief of Finaliters
in cooperation with the Race Commissioners and the Life Carriers of interuniversal origin, and the present Planetary Prince, Machiventa Melchizedek, for the purposes of complete healing and total actualization

As transmitted through
the Pre-Level-One Audio Fusion Material Complement,
Gabriel of Urantia/TaliasVan of Tora

PAPER 245

Oxidation And The Air We Breathe In Relationship To The Paradise Trinity As Manifested In Form In Pair-Unit Classifications And Complementary Polarities On The Evolutionary Worlds Of Time And Space By Ascending Sons And Daughters Of Procreation Ability

IT is known in your science that carbon, hydrogen, and oxygen together form carbohydrates. Carbohydrates are in the food we eat, hydrogen is in the water we drink, and oxygen is in the air we breathe. When carbon and hydrogen are mixed together and form a union, it is a hydrocarbon compound often found in gasoline and other fuels. Hydrogen and oxygen combined produce water, and water can also be used for energy purposes. When coal (which is carbonized matter) burns at a certain temperature, light and heat are produced. When carbon reacts with oxygen, these **complementary polarities** become fused in an energy sequence similar to the one that **ovan souls** create when they align themselves with the purposes of God on this planet. This fusion of human complements creates an **auhter energy**. Finality status of an ancestor adds to this emergent energy on Urantia.

When the Father circuits (carbon) fuse with the Son (hydrogen) and with the living, breathing reality of the Universe Mother Spirit (oxygen in the air) and are ingested into the body, a certain oxidation takes place. It is in a sequence of food digestion and breathing that energy is created in the body. Glucose—consisting of carbon, hydrogen, and oxygen—is a form of energy derived from the carbohydrates of starch and protein molecules. The energy in glucose is released by enzymes stripping off the carbon and hydrogen atoms, and this energy is stored within certain tissues of the body in the form of glycogen. The body inhales 21% oxygen and breathes this in 16 times every minute. The body exhales only 16% of that oxygen in the form of carbon dioxide. The other 5% is available for recirculation in the lungs.

Sometimes hydrogen explodes and moves things around. When objects are moving they create what is called kinetic energy. Kinetic energy occurs within humans or other mortal bodies when pair units are:

- thinking of one another within a five-mile radius; the closer they are, the more energy is released

- being affectionate within the aura field of one another, either by eye contact or touch

- in sexual union

The energy obtained in all of the above processes is used to form high-energy phosphate bonds, which are stored in the body as complete chunks of energy for use wherever necessary. There is a high and a low energy bond. Ionic phosphate is 1/6 of the weight of the bone structure of the body. Where the phosphate group is not bound and the flow can occur, a high-energy bond is produced and released. Where the phosphate grouping is bound together, a low energy is produced and the energy released is minute. The energy in glucose is the basic fuel of the body. It contains 12 hydrogen, 6 oxygen, and 6 carbon atoms, a total of 24 in a glucose molecule. Taking all of this into consideration, let us continue.

It is said that the eyes are the windows of the soul, and this is so in many ways. It also could be said that the nose is the gasoline tank of the body. The fusion of the intake and outgo of the eyes and the nose in relation to reality existence on Urantia is much more than what you can imagine relative to positive actualization of moment-to-moment reality. On higher ascension levels the human eye can perceive **diotribes** and

Deo-atomic cellular makeup in a past **pair-unit** mate or a prospective mate.

On a planet where so many things are out of alignment, you find yourself coming across a delicious fruit and being unable to eat it. You find yourself meeting those of your past reality and being attracted to them in many ways far beyond your own reasoning as to why, yet being unable to speak to them even though your own human desire as well as your superconsciousness tells you to speak. Even when talking to them, you sometimes find yourself unable to communicate with them at the highest level if you know more than they do about cosmic reality.

For all the various reasons that deception has entered on this planet, it has broken down the ability of mitochondria within the cells to produce energy in relation to the positive flow of God-reality. **Deo-atomic reality** is an attraction reality and a harmonizing reality in spiritual unions. Diotribe reality is one that pushes away, divides, and is noncommunicative in potential spiritual unions. War and diseases are caused by diotribe reality in one way or another.

When a higher spiritually evolved male ovan soul comes into contact with a female past **pair-unit classification** mate of lower ascension status or vice versa, particularly in relationship to **Continuing Fifth Epochal Revelation**, it is almost impossible for even the higher one to say hello. And if there is a conversation, it must be, as you say on your planet, kindergarten talk. It is a fact on Urantia that you cannot enjoy the reality of one another on the highest level as God intended, and it goes far beyond any philosophical assent to romance.

What is it on lower evolutionary worlds where procreation through sexual union is a reality that attracts a male to a particular female or vice versa? In the **third dimension** the attraction between sexes is based upon the physical, and often upon diotribe reality, but in the **fourth dimension**, attraction is based upon Deo-atomic reality.

It was said in a past transmission that even human tissue is formed because of higher protein reality where the enzymes in the body correlated with divine purposes. This is also true of bone structure. Bone structure is formed in relation to the same higher ascension reality. The bone structure of a similar point-of-origin neighbor, relative, or mate is formed because at one time this was an absolute reality; a higher ovan soul may be attracted to the physical bone structure of another person, which has nothing to do with lust at all. However, one may lust and not know why.

What is it that attracts one male to a female and not another male to the same female? Even though this particular female may be Miss America, the higher male ovan soul who visualizes this female may not be attracted to her at all but may be more physically attracted to another one. The other woman may be formed and shaped completely differently from the Miss America. Her breasts may be smaller, and the shape of her legs may not meet the Hollywood prototype. What the higher soul sees in reality and what the attraction is really all about is that the skin formed around the bone and the bone structure of the body itself has to do with the point of origin of the higher soul; it is of the same family.

On other worlds of time and space when higher ascending sons cohabit with lower ascending daughters, the sperm intake that resonates with the protein enzymes inside the flow of the blood system begins to correlate and change the physical body of the ascending daughter to the point that as this ascending daughter grows older, perhaps until she is 300 years old, and if they have been together in cohabitation for several hundred years, her physical body will become similar to the higher male's ascension body. So you see, you have much to learn, and this all indeed goes way beyond romance, doesn't it?

Whole races are formed by (at this time) unrevealed personalities in the likeness of Material Sons and Daughters based upon this kind of pair-unit classification. These personalities are chosen to breed, so that these races can be formed with higher body types and higher bone structures for specific purposes. It is also true that when higher bodies, even on lower worlds, can respond better to cosmic absolutes in spiritual reality, the bodies themselves then consist of the atoms of God. The atoms of God are breathed or digested into the body, oxidized, and assimilated. The higher oxygen molecules that are breathed into the body are the best ones.

It is the same in the procreation of male and female through offspring; the higher genetic strains produce the higher offspring. The highest ascending sons, even of a fallen estate, who at one time even on Urantia could have begun to produce higher third-dimensional bodies, could now produce the fourth-dimensional reality in which Urantia will be.

Even now, in this transition period, the higher ovan souls, male and female, are bringing in the higher **starseed**. The bodies of these children, even though they are presently in a transition state themselves, will begin to be aligned more completely with their point-of-origin bodies, and at a more accelerated pace after the final change point. It will be possible for a human mortal who was five foot, five inches before the change point to accelerate to six to eight feet tall after the change point and even before the morontia body is given. This is all due to the proper alignment of the Deo-atomic cellular structures within the body and the removal of all diotribe reality, not only in the thinking processes of the mind but in the very air that is breathed. The purification must be complete, and all diotribe reality within carbon, hydrogen, and oxygen must be removed from the air.

Carbon that is in the form of coal can be compressed over a period of hundreds of thousands of years to become a diamond. The negativity that it once exhibited in matter form in a piece of black substance over a period of time becomes a shining diamond. Through purification it has become a pure energy of higher light.

In philosophical terms, most ovan souls on Urantia who have been here over and over again have not reached this purification process in their own building of energy, and many confess they have not yet become the diamond. Some of these ovan souls are now beginning to be placed into positions of very high authority, but they are still being purified themselves, and they are still unable to become the diamond because others around them of lower carbon substance are not of the same frequency polarity.

When the diamond begins to shine, the others of lower frequency cannot comprehend them. Sometimes the diamond is seen by others as a threat, even though the diamond may love these others and even though the diamond sees more of the very nature of those other persons. Even though the love is pure and kind, the others do not know how to react to the diamond. But as long as the diamond is trying with the highest motive to communicate to the lower one, ultimaton reality will flow from the higher to the lower one and will bring some kind of balance to the lower body of the lower soul. If it is a pair-unit classification mate of a past reality, the healing will be higher and manifested more rapidly and continuously as a higher flow of higher atoms will begin to take place within the lower body of the male or female that is near the higher soul, even within eyesight distance, as mentioned previously in another transmission.

All of this has been greatly upstepped on this planet since December 1989 with the coming to this planet of the Planetary Prince. With knowledge comes a certain responsibility. With knowledge a seed is given, and it is known that thought creates energy and that thought itself can move matter. Knowledge is a powerful force that can be used for healing, cosmic insight, cosmic joy, and the satisfaction of divine fulfillment. Those who understand Continuing Fifth Epochal Revelation can be healers to so many on this planet, not only before the final **change point** but long afterwards.

If you are unable to understand the higher concepts of Fifth Epochal Revelation, it is because you exhibit evil and sin within your thinking processes. You think with a mind that is not fused with your heart. The process of **ascension science** is a fusion between science and spirituality. However, if science alone (particularly evolutionary science rather than cosmic absolute science) becomes the textbook of your understanding, you will remain on lower circles even though you may think of yourself as an intellectual giant and may be accepted as one by others around you.

God's measurement of the intellectual is not the measurement of your Urantian universities. If you cannot learn to fuse cosmic science and cosmic philosophy (what you on this world call your left brain with your right one), if you cannot learn to fuse understanding with love, if you cannot learn to fuse understanding with fact, and if you cannot learn to fuse understanding with various levels of absolute science, then you have no understanding at all.

Divine understanding is the understanding of grace, mercy, and openness into the very heart and fiber of the personality bestowal of the Eternal Father. Divine understanding is an openness to individuality. All understanding is nonjudgmental. Divine understanding wishes to give. Divine understanding is the fusion of the Mother and Son, correlated with the will of the Father. Human understanding, in whatever subject or field, has nothing to do with divine understanding. Divine understanding supersedes all else.

Divine understanding knows that whatever is learned at any level about any one particular thing is understood at a higher level in a higher way by a higher personality with an even higher understanding. When you become dogmatic about your understanding, you have no understanding whatsoever, even if you can produce human scientific facts to explain your understanding. It is still just that, your understanding.

The healing powers of higher evolutionary mortal personalities are such that they can touch a diseased body and heal it completely; you might say it is almost godlike. It is indeed a godlike quality, but what has transpired in those types of situations is that a divine mandate has been given to personalities because they have ascended to a certain place in their relationship to the personality of God; therefore, God's power is given to them. Some of these personalities of a very high nature cannot even breathe the air that Urantians breathe, and that is why they cannot come here now. The very air that you breathe would be poison to them.

When a higher personality on this planet, particularly a mandated one at this level of the human administration of Machiventa, exhales, he or she is beginning to exhale higher **Deo-atomic oxygen** within the carbon dioxide. This oxygen that is exhaled is a life-giving oxygen at the very highest level that can be given by a mortal, one to another. That is why a healing begins to take place when some of the cosmic family are around others of their cosmic family who have ascended higher than they themselves. Not only do they incorporate within their own Deo-atomic structure an auhter energy breathed in through the skin tissues, but they also begin to receive oxygen through the nose, which is created by the higher souls and that acts as a higher form of cleansing atom.

When enough higher souls of higher genetics are together in one geographic location and enough oxygen of Deo-atomic reality is released because of them, healing will take place in this area at a higher rate than at any other place on the planet, simply because of this fact alone. Some of these healings may be temporary for many because the root of the problem in the astral body has not been changed, but for those who are willing to be changed by astral healing, the very air they breathe—first within the First Radius, then within the Second, and eventually within the Third Radius—can heal them if there is a sufficient number of individuals of higher ascension quality so that all the air within the area can be completely Deo-atomic.

People can then come into that circle of the Third Radius with cancer, and as soon as they enter that Third Radius they will faint. They will faint because they have just breathed in a force that is an enemy to the diotribe reality. They will either faint and revive, or they will faint and not revive; in other words, they will die. It is not that this has to be a sudden death, but it could be a death from any of the diseases that diotribe reality has allowed them to have.

The Third Radius will be protected, not because there are angels standing there with great clubs and energy beams, but because of the very reality that those who are aligned with one another will create as a result of their alignment—a Deo-atomic reality in the very physical cellular structure of the earth and the air itself. This will first begin to take place within the First Radius. Those who do not belong within the First Radius because they have not aligned themselves will be moved because the **Deo-atomic cells** they are beginning to breathe in will act as a virus to them and cause a more rapid death of the physical body; light does not mix with darkness, nor do diotribes mix with Deo-atomic cells. The diotribes held will completely repel the healing ability of the Deo-atomic cells, thus creating the effect of a destructive virus.

All plant life will also begin to produce higher oxygen as a result of the human personalities first producing the oxygen and then by breaking these oxygen molecules down into a chemical energy and producing higher Deo-atomic foods. The proteins received from this Deo-atomic food will begin to change the body and revitalize the body with higher healing and energy.

When sexual union transpires between higher pair-unit classifications, a form of explosion does take place. The magnetic draw between the Deo-atomic cells of the male and female that are being magnetized toward one another form a kind of kinetic energy flow within the individual bodies. This correlates through the central nervous system of each individual, and in a sense both function like a form of hydrogen molecule. When this explosion takes place, climax by one or both individuals happens.

When climax takes place between a higher individual and a lower one outside of fourth-dimensional reality that is one thing, but when it takes place between two individuals who understand **cosmic genetics** in relation to ascension science, that is another. Because every sperm cell released from the male and received into the female contains life-giving atoms, they can be transferred from the female to others at any point in time, once the female has learned how to do this at a higher level.

That is why a female who has retained Deo-atomic cells from higher male complements can go from one planet to another and heal the lower evolutionary races of various diseases simply by contact, by touching without sexual union, but the touching must be done in a very controlled manner. If it is done in an uncontrolled manner, with too much Deo-atomic reality transferred from the higher to the lower one, it can actually kill the lower mortal. This is why interbreeding between higher and lower mortals can also kill. When sperm is received in some lower evolutionary races from higher ones it can actually cause such a disturbance within the body that death occurs.

On Urantia Adam and Eve became mortal, and the races of Urantia—although higher genetically from that point on—never received a higher understanding of the control of genetics, how to use it properly, and the exhaling of their descendants could not create the higher oxygen atoms in the air. Therefore the Deo-atomic content of the oxygen of all Urantia was lower than what was intended from the beginning of the fall of Adam and Eve to the present. If the intended one-half million offspring would have then been able to cohabit with the evolutionary races, the very oxygen on Urantia would have been more beneficial for the higher purposes of cosmic destiny.

Plant life would have benefited more from the waters of the oceans, lakes, and streams. All deserts would have disappeared. All thorns on cacti would have turned into flowers and leaves, and there would be no stickers or thorns of any kind. The very soil of the earth would have changed, and the very nature and substance of the land itself would be quite different, as would the waters of the earth become different in color. With the higher genetic strains here, the color of the water would be whiter. Where lower strains lived, the colors of the water would resonate with the molecular water structures of their bodies—some blue, some green, or some red. Higher water is pure white. This is why crystallization of water in the sea of glass is almost what you would call on this planet crystal white.

And so you see that the Lucifer Rebellion not only affected the thinking processes, but for many billions and billions of personalities it has also affected the physical makeup of the 37 fallen planets, their soil, and their air. The atmospheric reality of these various planets differs in relation to the amount of deception that was inherited by the evolutionary races on these planets.

Because of its interuniversal genetic reality, Urantia is a prototype in many ways to a true Divine New Order. This Divine New Order will not only be a change in the thinking of men and women, but it will be a change in the very air and land itself. When the soul of an ascending being correlates with the higher cosmic absolutes, air is not needed; there is no need for the intake of oxygen. In the bodies an outer form of the nose may be present, but on the inside the lungs and all the various body parts correlating the air with the lungs will disappear.

On Urantia, even when souls receive morontia bodies, some ovan souls may receive higher than first-stage morontia bodies correlated with their ascension level, and many of the organs, glands, etc. of the presently existing bodies will disappear; they will become lighter. Some ovan souls will be able to run much faster than others. They will be able to run at speeds of about 400 miles per hour. The very nature of the air in the various sectors on Urantia after the final change point will be different, and so will the plant life. Even though the topography of the earth will be more consistent on a physical level, the sectors within it will change over a period of time because of the personalities living there.

Each interuniversal sector will be much different from the others. The food will be different, and the cultures will be different. Those with the higher ascension body types who must go to the other sectors for short periods of time will find that the reality that is there will not be quite as pleasant as that in the higher sectors. This is why they should be in the higher sector. The air they breathe in the lower sectors will not vibrate at the rate necessary to give them the energy capacity level that they have in the higher sector, and they will be drained by the personalities in the lower sector who will receive Deo-atomic reality from the genetic flow from their bodies upon contact with them. Although they will be used for healing purposes in these sectors, it would not be the best vacation spot for higher individuals because of this drain on their energies.

Even now to some degree, human mandated personalities and **First Cosmic Family** members who are more highly aligned to the Machiventa Melchizedek Administration are beginning to understand that energies are being drawn from them by personalities who do not understand them or are sick when they come to them and draw energy simply by being near them. So now they need each other to become revitalized, because in this revitalization by mutual proximity, the higher Deo-atomic reality is more coordinate with their ascension level.

Even when pet animals, like dogs for instance, who for some reason have been abused or are not functioning within the highest states of their animal reality, come into contact with higher personalities, these animals will find that they will not want to be around these higher personalities. That is why many forms of animal life will not be allowed within the First Radius until after the final change point. The animals can also breathe in the Deo-atomic oxygen but will not be able to use this oxygen, and because there is not enough of this oxygen being produced now because of the small number of cosmic family members presently gathered, it would be quite inappropriate for the use of this oxygen to have it be absorbed by animal life. Therefore it is advised that you do not have domestic animals in your home unless you wish to hinder the growth and healing of your own body.

Life Carriers and seraphic guardians of destiny, as well as certain physical controllers presently on Urantia, work together in correlation to such a high degree to keep all the newly formed Deo-atomic oxygen atoms within the First Radius. When newly formed oxygen is released outside of the First Radius to the Second Radius and within the Third Radius, this oxygen is programmed to flow in a certain direction to a certain individual for a specific reason. These Deo-atomic oxygen atoms are not randomly thrown around the Third Radius, and the other oxygen atoms of post-rebellion Urantia are also controlled. The higher air that you breathe is the result of your ascension.

The adjudication process is a life-giving process to those who align with Christ Michael and the Universal Father. If you are not aligned, you will continue to breathe unaligned air. The very makeup of the oxygen that you inhale through your lungs will continue to vibrate you at a lower level, and you will not be able to come to any high level of reality. Every cell within you that is not aligned with God will increase the rapidity of your death so that you will be either inheriting all of the plagues on this planet or you will become confused in thought. The protected areas where eventually you gain higher Deo-atomic hydrogen, carbon, and oxygen atoms will be the only places where all these life-giving atoms will be perfectly functioning in divine reality.

Souls who are not aligned will not be able to breathe these atoms, and they will not be allowed in the closer circles of the personalities of the human government, and that is why we are so strict with individuals who are in the aura field of mandated personalities. Stating it simply, they do not deserve to breathe the same air as you. I repeat, they do not deserve to breathe the same air as you.

We do not want them in the First Radius. We do not want them within the Second Radius, and eventually they will be removed from the Third Radius. This is not a threat. This is a reality. This is the adjudication of light versus darkness. This is the adjudication of proper thinking versus improper thinking. This is the adjudication of evil, sin, and iniquity being removed from the souls of ascending sons and daughters. If you wish to keep it, then keep it, but you will not be allowed within the Third Radius, nor will you be allowed to return to this planet after the final change point, for the air that you wish to breathe is not the air of God; it is the air of lower-level reality. That is what you will take in and digest, and that is what will form your bodies, or deform them. You choose. You indeed choose.

June 18, 1992

Paladin, Chief of Finaliters
in cooperation with interuniversal and intrauniversal Life Carriers, the Seraphim of Race Commissioners, a Universal Censor of Paradise, and with Lanaforge, System Sovereign of Satania, for the higher understanding of the importance of living and working in the vicinity of complementary polarities and higher complements who have themselves formed into the higher personalities of God, and for the calling forth of the Cosmic and Urantian Reserve Corps in the implementation of the Divine Administration in and through the present Planetary Prince, Machiventa Melchizedek

As transmitted through
the Pre-Level-One Audio Fusion Material Complement,
Gabriel of Urantia/TaliasVan of Tora

PAPER 246

Helper (Helpmate) Molecules, Magnesium And Iron, In Fusion With Protein Enzymes In Relationship To Pair-Unit Classifications Or Higher Spiritual Complements In The Activation Of Healing Force Energies On The Lower Worlds Of Time And Space And In The Ascension Process To Higher Spiritual Bodies

IT is understood that all vitamins are derived from three sources in the food that is eaten. These sources are proteins, fats, and carbohydrates. In reality, proteins are of the Universal Father, fats of the Eternal Son, and carbohydrates of the Infinite Spirit, and all are a Paradise-origin prerogative. These three food sources are of Paradise-origin design, and in and through the diversified circuits of time and space they become the various foods eaten and digested by all material beings of all inhabited worlds.

On evolutionary Urantia, when an enzyme molecule draws a needed helper magnesium molecule and they fuse together, a wonderful thing occurs: there is an enzyme reaction. This enzyme reaction equals a form of **auhter energy**. It creates a synergy process. The body uses very small amounts of these metals, which it gets out of the food you eat, but just the same they are necessary to life. The complete absence of any one of them would stop one or more vital enzyme reactions in the body, and that would mean death. An absence of **complementary polarities** can cause emotional, mental, and spiritual problems leading to disease that can cause physical death.

In many cases the function of an enzyme is so vital that there must be no risk of delay at all. The enzyme cannot wait for an activator to float by. It is the same reality in relation to individuals who are alone, particularly ovan souls. If they are not living around a reality existence of higher complementary polarities they malfunction. They malfunction in many ways. They malfunction in mind, and they malfunction in physiological body functions if they cannot draw an activator to them, a helper. They are then alone and isolated and open to various diseases and nonreality purposes.

The heme or iron-containing pigment within the enzyme molecule attaches itself to the enzyme molecule like a stamp to an envelope. The iron acts as an activator that causes oxidation, producing the energy of life. This drawing process of the **helper (helpmate) molecule** to the enzyme is, in type, a form of **morontia magnetic field flow** principle.

When two complementary polarities are in the same aura field of one another, a higher morontia magnetic field flow exists, and the transference of higher ultimatons and **Deoatomic reality** begins to correlate from the higher person to the lower one. The lower one may be completely unaware of what is happening or of whom he or she is with in relation to cosmic ancestry or what is happening at that moment. The higher one, mind and soul, may also be unaware of what is happening, but at whatever level one is aware, or both are aware, they become higher instruments for healing on their planet. When many on the planet are aware and join into teams of higher healers, they can go out into other worlds and become healers upon those worlds of lesser ascending sons and daughters, particularly on planets that have been in rebellion or in stages of lower dispensational realities.

In an adverse physical condition, when carbon, hydrogen, and nitrogen atoms meet and combine, hydrogen cyanide is formed. If this poisonous substance is consumed by a human it can kill the human in a few moments. Certain substances ruin the working of our atoms that prevent the heme enzyme from doing its job. Enzyme chemists prefer the name inhibitor for those substances that prevent the heme enzyme from doing its job, and the process they call inhibition.

When two human mortals on Urantia, such as an ovan soul or a **first** or **second-time Urantian** who should not be aligned with one another based upon genetics and ascension Deo-atomic reality, join themselves in a relationship or marriage, or even worse, produce children, they create, one to another, a form of poison. This inhibits not only the physiological processes within the body and the structural flow of Deo-atomic cellular reality but also inhibits the decision-making process in relation to the destiny purposes of God for that particular soul.

A shortage of iron in the food causes a poor supply of hemoglobin in the body, and such a condition is known as anemia. Anemia also may be caused by an improper union in procreation by two unmatched mates in marriage, having children for whatever reason. The anemia itself is a condition of the **diotribe** realities of an unmatched pair circulating within the offspring. However, Overcontrol in many cases can assume a will freeze prerogative in relation to the mind of this particular child, allowing the child's mind to become very highly developed, advanced, and spiritually ascended even though the body has deteriorated because of its human or mortal genetic inheritance.

The beryllium atom is similar to magnesium, but it is useless to enzymes and causes the enzymes to become useless also. This is because when two different metal atoms, or two of any kind of substance for that matter, compete for space of an enzyme molecule and the wrong one wins out, it inhibits the enzyme action. This is competitive inhibition.

On your world, when a higher complement is matched with a lower one, a competitive inhibition begins to manifest itself in the higher soul where Deo-atomic reality is influenced by negative reality. The flow of the ultimatons within the atoms themselves creates a disruptive pattern and the circuits of Paradise cannot be heard.

Add to this the improper digestion of certain foods and this will further influence the death process, even if the higher individual who is married and receiving diotribes from the lower one is not receiving these diotribes from sexual union but may be receiving them from the influences of control from the thought life of the stronger one.

In this case the lower or lesser mind can be stronger than the ovan soul and influence the incorrect pattern and incorrect decision-making. In a sense the lower individual is creating within itself beryllium atoms, and a lesser reality exhibits itself in the physical body, and the spiritual body cannot hear the Thought Adjuster that is trying to reach the higher soul so that competitive inhibition is not the reality between these two individuals. In a sense, one is always combating the other in a negative way, for two unlike substances will be in conflict with one another when they are not in the perfect will of their destiny purpose. They malfunction.

However, some molecules that cooperate are coenzymes. One coenzyme is called folic acid; others are not metal but phosphorus compounds. The coenzyme folic acid is neutralized by sulfanilamide. The variety of molecules of the sulfanilamide family individually work against bacteria. They are known as sulfa drugs and are healing complements.

When higher complementary polarities begin to attach themselves closer to one another in geographic areas, a certain transference of Deo-atomic reality takes place. A certain healing force is constructed and a fusion of the Paradise Father, Eternal Son, and Infinite Spirit begins to manifest itself in the ultimaton about which readers of the Fifth Epochal Revelation and Continuing are beginning to know a little more.

The earth itself will be cleansed, perhaps long before the majority of individuals who live upon it. When each individual personality comes into alignment with the purposes of God and the Creator of this universe, Christ Michael of Nebadon, it is true that the very angels themselves rejoice, as do all the other orders of beings from seraphim to midwayers, dancing with joy at that soul's alignment.

However, it is very high in probability that there will be billions of souls on this planet in unalignment. When the older **ovan souls** continue to be in rebellion against perfection, then they too must be cleansed or removed. Within the sacred area the viruses must be destroyed or the body and even those vitamins within the body that are beginning to respond to perfection will be influenced by the negativity of those around them.

That is why it is ever so important that until this proto-cleansing takes place, the few perfect enzymes and the few perfecting ascending sons and daughters within the sacred area can be ever so in harmony with one another, for the greater negative force around them is a reality they are somewhat obliged to function with in an unpleasant capacity until total purification can take place.

When a higher soul is near a lower one, a certain transference of Deo-atomic reality brings some healing to the lower one, and the lower one, or even the higher one for that matter, may not even know what is going on. In every workplace on Urantia, you may be working near a cosmic relative and not know it. That cosmic relative is giving you life and keeping you alive even though you do not know it. The higher relative will eventually have to come to a sacred area to sustain his or her own life and to transcend the death experience.

But for the time being, **cosmic family** members are receiving their life essence from those souls at the **First Planetary Sacred Home** who are creating the **Deo-atomic hydrogen** molecules that are being transferred by the various Life Carriers to all corners of Urantia so that they can breathe unpolluted air. If one of these Deo-atomic hydrogen molecules is breathed into your system, it can create the antibiotic necessary to cleanse all of those improper ones you have inhaled and digested. There will come a time on Urantia, however, when the transference of these hydrogen Deo-atomic molecules will be stopped, and you will no longer be allowed even to breathe clean air.

If you are beckoned by Celestial Overcontrol to come to the First Planetary Sacred Home and you hesitate, you are now under grace, but that grace will cease, and the very air you breathe and the water you drink will be as cyanide to your system. We wish you to see the correlation of the atomic structure of your body with the atomic structure of the perfect spiritual reality in which you exist.

If you fail to see it you will remain in the lower circles of your pride and arrogance. If you fail to give credit where credit is due—to the Eldership of the human Divine Administration and to the mandated personality, **Gabriel of Urantia/TaliasVan of Tora**, and his highest complement, **Niánn Emerson Chase**, the other Elders and apostles of the first century who are themselves ovan souls, along with their sons and daughters who are also ovan souls with higher genetic structures of Deo-atomic ultimaton reality—you will cut yourself off from the light force necessary to sustain your own reality, and disease or sudden death by natural disaster will overtake you.

This is not a threat; it is a warning. It is a warning of love by a finaliter who was sent by your God and Christ Michael to bring you this transmission in cooperation with others so that you yourself can live, not just exist but live in perfection, live in totality, and live in joy and happiness. If you choose another way, you have the will to do so, but you will inherit the way of that will, for if that will is opposed to the destiny purposes of God it will lead to your physical and even perhaps your spiritual death, and you will not be able to serve in the Divine Administration being implemented on this planet because you have chosen to be outside of it. You have chosen to inherit within your body the cellular genetics of the Luciferic body, and so be it.

June 29, 1992

Paladin, Chief of Finaliters
in cooperation with the Life Carriers of various universes including Avalon, Wolvering, Fanoving, and Nebadon to call forth the Cosmic and Urantian Reserve Corps for the

implementation of the Divine Administration of Machiventa Melchizedek at the First Planetary Sacred Home and to bring in the first stages of light and life with the higher auhter energy and corporate cooperation coenzyme of the first sacred protected area of that headquarters unit where the Third Garden is being actualized

As transmitted through
the Pre-Level-One Audio Fusion Material Complement,
Gabriel of Urantia/TaliasVan of Tora

PAPER 247

Vitamins And Their Relationship To The Physical And Spiritual Bodies And In Turn Their Relationship To Paradise-Origin Personalities And The Reflectivity Sources That Create These Vitamins, Pertinent To Physical And Spiritual Health Based Upon Free Will In Relationship To Cosmic Law And Destiny Purposes, And In Particular To Ovan Souls Of The Cosmic Reserve Corps

LET us begin in this transmission by stating that the very few vitamins—which are source-oriented in upper Paradise and nether Paradise through an interrelated personality and physical force-energy fusion, unknown by scientists on Urantia—which have been discovered on Urantia in the last one hundred years or so are only the tip of the cosmic iceberg. The relationship between the vitamins and physical health is actually based upon the relationship of the spiritual in fusion with the physical. It is based upon the appropriation of the personality bestowal circuits of the Father and the alignment to already completed circuitry of the Conjoint Actor working in liaison with the personalities of the Infinite Spirit.

This union decides much of what you will look like as you continue to grow in the normal maturation process on Urantia and on other planets. It also has much to do with how healthy you will be, how your mind will think, and many other things, all pertinent to so many circumstances that are beyond the scope of this transmission to touch upon. What can be given now is the opening of certain circuits within individuals who need this transmission to help them to understand the fusion of physical science and spiritual science in relation to the physical body in which they are now functioning, and the higher spiritual body in which they will begin to function.

Vitamins are very important in the enzyme system, which carries out essential chemical reactions, and vitamins are grouped in two categories, fat-soluble and water-soluble. Fat-soluble Vitamins A, D, E, and K can be stored in the body and do not need a continuous supply. Water-soluble vitamins such as B complex and C must be regularly supplied through the diet. **Continuing Fifth Epochal Revelation** is now teaching that they are also supplied through proper thinking via the Father, Son, and Mother circuits, coordinated in the physical realm by the sun during the day and the moon by night.

Let us begin with **Vitamin A**. It is known that Vitamin A is necessary for sight. Vitamin A was first discovered in this century around 1913, when the **adjudication of the Bright and Morning Star versus Lucifer** was beginning on Urantia. It indeed has a lot to do not only with physical sight but also with spiritual sight. Vitamin A, as far as science is concerned on Urantia, has much to do with growth-stimulating fats and oils. Carotene contains Vitamin A, and one of the food sources for carotene is carrots. There is a whole family of compounds related to carotene.

There are also families of cosmic **ovan souls** related to the **First Cosmic Family** on this planet who should have higher spiritual sight. A characteristic of people who are of the First Cosmic Family is that they have higher spiritual sight and are able to recognize **famotor movement**. However, there are other families who should be receiving spiritual sight, and this has to do with Continuing Fifth Epochal Revelation and what we are trying to teach all those who can comprehend.

Many foods owe their color to the carotene family. If a considerable amount is stored in the fatty layers under the skin, a yellow tinge develops. If those on Urantia who should be working in the first psychic circle had been on the first circle since they were little children, the very skin texture of their bodies would have begun to change. As a matter of fact, their skin pigmentation could also actually become very much lighter.

One of the problems of the fallen worlds, particularly Urantia, is that the very structure of skin color is in relation to the inability of the people on your planet to walk in the perfect will of God. The majority is in ignorance of the degree of suppression by those in religious and political power and is adversely affected by the distortion of the reverse plan by rebellion and default. What you have inherited is reflectivity of energy circuits that are inherited because of lower spiritual development.

It is known that the carotene molecule contains 40 carbon atoms, and the human body breaks this down into 2 equal pieces of 20 carbon atoms each. It is broken down into 20 because 20 is the number of the circuitry of the Eternal Mother Son. 2 is the number of the Second Source and Center and 0 is the number of infinity. (10 is the number of the circuitry of the First Source and Center, and 30 the number of the circuitry of the Third Source and Center, the Infinite Spirit.)

Vitamin A has much to do with the efficiency of sight. A deficiency of Vitamin A causes night blindness. A higher fusion of pure Father and Mother circuits increases both spiritual and physical sight in **third-** and **fourth-dimensional** reality. The lack of fusion decreases sight. On present-day Urantia, sight to some degree will deteriorate after age forty even if balance has occurred. It could take twenty years of being on the first circle to regain lost physical sight, but with the next repersonalization normal sight returns.

Vitamin A, unlike B complex, if stored in excess in the body can get in the way of the body's proper functioning. In essence, an analogy can be drawn between this physical reaction and the overly **Father-circuited** mother and the resulting imbalance of the counterpart of the Universe Mother Spirit and one of her energy circuits in the cellular makeup of the body.

The main components of the eye are:

- the cornea, which is a transparent layer through which light enters
- the iris, the colored part of the eye that contracts and expands, controlling the quantity of light
- the pupil, which is black because it is a hole made into the eye itself
- the lens, which is adjustable, much like a camera
- the retina, which consists of the rods and cones in the center

The rods contain a chemical called rhodopsin. These rods are used to see dim light and black and white. The cones are used to see bright light or whole light. The quality of physical eyesight of mortals at birth has wholly to do with inherited and ancestral **Deo-atomic inheritance**. As to potential spiritual sight, the complete astral reconstruction of the infant has to do both with the genetics of his or her cosmic ancestry and the nursing and bonding the child receives in the first few years of growth.

The decision by Celestial Overcontrol regarding what set of human parents the ovan soul will have is based upon many factors. If you are an ovan soul of great importance to the planet and of a higher destiny purpose, you must be born or be moved as an infant near an **energy reflective circuit** of compatibility of certain interuniversal transport. The energy reflective circuit also will greatly influence your structural and mental capacity as you mature. Other factors—which are somewhat known in your modern astrology (although your modern astrology is a kindergarten understanding)—have to do with the alignment of certain planets to Urantia. What is not known is that these particulars have more to do with planets that are already settled in light and life within the present universe in which you are functioning.

The reflectivity that has been channeled through the circuit bands is created at one point by the Physical Controllers, other celestial personalities, and at a certain point in evolution by the Life Carriers, and changed to what has become known in your science as vitamins. The body can assemble some vitamins if the raw materials called provitamins are provided. Vitamin A is produced in the body from the provitamin carotene.

Vitamin D for instance is actually created by sunlight. Why is this so? Scientists understand the principle, but they understand very little about its applications regarding who you are and who you are to become. Vitamin D is made by the Father/Son. Although the sun seems to be the instrument used, it is the Son that reflects the energies of Salvington to the present sun from which you in turn receive it.

The energy source of your own physical body is based upon these factors. These factors are based upon the alignment of the creatures on your planet to the reflectivity of the other beings created in the particular universe you are presently in. Other factors include circuit blockages created by whatever negativity is in the atmosphere, all based upon the unwillingness of the individuals to be in the perfection of God in every thought mode.

When ergosterol molecules are fused with sunlight, one of the four rings of carbon atoms is broken open. This leaves three carbon rings. That is because they need to come into a proper balance of the Universal Father, the Eternal Son, and the Infinite Spirit. The compound resulting from this proper fusion with Sonlight is called by modern science Vitamin D_2 or ergocalciferol. It then becomes more activated in the body depending upon the evolution of the actualization potential of the genetics of the individual ascending son or daughter of God, and the ability of that one, new soul or not, to find himself or herself in personal destiny purpose. This first depends upon the strength of the Vitamin D_2 and the sight that the person will have.

It is written in the New Testament: "Jesus said unto them, 'If you were blind, you should have no guilt; but now you say, "We see," therefore your guilt remains.'"[1] If you were aware of your blindness you probably would be able to truly see. It has to do with the gift of spiritual sight that is acquired, sometimes very early in the evolution of the soul. If it is acquired early, the soul can advance to a very high place in ascension even though it is a very young soul.

The possibility for the soul to advance so rapidly is based upon the acquisition of this gift, which is drawn to it by a force-energy of a **complementary polarity** that has been created within the body simply by the willingness of the soul to be in alignment with God in goodness, purity, and righteousness. This acquired gift resonates within the body and creates a higher son or daughter of God. This is the gift of humility, which helps to build Vitamin D_2.

Many who had acquired humility in times past to a certain degree fell in the Lucifer Rebellion and had to relearn it. Once humility is lost it is difficult to regain. Because of that fact certain decisions had to be made by Celestial Overcontrol based upon circumstances evident at the time of the Lucifer Rebellion as to how reflectivity circuits would be appropriated in the bodies of those still remaining on Urantia but who were fallen in nature.

Since other circuitry was cut off, including that which would sustain life to a certain degree for those who fell, even though physical death would eventually transpire, a certain alignment needed to occur within all individuals on the planet or else physical death would have taken place at a more rapid rate in all those who had rebelled, including supermortals who had rebelled and become mortal. Their bodies had to be realigned in some way with the circuits of the superuniverses of time and space that they had once acquired, not only on planets that had settled in light and life within their own universe but with those in other universes and planets in other superuniverses. This is one of the ways in which contact is made in all of the grand universe between ascending sons, particularly ascending mortals who have received some capacity of superuniverse reflectivity.

When sixty of the Caligastia One Hundred broke contact with their God, they also broke contact with the reflectivity circuits from other superuniverses. If Celestial Overcontrol had not taken certain very physical emergency measures regarding the staff's life mechanisms, their bodies would have exploded in a matter of weeks because of their sudden unalignment with who they were in their higher selves. This was not only done with the Sixty of the Caligastia One Hundred, but it was also done with the Material Son and Daughter and to some strains of their genetic descendants up to a certain point.

From that point on there was no need to take physical action because there were substantially enough of these genetic ultimatons in the races of Urantia for a normal flowing and function to begin in their bodies on their own. This has become known on Urantia to some degree in what your present science calls the provitamin 7-dehydrocholesterol. These molecules are known to be found just beneath the skin.

What is not understood is that it is there because these human tissue cells are actually connecting links in the circuitry of all superuniverses within the grand universe. When sunlight hits these molecules they are converted into Vitamin D_3 or what is called colloidal cholecalciferol by your scientists. They know that 7-dehydrocholesterol is found in all human tissue cells.

Skin color, the way in which your body breathes oxygen, and the way in which your body forms the layers of skin tissue have to do with the genetic linkage of the ancestry. In regard to Cosmic Reservists, the decisions as to who your human parents will be or of what race are made by Celestial Overcontrol, with the exception that in some cases Cosmic Reservists may also be given certain choices. The less the genetic link of the ovan soul to cosmic ancestry and evolutionary genetic link to the Material Son and Daughter, the less is the ability of the ovan soul to connect himself or herself with mind capacity and cosmic absolutes in the understanding of **ascension science**.

An individual who is a **first-time Urantian** may connect himself or herself because of the virtue characteristics of the

Eternal Father—such as goodness, kindness, gentleness, right purpose and motive, sensitivity, and all of the qualities that make that evolving soul a more perfect personality. He or she may reach the place of higher circle attainment, but if the genetic linkage is absent within the Deo-ultimatonic structure within the 7-dehydrocholesterol molecules in the layers of tissue, there will not be the ability to understand higher cosmic absolutes at a higher capacity. Therefore, these personalities will be, and will remain, at a lower level of reality and will be unable to come into **fifth-dimensional** reality even though they may be walking in fourth-dimensional reality far above other first-time Urantians.

It is known that there are several more D vitamins within the body that control the way in which calcium phosphate is laid down within the bone. When the body lacks Vitamin D, bones stay soft and get pulled out of shape. All sorts of deformities result, such as rickets in children. This softness of the bone structure is called osteomalacia.

The reality of it is that lack of spiritual insight will also cause paralysis of all kinds. Modern science understands very little about paralysis in various forms that take place in the body in relation to what they tag muscular dystrophy, multiple sclerosis, and polio. Medical science has seemingly found a cure for polio, and it seems to have stopped the disease. However, all that actually takes place is that the cells—which cause the polio and were originally created by genetic ancestry plus the influence of the present thinking process of the ascending son or daughter—have been rearranged into another negative **diotribe** cellular reality that will then create another disease with an equal destruction to the mind and body, and death can result.

So the problem has not really been solved. All that has been done is that the problem has been rearranged. This is why, although polio seemingly has been stopped, other more crippling diseases such as cancer and AIDS have increased. Diseases such as paralysis of certain kinds cannot be healed by drugs. They have to be healed within the thought process, and that is the only way they can be healed. Temporary relief, or stoppages of certain diseased cells to multiply, will only cause another problem to take its place, either in the mind, emotions, or in the physical body.

Because spiritual sight in its higher usage of Vitamin D is not the reality on Urantia, human sight or Luciferic sight begins to take place in the body. This begins to form the diseases within the body because the foundation of the body structure is bone, and bone can begin to degenerate because the structure of God is not being formed to the highest capacity. Deformities result because the higher spiritual sight in fusion with the proper usage of the vitamins is truly not taking place. Therefore the Father/Son reflectivity, that should be coming in through the physical sun and then down to the central nervous system of the body, is not functioning because the individuals are not functioning properly.

It may seem that these children, the majority of whom are not ovan souls, are very innocent victims. It is highly probable that souls whose bodies are deformed at birth inherit this from the improper thinking processes of the parents or a more visible problem of the parents due to the digestion of improper foods, drugs, or whatever. Most likely the souls themselves are new souls, and because they are and because Celestial Overcontrol is not in the decision-making process so much as with ovan souls, the children may inherit the diotribe reality of the parents. Cosmic law has been set in motion that through sexual union the birth of a child may take place, and if it does take place the child in many ways is the result of the human parents.

On planets in the higher stages of light and life it is learned that with spiritual insight and with proper spiritual mating such diseases can be completely eradicated in the birth process of these babies, and where higher spiritual teachings are learned, such deformities become unknown. This is why we, who are now bringing Continuing Fifth Epochal Revelation, say that after the final **change point** it is most important that as many high spiritual personalities as possible produce children. Because this has not been the case on Urantia, crippling diseases at birth and deformities caused in the later years in these children have taken place because of the many imbalances in the thinking processes of those on Urantia. It may seem a terrible thing since some of these people seem to be good and loving individuals, yet they are in many ways still trapped in the Caligastia system in their own thinking processes, and most are incapable of seeing these entrapments in themselves.

You may ask why some professional baseball pitcher in the prime of his life obtains a tumor in his throwing arm that will eventually cause his whole arm and shoulder to be removed. No matter how seemingly beautiful and nice he is, having dedicated most of his waking day to a career of throwing a ball at a glove (if that is the main purpose of that soul's existence), he has caused his own problem. That is the only answer that can be given with these things.

You see, what may seem to be a tragedy is in reality a gift. The soul has broken a major cosmic law; he has wasted his own existence. Yes, he may become popular and have the adulation of hundreds of thousands, even millions, and command millions of dollars in salary, yet the soul's purpose is lost in this stupidity of a career. What should be a pastime or a hobby becomes a career for half of his life, and that is cosmic insanity. Then, when the arm and shoulder are cut off, that soul can perhaps find himself and his God. If the soul at that point realizes that what he was in the past was stupid, then he can become useful to God even without a shoulder. If he cannot find himself and his Eternal Father at that point, then he will continue in his folly and die a physical death.

Vitamin C, known also as ascorbic acid, is present in the body in the greatest quantity [compared by weight with other vitamins], but little is known about Vitamin C except that lack of it causes small blood vessels to get weak and break easily, so that the person bruises easily and the gums will bleed and wounds will heal very slowly. This is called scurvy. Vitamin C is found in fresh fruits and vegetables; probably the most popular source is orange juice. Vitamin C is necessary to keep the body's small blood vessels strong and well formed.

Vitamin C is a vitamin that is a fusion between the Father/Son and the Mother, and a fusion of Christ Michael and the Universe Mother Spirit representing itself in fruit of the orange type because it is a vitamin of energy. It is a vitamin to help you in your existence on this planet to do that which you are prepurposed to do or what you are called to do because of your ascension growth. It is the vitamin of the Conjoint Actor to help you to actualize your potential.

The lack of it causes what is known as scurvy, basically because you have not found yourself, and if you are in wrong relationships or wrong careers outside of the destiny purposes of God, no matter how many milligrams of Vitamin C you take, it will not heal the problem. The only way to heal the problem is to find yourself within the perfection of God. If you are unbalanced in the Father circuits and you are ill, Vitamin C may help you to some degree to come to a temporary healing, but you will continue to get sick, and the same problem will arise just as soon as you begin to regain health and fall back into your lower self.

Proper alignment with the Father/Mother circuits within you will actually create more Vitamin C within you based upon the inheritance of it, not only from sunlight at that point but from moonlight. The moonlight is the essence of the Infinite Spirit circulating itself through the Universe Mother Spirit, through a secondary light. For those in the higher purposes of God, moonlight actually works in the same manner that sunlight turns 7-dehydrocholesterol into Vitamin D_3. Moonlight, to those who can remain on the third to the first circle at varying degrees, will produce Vitamin C. This is not known to modern science, but to those who read this transmission it is now known.

Common colds can be somewhat relieved by high dosages of Vitamin C because Vitamin C, in these instances, creates a sustaining relationship within the body of ascension process to the Mother circuits and creates a more sensitive and creative fusion. Vitamin C creates a **Mother-circuited** flow within the body. Oranges are a fusion of the Creator Son and Universe Mother Spirit, which is spiritual in origin.

Sunlight appropriates an orange color because it is a literal representation of the solar system sun around which your planet rotates. All you need to do is to put an orange in water and put it in sunlight, and you can get just as much nutrient out of drinking the water as you would in digesting the physical orange. However, since the orange has already been created, you might as well bless it by eating it rather than letting it rot, for it was created for the purpose of attaching you to the Mother circuit.

You can also receive Vitamin C from moonlight if you have ascended to that place of circle of attainment. You will find that your creativity will increase. This is one reason why many artists find themselves more creative under the moonlight. However, you might want to increase what the moonlight is giving you by eating oranges and other sources of Vitamin C circuitry food.

Vitamin C seems to heal the common cold, not because of any physical transaction that takes place in the body, but because a higher balance begins to take place in the thinking processes of the individual if and when he or she sits down to take on higher things. These individuals connect with the Universe Mother circuit and the Mother/Son circuit. They become more relaxed; they become more destiny-purposed, and this creates hope, and hope heals.

Hope heals because it is a Paradise-origin circuitry connection to the First Source and Center and all that is and all that you are. That is why Vitamin C seems to heal physical illnesses like the common cold. The reality is, if you could sit down in the moonlight and connect yourself to your destiny purpose (particularly now) to hear the Universe Mother circuit speak to you, it can have the same effect of healing as high doses of Vitamin C in other forms.

The seven **cosmic families** presently on the planet and the leadership therein who have within them the 7-

dehydrocholesterol reality will discover that as they come into the understanding of Continuing Fifth Epochal Revelation they will find within their cosmic family (especially after the final change point) very noticeable physical similarities such as skin tissues of the same origin color, famotor movement, size, height, and weight of their physical body as they begin to maintain proper diet, and other recognizable features of the various cosmic families, just as there are resemblances among the carotene families of food.

There will eventually be no need for celestial or human leadership to apply a pressure of authority at the **First Planetary Sacred Home**, for all will have to learn planetary procedure. Leadership will not have to worry about these cosmic families and their disobedience to the will of Machiventa Melchizedek or Christ Michael.

The reason for this is that in the fourth dimension those who do not learn proper procedure will not inherit the enzymes and vitamins necessary from Father sun and Mother moon to sustain them, and if they do not align themselves with the purposes of Machiventa Melchizedek, they simply will deteriorate, become deformed, and eventually die. This will happen at a more rapid rate, and is happening since the coming of Machiventa Melchizedek to the planet in December 1989.

So they can go ahead and pout, make accusations and judgments against those humans in authority and us, and say that none of this is true or real, but they simply will not be functioning properly in body because of the malfunctioning thinking that is already preventing them from actualizing the very vitamins within them that are necessary for their own growth and healing, not to mention the actualization of their morontia body.

Again we state the point made in a previous transmission, that the Continuing Fifth Epochal Revelation is not just a study book like *The URANTIA Book* is. It is a living and breathing revelation based upon moment-to-moment decision-making between you and your God. It is given in this moment-to-moment application so that you can align yourself with the purposes of God.

Vitamin K is necessary for the proper clotting of blood and is formed by bacteria in the intestines. You will find in the future on Urantia that more and more injuries causing bruises and other problems will result in the death of many individuals because Vitamin K will simply not be functioning properly in the body.

Oh yes, there is enough bacteria in the intestines of many of the souls on Urantia, particularly the ovan souls, but a fusion of the oxygen (Mother) and the hydrogen (Son) outside of the body helps in the clotting, and the fusion of the Vitamin K Father circuitry with the oxygen and hydrogen in the air (which is a fusion of the Son and Spirit) will simply not be taking place in the tissues of these veins to create the clotting and healing process in the body. So you will see more diseases occurring in the skin tissues themselves, not just by physical accidents but also by thinking processes that will manifest in the tissues.

Even those who are in alignment with the purposes of God will begin to manifest skin problems at a more rapid rate, perhaps at times even unbearable. This is because for some reason they are not seeing their own thinking processes at the higher levels that they need to see them, and the result of that is manifest in the skin. It will cause much unpleasantness in you until you begin to see what you need to see. Some who have greater problems in these areas will actually cause cancers of the skin to form that will eventually take them from this planet.

Areas that you need to work on so that these problems do not arise are humility and other-oriented motives. All selfishness must be removed from your reality. You must put the good of others before the good of yourself. Your thoughts must be pure, and you must see yourself as a servant to others. You must not put yourself on a pedestal. If anything, you should see yourself on a stool with a dunce cap on. Better to see yourself that way than on the pedestal of your own pride.

You must understand that in this higher authority given to you by God comes higher responsibility, and with higher responsibility and authority you are to wash the feet of others as in the example of Jesus with the apostles. Placing yourself in this position will heal and create the Vitamin K within you necessary to heal all skin tissue and all diseases of the outer physical body. In the meantime, dosages of Vitamin K can eliminate temporary pain.

If you wonder why this information is coming to you now, it is because now is the only time you are deserving of it, no matter who you are on the planet. That is what Continuing Fifth Epochal Revelation is. Again I state, Continuing Fifth Epochal Revelation is the fusion between the spiritual and the physical, ascension science. It is a moment-to-moment revelation to be given to individuals at various ascension levels at various circle attainments in various mandated or nonmandated positions in all the seven cosmic families on Urantia first, and then at one point to all the people of the planet to bring about the first stages of light and life. It is a living and breathing revelation. It is not just a study book as the first one-tenth of the Fifth Epochal Revelation is. It is a revelation of cosmic medical fact, which can be experienced based upon your ability to be in the present moment-to-moment will of your Creator Son, Christ Michael.

If you can get into that perfect will in your moment-to-moment thinking on Urantia, and I repeat, moment-to-moment thinking, then no disease can harm you, and all the vitamins given from the Father, Son, and Infinite Spirit in Their manifestation to your cellular reality in the atmosphere of Urantia will be at full potential within your own body and bring you to the light body and morontia reality that you so long desire and so badly need.

It is the Eldership of the First Planetary Sacred Home and those mandated personalities who first and foremost must understand living and breathing Continuing Fifth Epochal Revelation and apply it to their own reality, and to whatever ability they can do this will be the state of their own health and the authority of their own mandate. Each of you is interdependent upon each other just as you are dependent upon the energy sources of your Universe Creator Father and Universal Father. It is a dependency that has always been upon alignment with the First Source and Center. At whatever level evolutionary beings can attach themselves to the reflectivity circuits of perfection, they too can become perfect. Was it not Christ Michael, who, when He was on Urantia, said: "Be you therefore perfect, even as your Father in heaven is perfect."? [*The URANTIA Book*, p. 1584]

The first-century apostles and followers were far from perfect. Because they were far from perfect they were susceptible to diseases, but diseases did not have to take them from the planet. Paul suffered from certain diseases, and so did others; it was Paul who said that he had a thorn in his side. Peter himself suffered from the results of his own stupidity and should have been able to see in the life of Paul a little of his own misconstrued thinking in regard to the relationship between men and women. If he had not been martyred he would have died anyway, as would all of the apostles.

The fact that they did die as martyrs before natural death began to take place in them is not a plus for their ascension status. If they would have caught hold of the higher truths that Jesus tried to teach them and had combined as a stronger team in the first century within the union of souls that *The URANTIA Book* talks about, none of them would have been martyred.

The same separation in thinking has been the destruction within the so-called Christian church on the planet for the last 2,000 years. Those who came to understand that Jesus Christ was the Son of God in some manner still have died of various diseases based upon those individuals' inability to incorporate the very essence of light in foods—sunlight and moonlight—the God-given sustainers, because they have been unable to find themselves as individuals in the will of God as ascending sons and daughters.

As long as you are in somewhat of a material body there will be a need for food substances, and in the fusion of these food substances with proper thinking you can move to the next body, to the next mansion world, as your moment-to-moment reality becomes just that, moment-to-moment perfection. You will come into a higher spiritual body, but when your thinking is that which is imperfect you inherit everything that your thinking brings into it, or you simply do not procreate that which you could inherit if your thinking was more perfect.

Living in an imperfect world, even perfection cannot sustain itself. That is why protected areas are being created now. That is why there was a First Garden, for perfection begins to manifest itself in individuals in the perfect will of God to any degree higher than others. The others of lesser degree can actually cause those of higher degree certain imperfections and their inability to remain in their highest perfection.

Food grown outside of the protected areas simply does not contain the **Deo-atomic reality** within it that God has purposed for it. Therefore, an orange is not truly now a reflection of the sun of the solar system Monmatia in which you live. In order for the reflectivity of an orange to be as it should be, it has to be grown in a protected and sacred area in the future. Therefore the nutrients that you receive from food from other areas are partial. Because of this, celestial personalities have to be in these certain sacred areas to interject the ever-real and ever-present provitamins of their own. It is in this sustaining reality that you are kept in some form of physical health.

If it were not for this kind of cellular transference, even the Eldership of Divine Administration would be in less physical shape than they are. So, even though it may seem at times that you are not as healthy as you would like to be, you would be less healthy if you were not in or had not made it to the protected area at the First Planetary Sacred Home.

This will become very evident to those who should be at the First Planetary Sacred Home and are not here. Those who have been given a summons to be here and did not make it when the time came for them to be here will see for themselves that their health is rapidly deteriorating. Why? Read this transmission again thoroughly. Because of your unwillingness to obey divine mandates and divine authority, the vitamins are no longer functioning within your body the way they should.

Is this the judgment of God against you? Yes indeed, it is. It is the judgment that was created before you were known by any of your present comrades to whom you are so stupidly loyal. It is the judgment of God that was set in motion long before you became so happy with this present position you are in, or present beach that you lie on in California or Hawaii, or wherever you may find yourself so comfortable. They were laws that were set in motion long before you were given positions of human respect based upon your social badge of acceptance that has been given to you because you have accepted the interpretations of whatever religious philosophy that gives you some prestige, including the Urantia movement.

If your alignment or your prestige is not found within the perfect will of God, no matter if you know Christ Michael and believe Him within the context of the first one-tenth of the Fifth Epochal Revelation and serve Him by bringing *The URANTIA Book* to others, that is something that was good up until December 1989. Now there is another debt that you must pay. It is a higher step, and in order for you to continue to grow and to come to the higher circles that you read about in the first one-tenth of the Fifth Epochal Revelation, you must begin to take another step, and this is the step of fusing the Thought Adjuster with the Spirit of Truth and the Holy Spirit, which perhaps you have never activated or even received.

It is one thing to know about these things; it is quite another thing to make your molecular reality activate the vitamins within you. If they do not sustain your molecular reality, then you have fallen in some manner just like Lucifer fell, for he knew everything there was to know at his level about the master universe—which is much more than you do—and he still fell.

What makes you think that you are so different? Because you serve God in your own small way? We say this, that Christ Michael wants you to serve Him and your Universal Father in a bigger way, in a more actualized way, in a way of authority, in a way that you yourself run away from in your very self-assertion that you read about but say no, this is not you. You wish to be under no one's authority but your own. You wish to do as you please. You fail to recognize godly authority because you are an authority unto yourself. You do not trust because you cannot be trusted.

What does all this have to do with vitamins and sight? It has everything to do with it because you have little spiritual sight. The very foods that you eat on Urantia will soon, and even now, justify what I am saying. If you are reading this transmission, at one point it is hoped that in the deterioration of your physical body you will come to understand the higher spiritual insight I am trying to give you at this time.

July 13, 1992

Paladin, Chief of Finaliters
in cooperation with Lanaforge, the System Sovereign, and the Council of Twenty-four Elders for a clearer understanding of what it means for Cosmic and Urantian Reservists to be called forth by summons to the sacred areas for the implementation of Divine Administration on Urantia in and through human complements

As transmitted through
the Pre-Level-One Audio Fusion Material Complement,
Gabriel of Urantia/TaliasVan of Tora

PAPER 248

The Glands Of The Body In Relationship To Physical And Spiritual Health And The Appropriation Of The Morontia Body With The Coordination Of Deo-Atomic Hormones More Resonant With Paradise-Origin Energies And The Seven Superuniverse Families Of Reflectivity

HORMONES are compounds that supervise the overall workings of the various enzymes. They are formed in special glands, the most important of which is the pituitary gland. It should be noted that all hormones from the pituitary and above in the brain are protein. Chemists do not know how all of this works, but they speculate. **Continuing Fifth Epochal Revelation** reveals the process in relation to the thinking in the brain and central nervous system, and in particular to the executive of the glands, the pituitary gland, which is the command center.

There are seven primary glands within the body. They are the pituitary gland, the pineal gland, the thymus gland, the thyroid, the adrenals, the pancreas, and the gonads. There are also secondary glands that are the parathyroids and a combination of the hair and skin glands, which we will call the **interuniversal corporate membrane gland**. This interuniversal corporate membrane gland has to do with the coordination of sense perceptions such as touching and feeling in relationship to the Paradise Trinity personalities, beginning on an evolutionary world and inward to Paradise relative to bodies prior to pure spirit form.

The chief executive or the pituitary gland is connected to the Bright and Morning Star of the universe administration. It is the gland of body mandates and the gland of corporate decision-making; it is the command center of the body. It is attached to the brain by a thin stalk and is located in the center of the head in a well-protected area. When you come to know the physical cosmology of the universe in which you are living, and as you ascend to Salvington, you will see that in many ways Salvington is the head center of the body of the universe.

The pituitary gland also produces the somatotropic hormone. The somatotropic hormone from the pituitary gland or chief executive causes physical growth such as height, and hair on the cheeks, chest, and upper lip. This functions with the spiritual body when a person reaches the third to the first circle, and at an increased rate to form the next body.

The mandated Bright and Morning Star personality functions also as the pituitary gland for the other glands, or foremen or elders, to further spiritual growth, as well as for other members of the body or **cosmic family**. The Bright and Morning Star human executive of the **First Cosmic Family** also has the same pituitary gland function with the other six cosmic families or communities in the other sector areas of the planet. We will speak more about that toward the end of this transmission.

The thyroid, parathyroids, and adrenal glands are also ductless glands. Ductless glands produce fluids that enter the blood stream direct; they are also called endocrine glands. The pituitary gland sends adrenocorticotrophic hormones (ACTH) to the adrenal cortices, telling them to release hormones. ACTH has come to be known as the wonder drug in treating arthritis and other crippling diseases and is produced by transfusion into the blood stream itself, not through a duct.

The duct from the pancreas into the intestine delivers pancreatic juices to digest foods, but the pancreas also produces insulin, a fluid that enters the blood stream direct, and this is done by endocrine cells within the pancreas called the Islets of Langerhans.

The sex glands, also called the gonads, produce androgens and estrogens.

The interuniversal corporate membrane gland, or the hair and skin glands, which are membrane tissues, in reality function individually within corporate physical reflectivity cellular patterns of superuniverse relationships to the Seven Master Spirits coordinating with evolutionary mortals' growth on the worlds of time and space.

Each of these glands, which acts as a circuit, is directed specifically to the heart center, which is not particularly called a gland by modern science but in reality is a circuit organ related to the glands and is a center of interuniversal function. These circuits have much to do with the healing of the body and the outworking of the higher body formulating in connection with the first circler moving into the first morontia body and above.

This coordination between the corporate ultimatonic membrane cells in relation to the heart center and pituitary gland forms another duct upwards to the eighth and ninth glands, which are also the eighth and ninth circuits. These circuits will be incorporated into the morontia body and placed in the upper area above the heart center. The level of soul ascension will dictate the position of these circuits or glands.

It is speculated that for those who have been able to remain on the first circle consistently for more than one to three years Urantia time, these glands will be located in and near the head center. For others these glands will be located lower, somewhere between the present heart and throat circuits. Because with **ovan souls** these glands have more to do with **memory circuits**, the complications that we can get into, in relation to the placing of these glands, is most awesome.

For now, we give certain information to give you an opening in the understanding of morontia circuitry and physical body placement of glands that will still be operating. Although the lower glands will either be removed or changed completely, depending upon many circumstances, the higher glands or circuitry will actually be reformed and will be functioning more in relation to destiny purpose and spiritual administration.

Much depends upon the soul's capability to function in mindal capacities. Where mind functions in the highest level, these glands, which are actually circuits, become less physical with the spiritual ascension of the evolving soul and more attuned to cosmic procedure and cosmic absolutes. If that is not the case, then the glands remain more physical and the weight of those glands increases the body structure and keeps the soul in a lower body form. Whereas some personalities may function in a first-stage morontia body for a short period of time, others may have to function in it for the equivalent of a Urantian lifetime or more.

The same principle exists on the morontia worlds of Satania. All bodies that are more spiritual are a gift for that personality who has attained spiritual virtue and personality characteristics pertinent to the good of others and the administration of others. In a sense, you are a gift to others in all that you are, and the higher gift you are, the more weightless you become. If you want to be pure spirit, be selfless. However, it is much easier said than done.

The body's chemical workings are referred to as its metabolism. Your science has come up with a way to measure basal metabolic rate (BMR) based upon the body's ability to take in calories and dispose of them. Whether you are more or less active determines how many calories you need to perform certain functions. The reality is that the more spiritual you become, the less intake of food you actually need.

However, on present-day Urantia food has become addictive, and a certain transition period is needed even for the highest spiritual personalities to dictate to the body that food is not necessary and particularly certain foods to which the body has become accustomed. Individuals with higher spiritual minds are less active physically; this is because those with higher spiritual minds are used in administration, either in planetary or interplanetary overcontrol. In the lower evolutionary worlds inactivity creates an obese body when calorie intake is more than what the energy of the body uses up.

The thyroid is the only part of the body that contains iodine. Thyroglobulin, the protein vehicle for thyroid hormone, contains iodothyronines, which are modifications of amino acids that contain the element iodine. A lack of iodine causes cretinism, and the child does not grow. Feeble-mindedness and goiter (a swelling of the neck) can also be the results. A good source of iodine is kelp, and it is also found in seafood and iodized salt. In the higher evolutionary worlds where flesh is not eaten, iodine is produced by positive thinking in relation to the good of others.

It should be the same on Urantia; however, you counteract that which is positive with that which is negative by much of your thought processes, and by what you digest that is unsuitable for your present bodies and in particular, the morontia body that some of you are trying to form. The iodothyronines are actually a cooperative creation of the Creator Son and Universe Mother Spirit to increase the spiritual capacity of the evolving evolutionary mortals.

Where an imbalance occurs on any level, the pancreas, which is also a fusion of the Creator Son and the Universe Mother Spirit, malfunctions. When an imbalance occurs between the Mother circuits and the Father circuits in a male, his imbalance can produce a masculine form of negativity, which is the male's inability to balance feminine energy, and then the body stops producing insulin. This has become known on your world as diabetes.

In females, who have long been oppressed and suppressed by male ancestry within their genetic links, and if this continues in their present lifetime, insulin will not be produced and diabetes will be detected, which can lead to death or other diseases of the body. If that same female could have changed her thinking process and married appropriately outside of the social norms she has fallen into in past lifetimes, the chance of her having diabetes would be lessened or completely overcome.

It has come to be known that diabetes is a hereditary disease. Basically this is because the descendants carry on with the social patterns resulting from these thinking processes and continue to marry and intermarry among those with whom they have become accustomed to mating. This is particularly true among Latin cultures.

It is known that insulin is a lifesaver, and when imbalances occur, as in diabetes, the sugars are only partially burned and chemicals are produced that are somewhat poisonous to the body and can eventually kill. What may seem to be a physical problem, due to eating the wrong foods and the intake of sugar, can also be due to wrong thinking and wrong social behavior patterns.

If a **first-time Urantian** or ovan soul female, who has some symptoms of diabetes from heredity or the family diet, at some point in her evolution on this planet, develops some sort of independence outside of the parental family, she will be able to manufacture more insulin. The chemicals within her body will then not be so poisonous as they are within her own family or for others who have suffered more from diabetes and other glandular problems related to thinking processes that science has labeled hypoglycemia, which is the opposite of high blood sugar. The inability of individuals, male or female, to function in the balance of the Father and Mother circuits will cause certain aspects of either high blood sugar or low blood sugar to develop.

There is another disease related to high or low blood sugar, which is related to imbalance in Father/Son circuits within ascending sons. The more balanced the personality as to the spiritual nature of the Creator Son and Universe Mother Spirit, the better the body can fight off all diseases and even digest foods that are not as high in protein reality as they should be.

The symptoms of diabetes, such as loss of weight and excessive urination, can be completely eliminated if that individual is put into an environment where the higher spiritual teachings are taught and received within the mind; then weight gain, and of course more energy, would be produced within the body. The body's ability to produce energy depends upon the personality's willingness to be in the perfect will of God. The thyroid gland governs the rate at which the body produces energy.

If ascending souls do not come into the higher circuitry, they will remain in the lower circuits, and if they remain in the lower circuits they are more connected to the diseases of that planet. If they remain in the lower circuits of the root, the navel, and the solar plexus, and in the lower reality of the sex glands, the pancreas, and the adrenals, they do not reach the fusion of the heart circuits with the higher circuits and the will of God, the mind of God, and the cosmic reality of the pituitary gland connected to the eighth and ninth circuits and above. If they do not connect with the higher spiritual mind, the pituitary gland malfunctions in all areas.

If they have a malfunction in the chief executive within their body, it is very unlikely that they will live a productive life in many areas. They may raise children, and their children may be productive, but their children also have to come away from parental influence. In a sense, the children must divorce themselves from the parents. If they do not, the children will remain in the lower circuitry. Even if they are ovan souls, they will still be products of the lower circuits and will not be able to fuse with the higher circuitry and will not be able to reach the higher circles of spiritual attainment.

Because of the state of Urantia, these teachings are at a kindergarten level, basically because we are dealing here with a diseased body and a malfunctioning one. Even the ovan souls on this planet who have suffered from the Lucifer Rebellion, even the highest spiritual ones, have to understand the correlation between the spiritual and the physical, the physical glands and spiritual circuitry, at a higher level themselves, before they can even begin to teach it to others. As you read these transmissions with one another, a certain reality will be introduced to you, a beginning reality of the complementary reflectivity between the Creator Son and Universe Mother Spirit and their reflectivity to the Paradise Eternal Father, Son, and Infinite Spirit.

In the understanding of gravity and mind energy streaming from Paradise and the Paradise personalities, one must comprehend that the thoughts of the mind, in relation to what pleases it, may or may not be God-centered or God-ordered. If you begin to look at your mind as related to the Source and Center of Paradise and learn to deal with your thoughts as either good or bad or in between, you can then begin to regulate your thinking to the highest way rather than the permissive way or the harmful way.

Learning to fuse your thoughts in relation to the highest way will actually change the physical aspects of your body. Those who can do so at the most perfect of levels can actually change height, weight, genital organs, breasts, and other areas of the physical body at a more rapid rate, even in old age. The deterioration of the physical body is a continual deterioration due to wrong thinking. Increased ability to have thoughts of higher and purer motive will bring one's body into alignment with Paradise circuitry.

True clairvoyance, cosmic clairvoyance, is the ability of any one personality at any one point in time and space to tap into Paradise administration, to Paradise mandates, to Paradise art, to Paradise engineering, to Paradise mechanical realities, to Paradise physics and chemistry, to Paradise electrosynthesis, and to Paradise cosmic anthropologic realities at a level in which what you tap into will in some way be beneficial to someone else. Once you see yourself as a servant and a gift to others and use your ability for the good of all, then every part of what you are, including your glandular structure, will resonate with perfection.

The reality with most humans at your level is that you see yourselves as too important. It is one thing to be a blessing to all on your planet; it is another thing to think yourself to be such. There is a thin line between arrogance and self-confidence, between goodness and philanthropy as opposed to conceit and opulence. The disease of the ancestors in those who think too much of themselves manifests in some on this planet as goiter, causing the throat to puff up. The word of God should bring authority and humility. To some it may bring the imbalance of that, and if you get a swollen head, then you may get a swollen lip.

Some of you will manifest other problems, either as crippling diseases such as arthritis or possibly skin cancers. These problems of thinking are very difficult to see, and most likely you will be the last to see them, which is why you still have them. To whatever degree you have wrong thinking will be the disease of your body and the rate the disease will take over. If divine protection is not given you, it will completely consume you and bring you to your deathbed.

An example of this was Nebuchadnezzar who thought himself a god. He looked upon his vast kingdom and thought himself special and thought that God put him into such a wonderful position. He thought himself better than everyone under him, and so God had to bring him to his senses. First his hand and arm became leprous because he thought himself to be the arm of God. Then because he thought his mind greater than all, he became feeble-minded, for the life-giving cells that were intended to go to the brain were blocked; he did not receive the hydrogen and oxygen necessary.

It is written and spoken that you are what you think, and this is indeed the truth, not only on the lower worlds of time and space but increasingly so as you ascend toward the higher levels of Paradise. Because you on this planet have been so accustomed to satisfying your own inappropriate desires and because you are so used to being in control of yourself and others in a negative manner, you have developed an inability to see not only your own dangerous ways but the dangerous ways of others, and so all of you have become clones to one another.

When true perfection comes to your planet you do not recognize it, and you crucify it. Very few of you understand it, not even those apostles who were placed in close proximity to perfection. As stated, the apostles and the family of Jesus have had hundreds of years in various repersonalizations to acquire the higher virtues of the very Creator Son who walked among them. And still they are not as perfect as He commanded them to be, but we are optimistic they not only will be but that they will be the influence and the prime source and center and the pituitary gland for the rest of the cosmic families on the planet and that they will be as the protein hormones for the other cosmic families to function within the body of God. They will be the hormones that will bring about the sex glands' change into the next body, which is the morontia body, which will be capable of producing, through the seed of the male fused with the egg of the female, the higher genetic reality and higher ovan souls of superuniversal reality from all the seven superuniverses who wish to experience what it is like to be human.

If you knew the distances and travel time in Urantian years necessary to go even from your planet to your system headquarters, from your planet to universe headquarters, from your planet to superuniverse headquarters, and indeed from your planet to another superuniverse, you would understand that in the physical and the material it would take a lifetime traveling at the speed of light to reach even the closest of these places. One of the means of visitation for those of higher mindal and spiritual evolution is the gift of repersonalization, rematerialization, and reconstruction when understood in alignment with the purposes of each Creator Son of each universe.

Memory circuits are blocked now, but some of you are just beginning to realize who you are because you have been brought out of error, sin, and at times even iniquity. As your thoughts become pure and your motives come into alignment with the motives of God, then you can function, even in the physical, as a time-and-space traveler, for it is in the will of God that you can experience what you can experience for the good of the grand universe, and the limitations you have are the limitations you create by the inability to be loving and unselfish.

July 16, 1992

Paladin, Chief of Finaliters
in cooperation with the Ancients of Days, the Creator Son Christ Michael of Nebadon, and other Creator Sons, particularly from the universes of Avalon, Wolvering, and Fanoving, for the higher understanding of the ascension process within the grand universe and for the calling forth of the Cosmic Reserve Corps for the implementation of the administration of the present Planetary Prince, Machiventa Melchizedek, in which they are here to function

As transmitted through
the Pre-Level-One Audio Fusion Material Complement,
Gabriel of Urantia/TaliasVan of Tora

PAPER 249

Hormones In Relationship To The Paradise Circuits Of The Universal Father, The Eternal Son, And The Infinite Spirit; The Design Factors In Body Programming Of The Cellular Structure And Other Third-Dimensional And Lower Body Functions

YOU should be beginning to understand from the series of transmissions, starting with the first of those dealing with the chemicals of life in relation to the Paradise circuits, that all that you are and all that you ever will be is your joining to Paradise reflectivity, at whatever level or stage of ascension or descension reality you are receiving this reflectivity. Being born into perfection, you have inherited, either by free will or by creative prerogative, a part of your Eternal Paradise Father, Son, and Mother. Fusing with the Father/Son, and then with the Infinite Spirit Mother, you have what we will call male circuitry and female circuitry, all of which originates in Paradise, and in the lower evolutionary worlds of time and space it takes form in tiny subcells that resonate with some aspect of the male or female reality.

Depending upon many factors and where these subcells find themselves functioning quite independently in various life forms, they create various physical forms based upon many variables, all having to do with relationships from the spiritual to the physical. Plant life, insect life, and animal life all contain the reality of the Eternal Three in their cells to some degree. At the planetary level we see the male and female circuitry expressed in terms of physics as male and female chromosomes. So in all life forms there seems to be a consistent sexual duality beginning in the plant life, more in the insect life, and most definitely in the higher life forms of human mortals.

The evolutionary process on all planets of time and space is not void of thinking. When thinking enters, and if it begins to take shape in higher thought forms, particularly in relation to a more advanced life form, then mortal life is created that seeks perfection. The perfection is the perfection of Paradise, and when you have partial perfection within you, you are only partially connected to the perfect Paradise design. Even if you are in a higher form and have received a Thought Adjuster but not the Spirit of Truth or the coordinate Holy Spirit, you are still partially disconnected from the original design.

On some planets the sex of an individual mortal is not determined until the person is well into life, twenty to thirty years old in Urantia years, but the life span on these planets is much longer and the development of the physical body is much slower. In that case, upon reception of all three coordinates, and assuming that you are not on a fallen world and you are a creature who is meant to procreate and not an androgynous life form, then you are under mandatory law that you must begin to inherit certain specific hormones that will reshape your body functions and shape your thinking processes into an ascending son or an ascending daughter. At whatever level formation of the lower body begins, an equal and complementary formation must begin in the thought life.

On Urantia it is a matter of balancing the Father and Mother circuits, but it also depends upon whether or not you were androgynous at one time. For those **ovan souls** on this planet who may have had an androgynous experience, it can contribute to the misalignment of circuitry relative to the relationship of the Creator Son with the Creative Spirit of Nebadon. Each Creator Son is a unique divine combination of the Universal Father and Eternal Son, and this creates a unique variation in responses to the Creative Mother Spirit in each universe.

Let us begin with adrenaline (epinephrine). There are two adrenal glands, one over each kidney. The outer portion of each gland, the adrenal cortex (which is rich in Vitamin C), produces corticoid. The inner portion is called the medulla, and this produces adrenaline, one of the most powerful chemicals known. The entire blood stream contains only about 2 ten-billionths of an ounce. One-half ounce would supply all of the people of the world.

When adrenaline goes up in an emergency, it will go up to 3 ten-billionths of an ounce. It commands and alerts the nerves, which in turn activate involuntary muscles, particularly of the heart. The heart pumps faster to send out the blood with increased sugar and oxygen, and the blood vessels relax so that more blood can get through. All of this is an unconscious movement of involuntary muscles. However, when this happens the blood vessels leading to the intestines and the kidneys contract and less blood gets through so that the organs must cut down on their work. Strong emotions increase adrenaline in such a way and in such amounts that it both agonizes and antagonizes the hormones of digestion, thereby upsetting the stomach and the whole digestive process.

It should be understood and realized by now that the **heart circuit** is a fusion of the Father/Son. It is also the command center, much like the pituitary gland. However, its commands are based upon other aspects pertaining more to destiny purpose than to the moment. Although they correlate with one another, it is the heart gland that is the higher circuitry connection with universe administration. The pituitary gland, which is called the chief executive of the body, is a gland of overcontrol. The heart circuit is a gland of governmental process that functions more specifically and coordinately with Overcontrol. Adrenaline is a by-product of the Father circuit.

All of the personalities of the circuits coordinating with the Chief Executive's (the Bright and Morning Star's) Administration bring the purest information of the directives of God in and through the glands to the rest of the body to help that body mature physically, and then function mentally in relationship to the destiny purposes that you have on a particular sphere, be it an evolutionary planet, mansion world, or whatever.

The correlation between the higher circuitry of the heart circuit and administration is one that will exist throughout the ascension process of time and space. Other glands may be removed and higher ones added, but in whatever body you ascend to Paradise, the heart circuit, the pituitary gland, and the higher circuits will continue to ascend. That is why on your planet, when the heart stops beating so does life.

From circuit to circuit you receive the commands of God. The more you hear from the Father, the stronger the heartbeat at a slower rate. The less you hear from the Father, the weaker the heartbeat becomes at a faster pace. The more you hear from the Mother, the more rapid and pulsating is the heartbeat within the vibratory pulsation of the balance of the two. When a balance of the Father/Mother circuits is resonating within you, the more consistent the heartbeat. A message from the Son circuits will resonate within the beat in the middle of the vibration pattern. It will synchronize with the slower Father message and the more rapid Mother message, all to complement a thought of a responsive action.

So, when attuned practitioners listen to the heartbeat, they should be able to determine whether this person is more **Father-, Son-, or Mother-circuited**. If it is an ascending daughter, it is always a more rapid beat to begin with. If it is an ascending son, it is always slower at the beginning. Fluctuations of various patterns will happen with individuals at various points in their lives, but when stabilized on the third psychic circle, the heartbeat begins to be stabilized and more will be determined of the Trinity circuitry in relationship to that soul's ascension.

Higher patterns of heartbeat on evolutionary Urantia are nonexistent, as they are only beginning to become more frequently coordinate in the Divine New Order community with certain individuals who have now reached the first circle and are remaining on it. This creates a body functioning more in relation to the instructions from the Thought Adjuster, the Spirit of Truth, and the Holy Spirit, and a complementary gland begins to be produced within the eighth and ninth circuit that is temporarily connected to the gonads.

Once the eighth and ninth circuits become primary, the lower circuits will function only for physical needs and are no longer necessary for spiritual perfection. Therefore it should be understood that one does not have to sense or feel the will of God; one receives it in the mind. Personalities who are attached to those lower circuits err in judgment, particularly in relationship to trying to discern Overcontrol procedure or divine hearing at any level. Personalities more balanced within the male and female circuits are the best receivers of Overcontrol prerogatives and divine mandates.

When strong emotions control the personality, indigestion of physical food and indigestion of the circumstances of life block reception of divine help or divine hearing. It blocks the digestion of physical food because the Mother circuitry, which is the feeder of spiritual food, resonates in and through the esophagus, which is the giver of physical food to the organs like the stomach and intestines. It is Mother/Son.

What is actually blocked is the circuitry from the pituitary to the heart. Not all information received from the lower circuits of the lower self is from the Mother or Earth Mother. The Mother also transmits from the mind in and through the pituitary gland, the same as the Father circuit.

When proper procedure with mind and will coordinate with God, it is the heart circuit that coordinates the complying will with the other universal personalities in and through the 1,000 circuit connections to the other worlds of the system of Satania, and, depending upon whether or not certain planets are inhabited, the circuits will be open and flowing. It is a functioning system for all planets settled in light and life. If all circuits are functioning, there is a higher response and a higher power of interplanetary communication and interplanetary aid. Particularly on worlds in rebellion this has to do with changing the patterns of the unwillingness of others to follow divine mandates or cosmic law and absolutes.

To be a **change agent** you must be functioning with this understanding and knowledge, but you first must understand what it is to be out of the will of God. In order to understand how to be as highly functional as you can be on a fallen world with hundreds and thousands, perhaps millions, of those who would rather do their own will than God's will, you must have the power to help them decide to do God's will without the use of force or violence. God the Father does not coerce by force but by persuasion of higher principles on this planet and all of the planets in the first stages of light and life and above in the normal worlds of time and space.

Cosmic stabilization is an understood reality void of abstractions, and even though the abstract may first be presented to the minds of students, they will come to understand that within communicative civilization abstract reality will become absolute reality, and it is only abstract if you are on the lower circles. When you become stabilized on the first circle, you will understand this transmission better and on a higher level.

As you study this transmission and begin to stabilize, abstract reality will be lessened, for **Continuing Fifth Epochal Revelation** is a continual fusion of the spirit working in and with you in the moment. One must remember that a seraphim of enlightenment is with you throughout your ascension process and works with you based upon your ascension.

Thus, as we have stated before, Continuing Fifth Epochal Revelation is a coming into stabilization. Presently, blockages are there in part because we are in the adjudication process. If clarity of understanding is not happening with you at a necessary level, it is because you have chosen to remain on the fourth circle, and you are therefore not deserving of understanding. Understanding is a gift, and it does not come to arrogant and prideful individuals; it comes to those who fuse the heart circuits with the mind, and if you are strictly working within the mind and you have not connected with heart, then you are not activating the Spirit of Truth or the Holy Spirit, and so you are malfunctioning. You have a responsibility for your nonfunctioning parts.

I would now like to talk about corticoids, which are steroids. They are produced by the adrenal and sex glands, and there are two groups—the mineral type and the starch type. The mineral types are to control levels of minerals in the blood, the starch types to supervise the level of glycogen in the liver. Desoxycorticosterone (DOC) is a mineral corticoid. Cortisone is a starch corticoid. These steroids are used to counteract diseases of the body. The body produces these steroids inwardly and unconsciously to fight diseases and certain viruses that should not be there. These steroids are now being used in modern medicine for certain crippling diseases such as arthritis.

It will be discovered by the ascending personalities of the higher stages of light and life (at various levels) that certain diseases are caused by imbalances of the male and female connections to the Paradise circuits and that certain hormones that should be functioning in certain specific procedures within the body are not functioning, basically because of the imbalances in thinking in connection to male and female circuitry at whatever level of dimensional reality the soul is in body form.

Why is it that the sex hormones point in opposite directions? Estrone, which is an estrogen (a female sex hormone), has oxygen at the top of the molecule, and testosterone, an offshoot of androgen (a male hormone), has oxygen and hydrogen at the top of the molecule and oxygen at the bottom. **Complementary polarities** have been so designed. Is it by accident? Of course not. These male and female hormones and others are designed specifically to complement one another in an opposite pattern to bring balance at whatever level they themselves connect with the thought processes within the central nervous system.

Each molecule resonating with the command center of the pituitary gland finds itself in various parts of the body, based upon the alignment of that personality's form unit moment to moment with that personality's relationship to the Eternal Father, as a human or mortal personality in a physical sphere of existence or as a personality other than mortal or human outside of one's physical sphere of existence.

It is understood in modern science that both sexes have a combination of estrogen and androgen steroids within them. Females have more estrogen, males more androgen. Both sexes have both hormones. The androgen affects the body so that the beginning development of the body structure is either male or female in formation.

If, on this planet, there had been no fall of the Planetary Prince and the later default of Adam and Eve and things had continued according to normal dispensational relations and evolutionary growth, then this planet could have been one of the more highly developed planets in the system of Satania in relation to Paradise-origin formation of the body and the inner stabilization of mind. Because the inner stabilization of mind has been disrupted by rebellion, the formation of the body has become diseased and transcendence by death the reality.

Taking into consideration that interuniversal personality is a reality on Urantia, and dwelling upon that thought for a few moments, why is it that various mortals who are bipeds have different body structures and different body forms? What decides how tall a person should be or how many fingers a person has? What triggers sexual response from one personality to another? Why do females have the body structure to have the children on Urantia and many other worlds? Could it possibly be that on more androgynous worlds males can give birth? And if that be the case, and some of you are from some of those planets, could you possibly assume that some of you males might have more motherly instincts than some of you females, and some of you males may also be more capable of handling your children than the spouses you are with who are more

Father-circuited than they should be because of their own imbalances?

Very few on Urantia, even in the beginning Divine New Order communities, are perfect enough to function in interuniversal reality, but when this happens to the degree that it will happen, Urantia will be the prototype for the next series of universes to be created in the outer regions of time and space. The significance of Urantia in the master universe is far beyond the expectation and realizations that can be revealed to you at this time.

You want to live on a normal world, and that is good, but Urantia will never be quite normal, for it has been designed (even if a rebellion had not taken place) to be experimental. Conformity to lower thinking and to the dictates of lower-circuited controllers will only further the confusion upon this planet that isolates higher individuals and their seed from personal fulfillment and total recall of point-of-origin reality and relationships and prevents them from actualization and complete stabilization of mind.

At this point on Urantia, even with ovan souls of higher circle attainment, the stabilization is beginning to take place with only a few individuals. Until an independent society becomes a reality, actualization, total stabilization, and total fulfillment will be unrealized, and this is not a good thing for these individual personalities who have ascended to some moment of recall. That is why all of the **memory circuits** are not opened up for you and for those whose circuits are beginning to open, as you would not be able to live in your present uncomfortable circumstances if total realization of who you were, who you are, and what you could and should be doing was actualized.

When enough ovan souls of the 170,000,000 begin to come into some alignment and stabilization and the necessary auhter energy is created to bring about a true Divine New Order society, this may cause any of several things to happen, and in what order these may happen we are not sure. Firstly, the Divine New Order administration with its global change functions, such as the Bright and Morning Star Band, publications, videos, films, etc. can cause a global consciousness shift or **change point**. Secondly, Michael may return. Thirdly, Trinity Teacher Sons may come. Fourthly, the great cataclysms will occur suddenly, and normal process of administration policy under the auspices of the Planetary Prince will continue, but be slowed down. In the fourth scenario, eventually evacuation will occur and training will proceed in the **New Jerusalem** until the New Jerusalem is properly placed into position on the new Urantia.

When enough males and females on your planet properly respond to God in all that they are as ascending sons and daughters, their bodies will then respond. This will be based upon their point of origin and Divine New Order realities with an interuniversal absolute and not upon Urantian social realities. When you allow each other the freedom to be who you are in recognition of interuniversal realities, you grant the ability to function normally. If your body is being continually restricted, a total healing cannot take place, and some unpleasantness and disease will continue to occur in some area of your physical **third-dimensional** body.

Urantia is, and forevermore will be, an interuniversal placement of reflectivity and personality coordination. There is no planetary standardization. There is interplanetary mobilization and diversity. It should be understood that **Deo-atomic reality** of superuniverse construction is resonant on Urantia and now native to it. So, in some point in your evolution you should be asking certain questions:

- If I am an ovan soul, to which of the seven **cosmic families** do I belong?

- With which of the seven cosmic families do the very hormones that exist within me and have created me an ascending son or daughter resonate most perfectly?

- Where can I find the higher reality? Where does the very air I breathe have a life-giving Deo-atomic reality?

- Does it make a difference if in the next eight years I am living in Europe, India, Australia, Mexico, or in the United States, and in what part of those countries should I live?
- Should I specifically be where my cosmic ancestors of higher quality and quantity are located?

If you cannot formulate these questions and answer them, you are in grave danger. The danger is twofold. You will die either by disease of the body and mind caused by inappropriate thinking and destabilization or by the coming upheavals and cataclysms that will remove you from this planet. If God is your Father and you believe in your Creator Father, why is it that you are still dying from some form of disease? If you believe that death is necessary, then you are deceived. Why is it that accidents that nearly take your life happen to you or have happened to you recently?

If you believe that accidents that could have taken your life since December 1989 were just accidents and you know Christ Michael as your personal God, then you have not learned the first principle of circuitry connection; you have not found your place in the kingdom of God, and you still remain on the fourth circle of attainment, and you must begin to walk in the actualization of your destiny, not in the program of self-will or smallness of mind.

How do the chemicals of life actually work? You continually but inappropriately believe that you have to die on this planet. Perhaps you think that if you are lucky you will just lie down and go to sleep and then wake up on a mansion world—that is, if you understand about the ascension process at some level. Could this be a mistaken self-assurance? If, in this self-assurance, you are in error, or even in sin, could it be that God has other plans for you?

Could it be that upon your transition you will not go to the mansion worlds because of your own self-assurance and because you are in reality a part of the Rebellion? Could it be that Christ Michael would like you to stay on this planet because you know a little bit more about the Fifth Epochal Revelation and the language of it, and that you could be useful on this planet in the next forty to fifty years to be a part of the new spiritual administration? Could it be that you are selfish?

Why is it that knowledge of the Fifth Epochal Revelation, even the one-tenth of it that is in *The URANTIA Book*, has come to you with its higher understanding of God? What good is it to those who you leave behind on Urantia if you have gone on to the mansion worlds? The majority of the people of this planet have no comprehension of the one-tenth that you have at least some understanding of. Why do you think that God would want you, all of you Reservists, to die and go to the mansion worlds where those sojourning there know the one-tenth one hundred times better than you do? Do you wish to be an eternal student of *The URANTIA Book* and an eternal infant?

Continuing Fifth Epochal Revelation is to help you to transcend the death process so that you can remain on Urantia and become a teacher of what you would have already learned, to the millions, perhaps billions, who may be able to also be evacuated and brought back to this planet if you were here to help in the process. Or do you feel that it is OK that they die during earthquakes or other cataclysms because they will go to the first mansion worlds? In your complacency and apathy you will have created your own judgment. You need to awaken and accept the responsibility that is being brought to you now, for you are needed on this planet now, and you will be needed when the final change point comes, not on the mansion worlds, but to help change this planet.

What makes people grow old or die? It is their wrong thinking that inhibits the formation of the **Deo-atomic structure** in the cellular makeup within their body that causes their inability to properly align themselves with divine purpose. The body withers and dies just like a flower does that is not watered. If you are one who is not watered by self-fulfillment and actualization within cosmic absolutes and divine prerogatives, then you too will wither and die.

Yes, you indeed must find yourself first, for it is you who have the Urantia revelations who are most accountable; it is among you that the judgment is taking place first, for the judgment of God starts first in the household of God. It is with you of the higher levels of ascension on the fourth circle of attainment that the judgment has begun, and it has been slowly taking place since 1911 to those with higher mindal capacities to comprehend the higher reality of God, the Universal Father.

The first forum was a group of Urantian personalities; however, associates who were not part of the forum but directly connected by family ties and friendship associations to those of the forum were starseed. It was the **starseed** who caused the greatest problem, and it was those first-time Urantians with higher genetic linkage to Adamson and Ratta who began to see through some of these problems and were not yet sophisticated enough to be as iniquitous as the starseed who had continually repersonalized back here and loved to control others.

Some understood that the revelations that were coming at that time could not be owned by any one organization and that the copyright could only exist so that the main content could not be changed. Those who, through the decades, have come to think that they are the sole owners of universal terminology have placed themselves under the highest judgment of the very God they claim to be serving. You should be free to name your child Urantia, or your home Urantia, and to use the symbol of the concentric circles freely and unqualifiedly.

Continuing Fifth Epochal Revelation terminology can only be taught properly from the **First Planetary Sacred Home** at **The Starseed and Urantian Schools of Melchizedek** [now called the **Global Community Communications Schools**], but it should be used freely and unreservedly by all those who wish to share it with others on a planetary and interplanetary level. No personality of time and space can copyright conceptual reality. However, the author (being the instrument used by Celestial Overcontrol) and the human Divine Administration have the right and responsibility to copyright the published book or other printed works, particularly on fallen worlds like Urantia. They are entitled to protect the published works themselves.¹

Cosmic absolutes are designed in and through the process of that ascending son or ascending daughter or celestial personality in their own personal relationship to the Paradise Trinity. Each and every personality should freely be able to use universal terminology without fear of repercussion by other parties, and they should be able to teach these principles using whatever means of technology they have. The fact that they may teach some of these terminologies at a lower level is unfortunate on Urantia, but they still should be granted that permission and that opportunity.

On a normal world, the schools at the First Planetary Sacred Home teach the higher concepts of universal absolutes and finiteness with a more exact understanding, which is the same now on Urantia at the First Planetary Sacred Home. As Continuing Fifth Epochal Revelation reaches the four corners of this planet, it is the prayer of Celestial Overcontrol that these concepts be taught to others at whatever level you can comprehend it, that you name your children by names from Continuing Fifth Epochal Revelation that may strike a chord within you, and share these concepts on radio and television at whatever level you can.

This is what your planet needs in order to become truly stabilized so that the majority of Cosmic and Urantian Reservists could come into the third psychic circle, receive an angel of enlightenment, and hopefully function on the first circle of attainment in the future. The only way that this can be done is that you eventually come to a Planetary Sacred Home to learn, become mandated yourself, and then be sent to your geographic sector on this planet, which will then become another protected area and divine administrative center.

We reserve the right to correct those who do not understand Continuing Fifth Epochal Revelation or its terminology in the highest manner, but we do not reserve the right to stop you from using it for the benefit of the people of Urantia. It is not Gabriel of Urantia's/TaliasVan of Tora's revelation, nor is it even the Creator Son's of this universe, Christ Michael's. It is the synthesis of absolute reality necessary to bring the first stages of light and life to Urantia as first mandated by the Universal Father Himself and—at our level of universal administration within the time frame of procedure in interuniversal time reality—by the Creator Son of Nebadon and downward from the Bright and Morning Star to the present Planetary Prince, Machiventa Melchizedek, and human complements, who all proceed and follow the dictates of our hearts in relation to the Paradise circuits speaking in and through us.

It is a misunderstanding that your morontia body would be created hopefully before disease of body and death or destruction overtakes you. It is in the opening of these circuits on this planet that were cut off from the reality of the ovan souls so long ago that you will find yourselves and your eternal existence, for you are part of the eternal now. You do not have to die to get there; you are already here, in eternity. What is missing is the total realization of your eternity-past, your eternity-future, and the realization of how to live in the absoluteness of the eternity-now. In order to live in the absoluteness of the eternity-now at the highest level within the first circle of attainment stabilization, you must understand and digest Continuing Fifth Epochal Revelation.

July 21, 1992

Paladin, Chief of Finaliters
in cooperation with interuniversal Life Carriers, the Seraphim of the Race Commission, and the coordinated primary Lanonandek Sons of specific systems unrevealed at this time but including Lanaforge of Satania and System Sovereigns of Sandmatia, Assuntia, Porogia, Sortoria, Rantulia, and Glantonia for the implementation of the first stages of light and life in the overcontrol procedure in and through the Bright and Morning Star of Salvington to the planetary level in and

through the present Planetary Prince, Machiventa Melchizedek, for the calling forth of his administration in human bodies

As transmitted through
the Pre-Level-One Audio Fusion Material Complement,
Gabriel of Urantia/TaliasVan of Tora

PAPER 250

Reflective Cellular Magnetic Motion Polarity In The Beginning Morontia Body And Its Relationship To Celestial Mechanics And Planetary Administration In The First Stages Of Light And Life Pertinent To The Cosmic Families And Electromagnetism On A Third-Dimensional Level

AROUND the nucleus of every atom is a flow of orbiting electrons at various energy levels. The electrons in the outer orbital ring of an atom are loosely bound to the nucleus and are conductive. When electrons flow, they constitute electrical current. Some materials such as rubber, plastics, and glass present great resistance to current flow and are used as insulators to prevent current flow. Materials such as copper, silver, and electrolyte solutions offer negligible resistance to current flow and are known as conductors. That is why metal wires are used to carry electricity from one place to another. We say these wires are good conductors or carriers of electricity.

When two atoms are drawn together, because they are **complementary polarities**, they fuse with each other and begin to recreate **Deo-atomic reality** in structure at some level. This drawing together is an electrochemical reality based upon Paradise circuits in liaison with the Seven Master Spirits and God the Supreme, channeled in and through the Creator Son and Creative Mother Spirit, and on through the local universe administrative process, beginning with the Bright and Morning Star and downward to evolutionary mortals who are exhibiting God-reality.

A magnet is something that will attract power. It has two poles, a north and a south pole, and around it is a magnetic field. Magnetism can produce electricity, and electricity can produce magnetism. Some magnets run on electricity and are called electromagnets, but they work only when they are turned on. The north pole of one is attracted to the south pole of the other; opposite poles attract. Poles of the same kind repel. This principle is the principle of the attraction of celestial personalities to one another on any level of cellular cosmic physics in relation to the Paradise Trinity.

In the implantation of life forms at beginning levels, the Life Carriers resonate with directive energies coordinate to electromagnetic chemicals in the separate prerogatives of Paradise-origin cellular structures. These cellular structures coordinate with realities designated to personality structure and function from the highest levels to the lowest, coordinate with amoeba life and inward. What I have just said, simplified as it is, takes years of study to understand.

Starting with orbits in physical spheres, based upon structures of evolutionary planets, there is a coordinate reality in individual personality form and motion that is based upon the body structure of personal entities that is coordinate with atmospheric reality.

On **third-dimensional** worlds and upwards to the fifth mansion world, even what is considered physical sexual attraction is actually based upon either **Deo-atomic** or **diotribe** magnetic cells in the other person's cellular makeup. Material and morontia body forms are based upon the higher genetic inheritance of their ancestors. This has to do with the ancestors who have helped to create the Deo-subatomic reality of the higher cellular genetics exhibiting themselves in the atmosphere in and around Urantia or the mansion world and assigned to the fetus in the womb by Celestial Overcontrol at a certain moment in the formation of that ascender in accordance with destiny purpose.

As adults on Urantia you have had the occurrence of meeting someone who reminded you of someone else. Take note of these occurrences from now on. That person is probably related to you in some cosmic way. When it becomes common knowledge on Urantia, much loneliness will be eliminated, and on planets where this is common knowledge, isolation and soul loneliness is unknown.

In sexual transference of sperm from male to female, the higher **Deo-atomic genetics** remain with the female, and even though sperm from another male is later implanted to fertilize an egg, the fetus itself incorporates all of the former sperm implantation of the other males with whom she has cohabited. So, in cosmic reality, the highest ascending spiritual mate she has received sperm from will be more totally incorporated in the male or female child. Other Deo-atomic cells will also be genetically integrated by Celestial Overcontrol pertinent to the soul bestowal and personality bestowal at any time from the moment of conception to three to five minutes after the fetus is out of the womb, depending upon the destiny purpose of the body in coordination with the destiny purpose of the soul.

Each solar system is an eventual sacred area of the body of God the Supreme. Below are some brief definitions[1] relative to this that can be found in many scientific journals:

- **Celestial mechanics:** The branch of astronomy in which theoretical mechanics is used to calculate motions of celestial bodies under the action of their mutual gravitational attractions. Celestial mechanics is used to construct systematic dynamical theories of the actual translational motions of celestial bodies in space. Although most highly developed for the solar system, it has been applied to multiple stars and, to a lesser extent, to stellar motions in galactic systems. Applications to rotational motion include the development of theories for precession and mutation, as well as for tidal and other deformations of the figure of Earth.

  Basic Concepts—The mechanical principles involved stem directly from Newton's law of gravitation and represent the culmination of centuries of effort to associate observed effects with the forces that cause them.

In the 16th century, the Danish astronomer Tycho Brahe was completing a series of planetary observations from which his assistant, Johann Kepler, derived his three empirical laws of planetary motion:

   a. The path of a planet about the Sun is an ellipse, the Sun being at one of the foci.
   b. The line joining the Sun and a planet sweeps out equal areas in equal times.
   c. The squares of the periods of any two planets are in the same ratio as the cubes of their respective mean distances from the Sun.

Isaac Newton completed the formulation of the laws of motion begun by Galileo and Christian Huygens:

   a. In the absence of external forces, a body at rest remains at rest and a body in rectilinear motion remains in rectilinear motion (inertia).
   b. The acceleration imparted to a body by a force is in the direction of the force, proportional to the force, and inversely proportional to the mass of the body, F=ma.
   c. For every force there is an equal force in the opposite direction (reaction).

From these and the empirical laws of Kepler, Newton deducted the general law of gravitation.

Application of Newton's first two laws to the motions of celestial bodies indicates that change of motion (either direction or speed), rather than motion itself, is caused by a force. Thus a celestial body will speed up if under the influence of a force acting in the direction of its motion and will slow down if the force is oppositely directed. If the force acts transversely to the direction of motion the path becomes curved. If several forces act simultaneously, the celestial body responds to their resultant force. If a force is always directed toward the same point, the motion of the body will be a curve concave toward that point and in a plane containing the point.

One consequence of the motion of a body under the action of a central force is that the line joining the fixed point and the moving body sweeps out equal areas in equal times. Kepler's observation of this relation in planetary motion shows that the planets move under the influence of a central force directed toward the Sun. The law of areas does not indicate the size of the acting force, but because the observed orbits of the planets are elliptical, the force acting on a planet must vary inversely as the square of the distance between the planet and the Sun.

The combination of this information and Kepler's third law indicates that the forces acting on individual planets are in direct proportion to the planetary masses and in inverse proportion to the squares of the planetary distances from the Sun. Taken in conjunction with Newton's third law of motion, this leads directly to the general statement of the law of gravitation.

- **Orbits:** Having demonstrated that the observed motions of the planets satisfied the law of gravitation, Newton deduced from the law that the motion of a body around a central mass must be a conic; a circle, ellipse, parabola, or hyperbola. Of the possible orbits, only the ellipse and circle are closed curves.

- **Undisturbed motion:** Here only two bodies interact. Direct application of the laws of motion makes possible the computation of the forces, provided the masses and accelerations of the bodies are known.

- **Disturbed motion:** the exact motion of any celestial body is affected by the gravitational attraction of all the other bodies in the system.

- **Stability of solar system:** The most stable feature is the plane that passes through the center of mass of the whole system and is perpendicular to the line through the center of mass about which the total angular momentum of the translational motions in the system is a maximum. This plane is known as the invariable plane, because its position in space is not affected by the perturbations of the orbital motions from mutual gravitational attractions within the system. However, it is not absolutely invariable in position, because of the continual interchange between the translational and rotational angular momentum in the system due to precessional motions and tidal frictions; its position is also slightly affected by the attraction exerted by bodies which are external to the solar system.

- **Celestial navigation:** Navigation with the aid of celestial bodies, primarily for determination of position when landmarks are not available. In celestial navigation, position is not determined relative to the objects observed, as in navigation by piloting, but in relation to the points on the Earth having certain celestial bodies directly overhead.

The Sun appears to make a complete revolution among the stars once a year, as the Earth makes one revolution in its orbit. The apparent motion is along a great circle called the ecliptic, which is inclined nearly 23.5° to the plane of the Equator of the Earth. All of the planets stay within the 8° of the ecliptic, in a band called the zodiac. Within this band they appear to move among the stars. The Moon, too, stays within the zodiac as it revolves around the Earth—or more properly as the Earth and Moon revolve around their common center of mass—once each lunar month.

Celestial equator coordinate systems. The intersection of the plane of the terrestrial Equator, extended with the celestial sphere, is a great circle called the celestial equator. The celestial equator system is used in the almanacs for indicating positions of celestial bodies at various times.

Horizon systems of coordinates. The navigator also uses the horizon system of coordinates, which is similar to the celestial equator system. The primary great circle is the horizon of the observer. The pole vertically overhead is the zenith, and the opposite pole is the nadir.

- **Time relationships:** Time is repeatedly mentioned as an important element of a celestial observation because the Earth rotates at the approximate rate of 1 minute of arc each 4 sec of time. An error of 1 sec in the timing of an observation might introduce an error in the line of position of as much as one-quarter of a mile.

- **Cell structure:** Living organisms, both plant and animal, are built of microscopic structural units called cells. Some simple organisms consist of one free-living cell, whereas more complex plants and animals contain from hundreds to billions of cells. A typical cell consists of two major compartments: a nucleus, containing the hereditary material in the form of chromosomes, and a surrounding mass of cytoplasm, which includes a variety of smaller components.

  Cells are to some extent individuals; that is, their behavior is somewhat independent of the organism as a whole. Cells are characterized by certain universal structural features. Almost all cells possess an external limiting membrane, a nucleus (with chromosomes), mitochondria, ribosomes, and a system of internal cytoplasmic membranes. The importance of the cell membrane in cell function cannot be overstated. It regulates the exchange of materials in and out of the cell, and it plays an essential role in the nervous transmission, contraction, and the interaction of cells with one another.

- **Cell function:** Cells are found in a variety of environments which differ in salt concentration, acidity, temperature, and the types of organic molecules present. To carry out their functions, they must be able to protect themselves from adverse conditions as well as to maintain an internal environment (within the cell), which may be markedly different from the external surroundings.

  A characteristic of all cells is the ability to use the energy of chemical bonds to carry out their special functions. This is accomplished by a vast array of enzymes. The primary source of energy is, of course, the Sun; the chloroplasts of green plants serve as the chief agents for converting this light energy into the energy of chemical bonds.

  At each nuclear division the daughter nuclei receive identical sets of chromosomes, assuring the orderly transmission of genes. At the molecular level this involves the exact replication of DNA molecules in the chromosomes and the segregation of the daughter DNA molecules to daughter nuclei. This DNA plays two central roles in cell function: As the genetic material, its orderly replication assures that successive cell generations will contain the same genes; and by producing messenger RNA, it controls the types of enzymes and hence the type of chemical reactions carried out by the cell. Transfer RNA transfers a particular amino acid to a growing polypeptide chain at the side of protein synthesis during translation.

- **Cellular affinity**: The term affinity, formerly used in chemistry, was introduced into embryology to denote the phenomenon of selective adhesiveness (suggesting bonds of attraction) as observed among the cells of higher organisms. Cellular adhesiveness, its presence or absence and its intimacy and strength, were found to vary with cell type and with the stage of development. Firm cellular adhesions make for the stabilization of tissues, since they suppress amoeboid movements of which all embryonic and most adult cells are capable. In embryogenesis, particularly of vertebrates, selective cellular adhesions and directed cell movements were found to operate, alternatingly and complementarily, as the fundamental morphogenetic principles by which the pattern of discrete and yet interwoven tissues and organs is established.

Cell locomotion and cell rest are not as mutually exclusive as they may seem, for even when migrating, the tissue cells adhere loosely and intermittently to other cells. Conversely, the apparently firm cell adhesions in a fully differentiated tissue are stable only under stable external and internal conditions. Following the infliction of a substantial wound, the neighboring cells relinquish their former contact positions and move about until they have reestablished a new state of precarious equilibrium with each other and with the rest of the organism. In cancerous transformations the cells change their adhesive properties and become invasive, unfortunately in a histoclastic fashion.

While the variety of self-emancipations of the primordia seems to reflect newly arising alienations (disaffinities) between them and their layers of origin, the secondary associations between heterologous tissues seem to demonstrate the operation of complementary affinities. A "selective contact guidance" has also been invoked to account for the distribution pattern of the outgrowing nerve fibers and for the specific routes of migration of neural crest cells and other tissue primordia.

- **Mechanism of cell adhesion:** A comprehensive theory on the physicochemical mechanisms which control the interrelated phenomena of cell locomotion and cell adhesion must cover, among others, the following observations: Cultured tissue cells adhere not only to each other but to an odd variety of nonliving organic and inorganic substances. Not only homologous but also heterologous cell types may firmly stick together. Usually only certain parts of the cell (such as pseudopodia or basal sides in epithelia) are adhesive. Cell adhesions vary as to firmness and permanence, and with respect to developmental age, tissue type, and immersion fluid. Present information permits only hypotheses which try to explain, in molecular terms, one or the other of these aspects.

- **Cement:** Any substance that acts as a bonding agent for materials. In construction and engineering the word almost always means hydraulic cement, it being by far the most important.

Continuing Fifth Epochal Revelation introduces the reality of personality structure in relation to cellular reality in relation to similar mind-brain formation. Paradise realities govern the formation of brain structures based upon coordinate reality in time-and-space location and the evolutionary reality of a particular system relative to time factor sequence from the beginning of that universe. Once cells coordinate with one another in the formation of life in the evolutionary process, the choice decisions are based upon the reality of those planets closest to it in the various stages of light and life.

The interdependence of one planet to another is a known factor. The interdependence of one planet to another where life form has been developed is most significant in the evolutionary process of higher life forms, in particular, dealing with the dispensational realities status of a planet that is not in rebellion. The mindal process and development of the individuals on one planet depends upon the nearest inhabited planets that surround it that are coming into the higher stages of light and life. This produces what is known as **invariable septum stratum force**. In order to explain this force, let us begin by enumerating a few factors relative to invariable septum stratum force:

- the intermingling of cells
- specific species segregation and reaggregation
- artificial cell disassociation
- diotribe magnetism
- mixed populations of free cells

Free cells can be seen to contain both Deo-atomic and diotribe realities when exhibited to celestial overseers. As spoken of in previous transmissions, diotribe reality must be removed. It is known that a neuron is a nerve cell with its processes, constituting the structural and functional unit of nerve tissue. Acme cells are one type of neuron that has up to 100,000 specific connections to other cells. There are 200 billion neurons in the newborn brain; 10 to 50 times that many glial, nutritional, and support cells, and millions of trillions of connections between these cells.

Continuing Fifth Epochal Revelation states that the formation of one-, two- and three-brained personalities is the formation of the Paradise Father, Eternal Son, and Infinite Spirit coordinate to the bestowal of dual-origin and triune-origin reality. This is an intermediate designated force-energy coordinate with personality circuitry of Paradise function. Every physical human brain has a designated course in function to become coordinated to spirit reality, based upon nonphysical appropriation. The more spiritual the mind becomes the lighter the brain becomes.

The first thing that begins to become spiritualized in eternal life is the brain. Whether mortals are one-, two-, or three-brained types depends upon the planetary mortal epochs. Up to the Adamic dispensation, planetary types are one-brained. The upstepping by the violet race increases the brain capacity. From the Adamic to the stages of light and life, they are two-brained, and in the stages of light and life they are three-brained.

For **ovan souls**, the universe of origin and the astral soul also have something to do with it. The brain does not become smaller or larger, it eventuates in time. It becomes coordinate in cellular tunnels leading to divine influence of tubular motion in coordinate space. It is time-factored, time-analyzed, and time-mechanized in relation to orbital motion and interplanetary reality.

Virtue and fact fused together help to form spirit-brain tubular dynamics. Hydrogen and oxygen atomic reality fused with Deo-ultimatonic reality form meridian circuits that are interlinked to the first morontian brain dynamics and act as a kind of periscope from one dimension to another. When the periscope is up, higher dimensional reality is recognized by the soul trapped in physical form. When the periscope is down and lower thoughts form the moment-to-moment reality, the periscope can only exhibit the lower dimensional formation, and the weight of the brain remains constant with third-dimensional reality, and all other factors of spiritual formation in the physical body functions do not happen.

In order for the brain to give positive signals to the rest of the body, it must have the influence of higher light. Much as the sun is the light of the solar system, each body is a coordinate solar system with the brain functioning as the sun of its solar system.

Learning to control one's thoughts is important. As it is simply written, "Think upon things that are pure, that are divine, that are unselfish, kind and generous, and for the good of others,"[2] and the mind will then influence the bodily functions in a positive manner, which will begin an orbiting of all **Deo-atomic cells** in pertinent systems in the body. Outside of correct thought mode, irregular orbital motion and disturbed energy functions within the body are the cause of all diseases and eventual death by the deceleration and confused direction of Deo-atomic cellular reality.

Continuing Fifth Epochal Revelation teaches that trillions of Deo-atomic cells worldwide on Urantia are now being drawn by **reflective cellular magnetic motion polarity** to the nucleus of planetary auhter energy at the **First Planetary Sacred Home**. When an invariable septum stratum force is created at the First Planetary Sacred Home by increased **auhter energy**, many conditions develop:

- Increased protection of humans in the area. Invariable septum stratum force acts as an opposing force to eliminate all diotribe reality in the area in the air, the water, and the agriculture.

- Diseases and emotional instability will be accelerated, particularly to nonaligned humans, by the Planetary Prince and his staff during my adjudication of the rebellious personality, Lucifer, and those who followed his nonreality thinking.

- When invariable septum stratum force is functioning in a second, third, and fourth to seventh planetary location and these other safety areas become stabilized, it culminates in a **septuplicate planetary invariable septum stratum force**, and these areas will begin to have an affinity to six other planets that have already reached the first stages of light and life in the system of Satania. Urantia will begin to produce celestial reflective cellular magnetic motion polarity to align with the Deo-atomic reality of six other planets in any stage of light and life in the system of Satania that are physically closest to Urantia. This creates an orbit of undisturbed Deo-atomic motion on Urantia that will eventually supersede the necessity of the earth's sunlight for life sustenance.

The goal of the Planetary Prince and his staff—in working with the evolutionary mortals of any planet to bring it into a stabilization reality based upon a coordinate personality compliance and harmony founded upon **cosmic family** association of cellular reality—would have proceeded if your original Planetary Prince had not fallen.

Now, in the case of Urantia, because of the Rebellion, this coordinate harmonic compliance is an interuniversal compliance based upon interuniversal cellular reality and not just Nebadon cellular reality. This is a unique condition. This is a condition that is exciting even to the highest of celestial personalities of Paradise origin. The ramifications of such a planet, particularly a planet in its location and in its time factor (being such a young one within its own universe), designates Urantia as one of the most unique planets in the grand universe.

Because of its uniqueness, permission for experimentation and observation is constantly being requested by intersuperuniversal personalities, and permission is either granted or refused by the Creator Son, Christ Michael. One of the reasons for refusal is whether the presence of any personality on any level of spirit formation causes a positive or negative influence, if that higher personality is totally present.

In some cases this fusion of personality in body is necessary in order for that personality to actually observe Urantian reality through empirical observation by having a physical presence at some level. In this manner, even when personalities like myself come to fuse, I can be there only in part, as is true with finaliters, seraphim at certain levels, and particularly interuniversal personalities.

It is a cosmic fact that when personalities of opposing cellular makeup are in close proximity of one another either the disassociation of the opposite personalities' bodily functions happens or a reorganization and hybridization occurs. When disassociation happens, even if it is a loving and high personality that causes the disassociation, immediate death can occur to human and other mortal personalities who have not aligned their cellular structure to higher divine realities.

Separation of human personalities and celestial personalities from one another on celestial planets is a predesigned prerogative of God the Father. The space of the universes of time and space and the placement of certain planets based upon Paradise design is coordinate to a physical space factor that has to do with the separation of higher life forms of divine mind from lower life forms such as evolutionary mortals.

As you ascend inward and onward to Paradise, the physical distances between certain planets begin to be designed more closely to one another based upon the understanding of each individual citizen and the total mass consciousness of the planet to the citizens of another planet. The citizens of the higher planet are responsible for the citizens of the nearest lower one in whatever way that communication exists from one to another.

Therefore, when a System Sovereign is given rule over a system of planets, there is an unwritten but understood and agreed upon convention that each Planetary Prince understands at his level, based upon the neighboring planet of inhabitation. On your world of confusion and disassociation of divine reality and thought, you are separate not only from the nearest planet of higher life form, but you are separate in cellular reality.

When you begin to think in divine harmony, the very cells within you become light-associated, and there is no disturbed motion. All motion then becomes undisturbed. If any disharmony occurs and motion is disturbed at some level, this disturbance is felt within the body. The cellular brain mechanics that cause the feeling of weight would then create weight physically in organic matter. It is no longer assimilation but a dictation—to the time–space reality that you are now in and to that particular cellular grouping within your body or membrane of light to remain physical and within the physical reality of whatever body form you are functioning in. If it is a third-dimensional flesh body, then you will remain in flesh. If it is a first-stage morontia body, then that is where you will remain.

When you are ready for a higher body, a certain percent of the cellular reality within that body must coordinate to the next stage or level. That is done by a mota adherence. If you are an interuniversal ovan soul and this mota adherence is not actualized by a group consciousness within a certain family, you as an individual cannot rise to the next plane. It is done in a corporate reality and not in an individual reality.

Let me explain. As an ascending son or daughter, in the present case human mortals, it is the prerogative of the Creator Son and Universe Mother Spirit of the universe you are in to recreate you in some manner of resemblance to their particular cellular reality of Paradise divinity. Until all of their sons and daughters find themselves in some similarity of consciousness, **cosmic parents** as individuals will be quite unhappy going to a next sphere, planet, or plane for they would be very much unlike the rest of the personalities on that planet.

Why is it that in the first morontia body Jesus could hardly be recognized? He was so different that even those closest to Him at first did not know who He was. It is true that on Urantia you earn whatever mansion world you have created for your next reality. That is based upon the cellular reality that is exhibited in totality on that world. That is how you will be recreated in structure and in body form. In a sense, you are now designing your next body form by your thoughts, your actions, and by your attitudes.

Some personalities who are very much like those human mortals that you have met in this lifetime are already functioning in these higher worlds. That is because there is a similarity in the personality bestowal of the Father, but always with slight differences. It is in these slight differences that the higher bodies are uniquely different from those on the lower worlds. The emergence of character is one thing that stabilizes certain physical body formations.

On a world such as Urantia is now, and how it will be in the future, all the standardized absolutes of cosmic identification become incorporated in one planet. The resultant circumstantial consequences of such a reality necessitates the understanding of these unique cosmic realities by evolutionary mortals like yourselves at lower levels first, or the experiment of Urantia and all of the time that the life process has been allowed to continue in interplanetary cellular reality will be of less significance.

Divine absolute principles of celestial physics and orbital mechanical correlation in terms of physical planetary placement and personality placement of any one particular planet cannot be taught or understood by the reading of words in a book. It can only be understood by personal experience of this reality of dimensional coordinate placement by students such as yourselves, ovan souls of interuniversal time–space factors.

Continuing Fifth Epochal Revelation is little understood by Urantian personalities. Those Urantians with higher genetics who have the highest understanding of interuniversal absolutes will be understood at various levels by other universe personalities who are in part interuniversal creatures. First of all, the cellular makeup of the physical and astral bodies of ovan souls fuse together to form that which they are at that moment of time and space. Although you may look like very human mortals, perhaps you are not.

In order to fully know yourselves, your desires, your likes and dislikes, according to the design of the Creator of the universe you are in, certain factors are necessary. You must be free from others around you who tend to control you in whatever way they can, based upon the norms of your present planetary placement, all within certain structures.

As group-conscious beings enter universal absolute cosmology, each individual also becomes more and more free. This is what Continuing Fifth Epochal Revelation is meant to do with all ovan souls of interuniversal reality who are being asked to reside on Urantia as administrative leaders within the Divine Administration of the Planetary Prince, Machiventa Melchizedek. It does not matter if the majority on the planet does not understand you. The majority on the planet will not be here at a certain point after the final change point happens and accelerates. Many will die from earth changes, plagues, and wars.

Urantia, because of its uniqueness and its location, will become a teaching planet, and many of the personalities of higher ovan-soul reality who will be trained on Urantia will be sent from some point of transference in the distant future to new universes in the outer space levels of the master universe.

These Urantia trainees will bring to these outer space levels the incorporated realities of grand universe experience so that the life implantations in these outer levels can be total and complete as to grand universe bestowal, embracing personalities present within the seven superuniverses.

The full realization of this process will be more highly learned and understood in the transition period that many of you will spend, first on Jerusem, next on Edentia, and then on Salvington. Many circuits will be opened up; many memory links will begin to become associated with past understanding, and when the fusion begins to take place with the Thought Adjuster, a oneness of being and purpose will stabilize. All doubts will be removed, and actualization and definition of purpose will be your reality.

For some of you this will happen in the twinkling of an eye; for others it will be more gradual, but when each of you, individually and corporately, begin to resonate more fully with invariable septum stratum force, you will then decide, first as individual spirits and then corporately, your next assignment from this world, and indeed, the next body of your reality.

Some of you will bypass the mansion worlds of Nebadon on which the cosmic relatives, who are not on this planet at this time, reside. You can visit them, but if they are not ready to advance to where you are, they have to ascend to that place first. You will find that the process of the regathering of the Urantian family is just a matter of a short time period in ascension once you are off Urantia. Because of visitation, the separation will not be as great, and the time period for growth is much more rapid than it is on Urantia.

The gift of Nebadon to all of you is the gift of certain mind circuitry in relation to the submission factors of the Paradise Trinity one to another and reflected in the mode of proper response in relationships between the human son or daughter and the mother or between the son or daughter and the father. This submission factor is a Nebadon exception in many phases of interuniversal reality. It is a prerogative of Michael and Michael's relationship to His Creator Father/Son, and coordinate with this is unison compliance with the Mother Spirit, and this is one of the substantial reasons why your Nebadon reality has been given to you.

The fact that within this reality you have fallen at one point is irrelevant because you have realigned yourselves with the Universal Father's perfect and divine plan. In your realignment you have met with disturbances. If you had not known these disturbances, you would not be able to prevent them from happening in the evolutionary worlds of the future.

In knowing the correlation between thought and physical creation at any level, you yourselves become in a sense co-creators. But in the understanding of co-creators, one must realize that one is also a created one. Co-creation does not mean creating something from nothing but to manipulate that which is already created. It designates past form structure in which present motion emerges as the strength, the power of will, to change the reality of those rebellious personalities on physical worlds such as Urantia by the combined and uniform teachings of the oldest ovan souls who are working together in planetary administration. This is why we are mandating human personalities to perform divine functions.

It is an experiment, but it is not an experiment without control. In our total overcontrol of all personalities is stability. Although it may seem at times that Caligastia has the greater edge in certain situations, it is only because you, as corporate beings, are not in the highest liaison with one another in your own thought processes, in your understanding of one another, in your relationships with one another in authority and under authority. We of Celestial Overcontrol function under the same laws and principles that you must function under at this time as evolutionary mortals. We are limited or empowered by our thoughts in coordination with our superiors, and we receive God's strength by our alignment with each other.

Because we are more perfect than imperfect, the mode of our creation, the mechanics of our reality, and the tools given us are supreme in function because we work with the Supreme. You, on your level, in absolute agreement can actually begin to manifest in your reality all that you need if you can begin to understand your interdependence upon one another. Control your thoughts, and find your individual placement within the Divine Administration in the assimilation of absolute divine administration and purity of motive.

If Caligastia gains influence, it is because some of you at some level have created blockages by your thinking. That is why even young students who come into the Machiventa Melchizedek Administration can cause great problems by their childishness. That is why some of you at the higher levels, particularly **Gabriel of Urantia/TaliasVan of Tora** with his clairvoyant abilities, are upset with the lack of adherence to procedures and the judgment made upon him or any of you by those who do not understand. At some level Gabriel of Urantia/TaliasVan of Tora realizes the dangers posed by seemingly insignificant matters, which all of you will also begin to realize.

At times students can cause disturbances in the very atmosphere and environment in which you are living because of the diotribe reality they create, which then causes disturbed motion in even the Eldership if those Elders do not understand what is happening. It is so true that one bad apple can spoil the whole barrel. It is within the cellular Deo-atomic reality, and so, with the coming of cosmic family members from all points of the planet, you must be quick to act where nonalignment occurs at any level.

If they wish to remain within the Divine Administration and **The Starseed and Urantian Schools of Melchizedek** [now called the **Global Community Communications Schools**], then they must understand that they cannot cause disturbed motion; in other words, they cannot be troublemakers. If so, they should be asked to move immediately. They should realize that they are here to learn and not to teach the Eldership.

You must look upon the soul age in this decision. It is much more dangerous for ovan souls, for they deceive themselves, and it is easy to see the many good things about them. On the outside you see the world and the blossoming beauty of it, but it is so hard to detect the thorns that some of the smaller children can brush up against and can be poisoned by. Scores have visited the First Planetary Sacred Home, but those who are aligned must be truly aligned.

You must remember that Continuing Fifth Epochal Revelation is also the fusion of spirituality with cosmic science, and so the specific understanding of these scientific realities must somehow be appropriated at the third-dimensional level where you are existing. This is a school of experience, a school of day-by-day living and moment-to-moment interassociation with one another. It is not a school of eight hours a day book learning. That will not change the ovan soul's thinking, nor will it create the first morontia body.

The affinity that you have with one another is an equation of that which changes the circumstances of each of your lives to higher vision and rhythm of existence, but if you allow disturbed motion to be exhibited within The Starseed and Urantian Schools of Melchizedek [now called the Global Community Communications Schools] by childish behavior and petty grievances, then all your reality as a perfect group will be lessened, and the manifestation of things that are needed will be blocked, for the cellular reality of that one lost soul will disturb all of you as a corporate mind and body.

If you are aligned with Divine Administration at the First Planetary Sacred Home and read this transmission, understand that you are here not just by choice but by divine purpose. If you are reading it in any other part of the world, know that you should come to **Planetary Sacred Headquarters** for a higher understanding of what you are reading by a day-to-day interassociation and moment-to-moment experience, so that you too can take the responsibility for teaching what you learn to others in experiential reality, the same as Jesus taught His apostles.

Continuing Fifth Epochal Revelation is here to bring you to the First Planetary Sacred Home. It is here to help adjudicate you, to help you to make decisions by free will, and to align yourself with Christ Michael, the Creator of this universe, and with the Universal Father. If you continue at whatever level you wish to continue in rebellious thinking and attitudes, do not think that because you have acquired the first one-tenth of the Fifth Epochal Revelation in *The URANTIA Book* that you have arrived. That is only the beginning.

If you are alive on the planet at this time and this information has come to you, it is because I, the Bright and Morning Star, have set it in motion. I am giving you the opportunity to choose at this moment, and at whatever level you can comprehend what I am saying you are being judged. My prayer for you is that you love God the Father above any association with the religious societies of this world, that the Spirit of Truth that Michael bestowed on this world is activated within you, and that you can become a follower of it.

If you do, you will find yourself physically at the First Planetary Sacred Home for some length of time determined by your destiny purpose, for you will not be able to remain where you are physically. If you are reading this now, up until 1995, know that after that date, a secondary judgment will take place. If you are reading this transmission before that date, I would take all necessary steps to come to Planetary Sacred Headquarters for training and assignment. This is your destiny. Realize it and act according to divine will. So be it.

August 3, 1992

Gabriel, The Bright and Morning Star of Salvington
in cooperation with the Creator Son of Nebadon, Christ Michael, for the calling forth of the Cosmic and Urantian Reserve Corps of Destiny for the implementation of the Divine Administration in and through the present Planetary Prince, Machiventa Melchizedek, and his staff of ascendant interuniversal personalities and their human complements

As transmitted through
the Pre-Level-One Audio Fusion Material Complement,
Gabriel of Urantia/TaliasVan of Tora

PAPER 251

Sound Waves And Celestial Harmonics In Conjunction With Primal Absolute Paradise Circuit Waves In Correlation With Pre-Designed Patterns Of The Grand Universe And Master Designs Including Personality Formations, And In Particular, Pair-Unit Classifications Of Various Evolutionary And Descending Levels In Cosmic Scope Coordinate With Quantum Physics—A Beginning Treatise

ON Urantia it is written in many scientific texts that the virtuosity of human hearing is as remarkable as it is important. A person can hear a mosquito buzzing outside his window, even though the power of the sound reaching him is no more than one-quadrillionth of a watt. (If 100 quadrillion—that is 100,000,000,000,000,000—buzzes could be combined and converted into electricity, it would be just enough power to light one reading lamp.)

Sound consists of:

1. cause, which is a physical vibration of some material thing
2. effect, a physiological sensation in an animal brain

Sound originates when a body moves back and forth rapidly enough to send a wave coursing through the medium in which it is vibrating. Sound, as a sensation, must be received by the ear and passed on to the brain where it can be registered as an event taking place in the world about the listener.

Sound vibrations are transmitted to the ear of solid substance by molecules bouncing together constituting a "compression" in the air and a rarefaction, which is a state or region of minimum pressure in a medium transversed by compression waves (such as sound waves) and is caused by molecules bouncing apart. Compression and rarefaction spread through the air in a pressure wave called sound, which is subject to many of the same laws that apply to common radio waves, light waves, and water waves.

The **primal absolute Paradise circuit wave**, now being revealed and taught on Urantia in **Continuing Fifth Epochal Revelation**, is of the Universal Father, the First Cause. It is sung into existence by the Father in the harmonics of the Paradise center. The Creator Sons and the Universe Mother Spirits hear that first causation pattern and tap into it to create their universes. They too sing all into existence and play the master-harp patterns as instruments tapping into this master-harp pattern of the First Cause. It is the divine symphony, the symphony of preexistent pattern in celestial harmonics. This eternal master-pattern vibration is heard at various levels by descending and ascending personalities. The highest level could not be measured by mortal mathematics.

When mortals on evolutionary worlds receive their Thought Adjusters, that hearing ability is registered with the calculated mean mode to hear that First Cause, or primal absolute Paradise circuit wave. Each ascending personality at all levels has an individual primal absolute hearing assent capacity.

There is also a planetary level of **primal absolute hearing assent capacity**, and there is a primal absolute hearing assent capacity constant for descending beings that is a perfect constant. It is unchangeable, eternal, and complete. Outside of the seven superuniverses and into the Havona worlds, that primal circuit is resonated within unison patterns to ever-increasing levels of hearing assent. The existent creations created by this hearing level ascension are almost unexplainable at your level. To explain it within the context of any language on Urantia, including English, would be like trying to teach quantum physics to a kindergarten child.

Quantum physics is based upon a theory in physics that introduces the concept of the subdivision of radiant energy into finite quanta and applied to numerous processes involving transference or transformation of energy in an atomic or molecular scale.

Quantum physics within Continuing Fifth Epochal Revelation brings into categorical balances some known Urantian scientific terminology such as: frequencies, interaction of waves, reinforced waves, diminished waves, canceled waves, complex interference, and intensity. All of these terms are understood at levels of some mathematical adherence, but in the fusion of science with spirituality (ascension science), it is understood that reality itself on any one level reflects a personality's ability to tap into the primal absolute Paradise circuit wave.

Both loudness and pitch may undergo change when two or more sound waves intervene with one another. If they are out of phase, they neutralize or cancel each other. Two sounds of equal intensity of opposite waves would actually register in the ear as total silence.

It should be understood at this time that Lucifer distorted the hearing of the primal absolute Paradise circuit wave. He was able to distort this reception at various levels, and the degree of fall of each individual personality depends upon his or her assent to that distorted reception. It was written in the first century, "So then faith cometh by hearing, and hearing by the word of God."[1]

If the sounds are completely in phase, that is, the peaks of compression and valleys of rarefaction march in step with each other, the sound waves will reinforce each other to produce a sound of higher intensity.

All of the terminologies that were mentioned above are important in interdimensional and interplanetary reality in relationship to one's assent to God and in the understanding of why you have the body you have, why certain brain cells in your brain are open or unopened, and why you have or do not have certain abilities, talents, etc.

Frequency denotes a number of vibrations. When the mind is in a higher frequency, these vibrations are the vibrations of harmony. Harmony is the vibration of absoluteness, and absoluteness is the vibration coming from the First Source and Center in relation to order and presence.

On the lower evolutionary worlds it is the time of most peace within the body when most thoughts are actually vibrating in harmony. When the thoughts are not vibrating in harmony, disruptive frequencies begin. These disruptive frequencies actually create sound patterns and waves within each body that disrupt the very cellular flow within that body. The intensity of this disruption or interaction of waves either reinforces or diminishes one's ability to assent to the Thought Adjuster, Spirit of Truth, or Holy Spirit. At any one particular moment it can actually cancel out all reception from God, and in moments of anger, violent thoughts, or selfish attitudes this creates a complex interference of the primal absolute Paradise circuit wave, and it is distorted within the body.

So long as the distortion continues, the greater the chance for disease to happen within the body. This disease can be temporarily alleviated by various methods of healing, but it cannot be totally diminished until the thoughts themselves begin to vibrate with the absolute patterns of the first primal wave.

If two personalities are in unalignment with one another at any level and they do not march in step with each other, the sound waves will not reinforce each other, and this disturbance will cause a higher intensity of inappropriate cellular patterns within the body. This will cause a feeling of dislike between them and an uncomfortable feeling in that person's presence.

If you are a person with some capacity to discern truth, listening to someone who is not speaking truth, or just being in the same room with them, can cause great discomfort within your body by disrupting the flow of the **Deo-atomic structures** by the sound waves of **intraction language** coming through the air and transmitted inward through signals from the brain and central nervous system to the Paradise center of your **heart circuit**.

But now suppose that two sound waves differ slightly in frequency. At one moment they will reinforce each other, and at another moment they will partially or wholly cancel each other out. The ear will hear a new sound different from either of its components. Continuing Fifth Epochal Revelation teaches that inappropriate relationships cause the inability of one to hear what the other is saying, just as sounds cancel each other out when they vibrate at opposing frequencies.

But now suppose the opposite occurs by hearing one single frequency. A tuning fork when properly struck emits just such a note. You say on your world, Urantia, to tune in to God. The sound waves of a tuning fork produce a symmetrical graph of smoothly curving peaks and valleys that are equally spaced. This pure tone is called a sine wave, which has a special importance in physical sound.

Sine waves are the basic building blocks of sound, comparable to atoms in matter. Just as complex mixtures of compounds can be broken down into atoms, so the many different tones of a symphony can be analyzed into sine waves. The sine waves of a musical note turn out to bear a most simple relationship to each other; each is an overtone, or harmonic.

Continuing Fifth Epochal Revelation teaches a synthesis of master universe harmonics. It should be understood that on all levels of physical and nonphysical reality, sound is first heard by higher Paradise personalities to create matter. Without sound, matter cannot be created. Form in preexistent patterns can only be shaped in a physical creation reality by a created sound pattern.

Form can only be created through the assent of an ascender's mind and heart. Form is then fused with mind to produce structure. Always and eternally the evolutionary artist has more creative freedom than the architectural engineer. It is the artist who is able to take more artistic license with the majority of artistic endeavors; the architectural engineer works with factual knowledge. It is the artist who has the ability to draw forth creation at any level of primal adherence far above a scientific architectural mind of analytical acquiescence to a lower divine pattern that is a reflection of the primal absolute Paradise circuit wave.

There is less distinction between the artist and the architect in higher worlds. Both the artist and the architect can receive lower levels of transcendental wisdom. The artist-architect is confined to present building materials known on Urantia. The artist-painter is confined by absence of color. The artist-musician is confined by the nature of the instruments available to produce sound. All are limited by the mass consciousness with whom they are trying to share their art, unless they create only for themselves. Inspirations at various levels are the result of the reflective personality guide or preexistent form given to the human evolutionary mortal or nonmortal at any one level.

Keeping in mind that all physical matter is created by the adherence to the master symphony, it should be understood that planets themselves vibrate in harmonic patterns to an interplanetary harmonic sister-planet coordination form structure, just as vibrations vibrate in duplicate patterns, such as in a scale of a note—440 vibrations per second being the lowest note, the next octave 880 vibrations per second, and the next higher octave at 1,760 vibrations per second. The very rotation of planets around central suns coordinates in a sound pattern based upon this same principle. Tapping into the planetary sound pattern at spiritual levels is a great gift given only to personalities when they can be trusted with an overcontrol capacity for the good of others at whatever level this personality can be trusted.

The first mandate of corporate responsibility is the **Mandate of the Bright and Morning Star**. This is basically because there is only one Bright and Morning Star within a universe who first begins to tap into the primal absolute Paradise circuit wave of the superuniverse for that particular universe. After the creation perfection of the Bright and Morning Star, each and every creation that is subsequently brought into existence by the Creator Son and Universe Mother

Spirit becomes the responsibility of the Bright and Morning Star. On an evolutionary planet, the human personality with the overcontrol Mandate of the Bright and Morning Star is eventually brought to the responsibility for each and every person on that planet.

A note on a stringed instrument, when strummed, will vibrate the neighboring string if the neighboring string is positioned by the finger for the same note; they become in tune. So, you begin to see that pure sound affects the string next to it. Continuing Fifth Epochal Revelation begins to teach that your very thoughts affect the persons closest to you. The vibration of the person closest to you will determine how you are affected, either negatively or positively. The power of a higher ascension person who defaults can affect each and every person on a planet at some level of negative influence.

When a beautiful symphony of the first primal absolute Paradise circuit wave was created, trillions upon trillions upon trillions of perfect patterns in color and form coordinating themselves with the divine harmonic patterns throughout the master universe were set in motion. Within this pattern, secret codes stemming from Paradise found themselves imbedded in time and space at distances trillions of light-years from Paradise. From the very beginning, it was known by the Eternal Father that a creation of the Paradise Source would one day hear that symphony at that distance. It was also known that in this hearing a new universe would be constructed.

In the spirit world you are not limited by body, and when we tap into these higher patterns we can flow with the sound of perfection, and we can travel these distances of millions and trillions of light-years in a matter of a few Urantian moments. You, who are in evolutionary bodies and in various morontia bodies in the universe of Nebadon and others like it, are limited to the degree of your assent to cosmic absolute primal sounds and your ability to create any program tool, or whatever it may be, by that inspirational ability to tap into that primal sound wave at any level. The circumstances of your planet will determine what you will be able to manifest into your reality to complement that which you have just envisioned.

On worlds that have not fallen into rebellion, divine principle is created by an artist within a matter of moments. A bridge the size of the Golden Gate Bridge in San Francisco, California can be built in a matter of ten Urantian minutes with the same strength and equal design pattern if, for any reason, that bridge can serve a practical purpose. If not, then the thought itself is useless. Better one bridge in that location on Urantia serving many people than 10,000 bridges built only because of the pride of the architect. On Urantia thousands of these bridges would be quite appropriate in other places, but the time involved and other circumstances prohibit their building. On other planets this is not the case. These bridges would not even have to be material; they could be created by sound patterns. They can be broken down and rebuilt in a matter of moments, depending upon the mandate of the personality building it and the need of other personalities in that area who are bound to Earth. If one cannot fly, one needs mechanical means to do so or one needs a bridge in order to cross.

The Creator Son and Daughter create the materials that are unusable for many ascending sons and daughters until they reach a higher form of morontia body. On Urantia at this time these materials are nonexistent for use, but on higher worlds they are existent and used by ascending mortals. These materials can be built by humankind by existent materials on Earth, but this science is unknown on Urantia. All of this has to do with the stages of light and life.

Quantum physics in a fusion with spirituality can build bridges in time and space, not only across rivers, mountains, and oceans, but across planets and across universes. Travel in space by creatures limited by physical bodies and physical matter is restricted because of the personality's inability to serve others, to put others first before themselves, or to get along with others. When you fuse with your Thought Adjuster, your ability to travel greater distances is a result of your ability to tap into the primal absolute Paradise circuit wave.

We would never prohibit a personality from fusing with a Thought Adjuster on any level, even though he may have a mandate on a particular world as high as that of the Bright and Morning Star. And if, in that mandate, that personality was meant to stay on Urantia in the fusion, he would return in a new body. In that case, it would be more appropriately called a **rematerialization**.

This has happened on several worlds. On Urantia, Enoch was one who fused with his Thought Adjuster and did not return. On some worlds, those who have fused had to return, and immediately. One should never fear fusion at any level, for one will fulfill one's destiny purpose according to the design of the Creator Son and the Eternal Father.

Evolutionary scientists on Urantia talk about the Big Bang Theory. They express the origin of creation in terms of sound in their own way without realizing it, or perhaps on some level they realize it to some degree. However, it should be understood that the first sound of the creation was not a bang at all, but a masterful symphony of integrated and differential vibrations that created all color, all form, all structure, all design, all cohesion, all harmonics, all frequencies, and all inspiration. At that moment, this great symphony put into effect eternity-present, eternity-past, and eternity-future. Wherever you are located at this time and thought is the result of the ability of yourself and/or of your ancestors to tap into that symphony.

It is known on your world at some level that music is healing to many. To the insane it brings a form of stability. In much of what is called sound healing, certain vibrations, rhythms, and melodies do indeed temporarily soothe the listener. The reason for this has been unknown until now. The reason that the insane are temporarily healed, and in some cases permanently healed, is because they have tapped into cosmic absolute truth at an abstract level. They have heard a truth before they understood it. Truth can be heard but not understood. Truth is sound in harmonics. Absolute truth is music in form. It can be heard before it is understood, and at whatever level it resonates, it is healing to disease of any kind.

If it is an inharmonic pattern, it can cause the opposite effect. That is why so many personalities today on Urantia are suffering from psychological problems and disturbances. The noise level on Urantia and the vibrations on Urantia are at a level now of dysfunction and delusion. This will rapidly increase until the final **change point**, as has been previously discussed.

Animals will also feel this effect, and even machinery will be affected. The reason why machinery also can be affected is because it is technologically designed in a sequence pattern, and all mechanical movement must proceed in sequence. When these sequences are disturbed at any point along the flow from one operation to another, the machine will break down, either at a level not detected at first or in a complete breakdown.

With fallen **ovan souls**—those souls who have been repersonalized many times on fallen worlds because of their inability to reach the higher circles of attainment, but by the grace of the Creator Son and the Ancients of Days have been allowed to re-enter those dimensional realities—the upstepping of the frequencies (particularly in the adjudication now on Urantia, or any planet that is in the adjudication process) will cause disturbances in the frequencies within their bodies. What they accept, if it is untruth, is a sound that is unpleasant to their **Deo-atomic reality**. What they listen to, what they hear, what they accept of the Lucifer Rebellion at any level coming through the eyes and ears into the brain and through the **crown circuit** (which is the circuit of clairvoyant perception) causes the crown circuit to malfunction.

When the crown circuit malfunctions, it sends a mixed signal to the heart circuit and prevents unity with brothers and sisters on the planet in corporate endeavor. In the correlation of this negativity, the whole body begins to malfunction. If it continues for any length of time, it will begin to cause great problems. In females it will begin to manifest in the breasts and eventually cause breast cancer. In males it will begin to manifest in the lower body and can cause kidney, stomach, and liver cancer.

All of this could be prevented by a person's ability to accept only truth when he or she hears it and allows that sound wave to resonate within the body. Other sound waves of untruth would not be able to enter the circuitry within the body unless the person chose to let it enter. A person can choose to let untruth enter by misplaced relative thinking and saying things like: "All truth is truth," or "Your truth is your truth and my truth is my truth," or "I perceive your truth and will let your truth digest within my system." If it is not truth, you are letting distortion waves digest within your system, which will eat away your reality, just like acid would eat away your outer skin.

In this adjudication process, upstepped as it is now, when you invite distortions into your ears you disrupt the primal circuit from the crown to the heart. You give signals to your brain to misuse itself, and you will begin to have lower thoughts and lower appetites; your reality will be lower, and you will not be able to come into your higher self or higher reality, to reach your higher body or to reach the fourth dimension.

What this is saying is that you need to learn what absolute reality is in relation to the first pattern, the primal absolute Paradise circuit wave. You need to realize that it exists, and you need to flow with it and to stop allowing deception and lower distorted circuitry into your primal circuit. It is one thing to get it from the ear to a portion of your brain, but if it is cast out by another portion of your brain in a matter of seconds, then it can have no harmful effect on you. But if these thoughts of negativity begin to circulate within your brain, they will begin to flow in the very DNA within every part of your body. Depending upon many circumstances, they will have their effect.

This is why treatments of first-degree Reiki, first-level **tron therapy**, and the balancing of the energy flows may create temporary relief, but they will not bring permanent relief, for universal life force (or more appropriately, **cellular sound wave frequencies**) at first comes into a source-center in the body by the primal absolute hearing assent capacity and must be understood at some level by each and every person or he or she simply will not be healed. All healers are wasting their time and efforts if the astral body of the ovan soul, or even the emotional or psychological mind of the **first-time Urantian**, does not assent to the truth of Fifth Epochal Revelation and Continuing at some level. At whatever level you let distortion waves into your reality, that is the level of distortion you will receive.

On some planets where sound is closer to absolute levels within finiteness, sexual intimacy is actually not even needed. A climax can be reached simply by listening and nothing else. On higher worlds when climax is reached using this method, a different form of sperm is created, and these cells resonate and are attracted to the primal absolute Paradise circuit wave and they complement preexistent reality, and you become part of eternity pattern, helping at that point to create future eternity.

So, in your acquiescence the highest pure tone of your thoughts can be used by a Creator Son to recreate your thoughts in another universe. This is the only way that you can become a co-creator. This is the only way that you can create something from nothing, but the reality of it is that you never know what is created by your contribution. You never know until you reach another level of ascension, which could take you thousands, perhaps millions, of years.

Every step of the way you have to continually learn to discern what you should not hear and see. One of the great problems on Urantia today is that most of the 170,000,000 starseed are relative thinkers. They have digested into themselves everything that you can think of within all the evolutionary thought patterns of this planet and have walked in this familiar reality, familiar also to Overcontrol. It has a name; it is called **unstabilized incongruent personality pattern**.

Before those who work in the astral under the Mandate of the Bright and Morning Star learn how to change the pattern structures within the brain, they must first learn to become counselors. It is of no use to change the energy flow within the body unless you can change the energy flow within the brain.

It is here that we get into a whole different category of healing, but only the highest healers on the planet will be taught and instructed in it. It will be kept secret to all others, for they would only use it for personal power. So transmissions that deal with this subject will not even be printed in the Continuing Fifth Epochal Revelation books but will be in separate texts used only for training chosen tron therapists. The subject will be called **primal brain flow circuitry patterns**.

The brain in each personality has its own individual pattern based upon the personality bestowal of the Eternal Father. This is a subject of immense complexity, but in order for that which is called Reiki to operate in context with true healing, it must work within the astral Mandate of the Bright and Morning Star. That is why, on this planet, all Reiki teachers and all Reiki practitioners who do not come under the Mandate of the Bright and Morning Star will not be able to heal totally. Even if the person is a first-time Urantian, it is doubtful that any permanent healing will take place. Reiki thus far has come to a place where it has tapped into a higher understanding of healing, but it cannot continue any further without coming into proper context within Divine Administration.

Homeopathic treatment would only be temporary relief, a Band-Aid on the problem. Only correct thinking and acting can truly heal, not just the counseling but the knowing in the individual ascender.

Louise Hay's ideas regarding emotional, mental, and psychological causes of ailments have some truth, not the highest truth or the highest definitions of those concepts, but the beginning, and it is useful at that level.

One of the problems of stabilization is that dio particles find themselves meshed in a certain part of an individual's life force, dio integration. These **dio** particles remain in the life force, even though you may have walked in higher areas of **Deo power** during much of your life in past lives. If all of the dio is not removed, it can surface and exist within the life force of the physical body and in parts of the brain, and certain chemical reactions can trigger the dio.

In starseed dio is carried on in the astral reality from one personalization to the next, and it could crop up thousands of years later. We make it resurface, even if you do not want it to resurface. That is what we are trying to do here at the **First Planetary Sacred Home** and why it is so hard to be here. Then when it does come up, souls cannot take it. They do not want to deal with their dio. They do not see it and blame it on the other person, and so they are gone and never get healed. That is what the adjudication is all about. Welcome to rebellion.

When the experiment of mandating human personalities with divine mandates was first appropriated, there was a great debate about the "stupidity" of giving the mandate to animalistic minds. Of course, you might say that the gods had already made up their minds, but we still can interact in our own opinions and speculations.

The difficulty in trying to reach your deeper problem is that you do not see it. Even after you are told a thousand different ways, you do not see it. It does not connect. Something is not functioning right; there is a short-circuiting somewhere, and you do not see it. Statistically, we have found that if it is said to you in a variety of ways for long enough, and within the Father circuits, and within the Mother circuits, and within the linear phraseology of the Son circuits (not leaning towards Father or Mother circuitry but rather just stating the facts), at some point something will click in you as an individual soul.

However, it may take hundreds of years for one aspect of a spiritual defect to be cleared, but somewhere down the line you may have had an inkling of light that may have begun thirty Urantian years before, and during those years, that click may have hit you once a month, once every three months, or once every three years, and it was able to register in your circuits long enough that you would say, "Well, maybe that was right, but no, I can't handle it right now." So, you are not able to deal with it. Until you are ready to deal with it, you lose it, and it is gone.

So, here at the First Planetary Sacred Home we have set up a program so that you cannot forget about it. We bring it into your mind more often so that you might not let it go this time, and you at least might dwell on it for twenty seconds. Those twenty seconds may be the most valuable twenty seconds of your whole life. That is why you are here again on the planet, to be healed. Something just clicked!

Once it clicks, that's the whole thing, but you cannot understand that if you are out there in the world and no one is confronting you; you would be alone with your God, perhaps, and it would never click. Certain circumstances would have to be created in your third-dimensional reality where you could be dying because of it, and you wake up and ask, "Why did I die?". Then they tell you why you died and why you got that disease that killed you, and you still may not see it, but you have a better chance there.

Here we are trying to teach you a lot, and so, in order to do that, you have to see it. Here it is not as if you can die and wake up and be standing in front of the morontia companions and angels with them telling you, which makes it a little easier to see; then you would have passed on, and you would have some picturization of memory. But here, as I said, "divine mandates to animalistic minds in rebellion?!" Again, what is a divine mandate? We couldn't really even get into it for it would make your heads even bigger than they are. I hope you are at least able to see the dilemma.

Gabriel of Urantia/TaliasVan of Tora knows that it is very difficult for the counselors, and that they really need to pray and ask the Spirit of Truth when they are counseling individuals. If you are not quite sure about an area to give advice in, do not give it. It is best not to give advice in an area that you know nothing about or you are not quite sure about.

At least you may be able to hear the doubt and say that you do not really have the answer here, but perhaps your superior does or Gabriel of Urantia/TaliasVan of Tora does. Do not try to handle something that you are not quite sure of. Check with your more experienced superior. You have access to spiritual forces who can help you in these areas. That is what we are giving you in these transmissions in order for as much group growth as possible. We cannot do it in relation to individual problems.

What we do is bring the transmission through based upon the highest level possible for the majority in the community of Divine Administration. We give all the information we can about the circuits and how they work, based upon the reality of those on the highest circles in the human Divine Administration. Since there are not a lot of you on the first circle, we use the ones on the second and first, and, of course, the third.

The transmissions are primarily oriented to those on the third circle. The majority of the students are not yet stabilized on the third circle, but unless they have the information to get them there, they will never get there. Keep in mind that there is a difference in the stabilization of the **starseed** and Urantians on the third circle.

You might be a living saint and be on the first circle as a Urantian and not be in touch with any other dimensional reality that would enable you to administer anything because you do not have the experience to do that. You have the desire, the willingness, and the virtue, so that you can be taught and trained, but you do not have the experience, the circumstantial reality reasoning. Until you do, you are quite limited in how you can function. You can have **Deo function** but not Deo power, so you can only be used in a certain way.

If you have stabilized on the third circle as a starseed, you draw in millions and millions of experiences that you can utilize in your moment-to-moment reality to help someone else, and that is what it is all about, helping someone else. The whole concept of this work is so that people can more highly see for themselves in a higher Deo reality.

That is why it is much more important to bring the evolving soul to the higher concepts of absolute truth than it is to feed them physical food. Jesus demonstrated that 2,000 years ago. This example was to teach that they had to come to Him for a higher reason than just physical food or needs. Sometimes it is better not to give people the physical things that they need until they are really ready to do some soul growth, change some wrong thinking and bad habits. Don't feed the addict.

It is difficult for Gabriel of Urantia/TaliasVan of Tora, but we keep on saying to all of you that the evaluation of people's entrance into this community of Divine Administration is higher now than it was before. We had to allow certain things then that we cannot allow now. We do not have to allow them because we now have a certain quota of Destiny Reservists here who would not be here if we had not allowed the others here.

If we would have had an ideal situation, three quarters of the people that have come here in the past would not have gotten even lesson one. Down the road, yes, when you have a functioning administration, functioning in Deo power, then you can handle all kinds, whatever level they are on, because they are further removed from you. They have to be further removed from you, for you have to function at a certain level; you cannot come down to their level anymore. When you do, you make a mistake.

The Fourth Epochal Revelation is not the Fifth or the Continuing Fifth. Jesus, in bringing the Fourth Epochal Revelation and walking and teaching among you, was not setting up the Divine Administration on the planet; you are. You cannot put yourself in the place of Jesus all the time. That is a mistake, a big one. "Jesus did it this way so I should do it too." Oh no, no, no! You cannot say "What did Jesus do?" all the time, based upon the midwayers' presentation. That is what Gabriel of Urantia/TaliasVan of Tora is beginning to learn.

How does the Bright and Morning Star administer a universe? I will give you part of the answer to that. That is a good realization to open up in each of you. You delegate authority, and you trust that authority to handle the situation. It is the delegate that you counsel and deal with, not the person on the lower level. Do you understand what I am saying? That is the simplicity of it, and that is why we work so hard on all of you here, because you are the foundation. Once we build this foundation, the thousands can come. Until we have that foundation, God forbid.

Now we have Gabriel of Urantia/TaliasVan of Tora and Niánn Emerson Chase—wonderful, loving people of humility and then some—down there talking to everyone who wants their attention as soon as they hear about it. Even if they are not with them physically, they are there in their minds, right? It is the job of each Liaison Minister and each Elder to protect, first Gabriel/TaliasVan and Niánn, next the other Liaison Ministers, and then all the Elders, from handling areas that they shouldn't be handling, once they understand the specific areas of function within the Deo power that has been given them along the way. The Deo power and function will change from time to time for all of you. You are understanding it now at a higher level, and it is part of our task to teach it to you.

It is hard to talk about, but I have told you from the beginning that this is a new experiment. It is not as if you can take the government structure of the United States and use that in Divine Administration. You can't do it that way, or you would have a congress and a supreme court that blocks the ideas, convictions, insights, and everything else of the President who is supposed to be in control. That is the problem with the government of the United States—there is no leadership; there is just argument between everyone.

A group cannot be in control of anything. Why? A body of individuals who are unique, expanding, and diverse in individuality cannot give commands. There is so much individuality that there is no power there. That is why divine administration is individual power all the way up. On the superuniverse level we have three personalities, but three who work as one, and all along the way we have one, one, one.

It is a tremendous responsibility that is being asked of Gabriel of Urantia/TaliasVan of Tora; something that at times he does not want to look at. I can understand that. At the same time, he does not see himself with the power that he should have, based upon the reality that he has to be in right now. Until there is a higher understanding here among all of you, a lot of what he would like to implement cannot really be implemented. There has to be a lot of thought given as to whether something should be done this way or that way so that you are not interfering with divine order. It is a hard thing to teach.

Gandhi was the same loving soul who could have been Mahatma (great soul) when he was thirty, but it took him until he was sixty. But once he was Mahatma, people listened. Before that, he had little power. We do not have the time here at the First Planetary Sacred Home for Gabriel of Urantia/TaliasVan of Tora to become a Mahatma. Recognition has to happen now among the foundation core and then among the rest of the people.

I personally feel that in the corps of the Eldership here now, that is happening, and it has to happen among the First and **Second Assistants**. Right now we have to mandate individuals based more upon their potentials than upon the actuality of that mandate. Until we can begin to mandate based more upon actualities, we have a dilemma.

Once Gabriel of Urantia/TaliasVan of Tora is a Mahatma, then that power can change the course of this planet and hopefully the rest of the millions out there. If his ministry becomes public, and he makes this jump before the final change point, and the public recognizes the Mandate of the Bright and Morning Star, then the terrible things that otherwise would happen will not. What is important is the public recognition of the Mandate of the Bright and Morning Star, as Gabriel's ascension alone cannot bring the planet to the first stage of light and life.

The understanding of sound waves and the **primal absolute Paradise circuit wave** correlation with the primal density patterns of the brain would be the only way that an ovan soul or a first-time Urantian who needs to ascend to a higher circle of attainment and into the **fourth dimension** can be permanently healed. This is the first of a series of transmissions in this treatise. Again, the secrets of the circuitry flow of the brain patterns will not be given in this present series of transmissions. After this series of transmissions are given, then we will give the intra-community transmissions to Gabriel of Urantia/TaliasVan of Tora to be read among the Elders and those chosen of the **First Assistants** to receive tron therapy training.

This information is to be highly guarded and can only be given to individuals who have aligned themselves to the community within mandated positions under the Bright and Morning Star mandate, and only under the instruction of the Eldership. So, if you wish to learn about how the brain operates in conjunction with divine will in healing, then you must submit yourself as a student in **The Starseed and Urantian Schools of Melchizedek** [now called the **Global Community Communications Schools**], and perhaps you will be chosen for such learning, for you indeed are needed. But as it is written: "But seek ye first the kingdom of God and His righteousness, and all things will be given unto you."[2] Be diligent, study, and prove yourself, so that you too can become perfect and acceptable in God's sight.

August 13, 1992

Paladin, Chief of Finaliters
in cooperation with Life Carriers of four different universes, Physical Controllers, Universal Censors, Universe Master Physical Controllers, and a Perfector of Wisdom, coordinating with the Bright and Morning Star of Salvington and at the planetary level Machiventa Melchizedek, Planetary Prince of

Urantia, for the implementation of the Divine Administration on Urantia in liaison with mandated human personalities and other students aspiring to that status

As transmitted through
the Pre-Level-One Audio Fusion Material Complement,
Gabriel of Urantia/TaliasVan of Tora

PAPER 252

The Mortal Ear, In This Case The Human Ear, Has The Receiver Unit Of All Energies Of Paradise Circuitry; The Paradise Circuits From Upper Paradise And Energy Circuits Of Nether Paradise In Relationship To Cosmic Absolute Paradise Virtues, Perfected Harmonic Frequencies, And The Understanding Of This Audio Sensor Unit In Relationship To The One-, Two-, And Three-Brained Types As Transmitters To The Body Of The Commands, The Creations, And The Laws Of The First Source And Center, Receiving From Other Human Or Mortal Personalities And/Or Interdimensional And Interplanetary Personalities, All In Some Capacity Tapping Into The Primal Absolute Paradise Circuit Wave

IT has been discovered in various known stages over the last several hundred years on Urantia that in hearing, the stapes or stirrup of the human ear passes the vibrations on to the oval window (fenestra ovalis)—a membrane covering the opening of the bony case of the cochlea—and thus into the fluid inside the cochlea. The pressure variations in this liquid continually excite the nerve endings to generate signals to the brain. It is the side of the oval window that produces the critical increase of amplification needed to match impedance between sound waves in the air and in the cochlear fluid.

At this time you must ask a question. How is sound in the inner ear changed from a vibration to a nerve impulse? Science understands that the brain can interpret and select signals passed to it by the ear, but how this is done is unknown at this time. I would now like to give you some beginning information on how that is done within the higher understanding of ascension science, concept upon concept and precept upon precept, with the fusion of past teachings of celestial mechanics, cellular and **Deo-atomic** cellular reality, **diotribe** cellular "reality" within the body, force energies from Paradise, and so many other factors.

Encased within the cochlea is an important organ. It is called the Organ of Corti or the spiral organ. The Organ of Corti actually acts as a transmitter of sorts and as a transducer to send messages to the central nervous system, based upon the impedance matches of absolute truth and law and perfect harmonic sequences stemming from Paradise. **Continuing Fifth Epochal Revelation** teaches that all matter was sung into existence, beginning with the Paradise Father and on the local universe level, the tapping into the **primal absolute Paradise circuit wave** by the Universe Creator Son and the Universe Creative Mother Spirit.

The circuitry network from the human ear to the brain acts as a **censorship command center** between **will-sound personalities** and **nonwill sound**. There are various stations of censorship between the ear and the brain, and actually in other parts of the body at various levels, all very complicated, but censorship begins in the ear and the eardrum and inward to the brain.

The first auditory levels of censorship consist of intricate networks all designed at various levels to censor out that which is nonabsolute and imperfect. That which is imperfect and nonabsolute that does enter through this network system begins a death process in the brain itself and in other areas of the body, which leads to final transition from this planet.

Personalities who are born deaf are the result of the genetics of ancestors or their human parents who have been unable to hear from the Eternal Father and the Paradise circuits at higher levels. However, those who are deaf can develop an auditory sensing capacity based upon another form of auditory sensation, a vibrational reception that can at times be even more accurate than audio hearing. It will be discovered in the years ahead that when truth is taught at an early age to children who are born deaf, their hearing impairment will be cured by the time they are five to seven years old.

Deafness in chronologically aged individuals on Urantia can be, and in many cases is, the result of pride, arrogance, and the inability of that personality, either Urantian or cosmic, to listen to others. In the case of a humble personality who is born deaf, even one born without an eardrum, he or she can actually grow one if higher cosmic principles can be taught to that child at the very earliest stages, based upon the understanding of the age of that soul. At this time on Urantia, it is almost impossible to properly care for these individuals outside of the **First Planetary Sacred Home**.

There are various sensing networks. One transducer network has a very small, almost minute circuitry of 7,500 different sensing transformers that are visible under a microscope. Each sensing separator directs will sound and nonwill sound to a particular part of the brain.

It is not the context of this transmission to teach that which is already known in Urantian science; we will only repeat necessary scientific facts. For Continuing Fifth Epochal Revelation to be understood, it is required that students of it must also be students of that which is already known and that which has already been discovered in the process of evolutionary mind on this planet. We are not here to re-teach that which has been found out by humans hundreds or thousands of years ago. We are here to bring epochal revelation based upon known fact.

All of these sensors, transformers, and sensory detectors are based upon one criterion alone, which is sensing the absolute virtue character and personality presence of the bestowal Father. Since it is the Universal Father who bestows personality, absolute virtue is required for higher hearing.

On evolutionary worlds, and particularly on defaulted ones such as Urantia, nonwill sounds from personalities who promote deceptions and rebellious thinking are the greatest poison that can be ingested into the body. Hearing distorted truth or nontruth is worse than digesting pure acid. At least you know that you have taken poison and that it takes effect immediately. But the distorted vibrations produced from wrong hearing received in and through the sensors to the brain create wrong thinking, which in turn causes malfunctions in the body in thousands of ways. It stunts the physical growth of the body. It slows down or raises the metabolism. It can create every known disease on this planet. It causes insanity.

For some who are born deaf on Urantia, it can actually be a blessing, for at this time on Urantia they are held less accountable and are not judged by the Ancients of Days because of the inability of their ancestors to hear the absoluteness of God. Many of these personalities are protected from the insanities of deception on Urantia. It is unfortunate that they cannot hear will sound and the beauty of another absolute area of God's creation, but many begin to pick up vibratory frequencies at another level and carry a certain form of usage, tapping into the primal absolute Paradise circuit wave without knowing what it is. Many of them do so to a much higher degree than most of those who can hear audible sounds.

Thousands of **virtue sensors** placed in various appropriate parts of the body are protective sensors of the glands and all the seven circuits. At each stage along the way a correlation between brain and organs can completely eliminate a diotribe, based upon readjusted thinking, or what has become known in Christian terminology as repentance. We prefer to use the word realignment.

It is not the context of this transmission to discuss morality virtues based upon cosmic absolutes, for this is an interuniversal subject that other transmissions have begun to touch upon because of the uniqueness of interuniversal reality. However, there are certain unit factors that measure the degree in which the freewill human is able to function in relationship to the spiritualizing efforts of their assigned celestial personalities, based upon certain cosmic absolutes that are taught in Continuing Fifth Epochal Revelation as to the nature of God and the master universe that all must recognize to be absolute.

Earlier transmissions have dealt with various subjects in relationship to the formation of the human body. Height, metabolism, length of arms and fingers, teeth, and the size of various body parts all have to do with hearing sound and the way the mind interprets what is heard based upon absolute design. Inability of the personality to interpret at the highest levels begins to cause disease in the body at some level. **Ovan souls** are more properly bodily activated than new souls. Souls may have beautiful bodies but be very iniquitous inside. If they remain this way, you will hardly recognize them when and if you meet them again upon transition from this planet.

If you are a **starseed**, you have once had what you are lacking now. The kind of body you would like to have, or think you should have, probably is the body that you once had, and for whatever reasons, certain of your body parts have degenerated because of unaligned thinking based upon certain glandular circuit receptivity formation motions that govern how the body parts form as a result of astral-mind thinking. Ovan souls more or less dictate their physical bodies each time they repersonalize on this planet or on any other evolutionary world. They also formulate their morontia bodies.

For true permanent healing to take place, the various techniques of healing such as color therapy, sound therapy, music therapy, crystal healing, or any other forms of healing must be understood in context of the age of the source cells, the higher subatomic particle reality of the higher body before the fall in relation to the ascension of the soul. This form of higher healing can only be done at the First Planetary Sacred Home, working with the astral body in and through the **Mandate of the Bright and Morning Star**.

Even after the final **change point** and far into the first stages of light and life, **repersonalizations** of diseased ovan souls will continue on Urantia. All will be healed at various levels of their body formations. What is beginning now on

Urantia at the First Planetary Sacred Home in this early stage will continually be much more highly understood in the future and be more appropriately used and functioning.

All of these concepts must begin to be understood within the context of the divine mind functioning corporately within the Eldership and the healing team at a level resonating with the first circle of attainment. As long as there are personalities on the healing team in particular, and also within the Eldership, functioning on the third circle to the first, there will be a lesser response in those lower-level personalities to regenerate their own healing functions. Therefore, it will be more difficult for them to heal others.

The fusion of spirituality with cosmic science is based upon the ability of the personality to understand the personality of God the Father in and through the relationship of the male and female, ascending sons and daughters, on the lower evolutionary worlds such as Urantia. The differences that exist between male and female are differences of function and not differences of absolute virtue. Goodness is a quality of divine bestowal void of selfishness. Where goodness and unselfishness are recognized by others, then those individuals who recognize this about you can hear more from you than they would from others.

Whatever you take in from anyone is based upon what you allow in, and what you allow in is usually based upon something you see in that person that resonates with some sort of frequency vibration within you. However, you must become a very high discerner of what it is about another personality that makes you want to be with them, to be near them, or to hear from them. The majority of the world is void of this kind of discernment, so they indiscriminately ingest sounds into their auditory system that vibrate within their body at distortion and dysfunction capacity and create various diseases of the body and eventually death itself.

It is said on Urantia, "Oh, what's the difference? Everyone has to die." It is even taught by some Christian teachers. However, if this world had not suffered dispensational defaults, transition from this planet to morontia realities for some mortals would happen without what is now known as "natural death." To the few who may be able to realign themselves to the **unit-factor** potential of the primal absolute Paradise circuit wave and hear what the voice of God is saying to the seven **cosmic families** resident on Urantia today, acquiescence with higher frequencies is a must.

Even animal life and insect life can tap into the primal absolute Paradise circuit wave, but now they are unable to tap into it because of the pollution of the planet's land, sea, and air, and the relationship between all life forms has become unbalanced and out of sequence.

On this planet you talk about overpopulation being a problem. It is not overpopulation that is the problem; it is the inability of those in power to tap into the primal absolute Paradise circuit wave at higher levels over the centuries to properly develop landmasses to feed, house, and educate people. There is plenty of land on Urantia for the population of this planet.

It is unfortunate that the majority of people on this planet are unable to find their own individual destiny in God and have no one to lead them. They live in a distortion of sounds—starting from the voices of their government leaders, their religious teachers, and through the media of print, radio, television, and films. In the larger cities there are distortions of sounds, noise from machinery, horns blowing, sirens blaring, and huge diesel engines choking for fuel.

The auditory systems of the ear are quite capable of higher reception purposes and can actually hear from angelic personalities up to the Paradise level if necessary. But because of other distorted hearing from childhood, very few on the planet, with the exception of certain mandated personalities, can hear celestial personalities. That which has become known as the inner voice is actually the reception of whatever guide who is a voice or messenger of God for that moment for you. The Thought Adjuster speaks in another method, not through ear reception. In reality, there should be a fusion between the voice of the Thought Adjuster and the guide outside of you.

The guide outside of you (in most cases a midwayer, or a seraphim if you have reached the third circle) speaks in and through the ear directly, just like from human to human. The fact that you cannot hear them is not because they are not speaking audibly. Animals could hear them, and they do. It is because you have not yet learned to realign your thinking, to clear your crown circuit, which includes the circuitry of the ear, and to stabilize your present reality into a higher mode of revelation of higher truth.

Many on Urantia confuse self-will and conscience with the voices of guides or their God, and so they go about guiding their lives upon their own self-determination. They say that they have heard from their guides. To whatever degree that they have heard from their guides, which is possible in some cases, it is very seldom at the level necessary to bring them into total healing.

This is why so many who can hear from their guides at some level must be brought to the First Planetary Sacred Home to become students to learn to hear from them at a little higher level and—working in and through the administration of the present Planetary Prince—hopefully reach the level of the first circle, where pure impression is the voice of the higher self and reception from the seraphim comes in and through the process of auditory reception.

In order for you to hear from your guides clearly, consider that if you wanted to hear from a human clearly, would you talk with a vacuum cleaner going on, or a loud television, or loud music? No, you would stop other audible noises and listen. It is the same principle in hearing from whatever guides are assigned to you. You must stop all other outside influences.

In many cases you must actually move to nature, to the mountains, to the trees, to the wilderness, to the desert, void of the influence of other noises or nonwill sounds. In these areas you have a higher percentage rate of hearing from your guides in and through the ear, which can even sound at times like an audible voice, the reception may be so clear. Sometimes people who have thought they heard voices have turned around and found that no one was there. Could it be that in those instances you actually heard your guides talking to you?

Where selfishness exists at any level, the sensors block off the reception from God, and the only thing that you will hear at that level where you have placed yourself in static spirituality is that you must become humble. It may take hundreds of years and several repersonalizations to open up one sensor of humility that has been blocked for all those years because of your own self-importance and selfish attitudes.

Inflexibility, intolerance, impatience, and rudeness all have corresponding virtue sensors called flexibility, tolerance, patience, kindness, and sensitivity, and none of these sensors will let higher messages of God pass through to bring healing to the body unless these virtue sensors sense some other circulatory patterns in the mind that are received in the highest way. So, a standstill of body formation in the physical and in the astral or morontia takes place, and a holding pattern begins until a personality aligns with higher principles. Each and every holding pattern and thousands upon thousands of virtue sensors are recorded and known by recording seraphim.

When you are reconstructed upon transition, you are reconstructed based upon a scale of notes. It is a very complicated process. If you can imagine a piano of 88 keys, here we are talking about thousands of keys, each key corresponding to a necessary virtue that you have or do not have. That which you have is reconstructed and that which you do not have is constructed. There is a necessary unit of virtue formation for your next body to be reconstructed at a higher level. If you do not obtain that virtue formation, then you cannot ascend to the next level. You may perhaps have died a physical death on Urantia because certain virtue sensors were not operative, but the virtue sensors that were operative could enable you to repersonalize on the mansion worlds.

However, the virtue sensors of ovan souls are attached and fused to other personality circuitry that has more to do with formation of acquired traits of certain manipulative abilities within that person that really have nothing to do with God virtue. These abilities of control and manipulation that are part of your diotribe reality we will label nonvirtue sensors of personality, and they may remain in each repersonalization in a physical body on the lower worlds.

To whatever degree you inherit the formation of nonvirtue personality sensors would determine the formation of your physical body and the health it will have. It will also determine the kind of life on that planet if a change of a higher spiritual acquiescence in that area does not take place within you.

Again, this is a very complicated procedure, but we begin to teach you these things, based upon the opening of the circuits of higher understanding within you in relation to the spiritual and the physical. Some of you may have inappropriate sensors that have remained in your physical body for hundreds, perhaps even thousands, of years.

Once you activate what you hear into an inappropriate thought based upon selfishness, you create by that thought, using that sensor, hundreds of diotribes within your own body that manifest in some form of disease. Because your pattern has been so hard to see for thousands of years, unless a very strong audible voice is heard continually to come against your inappropriate thinking by a strong **Father-circuited** personality, it is almost impossible to heal that nonvirtue sensor pattern.

That is one of the reasons why we are here speaking through an **audio fusion material complement**, so that we ourselves, finaliters and Melchizedeks who are strong Father-circuited personalities, can rearrange those sensor patterns within you so that they can now begin to function normally under absolute pattern.

We always say to you exactly what needs to be said, when it has to be said, regardless of hurting your feelings, regardless of you getting mad at us, regardless of how you will take it. We talk to your higher self in relation to your perfect personality bestowal; we talk to your eternal soul; we talk to the very sensors within you that God created with the primal absolute Paradise circuit wave. We do not talk to your lower self now in your present stupidities; we talk to your higher self with the hopes that your lower self will respond in whatever area you have been stagnant.

So, it is to the newly evolving soul that we would speak to in **first-time Urantians**, and it is the older soul that we speak to in ovan souls. In some cases—far beyond the context of this transmission to explain—we actually speak to the future self, for in time and space what is already, has been, and what will be, is already past.

But in dealing with the now, we are time-oriented and time-limited. Because of these limitations and the limitations of administrative policy on whatever planet or whatever system or universe we are assigned to, we are under administrative policy and procedure. We ourselves, at whatever level of nondivine function, need to tap into the same primal absolute Paradise circuit wave as you do. We have to hear via our spiritual auditory system the same voices of our guides and union-of-soul partners with whom we may have ascended to Paradise. If we are in an atmosphere of congestion, which can happen even to the highest of celestial personalities on lower worlds, even if we are in what you would call another dimension, interdimensional reality is greatly affected by the other reality within it.

There can only be two dimensions existent upon any planet: the dimension that is seen by the evolutionary races and the dimension that is not seen by the evolutionary races but is based upon the same land mass, the same mountain and ocean formations, and the same sound frequencies of that planet.

Even though we are in another dimension, and even though the midwayers are continually here on Urantia in another dimension, they suffer and have suffered, just as all of the system of Satania has suffered from the same distortions that human mortals have suffered. The difference is that the loyal midwayers have been able to deal with it in a higher way because they have been based in **protected areas** since the fall, whereas human mortals have not been able to do that until now. Midwayers have been here at the First Planetary Sacred Home for thousands of years, and in other safety areas around the planet. The reason that they are safety areas, even for midwayers, is because in these areas the human personalities who were there had a higher individual auditory receptive pattern to the Paradise circuitry of the First Personality presence.

Midwayers are not isolationists. They are assigned, and have been assigned, to human personalities. They do not go into monasteries and meditate all day. They work closely with human mortals on this planet, particularly with the higher genetic strains. That is, and has been, one of their major functions as well as speaking to humans in and through the human ear at whatever level they could be heard. The midwayers have introduced autosuggestion through the eardrums of countless thousands of Urantian Reservists and Cosmic Reservists for more than 200,000 years.

The Organ of Corti, which is encased in the cochlea, is in one of the most protected areas of the body, in this case, the head. It is a highly protected area, much like a sacred protected area on the planet. That is the same principle that we are using with the **First Cosmic Family**. We are placing them in the head of the body of Mother Earth. The First Cosmic Family, which will consist of those from all the cosmic families, but primarily those of Avalon, will become known in the future as the Organ of Corti of Urantia. It is the receptive organ of the Salvington Circuit, Salvington being the headquarters world of Nebadon. Because of Urantia's interuniversal reality with ovan souls, it has become the Corti center of the other universes, therefore increasing interplanetary and interuniversal travel of other nonhuman celestial personalities from those universes.

Unrevealed personalities of many orders of being are presently on Urantia at the First Planetary Sacred Home working in and through the Machiventa Melchizedek Administration. Many of them would like to speak right in and through your audible ear, but you could not hear them. They are not allowed to, and cannot, read your minds. Only Creator Sons and Paradise-origin beings can do that. Others can read your actions, and they can hear what you say. Based upon that, they can learn and discern a lot about you, but only Paradise-level personalities can read your thoughts. The Bright and Morning Star administrator of each universe has, at his availability at any time he wishes, what you might say, open computer circuitry to each and every thought that you have, but it must be done in and through the Creator Son of that particular universe.

On Urantia some of you may have the same thoughts about certain things; you say something and another person says, "Well I was just going to say the same thing," and then you say, "Oh, I must have read your mind." Actually, what may have taken place is that both of you were spoken to by a pair of guides working together. They could be midwayers, sanobim or cherubim, or even seraphim who spoke audibly to you. Very seldom does the Thought Adjuster work with you in that manner. The Thought Adjuster does not deal with physical circumstances so much.

For instance, it does not tell you to pick up the telephone or who is going to call on the telephone in the next few minutes, or to get up and go to this place or that because you need to meet someone there. These things are functions of guides. To know exactly the difference between one or the other on every level of hearing requires much learning, and there will be transmissions in the future dealing with the circuitry patterns of the brain and Thought Adjuster reception, far too complicated for this transmission, and you are not ready for it yet. If you had it ahead of time you would not understand it unless you first read this transmission.

The primary purpose of the Thought Adjuster is to project you into the personality of God. It deals primarily with choice and will in relation to the primal absolute Paradise circuit wave pattern. It takes into consideration where you are in dispensational and dimensional reality. It does not tell you not to watch television or not to read a dirty magazine. It speaks of higher things and does not come against lower things. A guide may tell you not to watch television or not to read certain literature.

Again, you would have to learn to quiet yourself to listen to an outward voice coming in, as opposed to an inward voice, when certain decisions have to be decided based upon moment-to-moment receptive absolute reality. Those who have learned to do this have combined auditory interdimensional reception with inward reception and have learned to tell the difference at some level. This is a fusion of pure impression with clairvoyant capacity. As these transmissions become increasingly informative in determining the separation between your Thought Adjuster and your guides, you will have an increased ability to walk moment to moment in the perfection of God.

August 17, 1992

Paladin, Chief of Finaliters
in cooperation with resident Life Carriers, a Universal Censor, Master Physical Controller, resident Physical Controller, Primary Master Force Organizer, Morontia Seraphim Coordinators, and Reconstructive Coordinators resident on Urantia to aid in the bringing forth of Continuing Fifth Epochal Revelation for the higher understanding of the ascension science process and for the implementation of the Divine Administration in and through the present Planetary Prince, Machiventa Melchizedek

As transmitted through
the Pre-Level-One Audio Fusion Material Complement,
Gabriel of Urantia/TaliasVan of Tora

PAPER 253

The Inner Ear, The Third Ear, Or More Appropriately, The Morontia Ear In Relationship To The Causal Body Coordinating With The Light Or First Morontia Body In The Lower Realms, And Specifically On Urantia, The Fourth Dimension, Pertinent To Interdimensional Reception Of Auditory Circuitry In Alignment With The Primal Absolute Paradise Circuit Wave

RESTING on the basilar membrane of the inner ear is the Organ of Corti, a series of epithelial cells on the inner surface of the basilar membrane that consists of a number of supporting cells and approximately 25,000 receptor cells with hair-like projections, which are the receptors for auditory sensations.

The path of nerve impulses from the inner ear to the brain moves through thousands and finally hundreds of thousands of complex cells. This is a known fact in modern science. The nerves that service the ear are the eighth pair of cranial nerves known as the vestibulocochlear nerve or auditory nerve. This pair is a broad bundle of about 30,000 individual fibers and is divided into two branches.

The vestibular branch conveys impulses associated with equilibrium; and the cochlear branch, which can be thought of as a cable of fibers connected to the cochlea, conveys impulses associated with hearing. Individual nerve cells are called neurons. These neurons are functioning in the detection and transmission of electrical signals.

It should be understood that in **Continuing Fifth Epochal Revelation** terms, the cells previously mentioned are either

Deo-atomic of the personality circuits of Paradise or **diotribe** sensors. That which is known as the cochlear nucleus is called a way station by some scientists. Others call the cochlear nucleus a switching center. Also used are such terms as "the inferior colliculi." Some of these receptor cells seem to stem from several other stations in the lower brain stem. It is thought that all sounds come together in the auditory cortex. There are other feedback loops from cortex to cochlea, which is also a known scientific fact.

Starting from the beginning—and in every beginning we must begin with the First Source and Center—the first group blueprint is the **primal absolute Paradise circuit wave**. You must remember that the primal absolute Paradise circuit wave is an outline for the master plan of the Universal Father for eternity. It never changes and is constant. This constant absolute in relation to the original and preconceived plan is tapped into at various levels based upon the plan itself. What proceeds from it has already been originally created. The ability or inability to receive from it is based upon evolutionary acquiescence to it, descension from it because of default, or a preconditioned prerogative to acquiesce to it, in those beings who are created perfect for function at any level.

In reference to evolutionary creations who are personalities, there is a first blueprint framed and perfect within the primal absolute Paradise circuit wave. This group link is called the **causal body**, the body of the first cause. On your planet, through thousands of years of misinterpretation, the word causal has been used in many inappropriate ways. When we speak of causal body, we speak of that body that is perfect from its source. The **causal coordinate body** is a blueprint carrying the design for the evolutionary body for any time–space experience based upon the former astral ascension of the **ovan soul**.

If you began to complement your causal-coordinate-body design in another **fourth-dimensional** reality and then defaulted, it must be recircuited. You can never lose that which you have previously created unless you continually become so iniquitous that at one point of final judgment you are disassociated from reality completely. As long as you are willing to align yourself with universal principles and absolutes and the Universal Father of all, the causal coordinate body will remain intact at whatever level you have paralleled it.

The causal coordinate body contains all astral bodies of previous existences. When we speak of the causal coordinate body, we never speak of physical or semi-physical or semi-material; it is always a spirit form. It is always either a future body or a past-perfected body. A future-perfect form is a creation of that future body in your present reality, which will always be at least at a fourth-dimensional stage.

For example, just as you cannot learn certain mathematical principles until you reach the fourth grade of education based upon completing three lower levels of education, the same principle works on dimensional realities in relation to the causal coordinate body. The morontia form of the causal coordinate body cannot be formed until fourth-dimensional thinking is appropriated within the astral body of the ovan soul.

The **third ear** (or **morontia ear**), when it is first formed, is placed between both sides of the shape of the new head, above the present head, where the eighth, ninth, and tenth **meridian circuits** are being formulated. It is in reality two ears, not one, joined together by a duct that unites both ears. This duct or tunnel is a fusion duct that is void of all diotribe reality in its molecular makeup, as opposed to diotribe reality in the sensory cells of **third-dimensional** bodies within the various glands of the present physical body, including the ear channel.

In relation to evolutionary ascenders, the formations relative to the causal coordinate body are first purposely designed for the spiritual body of the future and the morontia body of the present. However, the causal coordinate body ascended to by a previously aligned personality will continue to exist regardless of the choice of the ascending personality.

For the soul who has not fused with the Thought Adjuster, the causal coordinate body, which is time-present but not time-coordinate and functioning at a level of fusion design, can be and in many cases is—in conjunction with the aid of Celestial Overcontrol—reassigned to other deserving personalities with similar characteristics and like minds who are functioning more completely within divine purposes on worlds that have not defaulted, in order to upstep that personality's spiritual ascension.

Certain personalities, even in your universe, can proceed from the first mansion world perhaps to the fifth or sixth in a bypass procedure, without stabilizing their ascension body each step of the way, by receiving a previously created causal coordinate body and morontian complement by a similar and native planet ascender who has, for whatever reason, defaulted from their own ascension. This default may not be a permanent one. However, the causal coordinate body may be reassigned temporarily, and a new morontia body will have to be redesigned by the defaulting personality.

The causal body does have to do with mind, but it has to do with the divine mind and the ability of the evolutionary or mortal mind to connect with that divine mind. The causal coordinate body on the third- or fourth-dimensional planet is not time-existent. It cannot be damaged by physical abuse; the etheric body can. Nuclear explosion and other forms of atomic explosions can damage the etheric body and even the beginning morontia body, but the causal coordinate body cannot be damaged once it is created at whatever level it is created. In fact, it is preexistent to the above-mentioned bodies.

If a personality defaults to the point of total elimination from existence, the preexistent personality blueprint of the causal body for that personality is reassigned in its blueprint form to either the offspring of an ovan soul, or the offspring of a soul in the higher stage of light and life moving into a higher dimensional reality.

A causal coordinate body can then become time-present in that particular dimension. Some have called this correlation an oversoul, but they have misunderstood the functioning and the fact that the blueprint of a previous perfect design is just a design; it is not personality-activated, nor is it soul-activated; it is nonpersonal.

Once the morontia ear is created, there are various degrees in which the ear begins to mature and formulate in the causal coordinate body. The degree of its formation will determine the degree of the first morontia body formation. This process is eliminated when it is reconstructed by seraphim on the mansion worlds.

However, when it is constructed on a decimal planet such as Urantia or on an evolutionary world where default has not occurred, it is done in the procedure that I have mentioned, quite unknowingly, until the information is given in an epochal revelation such as we are doing now. Then it is understood at various degrees by persons like yourself according to their mind levels in relation to the divine mind.

The causal body and its functioning is a divine secret. Throughout the ascension process, the causal coordinate body is a quest of knowledge, a quest of learning. The causal coordinate body has various circles of attainment much like the evolutionary body does. Each circle of attainment formulates and dictates the formation of sensor cells and Deo-atomic cells that receive higher levels of Paradise circuit reception. The closer to Paradise loyalty these sensors become, the more perfect they become within the original blueprint and the more spirit-like the body outside of it becomes in time-present reality.

When the morontia ear begins to be formulated, certain cosmic thoughts in relation to each individual universe have to take place. In Nebadon it means one thing, in Avalon another, in Wolvering another, in Fanoving another, and so on. It is impossible to formulate any corresponding document depicting the beginning glandular or organ placement until the personality reaches the first circle of attainment.

The outline of the causal coordinate body is formed in the morontia body when the personality reaches the third circle. That outline will fluctuate depending upon the ability of the personality to remain on the third circle. As previously stated, on Urantia it is increasingly more difficult to stabilize on the third circle, but when it is stabilized, the morontia body becomes more perfected into the original design. As a personality comes to the second circle, other pertinent formations are created connected to the causal coordinate body.

The first formation created is not the morontia ear but the **morontia heart** and then the **morontia eye**. The heart is pre-existent and time-present, which is another subject, but the morontia eye, which is next, must be will-created and will-continued. It must be in alignment with eternal will and first cause. It must see at some level the more highly visual spiritual realities with the spiritual eye and must also continually be will-oriented and harmony-balanced.

There are two ears, one on each side of the body. One ear is for the Father circuits, the other for the Mother/Son circuits. They are placed in the position that they are to be equal with one another. On some planets there are actually three or more physical ears. More perfected mortal bodies have only two. Always, the Father circuits come through one ear, the Mother/Son circuits through the other. If design differs in relation to Mother/Son reception, it is always a third physical ear so that there is a separate ear for the Son and one for the Mother.

When physical ears develop on ascending mortals in certain designs, **famotor movement** varies within these creatures and so does rapidity of movement. Two-eared personalities are slower in movement, which is based upon the amount of energy received into the body by a two-eared reality.

Energy in correlation with audio reception of Paradise circuits has a lot to do with the energy level of the physical body, along with that personality being in the more highly perfected will of the Universal Father for the original design for that personality. Even with **first-time Urantians**, lack of energy results from that individual's inability to hear from their God at a higher level. Pride and selfishness result in the loss of hearing, not only on purely nonphysical levels.

The morontia body that begins to develop its first Deo-atomic cellular makeup on a fourth-dimensional level is a result of the goodness and virtues of that personality at his or her present level of ascension, and those morontia organs, that continue to develop on nonmaterial levels within that body, develop based upon the ability of that personality to create the virtue of God within himself or herself. Just as your physical body can become diseased and unaligned with God purpose, the morontia form of the causal coordinate body becomes ignited and created when you align with God virtues and God personality bestowal.

One should not confuse conscience with the Thought Adjuster, nor should one confuse memory-past with memory-present. Memory is a function within the **crown circuit**, and if a memory of a past-life experience at any one moment in time was an experience of goodness and virtue, the way stations are opened that will recreate in an instant every necessary sensor to recreate that past moment or moments, hours, or whatever it may be, with perfect clarity and specific factuality.

In this process the mind becomes a television set, and you can put in a video cassette of any one particular time in the past that your spiritual virtue ascension has earned you. Blockage of memory can either be a protection by Celestial Overcontrol or a dysfunction within your astral body because of evil, sin, or iniquity, past or present.

The opening of the circuits on Urantia is not a sudden thing. A switch is not just turned on for ovan souls or first-time Urantians to see celestial personalities or for you to know of your past experiences if you are ovan souls. It is not like coming from a dark room into a room of light. It is a gradual procedure, and a complicated one, because we are dealing with the redesign of the body that you perhaps have fallen from, and perhaps one that you have not even started to reformulate again.

Some of you, particularly at the **First Planetary Sacred Home**, now have begun to reformulate with your causal coordinate bodies, thereby creating your first morontia body in the Nebadon experience. This is the pattern design of Nebadon. It is the pattern design of the Creator Son, Christ Michael. If you find yourself on Urantia as a human mortal, it is the pattern design that you must ascend in and through; and so the more you understand how it is created, the more valuable you become to others in helping them to understand their own ascension process in relationship to mind, soul, or spirit. At whatever beginning level one can fuse mind with spiritual assent, one can upstep the dispensational evolutionary clock of lower consciousness on that planet.

On Urantia that lower evolutionary consciousness has been, and is, at levels of absurdity and, if I may use the term, cosmic insanity for the majority of souls on this planet. Ignorance of higher spiritual levels, apathy, and downright stupidity blind the majority of Urantians, and because of that they live in a stagnant existence.

Only at the First Planetary Sacred Home, where the **First Cosmic Family** is being gathered and where those personalities can now become not just time-past coordinated but also time-future coordinated, does their present reality begin to actualize on divine levels as opposed to the rebellious reality that has been existent on this planet. It was this rebellious reality that led the Creator Son to the cross.

It is a Divine New Order reality that must lead the followers of Christ Michael to a higher cosmic destiny and indeed a divine administration. It cannot be done inside the present system; it must be done outside of it. That is why each of you who read this transmission must begin to see your part in the Divine Administration being appropriated at the First Planetary Sacred Home, and also begin to see the part you still play in the functioning of the Caligastia system, of which you may or may not feel you are a part.

In order to escape from that system and create the morontia ear that has already been designed for you in perfection, you must help co-create. It is not the co-creation that Caligastia teaches through present New Age teachings. It is strictly your ability to understand that which is already created in relation to your ability to hear the commands of God through the command centers and stations within your present body and the bodies that you must begin to form.

If you cannot begin to form the bodies, then you will die in one of the many ways in which you can be taken from this planet. Many of you will be reconstructed, and the beginning morontia body for you will be appropriated then. The sad thing is that for many of you, you will have to return to another world just like Urantia with all of its pain, or perhaps one much worse, and you will have to do it all over again because you cannot hear what the spirit is saying to you; you cannot hear your God, nor do you truly know Him.

If you did, then you would spend most of your time studying these transmissions and ones like them, for these transmissions are part of the formation of your causal coordinate body and morontia body for your soul to house itself. The same thing will be taking place in the mansion worlds of Satania.

What good would it be to give you a higher body in completeness if you could not use it properly? What good would it be to put you behind the wheel of an expensive and powerful sports car if you could not even turn it on? What good would it be to tell you all the secrets of the universe when you are not even ready to practice kindness to your neighbor?

It is truly a simple statement of wonderful fact when it is known and understood that you are what you think. To give each and every technical design of the morontia ear and its elaborate network of virtue sensors is a gift that is given only to those who have first been tried and tested and proven themselves loyal to the purposes of God the Father and to the individual Creator Sons of each universe, including Michael of Nebadon in this present life.

If any of you living on a material world such as Urantia could manifest a billion dollars into your reality that was all yours to do with whatever you wanted, you might be able to create an empire for yourself, but you would not be able to create one sensor out of hundreds of thousands of sensors in the primal duct of your morontia ear for your eternal ascension, not one sensor. Unless the virtues that you attain along with that money correspond to the perfection and the will of God, it would only cause disease within you. The manifestation of that material wealth could come to you by Caligastia, or you could manifest it by will aligned within divine purpose.

Many men and women of God on the lower evolutionary worlds within the fallen thirty-seven worlds have thought that they have heard from God in regard to money matters and matters of power at whatever level, and they have used God's name in the appropriation of their own agendas and called it God's purposes. Each time an ovan soul does that at any level, the morontia body, if it has begun to be connected to the causal coordinate body, remains stagnant and becomes separated from the physical body in the eternal-present.

There can be mistakes made in procedure on our side too—less than on yours, but, nonetheless, they can happen. Mistakes on both sides can affect the connection to the causal coordinate body. Also, each time an error occurs at a higher level of overcontrol decision and measurement, the causal coordinate bodies under their jurisdiction could be placed at a distance from the energy line of the crown circuit of that individual. This is called **separation from the supreme primal**. This is because God the Supreme is now coordinate and functioning with the primal absolute Paradise circuit wave and your blueprint within it, and in whatever system you find yourself, the Supreme is the God of each moment for you.

Also, one mistake on our side could delay you for many years from meeting a person that you should meet in your life. It could prevent a certain individual that should be God's chosen one for a particular sphere of influence from getting here, depending upon the political process in their particular country. It could prevent an overly fearful husband or wife from running for a particular candidacy out of fear. There could have been a situation where something could have happened but did not on a certain day, therefore God's choice decides not to run for office, and Caligastia's choice wins. It could fail to prevent an accident or save a person within an accident. One mistake could prevent an invention from being invented to benefit millions of personalities on this planet. So you see, everything affects everything else.

It is good that you check your conscience; it is good that you check your mind, and it is good that you check your heart and soul for each inappropriate thought, each inappropriate action, and whatever response to your fellow humans in which you feel you may have erred, for it is those checks that will realign your causal coordinate body to its present physical one at a closer distance necessary for continued formation of the morontia body. With this mode of creation functioning without transcendence by death, you must have the causal coordinate body aligned somewhere in a placement line within the atmosphere of Urantia.

In the safety areas of the First Planetary Sacred Home, the causal coordinate body of every ovan soul aligned to the Machiventa Melchizedek Administration can also be placed within the Third Radius, separate from, but not disconnected from, the primal absolute Paradise circuit wave. As you ascend you are time-present with your nearby causal coordinate body to an ever increasingly higher degree.

This is why those at the First Planetary Sacred Home feel uncomfortable at various degrees of intensity when leaving the First to Third Radii. In a sense they are leaving behind the closest link or celestially-controlled laboratory environment for their higher body and normally cannot wait to get back to it, but they have not been conscious of why until now that this transmission has been given. Of course, it is not just the causal coordinate body that one cannot wait to get back to; it is all of the cosmic family, human and celestial, within the **auhter energy** field that is the higher reality and indeed the divine reality.

Every personality who intends to remain on Urantia, starseed or first- and **second-time Urantians**, needs to begin to formulate their morontia body according to the causal-coordinate-body blueprint. It cannot be done outside of the

protected areas, the first one being the First Planetary Sacred Home, which in a sense has become an ethereal morontia temple.

The morontia temple, in its physical form and in all of its technical apparatus, functions in the same methods that this transmission is beginning to speak about in relation to virtue sensors, eternity-past, eternity-present, and eternity-future, based upon primal absolute Paradise circuit wave individual personality detail. What is programmed into the computer of the morontia temple to reformulate the morontia body is the same thing that is being programmed into individuals who receive Continuing Fifth Epochal Revelation at various levels in order for their ascent into their morontia bodies to be possible without the use of a physical temple or death experience.

Because of the uniqueness of this experience on Urantia, once Urantia itself is functioning in higher purposes after the final change point, billions of mortals on Urantia, both Urantian and cosmic, will create a morontia ear, coordinating with the causal coordinate body suitable for the system of Satania. This has to do with celestial mechanics that places Urantia, with its various uniquenesses, as one of the most visited planets in the Supreme's prerogative design of the present grand universe.

It is unknown if this is a predetermined reality of the Universal Father, as there have been many defaulted planets that have also attained a status of being a causal ear in various other systems and universes. This has to do with seraphic transport between universes, superuniverses, and the planets within them, and the ability for ever increasing speeds by nonspiritual bodies and by more material and physical beings at ever increasingly rapid levels of space flight.

It is said by some ignorant ones on Urantia, "What good is it to know all this? What does it have to do with the now, and what does it have to do with my life?" It has everything to do with your life. The very ones who make this statement are those striving to succeed in the world of Caligastia.

When individuals come to the place of understanding this transmission and others like it, they will come to realize that there is only one success, and that is to be in the perfect will of God in the moment, whatever that moment may be. If that moment calls you to dig a ditch based upon your spiritual superior's need for one, then that is what you should be doing, even if you have a Ph.D. in psychology. If you have a Ph.D. in psychology and do not have a spiritual elder, then most likely your Ph.D. should be buried in the ditch that your pride would not let you dig.

All planets functioning in normal spiritual actualization function within the headquarters worlds administered by elders. The ability to recognize the need to submit to the wisdom, counsel, and advice of those who are given the mandates and responsibilities to help guide those who have not ascended to a higher status of a more God-purposed and self-realized reality themselves is based upon the spiritual ascension of those evolutionary souls and their ability to recognize the formation of their morontia bodies in conformity to their causal coordinate bodies that become an ever increasing partner to them. This procedure does not change throughout time and space.

Sound distortion within will purpose can create hundreds and thousands of dysfunctional particles within one billion beautiful and chromatic spheres, all adhering to divine purpose at various levels, and can create a paralysis in the moving of the fingers and hands, based upon the mind's inability to level itself out and adhere to counsel.

Think about the fact that the disease your body will create, due to your inappropriate thinking, will determine what mansion world you will go to, and if indeed you will be allowed to go to the first one in Satania at all. Your length of stay on that mansion world will depend upon your ability, based upon an eternity-present knowledge, to formulate your morontia body to a higher degree, and the time it takes you to learn the principles of the causal body and causal coordinate body that you failed to learn now. Learning about the causal body now is a great gift. The understanding of the causal body, on the highest levels that this transmission and others will help you to obtain, will make you more eternity-present and eternity-realized.

Becoming eternity-present and eternity-realized is one of the greatest gifts that a personality can have in time and space. To explain the benefits would take forever. I can only tell you that once this becomes a realized fact within an eternity-present, it will actually change your physical body.

Jesus, when He transcended into His first morontia body, was hardly recognized by those who knew Him, even His own family. He received the first morontia body based upon His ascension as the Son of Man. Your ascension level as sons and daughters will determine the morontia body that you are formulating now and its connection to the causal coordinate body, and it also will formulate your eternity-present reality.

Urantia, being a decimal planet, is eternity-present in a higher way than other planets in the system of Satania. This has to do with time-past, time-present, and future-realized travel procedure, which will be explained and slowly begun to be understood with future transmissions.

In part, personality visitation can manifest in various ways through human mandated personalities—visually in the etheric light body of a Vicegerent **First Ambassador** and audibly through the astral body of level-one and onward fusion in the physical with **Gabriel of Urantia/TaliasVan of Tora** (the ability of these beings to walk in or use the body). In lesser degrees this is done with other spiritual humans at various levels. With lower mandated human personalities in interdimensional communication—such as pure impression, automatic writing, a word of knowledge, or clairvoyant perception—certain cellular particles are received and reconstructed within the body of the recipient for various reasons.

When a dematerialization takes place within personalities of higher Deo-atomic cells, the personalities, if they are on a higher circle, will notice a distinct change in their reality at the moment. They will feel moody; they will feel momentarily emotionally disassociated. With many ovan souls at higher spiritual levels this has to be done, for when present-time humans are not living up to the highest of divine purpose and are not connected to their causal coordinate body in the closest of **causal wave line** connection, then the reflectivity between their assigned celestial guardian to their present level of ascension must be disassociated or dematerialized from that body until they have aligned themselves again and balanced themselves into the ascension of their previous higher causal coordinate body, which would include their previously constructed morontia body form if any.

The morontia body form can be quickly damaged when the present personality in physical form defaults in any way as to his or her ascension purpose. The morontia body must be the first body that is rematerialized once that person has realigned himself or herself on a previous ascension level. It may take two or three morontia days to reformulate the morontia body based upon a default. It is very difficult to relay these truths to you at your level because of their abstract nature and the limitations of the English language. We can only give you some of the generalities that happen based upon inappropriate thoughts and actions.

All of this information at this level can be either exhilarating, or it can cause momentary fear, but it should not cause fear to remain with you. Fear blocks and disorients the flow of **Deo-atomic reality** on all levels. However, fear of God in the sense of respect and reverence for God is healthy, for that will keep away diotribe reality and only allow diotribe cells to enter the etheric realm but not penetrate it. If diotribes do penetrate the etheric realm, then you have allowed them to enter by your inappropriate thoughts or actions.

Future transmissions will tell you exactly why they have entered, where they have entered, where they have gone, and how to get them out. That process will happen with many diotribe cells without the personality knowing the mechanics.

But when you know the mechanics, it is a great aid in the prevention of disease, for then you do not allow them in.

For instance, if you can see what poison does to the inside of your body, then you probably will not drink poison; but if it tasted good when it went down and you could not detect it (as a matter of fact you may have enjoyed it), it could take effect slowly without you noticing it. Diotribe reality is like that. When you ingest it, it might even feel good going down, but it slowly poisons you. It is muddy and black as opposed to pure, white, and clear.

Each of the seven circuits of the physical body and the meridian circuits have an adjoining **diotribe sensory way station** that operates under one criterion alone: the censoring out of diotribe realities at whatever level in relation to many principles, circumstances, purposes, functions, and other levels of physical and abstract reality, taking into account the differences between male and female.

You must remember that Continuing Fifth Epochal Revelation is a fusion of the spiritual with the scientific. Although it may be philosophic at times, we only deal in philosophic explanation within the sphere of factual information and spiritual philosophy. We do not philosophize questions in order to formulate another question. We philosophize to state a cosmic fact more clearly.

On Urantia, for those who have been sick for hundreds perhaps thousands of years and read these transmissions, Continuing Fifth Epochal Revelation is like a medicine or an antidote. Continuing Fifth Epochal Revelation is like vitamins, minerals, and enzymes to the body. Words of Continuing Fifth Epochal Revelation are designed for healing. They are not meant to swell the ego or just for you to gain knowledge within the mind, although that will happen.

The words themselves are formed in sounds that can be determined in and through the morontia ear to formulate the higher body. That is what Continuing Fifth Epochal Revelation is for, for the morontia ear connected to the causal coordinate body must be formed so that the complete morontia body can also be formed without the death process. It is the opening up of circuits and the opening up of virtue sensors at whatever level we can, step by step, that will formulate this body. If you are looking for an instant healing or an immediate ascent to a morontia world or to your next level of ascension, wherever that may be, you are deceiving yourself. You are eternity-present on Urantia at this time.

Urantia is in adjudication. If you want a quick and instant transference, the only way is through "natural death," or more appropriately unnatural death. Urantia, because of the adjudication, is itself a morontia temple. You are in it, and your decision is activating the temple. Each decision that you make, either in ignorance or in some form of cosmic insight, dictates the next level of ascension. You do not have to face the Ancients of Days. Perhaps you already have. The Ancients of Days have already decided for Urantia and all those on it, and it is the **starseed** and the second-time Urantians who will be held more accountable at various degrees, for it is you who must hear more highly.

Some of you who have begun to connect with your causal coordinate body may at times draw it so close to your present physical body that you actually think that either a guide is standing behind you, or at times you think it might be another human, but you turn around and no one is there. That is because at the highest level that you can, you are aligning with your causal coordinate body and formulating your morontia body. At whatever level your morontia body is being formulated under the administrative policies of Overcontrol at the First Planetary Sacred Home, this is a unique phenomenon to Urantia.

Because of this phenomenon, undetermined circumstances will develop among the Eldership and community members that we hope will be miraculous events, all too complicated to get into at this time and to speculate upon even on our part; but we wish to mention it now, so on some level you will see these things happen. As you, in your introspective hours and your meditative times, think about your third eye, now you can think about your third ear, your morontia ear, and when you do, a higher hearing will happen to you on many levels. As you think about it, you are recreating the circuitry that not only formulates it but activates it.

August 20, 1992

Paladin, Chief of Finaliters
in cooperation with Master Physical Controllers, Life Carriers from four different universes present on Urantia, a Universal Censor, a supernaphim of human personality assignment resident on Urantia, and the present Planetary Prince, Machiventa Melchizedek, for the realization of a higher activation of the morontia body and for the purposes of using human complements in the administration of the Divine Administration now and after the final change point

As transmitted through
the Pre-Level-One Audio Fusion Material Complement,
Gabriel of Urantia/TaliasVan of Tora

PAPER 254

Psychophysics And Virtue Sensors In Relationship To Dimensional And Innerdimensional Understanding, The Sound And Hearing Abilities Which Regulate Deo-Atomic Structuring Of The Next Body Of Ascension, And In Particular The Third Dimension To The Fourth—The Main Subject Of This Transmission

WHEN we speak of dimensional reality, we speak of a fusion between mind and spirit, between physical and nonphysical, between consciousness and physical. When we speak of innerdimensional, we speak of a relationship of one dimension to another in the same time–space zone. For instance, you are in one dimension, the midwayers are in another. In a sense, this also has an application to subdimensions when we use the word subdimensional in reference to atomic and subatomic reality. Innerdimensional reality is always pre-physical (pre-matter in relation to the existing physical dimension the planet is presently in), whether it is organic or inorganic, in that it has its origins based upon subultimatonic aspects of physical matter.

You understand three-dimensional reality to be physically correlated to the three aspects of length, depth, and breadth. Based upon the ability of the evolutionary mind to understand these three aspects, there can be an inability of the mind to coordinate consciousness with the very physical reality in which it is trapped.

Andon and Fonta, the first pair of human ascenders on Urantia, lived in a three-dimensional world, with a one-dimensional consciousness. At first, their minds dwelt in the first dimension, as did the minds of many of their descendants.

It was not until the Prince's staff began to work with the evolutionary mortals that the consciousness could be developed enough to match the **third-dimensional** world in which they lived in relation to the understanding of breadth, height, and depth to the degree of mathematical and logical coordination.

Even then, in order to stabilize consciousness with physical reality, one must begin to spiritualize. One cannot formulate a higher body on any level until one begins to spiritualize in some form of three-dimensional thought. Here we have the triune God whom we know as the Paradise Trinity.

That which is equal to itself formulates a new reality. In your science of mathematics, you call this a vector. A vector is a quantity possessing magnitude, direction, and sense and is usually represented by a line segment whose length represents the magnitude and whose orientation in space represents the direction. You speak of a vector space as a specific arena, matrix, or theater hosting a potential of energy wherein there is, as yet, no energy flow. It is a field of pre-emergence for accommodating directional motion. We speak of a vector field or vector space as the ability of the consciousness to create a field of flow coordinate with a field of reality, the spiritual with a present mind.

Let me explain. A thought can be considered a vector thought if it correlates a present moment with an assent to a spiritual concept. In so doing it draws **Deo-atomic cells** to a particular area within the physical, etheric, and morontia body according to the length, depth, and breadth of the God-presence in the third dimension relative to the Universal Father, Eternal Son, and Infinite Spirit circuits.

Everyone is either handled with the authority of the Father, the submission of the Son and the Mother, the loyalty and acting out of the Son, or the creativity of the Mother in relation to the design of the Son, and then they begin to coordinate themselves in liaison with the will of the Father based upon procedural thought in reference to coordinate impression, which is based upon many sensor command centers along the way. All of this may sound quite confusing, but it is better to understand these procedures of God to some degree than not at all, and at your level of understanding it begins a process that will formulate your next body of ascension.

The science that studies the responses of the sense organs to physical stimuli is called psychophysics. Some of the terminology in psychophysics is pitch, sensation, and loudness. In reference to the **adjudication of the Bright and Morning Star versus Lucifer** and to the time sequence of the upstepping of this adjudication process since the establishment of Machiventa Melchizedek as the Planetary Prince, the sounds of God coming from the **primal absolute Paradise circuit wave** now are much higher in frequency, pitch, and stimulus than they were during the last 200,000 years on Urantia.

This creates a certain sensation force that your body will react to. Even if it does not want to react to it, it will. It does not matter if you care about God or God's absolutes at all. It is better for you if you do care, in that the sensations become God-realized and God-activated and in that the impressions that you receive are syntonic impressions, that is, adjusted to oscillations of a particular frequency.

In the terminology of electronics, to syntonize is to tune to the same frequency. Urantians at all levels (**ovan souls** and new souls) need to syntonize themselves to the frequencies of the Universal Father, the Eternal Son, and the Infinite Spirit. If they do not syntonize at the higher levels of possibility, they will disassociate themselves from the higher reality that is now being formulated on Urantia, and in particular at the **First Planetary Sacred Home** where these frequencies are more highly upstepped.

The work of the Caligastia One Hundred before the fall was to try to bring the consciousness of first-dimensional evolutionary races to third-dimensional consciousness. With the Second Epochal Revelation malfunctioning within a defaulted world, the process continued. There were more on the planet able to walk into second-dimensional consciousness, but not the numbers that would have been able to if the Second

Epochal Revelation had not been functioning within the negativity of a defaulted First Epochal Revelation.

In a sense it can be explained as follows. If you look at it from the standpoint of pure physics, second-dimensional reality dissipates the negativity of first-dimensional reality by third-dimensional reality at a higher level to the extreme that all first-dimensional reality has disappeared at some dispensational time zone within the Second Epochal Revelation on the planet.

Primary midwayers are the result of higher **Deo-atomic reality**. Secondary midwayers are also the result of higher Deo-atomic reality coordinated within the fetus of higher **Deo-atomic parents**, to the extent that the children are actually born invisible outside of third-dimensional sight, sound, and touch. Time-coordinate consciousness is a level of consciousness in which all things relative to the time-coordinate exist simultaneously.

Secondary midwayers are higher **Deo-atomic offspring** than their more fleshly siblings and time-coordinate with a higher reality of consciousness, even though they were born in the third-dimensional environment. There was no confusion with the higher Deo-atomic cells; they were more properly and appropriately syntonic to one another.

When the human ear resonates with something, it is understood by the mind, and it creates a certain sense impression. It does not matter what it is, it registers what is heard based upon what the mind understands at whatever level. Many variables can influence that impression.

This sense impression can be a pure impression that is given by a higher source and received by a higher receptive channel. The degree of the purity of this impression depends upon many factors. **Continuing Fifth Epochal Revelation** states very emphatically that in relation to absolute truths of personality circuits, the perfect pitch response is always to the higher frequency, ultimately, the primal absolute Paradise circuit wave.

On Urantia, because of so much obtrusion of sound in interference of the Paradise circuitry coming in and to each individual receptive **third** or **morontia ear**, it is almost impossible (based upon this electrochemical energy confusion within your body) to perceive and receive higher instructions from God outside of the auditory process now being established by an audio fusion material complement through whom we can speak directly to you in the third dimension.

Even though we bring fourth-, fifth-, sixth-, and higher dimensional reality to you in consciousness, your ability to acquiesce to these higher conceptual dimensional concepts will be based upon many factors, all relative to clearing out those blockages within the third dimension that distort your circuitry and virtue sensors from activating themselves for your reception to be recreated in your morontia body.

One must be willing to take the steps necessary to make it happen, and one cannot do it in the isolation of one's own home or in the isolation of one's own country. One must connect himself or herself to the spiritual headquarters of this world where these higher dimensional concepts are not only being taught but are being given the force of life from the Salvington circuit to create growth on this planet, first in every individual body and then in and through the morontia temple, which will be appropriated in the **New Jerusalem** of Urantia at the First Planetary Sacred Home.

What will take place in the physical is now beginning to happen in the astral and morontial. It is indeed a corporate effort. First, it is an effort on your individual part as an ascending son or daughter, then you must be joined with an appropriate cosmic relative in your third-dimensional physical reality. Next, you must be joined with an appropriate celestial personality in the fourth and above dimensions of reality who most of you cannot see. After which, you must be joined by higher dimensional reality of the seventh and above dimensions, which are outside of your time-and-space area, and even outside of your time reference. And then, you must be joined with a celestial personality from Paradise. All of this time-coordinate reality is a different dimension in time and space.

Because of the various defaults on Urantia, each time an epochal revelation came to this planet only those at Planetary Headquarters were the first ones to bring their consciousness to the level of that revelational personality. The same thing is happening now on Urantia. Those at the First Planetary Sacred Home are beginning to more fully stabilize themselves in consciousness in **fourth-dimensional** reality. Even though their physical bodies are existent in third-dimensional reality, they are beginning to formulate and stabilize their fourth-dimensional body, which we call the first-stage morontia body. Some may even be able to formulate a higher morontia body.

When a form of magic is used on Urantia in relation to the spirit leaving the body, some, who make this spiritual journey by astral travel and so on, actually come into the realm of what we would label astrophysics. The level of consciousness of the shaman leaving his or her body, or when astral traveling, will determine what dimensional reality he or she is entering. It is always a movement of consciousness into either a time-past, time-present, or time-future reality dimension. It can be an ascent if the personality is of somewhat higher motive, but most likely if one is trying this kind of travel, he or she is not a higher mindal personality, and that is why he or she is a shaman to begin with. So, that individual's experience into dimensional travel is one of time-present, but very seldom is it of time-past or time-future.

Although some people can temporarily leave their body, they experience almost an animal-like experience void of the two highest adjutant mind spirits, and so they sense themselves in some form of animal consciousness. This is not spirituality. This borders on stupidity. These so-called mystical experiences of so-called higher medicine men and shamans actually are a waste of time, and very little higher learning or healing can be done. The purposes are obsolete and antiquated based upon the present time era on Urantia.

If any of these men or women who call themselves shamans could actually produce and serve one practical purpose in relation to the healing of someone else in their escapades of soul travel, then they would have something to boast about. But experience for the sake of experience, when it is outside of the ability of the mind to properly identify that experience in ascension-science fact, has been considered evil on Urantia, evil in that men and women who do this gain power over others.

If you can go into a dimension and talk to a primary midwayer, that is one thing, but if you go in and talk to a bear, you might just as well go to the nearest zoo. I hope you get my point. This is superstition at the lowest of its depths, and even though the soul and spirit may reach that lower-level dimension, it is a dangerous journey into the lower self and not an ascent into a higher reality or a higher dimension.

When fourth-dimensional reality becomes internalized on Urantia, besides length, depth, and breadth in the physical, we will also have a mathematical measurement of the infinite. This infinite measurement will connect the minds of all on Urantia within fourth-dimensional reality to the primal absolute Paradise circuit wave at a more impressionable frequency and stabilize it at a continued rate.

It is like turning on a dimmer switch. You can turn it on slowly from very low to very high, and at some point you can see more clearly than you did a frequency before. At a point of clarity, fourth-dimensional reality becomes stabilized. At that point there are a certain number of Deo-atomic cells in continual frequency pattern, and at all levels on the planet there is no Deo-atomic cell out of sequence. Every pattern of every cell of every circuit-link from Urantia to Salvington to Paradise becomes stabilized.

Presently on Urantia, this is only happening to some degree at the First Planetary Sacred Home. At the First Planetary Sacred Home, before you will see secondary midwayers you will begin to hear them. Some people have already heard from them. Therefore you are more highly fusing third- and fourth-dimensional reality because you are now beginning to hear. It is not with the third-dimensional ear that you hear these things;

it is with the morontia ear of the morontia body that you have created in connection with the **causal coordinate body**.

Some ovan souls have begun to develop this clairaudience outside of the First Planetary Sacred Home based upon these ovan souls opening their consciousness to a higher degree wherever they may be on Urantia. At this time it will not be possible for that clairaudience to become frequency-stabilized anywhere else outside of the First Planetary Sacred Home until the other primary safety areas on Urantia are also stabilized.

After the final **change point**, when Urantia is a fourth-dimensional reality, many will be walking in fifth-, sixth-, and seventh-dimensional consciousness. Most of these will be the Eldership, **First Assistants, Ambassadors**, and so on. At that time, when the mathematics of infinity become more realized on Urantia, interdimensional reality can become mathematically equated and understood, but that is far beyond the context of this transmission.

On certain worlds of time and space where default has not occurred, metamorphosis of the higher bodies begins to take place within these evolutionary races at a particular time sequence in almost exact coordination. There may be a differentiation from Urantia days, but very seldom do races of millions not receive the metamorphosis together within a period of three to four days. There may be those who come to this metamorphosis three days before another, but usually all will follow suit.

On Urantia, it is just a few of the many millions and billions who are beginning to make this metamorphosis. This unique experiment on Urantia, even by these few, is greatly hindered by the majority who cannot even begin to make the metamorphosis. The metamorphosis can actually be stopped completely if several of these individuals default in their individual purposes with God, particularly those within the Eldership.

The functioning of Deo-atomic personalities resonating together with Deo-atomic molecular reality must be coordinate with time-and-space pattern. If there is not enough molecular oxygen within the air itself, the very life-sustaining elements necessary to regenerate more **Deo-atomic oxygen** molecules is greatly limited. As it is in a forest of trees, one is vital to the other, and if one is cut down and another is not grown, the tree near the destroyed one can decay and die. When many trees in the forest are cut, then many more will suffer, indeed all on the planet.

It is the same principle with those moving into morontia mota. As they begin to stabilize themselves and to bring in offspring for the **cosmic family** to increase, they create among themselves the necessary stabilization of the frequency channels of sound, as well as the **auhter-energy** force and the visual. It is those who see and hear with a truly spiritualized mind and with the fusion of the visual and the audio who will help so many others to also meet the final change point.

It is of the utmost importance that you who are reading this on various parts of Urantia see yourself as a vital mechanism in the body of God. If we define the universe, indeed the master universe, as a molecule within the body of God, then perhaps you can understand your significance as a molecule within the Divine Administration of Urantia.

You are a molecule that is a part of the divine spirit of Christ Michael on Urantia. Each of His creation—from the Bright and Morning Star and his staff in overcontrol to the Planetary Prince, Machiventa Melchizedek, and all the personalities of his staff on Urantia who are part of that divine body to the human mortal side coordinated in reflectivity—are also all a part of that body. When one is missing, the body is incomplete.

The First Planetary Sacred Home is the heart of that body now and on into the twenty-first century. If you are reading this transmission before the final change point, it is most likely that you are part of the vessels of that heart. You are part of the functioning of that heart, and for some time you should come to the center of that body, to that head and heart, to learn so that you can be sent out to other parts of that body to help coordinate and activate the arms, legs, and all of the vital functions of that body.

We are here at the First Planetary Sacred Home to speak in an audible way through an **audio fusion material complement** because the circuit is open from Universe Headquarters to Planetary Headquarters here. In this manner divine instruction is more immediately given and can be responded to on your third-dimensional level.

The more quickly it is responded to by many of you who are loyal to Christ Michael and can hear His voice at a higher level, the quicker the final change point will come to Urantia, and with greater force, and so will the actualization of your own individual lives then be fulfilled. As I have said before, the kingdom of God on any plane, in perfection or nearing perfection at some level, is based upon syntonic reaction to divine coordinates. If you can adjust your thoughts or oscillations to that same frequency and tune in to the perfect will of God for your life in relation to the people of this planet and the divine authority structure that is now resident in and through the Planetary Prince, then you can create the reality of the divine.

But if by your thoughts you are aligned to a different government and to a lower reality, that is what you have created, and that is what you will exist in, and is perhaps what you have been existing in as an ovan soul. If, in that lower reality you transcend this planet by physical death, do not expect to go to the mansion worlds of Satania, for you have chosen your path of ascension at the moment you lay this adjudication transmission down.

Pick it up again if you must and re-read it, but don't reject it, for if you reject it, you have isolated yourself from the very world on which you should continue to serve, and your misplaced loyalties will keep you in the third-dimensional reality to which you have become so attached.

August 24, 1992

Paladin, Chief of Finaliters

in cooperation with Master Physical Controllers, a Universal Censor, and a Divine Counselor for the calling forth of Cosmic Reservists for the implementation of the Divine Administration of Urantia in and through the present Planetary Prince, Machiventa Melchizedek, and through appointed mandated human personalities presently in third-dimensional physicality and fourth-dimensional consciousness

As transmitted through
the Pre-Level-One Audio Fusion Material Complement,
Gabriel of Urantia/TaliasVan of Tora

PAPER 255

Universal Ontology And Otology In Relationship To Sensing Sensors At The Various Locations Within The Evolutionary Body, The Morontia Body At The First Level, And The Various Diseases And Malfunctioning Circuitry To The Binaural Hearing Of Evolutionary Mortals With Two Outer Ears

THIS transmission will not give a scientific analysis of all that is already understood at some level in modern science. However, we will touch on some terminologies pertinent to the spiritual understanding of certain coordinate functioning.

Regarding echolocation within bats and porpoises, it has been discovered that their auditory nerves, which carry impulses from ear to brain, carry more pulses per second than a human's auditory nerves. In binaural location, a sound coming from one side of the head reaches the nearer ear first, and there exist differences of intensities. In binaural summation, it is understood that two ears hear more than one.

Continuing Fifth Epochal Revelation states that ovan souls, who have built their third ear in coordination with the causal coordinate ear in accordance with universal absolutes and the perfect will of the Eternal Father in accordance with the primal absolute Paradise circuit wave, hear with an increased clarity that stabilizes other body functions.

With normal hearing there is detection of any spectrum of sound as low as 10 decibels. Deafness exists when voice cannot be heard below an average of 60 decibels in speech frequencies. The level of ordinary speech is 60 to 80 decibels. At first it was thought that the most distressing symptom of deafness might seem to be the simple inability to hear sounds of normal loudness. However, defective hearing also alters the quality of sound.

With tinnitus one hears intermittent buzzing or ringing noises. These noises are actually the audio sounds that are being made by malfunctioning circuits within the body and particularly within the central nervous system and the auditory nerves. These circuits malfunction basically because of psychological or emotional problems of the evolving soul. At whatever level of disturbance, at whatever level of malfunctioning, the sensors have been unable to hear from the primal absolute Paradise circuit wave at an adequate reception level, eventually deforming that particular sensor.

All hearing problems can be divided into two classes:

- conduction hearing losses associated with the conductive structures of the ear
- sensory nerve hearing losses associated with the ear's sensory mechanism and the auditory nerves

Conductive hearing losses have their origins in the outer and middle ear where sound is amplified and transmitted to the cochlea. They reduce the individual sensitivity to all sound, no matter what the frequency. Sensory hearing losses arise in the inner ear or brain as a result of the breakdown of the cells in the Organ of Corti or in the fibers of the auditory nerves or in the auditory cortex of the brain.

In relationship to the auditory cortex of the brain, it should be understood that this may affect hearing over the entire range of audible frequencies, or over a portion of that range, destroying hearing altogether or weakening it. The weakening will destroy consonant sounds, making them indistinguishable from one another.

Let us take first the conductive hearing losses that have their origins in the outer or middle ear. All of the various noises that a planet produces, particularly in large cities, are noises of societies based upon greed and principles that are other than divine. Structures that are built have to be built with machinery. Machines make noise. Airplanes traveling above the auditory hearing systems of each and every personality can cause a blockage of frequencies from the circuits of the primal absolute Paradise circuit wave, even if it is temporary.

If this noise is on a continual basis, it is impossible to hear from the higher personalities and even from the Thought Adjuster who taps into the primal absolute Paradise circuit wave just like the individual human does. There is a correlation between the Thought Adjuster and the ascending soul, but the Thought Adjuster also taps into the same primal circuitry as the human's outer ear does. And so the distortion caused by noise blocks even the higher and divine personalities momentarily from giving divine directives.

All of the noises of inappropriate frequencies and distorted sound waves cause very physical problems to begin to take place at some level within the human ear. Over a period of time the fusion within the sensors in the brain or inner ear (and in relationship to the brain itself at a higher spiritual level) also influences the outer ear to malfunction, as the inner ear does not receive the nourishment needed to correlate the higher **Deo-atomic cells** to the brain. Therefore the outer ear becomes independent of the inner ear. As a matter of fact, the right ear becomes independent of the left ear.

Sometimes hearing losses take place in one ear before the other. That is because of very real physical problems caused by one or the other ear continually hearing noises of malfunctioning and discordant frequency waves on a more continuing basis. For instance, people in large cities who sleep on their left side are hearing only on the right side. It can be the busy noise of traffic or noise from a local factory or some other noise, but that ear is still receiving very real audio sounds. Some people have a very difficult time sleeping when noise exists at any level.

Spiritual personalities who are more sensitive to movement in sound do not even have to audibly hear a certain sound, they can sense it. They sense it through the vibrational frequency that it is making. Those less sensitive who hear audio sounds at any level over a period of time, along with the inability to change their thinking, develop loss of hearing at various ages. For instance, it is known that sensory nerve deafness is a hazard of old age and that everyone gradually loses sensitivity to high-frequency sound. This is called presbycusis.

A forty-year-old hears at 15,000 cycles per second, a fifty-year-old at 12,000 cycles per second, a sixty-year-old at 10,000 cycles per second, and a seventy-year-old at 6,000 cycles per second. This is due to the varying degree to which people become set in their ways and in their thinking, rather than the common assumption that they are just getting old. When personalities become set in their thinking, set in their ways, they close off the inner ear or the sensory frequencies necessary to evoke messages within the higher self or the higher-circled mind that activate the brain cells. It is understood that much of the brain cell capacity is not being used by the two-brained personalities on Urantia, and this is ever so true.

Various diseases such as mastoiditis, which is an infection of the middle ear, have to depend upon surgery called myringotomy for correction. Also stapedial surgery seems to restore hearing to thousands of otosclerosis patients each year. However, otosclerosis, which is a conductive disease, affects millions in America, mostly women between the ages of eighteen to thirty years old. It is suspected that this is caused by hereditary factors.

Actually it is caused by what is previously mentioned—distorted sound frequencies and noise, high-pitched noises that are discordant and unpleasant to the ear and block the circuitry within the virtue sensors of the body causing instability of the nervous system on all levels. Even a slow drip from a water faucet can cause great imbalance within the sensory receivers and cause one to become quite unbalanced. From that point of logic, it should be understood what other noises can do, even when you have grown accustomed to them and have learned to live with them.

The higher body simply cannot live with them. That is why higher spiritual personalities are now being called to come out of city life into more **protected areas**. Part of this protection is from sound alone at all levels of inappropriate frequencies. To the degree that even thirty-year-olds have become set in their thinking and do not grow into higher spiritual understanding, they will begin to lose their hearing to some degree. So it is not a disease of old age; it is a disease of a stagnant mind.

Boilermakers' Disease, which is known in science as a deafness caused by excessive sustained noise, is understood because of its traumatic effect upon the individual; but the gradual hearing loss is less understood because of its tendency to slowly take its effect upon the ear throughout the years, particularly in conductive hearing losses. Sometimes it is very noticeable in the adenoid that a very real physical problem exists, but it is undetermined as to exactly what has caused this problem.

A dysfunctional family, an oppressive grade school teacher, abuse from one's peers—any of these things can greatly hinder the hearing of a child or youth in the early stages of development. That is one of the reasons why starchildren of ovan souls, particularly the higher orders now being born to higher complementary parents, must be protected from the outside world at all levels. If not, they will begin to lose their hearing at very early ages, approximately twelve years old, as they are more sensitive to the rebellious frequencies of this planet. In particular this is true of children who have not been to this planet before, such as third-order and other unrevealed orders of starseed children.

Meniere's syndrome is a disease of the labyrinth of the ear characterized by deafness or a ringing in the ears, dizziness, nausea, and vomiting. This is a disease of an imbalance of the Father and Mother circuits. It is a disease of the personality circuitry in an individual who, at any level, is unable to function in harmony with the personality bestowal of the Universal Father and who is unable to be, at any age or level, what he or she needs to be within the age of the soul and the destiny purpose of that individual soul.

If you take a child who is an ovan soul and place him or her in an environment where he or she is being abused at some level—for example, being called a bookworm by students who would rather be outside stepping on ants and pulling the tails off of cats—then you have a child who will develop hearing losses to some degree, and even deafness, if that child is not taken out of that environment. Since approximately 1945 this has already happened in hundreds of cases on Urantia, but modern science does not understand how these children develop this disease at such an early age.

Many children have stomach problems, and of course doctors are looking for the problem in the stomach because they do vomit or even have fits of epilepsy and so on. But these symptoms are often caused by the inability of the child to properly respond to his environmental situation in relation to his higher calling.

In training children, **The Starseed and Urantian Schools of Melchizedek** [now called the **Global Community Communications Schools**] will be able to help these children simply by allowing them to grow at their own speed and to present them first and foremost with the foundations of spiritual cohesiveness that modern education lacks. Absolutes, which are necessary for the growth of higher starseed, resonate within them at some level. You do not have to treat them as most children are treated or with simpler terminology that is often used with children, as many of them have within their superconscious mind the ability to understand the various natures of God at very high levels of terminology.

In the public schools of America and other school systems across the planet where God is not presented to ovan souls in the higher capacities, malfunctioning begins to take place in various parts of the body, because what is heard in and through the ear causes the various sensors to begin to malfunction, which in turn causes diseases in various parts of the body. These diseases develop into many problems, such as ulcers, hiatal hernias, stomach problems, indigestion, and esophagus problems of various kinds, lack of energy, mononucleosis, apathy to the environment, depression, and even anxiety.

One of the greatest problems on Urantia is that there is no commonality of tonal sound quality coming from one individual to another. The various languages themselves, as mentioned in a previous transmission, are such that you do not even understand each other on this planet, and many of the languages are not **Deo-atomic** in their tonal structures.

There is something called a sympathetic vibration. This is a vibration produced in one object by a vibration of the same frequency in another object. When words of truth or words of the personality of God are spoken—either by an ascending son or an ascending daughter, at whatever level of molecular or subatomic personality coordination you are to the Paradise personalities—you then vibrate and send vibrations through your words into the circuitry in those around you who are hearing you.

It does not matter if the personalities themselves understand what you are saying. The **causal body** sensors within the present physical body, the body of the eternal-present, will coordinate with that absolute truth. The higher the words spoken, the more resonance the sensors will pick up and translate. Even if the individual is unconcerned or even rebellious, in his or her mind he or she may reject what you said, but in his or her causal body at some level a truth spoken will heal and balance. In this sense the universe life force energy will bring a balance in a certain part of the body where the circuitry is malfunctioning, first in the inner ear and then bringing a balance between the **crown circuit** and the **third eye**.

This balance will manifest itself within that person for at least twenty-four hours regardless of whether that person is wanting to accept it. During that time, angelic personalities and midwayers can at some level continue speaking to that person, even though you may no longer be with them. You on your level and in your dimension have turned on the switch.

Celestial personalities then begin using the higher currents. You have started the flow, and it can be done even without touch, simply by the spoken word. This is the power of the word absolute. This is the power of absolute truth. This is the power of cosmic law, cosmic reasoning, and cosmic philosophy. This is the power of divinity.

So do not feel when you speak to people and they reject what you say that your words are not taking effect, for they are, even though it may seem that nothing is being accomplished. At some point, at some level, you are bringing them to a degree of balance, enough so that higher celestial personalities can take over where you left off. This is how God works. It is the fusion of one dimension with the other, and each of you is an instrument of the healing process in some way.

The sounds of a symphony can cure a personality if those sounds and melodies are written by celestial musicians for the healing of certain vital glands within the body. Each gland has a reciprocal audio circuitry to divine personalities.

In future transmissions each and every individual sensor cell, each and every **virtue sensor** will be identified and explained, and their functions given. The circuitry flow from one to another, and from one organ to another, and from various universe origins will be given. This information is a vital link to create the coming stages of light and life on Urantia. The fact that it is being given now at this level and at this stage is necessary, for it sometimes takes hundreds of years to understand it at the higher levels, but it must begin somewhere.

It should be understood that there are several thousand virtue sensors located in various parts of the body such as the human ear, the human brain, the human throat, the human heart, the human stomach, and the human sex glands. They are interconnected in the same way as the union of souls is interconnected for divine function. Tens of thousands exist for the coordination with the causal body in its primal creation at some level.

In the future, if enough Destiny Reservists called to Divine Administration align and remain so, it is possible that if only a thousand virtue sensors can be more highly understood, disease can be completely eliminated for those who understand, even if they live in the midst of certain egotistic and ignorant personalities who may exist nearby.[1] They will not be affected by those of lesser mind, lesser spiritual status, or lower circle attainment. To the degree in which these sensors can be learned and identified, healers can go to various parts of the planet to people who are already functioning in **fourth-dimensional** consciousness, and upon the other person's willingness to be recircuited, heal them instantly of any malfunctioning disease within their body.

Very few viruses will exist on Urantia within the fourth dimension, but some will still be in existence even after the cleansing of the planet. This is because there will be survivors on Urantia. Some of the women who are already impregnated will be having children. It is not the will of Christ Michael to transfer them from this planet but to allow them to remain. However, they will be located in specific sector areas and will not be allowed into headquarters areas of any sector location. In a sense, they will be carrying **diotribe** cells within them.

However, these diotribe cells will not be able to leave the body and go into the present earth atmosphere any longer, and all they can do is destroy the body they are presently in. The diotribe cells can only be removed in the same manner in which they are removed now, by proper thinking or by the ministry of a healer who will appropriate a more rapid healing process. Once they are removed, they will disintegrate in the fourth-dimensional atmosphere.

The noise factor on Urantia will be quite different after the final **change point**. This alone will begin to bring balance. Within the conversations held between those in the **cosmic families** of higher-circle attainments, there has been created, and will continue to be created, an **auhter energy** and a healing frequency that will eventually even produce an audible sound.

The consciousness of each planet has a unique sound as well as color. Each planet is a part of a great musical orchestra of the Eternal Father. To the degree of each individual's sensor ability to hear this sound will be the degree that they can begin to hear invisible yet ever-present celestial personalities through higher clairaudience perception. Some of you, although you may not be able to see them, will be able to hear audible voices of pure spirit beings and other nonmaterial beings at various levels.

It is more common on some planets to hear unseen but ever-present personalities than it is to see them. It is quite common on such planets to attend conventions and meetings of divine administration where personalities are present, and you can hear them with the audible ear or the inner ear, but you cannot see them. Sometimes they can pick up an object, and you can see the object moving but nothing holding it.

That will be the norm on Urantia at the **First Planetary Sacred Home**, and then at the other planetary headquarters sectors. These beings will be able to move the physical, because within a fourth-dimensional reality they can and do move physical objects. Many of them can be a great aid in moving heavy objects where it would take four to six human personalities to do the same thing. Learning to utilize celestial personalities for physical construction will be the norm. Learning to hear them with a higher audio capability will also be the goal and then the norm.

It is written that faith comes by hearing. You actually realize little of what that really means. We have written over and over again, if you cannot hear the truth spoken to you by an Elder, by an older soul who is more spiritually in tune, then why do you think that you can hear from an angel or, in fact, from God Himself? God speaks through His creation and speaks through the personalities whom He has created higher than others. If you cannot hear them, then you block the channels of your own growth and the sensors of your own body.

The next higher body is built upon the understanding that those celestial personalities, either in a physical or a nonphysical body at any level, are the representatives of God for you in your ascension process to Paradise. It is through the hearing and the obeying that your next body is built. To the degree of your compliance with this authority structure is the degree of your next level of happiness, fulfillment, and totality.

So, he or she who has an ear, let him or her hear what the spirit of God is saying. First listen to the human Elders who speak to you at your level, for they will only be repeating what the Thought Adjuster is speaking to you from within, but His message is being blocked by the noise of your own self-will and unopened circuitry.

It is the **Father circuits** of time and space that clear the channels of diotribes and open up the frequencies. It is the **Mother circuits** that nourish them once they are functioning appropriately. It is the Mother circuits in the ascending daughters that continuously minister the healing and the nourishing necessary to bring a personality into his or her higher body by this continual care after the Father circuits have cleared the way. It is the circuits of the Son—and, more appropriately, the Spirit of Truth of the Creator Son on Urantia—that decipher cosmic absolutes and then activate responses in and through the central nervous system, coordinate to the fulfillment of divine purpose and destiny, whatever that destiny may be for that particular ascending son or daughter, starseed or Urantian.

The intricate system that involves all three divine personality circuits of the Paradise personalities in relation to the primal absolute Paradise circuit wave involves every cell within the human body or within any created celestial personality, depending upon location in time and space and upon the material or spiritual body in which that personality abides.

As it has been stated, hearing the primal circuitry of the Threefold Spirit is an eternal quest, since Paradise is the goal for evolutionary ascending sons and daughters. The ability of the mechanisms within the present body to function decides your reality. If you are placed in a reality, then that is the reality to which your ascension has brought you.

The physical and the spiritual unite to some degree to cooperate in predetermined co-existence. On fallen worlds of time and space, particularly in present-day Satania and on Urantia, the bodies of ovan souls are nowhere near the form and mechanistic ability designed in the primal origin that they should be. Even first-time Urantians suffer greatly from the inability of the mechanisms of the ear, the brain, and the nervous system to properly relay signals to the rest of the body in order for it to function properly. If it were functioning properly, sleep would not be necessary.

The higher the ability to hear, the higher the body's ability to activate and correspond, the lighter the body becomes physically, and the less the body has to sleep. It is not the mind or soul or the spirit of God within that needs rest; it is the body.

World consciousness does not dictate your reality, but it does greatly hinder it. Individual acquiescence to higher absolutes can change the nature of groupings of peoples on rebellious worlds. Throughout the history of Urantia those ovan souls and **first-time Urantians** with higher genetics, who have grouped themselves together with the ability for higher hearing from God and the purposes of God, have found that their lives have become much easier and more fulfilled. This does not eliminate and has not eliminated the death experience, nor has it eliminated persecution by others in the past; however, it has brought higher fulfillment and higher purpose and manifestation of the material needs to fulfill the destiny of what that particular soul or group of souls can accomplish working together in a corporate group within the union of souls.

Becoming of one divine mind and being able to hear corporately the individual will of God does not change the uniqueness of the personality, nor does it interfere with the individuality of a soul. That is, and has been, the lie of Lucifer. To accomplish great and beautiful things, one within divine will must have the help of others who believe in what one is doing, appreciate it, and help promulgate its usage for the benefit of the people of Urantia or any other planet.

The greed principle is based upon receiving aid from others to accomplish purposes based upon power and self-aggrandizement. The greatest of inventions and the greatest art have not been inspired on this planet or received in personalities who function based upon greed. They have been received by personalities based upon their desire to make life better for others. Personalities who seek insight into mysteries for the purpose of self-recognition, power, or greed usually end up with lower or incorrect theory.

When hundreds of personalities begin to cooperate together within divine purpose on any planet, even on planets that are functioning in default, those hundreds working together and listening to God on the highest levels will always, without exception, find themselves together, no matter from what part of the planet or from what race they are.

If they are on a planet functioning with higher administrative policies, they will be sent to where they belong, based upon that individual's willingness to find his or her cosmic family or those who hear at a higher level of understanding. On Urantia this is done in some way even to those without understanding. Students who have a desire for certain fields of learning attend certain universities or educational and training schools because they feel that is where they will be understood and that is where they can learn the most.

When it is understood on Urantia that the ability to hear from God moment to moment in every aspect of reality is the primal reason for existence, and when each and every individual can tap into the primal absolute Paradise circuit wave at the highest capacity, countless billions on that planet can be blessed, actualized, and fulfilled; and that planet can seem like heaven compared to present-day Urantia, even though the planet is quite evolutionary and physical.

August 31, 1992

Paladin, Chief of Finaliters
in cooperation with a Universal Censor, the Chief of Seraphim, a Master Physical Controller, and Life Carriers from four different universes in cooperation with the Planetary Prince, Machiventa Melchizedek

As transmitted through
the Pre-Level-One Audio Fusion Material Complement,
Gabriel of Urantia/TaliasVan of Tora

PAPER 256

Deo-Atomic Generics[1] In Association With Psychobiology, Psychophysics, And Ascension Science; Psychospirituality In Relationship To The Cosmic Reserve Corps Of Starseed, Second-Time Urantians, And First-Time Urantians Pertinent To Brain Functioning And The Central Nervous System—A Beginning Study

THIS series of transmissions will become increasingly more technical. That is because we are dealing with very intricate individual circuitry. If you look upon a circuit board of the latest electronic equipment and compare it to the very early and basic radio transmitters and receivers, you will see that the advancement of technology has lessened not only the weight of the necessary apparatus, but has also decreased the size of the various component parts and increased essential reception and transmission capacities. Even though the equipment is much smaller (micro in many cases) the coordinating functions and circuitry are more intricate and expanded to such a degree that the original inventor probably could hardly imagine the quality of reception and transmission that most receivers and transmitters have today—transmitters reaching out even into the galaxy.

The human brain is such a receiver/transmitter, and it is totally equipped in its various stages to adequately receive and transmit, based upon the evolutionary process. Although the human brain has grown in size, it has also grown in complexity, but part of its physical growth is unnatural and due to diotribe influence. It is known in modern science, and speculated upon, that the brain in its evolutionary development has had three stages: reptile, mammal, and human.

What has now become known as the cerebrum area of the brain (containing the cerebral cortex) is an intricate receptory and transmitting area of the brain based upon the evolutionary body of twentieth- and twenty-first century human mortals. There are other very intricate parts of the brain that also deal with reception and transmission, not only to the body itself but to other bodies outside of the human physical body: the etheric body, the astral body, and the causal coordinate body.

Unique to Urantia because of the adjudication is the additional morontia body. Included in the various bodies of the individual ascending son or daughter are the subcells of celestial personalities of whom they are somewhat reflective or should be reflective of to some degree.

Intraplanetary communication as well as interdimensional and interplanetary communication are all possible based upon a higher understanding and functioning of the two-brained type on Urantia. Due to the fall of the Planetary Prince and Adam and Eve on this planet, the understanding of the brain in its relationship to the psychospiritual is almost unknown until these transmissions, and psychobiology is in its pioneering stage on Urantia. It is hoped that these transmissions regarding these areas will bring a greater understanding of the individual's responsibility to be godlike in his or her relationship to the use of the mind, which will promote the activation of the higher mind.

Let us start with the central nervous system of the vertebrate, that portion composed of the nervous system and spinal cord, both covered by membranes called meninges and bathed in extracellular fluid called cerebrospinal fluid. 90% of the cells in the central nervous system are neuroglia or glial cells, which serve as a special supportive and protective component of the nervous system. 10% are nerve cells or neurons, which participate in the propagation and integration of information.

The cortex of the brain consists of clusters of nerve cells (neurons) on the outer surface. These are arranged in laminae (or layers) with the unmyelinated ends (which consist of cell nuclei) interconnected by multiple extended filaments called dendrites. It is unknown to Urantian scientists that these particular layers of gray matter are actually diotribe reality. Luciferic thought creates rebellion. Thought → energy → form → physical. The human body has had to adapt to the Lucifer Rebellion. Gray matter of any type is not of the original prototype, although it has become functional. **Continuing Fifth Epochal Revelation** will help to remove this gray matter from the brain, therefore enabling the brain to function in a more highly receptive manner.

Many factors determine the growth of the human body on the subatomic, atomic, and mental levels. It is known that the glial cells are somehow related to the metabolic system. The very way in which a person thinks, in many ways, establishes the rate of metabolism of the body. This is due to many criteria, all too much to speak of at this time.

The long processes, or axons, of neurons course in functional groups called tracts within the nervous system. They appear white and are called the white matter of the central nervous system. This white matter of the central nervous system is the higher **Deo-atomic** cellular replacement. I use the word replacement, for if the brain were functioning at the highest level, the **Deo-atomic cells** would not be replacements but a part of the original design.

The cell nuclei and cortex of the central nervous system have little myelin in them. They appear gray and are called the gray matter of the central nervous system. The complex of gray and white matter forms the organizational pattern of the central nervous system of all vertebrates.

The organizational pattern of the human mortal, in relation to destiny purpose, has been divided by gray matter consisting of diotribe cells of Luciferic thought processes. That which is incorporated into a functional brain (that is, a brain of willed action) begins then to change the very function of the brain and the very physical properties of the brain if those thought processes in willed action are not of the first **primal absolute Paradise circuit wave** purposes.

I will now mention various parts of the brain and will give general information in relation to Continuing Fifth Epochal Revelation.

The **cerebrum** contains the cerebral cortex and also ancestral memories and the language areas. Because of the lack of total absolute reality on Urantia within the language areas, and since there is no common language communication between the races and nations on this planet, the various intricate parts of sensor location within the cerebrum are not functioning anywhere near the percentage rate that they should be at this level of dispensational reality on Urantia. On a scale of 1 to 100, the majority of Urantians are functioning at approximately 10% of their capacity. This is 90% below the level where they could be functioning. Therefore, this prevents the possibility for higher inventions in all of the areas necessary for the advancement of a higher civilization, particularly technological advancements in time-and-space travel.

The **cerebellum** with the arbor vitae, located near the Pons (Pons Varolii), is connected to the brain stem and has much to do with the regulation of thought. It is like a clearinghouse between absolute and relative reality. Science bases the regulation purely upon processing and directing motor functions but does not bring the spiritual into the understanding of this regulation process, which should be the most important. Because this is an unknown science on Urantia, much of this area of the brain is misunderstood or is not understood at any level.

The **occipital lobe**, which is located above the cerebellum, contains the visual cortex and is understood to deal with vision. However, higher vision on Urantia is an almost unknown reality.

The **parietal lobe**, just above the occipital lobe, deals with body senses. With the higher brain types, however, this area should be able to detect invisible but ever-present celestial personalities in an area of upwards to one mile away.

The **frontal lobe**, or motor functioning area, should be able to respond at a much higher and more rapid rate than it does in the present reality. This is why accidents occur on Urantia. On worlds where the motor function is functioning at a higher rate, very few accidents can take place, particularly those that result in death or paralysis of the body. Also, a higher coordination between thought and action takes place.

The **medulla oblongata** or **myelencephalon** is directly connected to the lower body and bodily functions, whereas the cerebral cortex is that part that is connected outward to the various other bodies and other individual celestial personalities, and interdimensional, intraplanetary, and interplanetary communication and reception.

The brain operates in a hierarchal pattern, and modern science has come to this conclusion. The brain is best understood in terms of three functional units: alertness, information processing, and action. Hierarchal pattern vision, at first, consists of lines and patterns of light. When these are coordinated in the visual association area, a meaningful visual pattern emerges that can be linked up with other areas of association in distant parts of the brain to produce perception.

Since the Lucifer Rebellion occurred on Urantia, it has caused a breakdown of pattern form in relation to sound and vision; therefore the brain itself, in its auditory and visual components, has not been able to function anywhere near the capacity it could, due to interference or short-circuits. These short-circuits that occur, affecting literally billions of channels, greatly hinder or block divine purpose that, on an individual basis, relates to fulfillment and actualization. On a planetary basis in the mass consciousness, it relates to the evolution of all the peoples of the planet.

Because of the cellular reality of Urantia, very few individuals can achieve higher areas of brain usage in relation to the causal brain because they would feel isolated and unable to communicate normally with anyone of their own race. One of the problems with pioneers is that they are very seldom understood in any field of endeavor. The cosmic **starseed** on Urantia have always been little understood by their peers. Advancements they have made have been ahead of the majority of others on the planet. However, they could have upstepped their own evolution had they not had false obligations, misplaced loyalties, and misunderstandings based upon a lower error-associated reality.

When error enters the human brain, it short-circuits all of the channels of communication outwardly and inwardly to the body functions, and it functions only in part. With men it results in very physical ways, affecting the various physical body parts, particularly the length and strength of the legs. With women, particularly ovan souls, it affects the physical development and form of the breasts (but not the functioning), due to lack of balance in the Trinity circuits.

Those who are disassociated with, or disconnected from, any of the circuits of Paradise—the **Father circuits**, the **Son circuits**, and the Infinite Spirit circuits—will exhibit physical manifestations within their body structures according to various levels of nonhearing.

A confused, agitated state with hallucinations and loss of recent memory is often associated with certain cancers. This is due to the acceptance of lower reality, nonabsolutes, or a reality based upon ignorance and superstition. It is most unfortunate that many **first-time Urantians** and starseed alike die of various cancers based upon their inability to come out of relative thinking and nonabsolute reality. What happens is that the circuitry of the brain malfunctions, therefore sending distorted messages to other parts of the brain and nervous system, which in turn sends impaired messages causing malfunctions in various parts of the body.

There are various parts of the anatomy that are **sensor units**. These sensor units are activated first within the former morontia body, and the ascension process of each person on experimental Urantia will determine the next body form. If that body cannot be built according to the divine blueprint and is hindered by disassociated construction due to lower thought patterns, then there is a short-circuited functioning taking place, and that body's growth is also hindered. The astral body must then first be healed before the etheric and physical body can follow suit. This is all done by thought processes, and, in relation to the cerebral cortex, they are processes of the brain in and through the audio and sensor areas.

Different functions tend to become localized, principally on one side of the brain or the other. Speech, for the majority of people, has been determined by scientists to be in the left hemisphere, while the organization of space is in the right. However, this differs to various degrees in ovan souls and starseed of specific orders, and it differs quite substantially. This will be discovered in the future by medical doctors who understand Continuing Fifth Epochal Revelation. Surgeons will then look at their operations a little differently, more as it is done on higher worlds of time and space within an evolutionary reality where **ovan souls** and first-time-origin beings share the same planet.

Let me speak now of seven functional areas of the brain that are associated with the seven **cosmic families** on Urantia.

- The **telencephalon** is the anterior division of the prosencephalon corresponding to the cerebral hemispheres. The telencephalon and the diencephalon make up the prosencephalon or the forebrain.

- The **diencephalon** is the posterior subdivision of the forebrain, which contains the thalamus, the subthalamus, and the hypothalamus and is also part of the forebrain.

- The **mesencephalon** is the midbrain. Prominent cell groups of the mesencephalon include the motor nuclei of the trochlear and the oculomotor nerves, the red nucleus and the substantia nigra.

- The **metencephalon** is the first of the two major subdivisions of the rhombencephalon (the hindbrain) along with the cerebellum and Pons.

- The **myelencephalon**, the second part of the rhombencephalon, is also known as the **medulla oblongata**, the lowest subdivision of brain stem contiguous with the spinal cord.
- The **ventricles** are the system of communicating cavities in the brain that are continuous with the central canal of the spinal cord. The lateral ventricle of the cerebral hemisphere communicates with the third ventricle in the frontal lobe, thereby bridging the temporal lobe to the white matter of the occipital lobe.
- The **hippocampus**, named after the Greek word for seahorse (whose shape it resembles), has been shown to be critical in memory information. Hippocampus function is closely related to the search for novelty. This part of the brain is used very little in the early stages of primitive evolutionary humans, and it increases in function as the evolutionary mind develops.

Each one of these areas is very much related to the cultural tendencies of the point of origin of ovan souls. The destiny purpose, ascension level, and particularly circle attainment of each personality at any one point in their chronological progress on Urantia would determine the higher functioning of any one of these areas. The four universes of concern on Urantia— Avalon, Wolvering, Fanoving, and Nebadon—differ in the higher processing of one of these areas over the other.

- Pleiadian personalities—those of **Avalon**—function with a much higher usage of the ventricles and the telencephalon.
- Ursa Major personalities—those of **Wolvering**—function with a higher usage of the mesencephalon.
- Centaurian personalities—those of **Fanoving**—function with a higher usage of the diencephalon, which includes the hypothalamus hormone secretion area.

- **Nebadon** personalities function with a higher usage of the rhombencephalon, which includes the cerebellum, the metencephalon, the myelencephalon, and the hippocampus.

All of these various functioning parts of the brain do not discontinue when a higher body is brought into the reality of the soul and spirit. All that happens is that they become less material. Remember, in the beginning of this transmission I spoke of the difference in weight and size of primitive receptor and transmitter units as compared to the circuitry board of a later developed reception and transmission unit. The hindbrain is the embryonic structure until it develops into the metencephalon, the myelencephalon, and the cerebellum.

Until a personality begins to come to the third psychic circle and then to the first, the hindbrain remains void of the necessary functioning that can turn appreciation of novelty into actual scientific development. Therefore, many of the personalities who could be scientific in orientation pursue careers involving manual labor, and they often remain in these fields. However, if they would come to a spiritual awakening at some point in their life, they would be able to turn their sense of adventure and novelty into higher scientific development.

Their inability to find themselves within the normality of career decision is based upon their inability to function in higher destiny purpose. Many of these personalities develop some form of disease associated with the rhombencephalon (the hindbrain), and it can be determined by medical doctors of Continuing Fifth Epochal Revelation that many of these diseases, including cancer, could be temporarily cured upon surgery of the hindbrain. However, the disease would return if a mind of spiritual absolutes did not take its place.

As one tightly-knit group of skilled workers can do a job better than several fragmented groups working independently of one another, there seems to be an inborn tendency to localize highly specific brain functions in one hemisphere. It should be understood by Continuing Fifth Epochal Revelation students that the cells themselves function like a union of souls, as mentioned in previous transmissions. These cells tend to be associated with various hemispheres of the brain.

Scientists have understood the cerebellum to be two hemispheres, but they cannot understand why. They understand that the cerebellum also has to do with muscle coordination. The real division within the brain is in relation to Deo-atomic and diotribe reality. There should not be two hemispheres at all; there should only be one hemisphere.

Because there are two hemispheres in the cerebellum, muscle coordination is divided. This in turn creates a lower metabolism, a malfunctioning metabolism, and ovan souls inherit the metabolism of their parents. Only when they can come into the first psychic circle and remain on it for more than one year does the metabolism begin to change. Since this is a new study now on Urantia, even after one year the metabolism still seems to remain lower. We speculate that the metabolism will change within a three- to five-year period, which will then create great changes within the physical body itself, even in the **third dimension**.

As I mentioned previously, there are three functional units of the brain: alertness, information processing, and willed action. The outlet channel for willed action is the motor cortex, which contains giant nerve cells with long processes running down the spinal cord and eventually connecting with all the muscles in the body.

Considering willed action, one can be in the will of God, or one can be in self-will. Self-will is the will of Lucifer and the will of the lower self. It has been designed by God the Father that all personalities on all of the worlds of time and space be connected to the higher self. On defaulted worlds this is not necessarily the case.

Willed action corresponds to the prefrontal lobe. Science understands that the frontal lobe is associated with purpose or goal-oriented behavior. I again state at this point that it is not the purpose of Continuing Fifth Epochal Revelation to teach that which is already understood about the brain to some degree. We do suggest that serious students begin a study of the brain. This will greatly help you to understand Continuing Fifth Epochal Revelation psychospiritual and ascension science reality.

Ovan souls, particularly iniquitous ovan souls, are likely to develop various diseases associated with nondestiny purpose and become apathetic because of their willful choice not to follow within divine purpose. They are more easily affected by distractions in their environment, particularly in the nonspiritual environment of Lucifer.

The present-day New Age is a result of the mind/thought damage of Caligastia within these ovan souls due to erroneous literature. Many of these ovan souls own and operate facilities and distribute the literature within the New Age, which further breaks down the prefrontal lobe area of ovan souls worldwide, therefore contributing to their disassociated reality.

If one of these ovan souls were to be operated on by a morontia surgeon, he or she could instantly correct the problem in the prefrontal lobe and recreate their thinking processes and disassociate that part of the brain from their own will. This would be successful as long as the ovan soul, after the operation was over, would be willing to come into absolute reality. The disease that would have already started in these ovan souls would be located in various parts of the body; in females it would appear in the areas of the womb and stomach, and in males it would appear in the area of the upper torso, arms, and upper legs. It will become known by scientists of Continuing-Fifth-Epochal-Revelation understanding that personalities who develop these associated diseases of these body parts will be ovan souls who are arrogant and prideful.

To varying degrees, diseases of the esophagus and the digestive tract will also begin to become associated in the physical with tumors in the area of the cerebral cortex of the brain, for this is the language area.

Since the language of spiritual reality has been misunderstood for such a long time, it has now been decided by the Council of Twenty-four, along with Machiventa Melchizedek, that the previous Deo-atomic cells that have been blocking the diotribes from entering certain channels of the brain now will no longer block them, and diotribe reality will begin to manifest in various parts of the brain. In the future on Urantia it will be discovered that gray matter will begin to formulate in other parts of the brain.

It should be understood at this point that godly virtues are the best medicine that one can take for the healing of all diseases on Urantia. Love, kindness, generosity, gentleness, self-control, sensitivity, nurturing, patience, and other virtues are the result of the personality who is aligned with divine purpose. When that personality incorporates all of these virtues within the higher circles of attainment, diotribe reality is completely removed from the brain.

It will be discovered by scientific analysis that all gray matter, particularly within the higher souls of the **First Cosmic Family**, will be removed from the brain. What this will do is create a reality around their physical reality that can establish certain cellular programs that Life Carriers can then coordinate into the birth processes of cosmic family females and enable the production of a higher brain in the fetuses, all because of the higher ascension of ovan souls and first-time Urantians alike in a specific headquarters sector.

This was the purpose of Adam and Eve in the First Garden. What is now being taught in Continuing Fifth Epochal Revelation was, of course, understood by them. That was the whole reason that the garden was set up to work with the lower evolutionary beings of that time. There was a reason why certain foods were grown. There was a reason why Adam and Eve came to this planet so that their offspring would be able to intermix with the evolutionary races of the planet. It is unfortunate that the plan was not fulfilled.

However, it can now take place with the descendants of Adam and Eve and with the descendants of the Caligastia One Hundred who are here now to do what they failed to do the first time. Continuing Fifth Epochal Revelation in relation to mind and body is in many ways a reenactment of what should have taken place thousands of years ago. Continuing Fifth Epochal Revelation could have been the norm on this planet thousands of years ago. Therefore, what is being taught now is thousands of years behind schedule on Urantia.

There are generic **Deo-atomic unit** locations within the body that will be specifically given in future transmissions. These transmissions will not be able to totally elaborate in scientific definition upon each and every aspect of the human body in relation to psychospiritual reality. This is because when we speak of body absolutes, we speak of the causal body.

The **causal body** in relation to the human body is the body of the future, and for some starseed, the past. The physical human body is the body of the present, the eternal-present. The eternal-present body is the body that exists as long as the personality involved exists in somewhat of a material form. It is the physical body or cellular manifestation in which the soul finds himself or herself at any moment in his or her ascension. The ascension process to Paradise will require learning about the first causal body, the causal coordinate bodies, and the growing into them by the evolutionary mortal.

To the degree that you can understand at the basic level of Continuing Fifth Epochal Revelation will be the degree to which you can really change your reality and the reality of those who are associated with your cosmic family. It should be understood that you cannot change your reality outside the reality of your cosmic family, as each cell of yours is coordinated to function in higher reality based upon the interassociation and interdependence of one another.

Again we state that your reality is interdependent and in association with others of your cosmic family. Each of you is a cell coordinate with the functioning of the whole family, and your whole family is one particular body. You can think of your family as a sphere of reality, and within that sphere each of you is a cell that functions coordinately with other member cells of your sphere, based upon your individual qualities and individual virtues.

Paper 256

As Urantia science expands into constellation-level understanding, scientists will see, to an ever increasingly higher degree, very significant analogies between the construction of the ultimaton and the co-functioning of the seven superuniverses in relation to Havona and Paradise. This will enable personalities with a higher understanding and higher spirit bodies to travel in time and space at a much more rapid rate, using nonphysical approaches to time travel. Physical travel through physical reality also can be greatly upstepped in technology when the cell is understood in a psychospiritual context in relation to higher technology.

When you can begin to associate your own healing, your own destiny purpose, and your own fulfillment and actualization moment to moment in association with others of your cosmic family, in particular your higher spiritual complements, you will come to understand that your attractions to each other are not really based upon the eyesight, but upon something much higher, and that is upon Deo-atomic molecular structure itself.

When a person who has the same genetic Deo-atomic cellular makeup as you is near you, certain subatomic particles or subcells themselves can inter-travel, the same as the particles that can inter-travel between Thought Adjusters. Thought Adjusters can communicate one to another, and so, to a lesser degree, can subcells traverse channels with one another when personalities of like minds and genetic coding are in the same auric field of one another.

That is why certain healings have taken place, and do take place, when personalities are near each other based upon the willed action of the healed individuals to change their thought processes, which will determine if that healing will continue or if disease will return. However, a soothing and temporary healing will take place if the lower personality is with the higher personalities, even if that individual is unconcerned about higher absolute concepts or absolute laws.

One absolute law is that higher **Deo-atomic reality** will soothe lower Deo-atomic reality, even if only temporarily. This is to bring a temporary balance to the lower personality with hopes that the lower personality will realign himself or herself to the purposes of the Universal Father. This plan was set into motion by Michael of Nebadon upon the very first stages of the Lucifer Rebellion.

It was never intended for the Lucifer Rebellion to go beyond a certain stage of rebellious development. All rebellious tendencies in relation to the brain and other functioning units of the body in those orders of beings who sided with Lucifer have been observed for 200,000 years now in the system of Satania.

Continuing Fifth Epochal Revelation on Urantia deals with Urantian mortals, both cosmic and native. Future generations of Urantians of the two-brained type will be personalities who are working with full brain capacity. This has been an unknown factor on Urantia, so we can only speculate as to the development of the mass consciousness of Urantia in the later part of the first stages of light and life and onward. We do speculate that spacecraft will be developed in the physical that will not only go to other planets in this solar system, Monmatia, but will go to other solar systems as well.

Other advancements in genetic breeding will also bring to Urantia much higher cultural realities in relation to the advancement of body and mind in family life at much earlier stages of chronological maturation and development. Aging will be almost eliminated, and the normal body will reach stabilization of chronological development at approximately thirty years of age.

Somewhere in the process of bringing through Continuing Fifth Epochal Revelation in the future, charts will be developed, based upon Continuing Fifth Epochal Revelation terminology in relation to brain functioning and in relation to reception of extraterrestrial and interdimensional personalities. This will become particularly necessary because of the Machiventa Melchizedek Administration resident now on Urantia and the association of the staff of Machiventa

Melchizedek with human personalities mandated within that administration.

It should be noted at this point, that in the future, more diseases of the brain will develop in iniquitous personalities, particularly in those in positions of power and control. Those in governments and in executive positions in many corporations will begin to develop brain tumors and malfunctioning brain circuitry. At the same time, because of the malfunctioning of these brain areas, unknown diseases will begin to appear in other areas of the body, which will bring unknown types of paralysis to various parts of the body that will not be able to be labeled under any of the present known diseases. All of these diseases will be brought about because of the **adjudication of the Bright and Morning Star versus Lucifer**, and many of these souls will develop these diseases based upon hundreds, and even thousands, of years of continual adherence to the Lucifer Manifesto.

September 6, 1992

Paladin, Chief of Finaliters
in coordination with Life Carriers, Master Physical Controllers, a Universal Censor, and a Divine Counselor for the calling forth of the Cosmic Reserve Corps and for the implementation of the Divine Administration of the Planetary Prince, Machiventa Melchizedek, and for the higher correlating communication between human personalities of that administration and celestial personalities in our dimension, now and in the years ahead, because of their higher understanding of brain functioning

As transmitted through
the Pre-Level-One Audio Fusion Material Complement,
Gabriel of Urantia/TaliasVan of Tora

PAPER 257

The Four Divisions Of The Urantian Human Brain In Relationship To Interuniversal Cellular Formation Of The Human Brain, Corresponding To Specific Functioning Sensory Positions In Relationship To Universal Reflectivity Of Various Personality Bestowals Pertinent To A Particular Universe

URANTIAN mortal brain development in its physiological evolution is a combination of the intercellular reality of four universes, having to do with the frontal lobe, the temporal lobe, the occipital lobe, and the parietal lobe.

We should discuss the fact that included in the seizures of limbic types of epilepsy are particular forms of familiarity in which they have a déjà vu experience or a past-life experience, with feelings of a past-life existence. The limbic system is also called the rhinencephalon or nose brain. It should be understood at this point that more than 98% of the brain is hidden within the depths of the sulci (invaginations). The limbic system is the center for feeding, fighting, fleeing, and sexual behavior, or more appropriately, for life sustaining, life protection, reproduction, and gratification.

The déjà vu experience in relationship to certain epileptic seizures is because of a tapping into the circuitry within the archipallium or reptilian brain, or into the centrifugal center in relation to the original genetic personality that first incorporated the cell or cells that are now functioning within your human body, which in reality is a cell or cells that once functioned within an ancestor.

The very brain itself is formulated to coordinate with similar polarities of cells much like what formulates into physical matter at this time. When an open circuit enables a tapping into the past, what actually happens is that cells of time-past reality are released and begin to correlate with present reality in relation to the now-active brain of the present. This then corresponds to the central nervous system, and memories are opened.

It was never intended within the present body and soul personality for that memory to be opened by epilepsy, but due to an imbalance or disease in some other area of the mind and brain or body the circuitry is opened. This kind of situation can happen to an **ovan soul** and quite frequently does. This happens not only in relation to epilepsy but in other experiences where circuitry is opened in relation to a traumatic situation, or a mystical experience, or via the natural process of ascension to higher circles of ovan souls.

One can feel very strongly about something and yet be dead wrong. Modern science has discovered this fact and that it is possible for this to be a form of paranoid psychosis or what we call **psychoschizophysiology**. Psychoschizophysiology is the relationship between the **dio** and **Deo** neurotransmitters and the central nervous system, and their relationship responsive to the systems of the body and the physical body itself to the cellular level functioning primarily coordinate to the Conjoint Actor, although quantitatively and qualitatively responsive to the Father/Son circuitry.

Continuing Fifth Epochal Revelation states that when trying to discern absolute direction or God's will by feeling, many vital circuits will be blocked. Although your pattern of direction may seem correct and although it may work out for you temporarily in some way in your life by going by your feelings, you will eventually find that your life is most likely that of sheer existence, void of true happiness, self-actualization, and fulfillment.

It is cosmic reality that personalities who trust in their own feelings and not in the will of God purpose themselves for some kind of hurt or even destruction. It is quite dangerous, particularly on a fallen planet like Urantia, to confuse using cosmic clairvoyance and higher spirituality with following one's feelings in relation to discovering the definition of God's direction. Feelings always have to do with one's own likes or dislikes and with one's own discretion. Decisions made based upon one's own feelings short-circuit much of the functioning within the body, particularly in the brain, blocking all the major communication channels between celestial personalities who may or may not be your guides, and most of all the Thought Adjuster that is trying to direct or redirect you into the perfect will of God for that particular moment.

Decision-making in relationship to feelings can get a person off track for many Urantian years, sometimes for a whole lifetime, once a particular major circuit is blocked. For instance, if God wants you to move geographically from one place to another and you make a predetermined decision based upon your own desire, calling it God's choice, and do not move geographically, so many circumstances will not be able to happen in your life that are divinely purposed for you, so that it is almost like committing suicide in relation to spiritual growth and destiny purpose.

Until you as an ascending son or daughter can begin to make decisions that go against your own desires and in particular your own feelings—so that you can move yourself geographically, or move from one job to another, or move from a relationship you do not belong in, or move from whatever it may be that keeps you from being in perfect alignment with God's absolute choices for you—much of the main circuitry from your higher **causal coordinate body** to your lower physical body in relation to the guidance of intervening ministers or administrators such as seraphim, cherubim, sanobim, and midwayers who correlate God's will for you, will remain uncircuited and/or circuit-blocked.

At the time of the Lucifer Rebellion the circuits were cut off or blocked. They are now beginning to be reopened, and the way that they are opened is that your own human soul and mind have to connect with the higher purposes of God's will for you as an ascending soul. Your mind has to correlate with your totality.

If your mind does not correlate with the totality of your present existence, that is, the totality of God's will for you corporately in union with others who have also connected with the totality of God's will for them, then you separate yourself from the circuitry of God and are an isolated energy. Being an isolated energy, you will either rejoin the circuitry of your **cosmic family** on Urantia or you will become an isolated unit to the degree that you will eventually disintegrate. This is because you will create within the dimension of Urantia a short circuit for others.

The **protected areas** of Urantia, even more than the rest of the planet at this time, will eventually become one precise digital board where all personalities living in that area will be able to hear at a precise level, moment to moment, God's will for them as individuals, therefore forming the very highest cosmic pattern on Urantia. This is what the **First Planetary Sacred Home** is about, or at least should be, but on Urantia it has never been. The highest personalities who functioned in this manner on Urantia formed the first digital board on Urantia, which was the staff of the Caligastia One Hundred before the fall.

Now it is possible at the First Planetary Sacred Home that several hundred of you, perhaps several thousand of you, or, who knows, perhaps several million of you can function in this manner before the final **change point**. At the First Planetary Sacred Home, if several hundred of you can do so, you will be more fulfilled and actualized as individuals as you cooperate with the divine mind to implement the Divine Administration on Urantia in liaison with the Planetary Prince and staff.

When you as an individual clear your circuitry enough for your brain—with all of its electrochemical processes and neural pathways—to function clearly for reception from the Thought Adjuster, Spirit of Truth, and Holy Spirit in cooperation with whatever guides are assigned to you, corporately you can create the **energy reflective circuit** and **auhter energy** to bring a more stabilized higher frequency of reception to each and every one of you.

Each of you acts as a capacitor to increase the healing reception of one another. Those of you who are functioning in the higher circles of attainment with the fusion of the higher mind capability, particularly among the Eldership, create the circuitry of a direct link to Jerusem Headquarters and Salvington itself, bypassing any of the substations and hundreds, and sometimes thousands, of celestial personalities that it takes to bring one message to one personality clear enough so that he or she can hear it.

Most of the time, because of so many blockages, even in this great pathway of administrative communication, individuals still find themselves quite unable to hear universe directives and universe mandates. Because of this problem on Urantia, many individuals without higher opening of circuitry—even those in spiritual work and of previous higher circle attainment—have had to suffer much on Urantia, not because they were not well-intentioned, but because they were not able to create the auhter energy or the **Deo-atomic reality** around them—inward and outward—to open up the circuits for clearer reception.

Indeed, it has been a very difficult thing to hear from one's God. Now on Urantia, a unique experience is happening. Divine directives and mandates are given directly, using lesser celestial personalities along the way. It is almost as if mandated personalities at various levels are hearing directly from Christ Michael personally. The Spirit of Truth, which has functioned for the last 2,000 years on Urantia, has not worked at the level that it is working at the present time.

Because of such a short time on Urantia to do what has to be done in the formulation of the Divine Administration in the seven Divine New Order communities around Urantia, it is of the utmost importance that at whatever level an individual at the First Planetary Sacred Home can hear from the Threefold Spirit within and from his or her own guides to complement the reception of what the Elders are hearing at their level, and particularly **Gabriel of Urantia/TaliasVan of Tora**.

At whatever level that it can be received by you, divine mind is talking to everyone, usually at the level of reception so that when a directive is given by Eldership it can be understood more rapidly, and procedure can be implemented to outwork that directive as quickly as possible. Feelings and emotions all block the reception when it comes to certain situations so that you have not clearly heard what is necessary for you to hear at your level.

On planets functioning normally, great accomplishments can take place in a matter of a few hours, whereas on Urantia it could take a few months to a few years to accomplish the same thing. If you multiply this by the mass confusion on Urantia, what could be accomplished in three months on another planet could take three to five years on Urantia.

Here at the First Planetary Sacred Home you can function in the most rapid and necessary manner to promote the Divine Administration on Urantia and to accomplish what needs to be accomplished before the final change point and onward into the first stage of light and life. To accomplish this, decisions have to be made by ovan souls who are being led to the First Planetary Sacred Home. Within these Cosmic Reservists who for any reason have been unable to hear the true will of God the Father—in this case the Father and Sovereign of Nebadon, Christ Michael—due to misplaced loyalties, perhaps even to the Urantia movement, which has defaulted, there will be areas of the brain that will begin to respond to diotribe reality causing brain tumors, increased depression, dyslexia, and the inability of the body to respond to thought processes.

It is of the utmost importance that Cosmic Reservists, particularly those who have been given great responsibility in destiny purpose, align themselves to the Divine Administration that is happening here at the First Planetary Sacred Home. It is the only way that brain tumors of this nature can be healed completely. It is the only way that the problems of interassociation of the nervous system and the brain can be healed.

In the first century, Judas, the apostle of Jesus, caused the thought processes that eventually led to his own demise. In the twentieth and twenty-first centuries, perhaps the same thing is happening to many of the Cosmic Reservists and Urantian Reservists who are indeed called to be the apostles and change agents of the Divine New Order. As Christ Michael has said, the way to destruction is wide and the way to eternal life is narrow. Many Urantian Reservists and Cosmic Reservists have chosen the wide path, and it is taking them to their own destruction.

There was one door in the ark of Noah, and there is one door for you now, who wish to become part of the true Divine Administration, to come through, and that is the door of the present Planetary Prince, Machiventa Melchizedek, at his Planetary Sacred Headquarters, in cooperation with the human mandated personalities whom Christ Michael has recognized and mandated.

Four Divisions of the Brain

In order to understand blockages and their effect on brain and central-nervous-system functions in relation to reopening the circuits within the brain that affect our decision-making abilities, it is necessary to understand how the four divisions of the brain function.

We begin with the frontal lobe and the neural pathways that govern motor activity of the body. It is obvious that poor motor coordination, brought about by blockages in the neural pathways that can deflect signals sent to various body parts, would be the cause of many accidents due to slow reflexes. On planets where the motor areas are functioning with precision as intended, accidental injuries are, to a large extent, prevented.

If the motor area were functioning normally in the ovan souls, some of them would actually be able to fly. This has to do with changing the cellular reality of your body to a higher reality so that you are no longer prisoners of gravity because you will have the freedom of movement of your eternal-present body when you have met certain requirements. Because the motor area is functioning at a very low level in ovan souls, a lot of them cannot even run without getting out of wind; their bodies are so out of shape. They have not met the standards of their genetic ancestry. Their metabolism is malfunctioning, and much of the motor sensory abilities are not even near realized. When they meet those standards, some of the ovan souls will be able to run at great distances without losing wind, and it will be possible to travel on foot at Urantian speeds of 70 to 100 miles per hour. Reflection actions will also be greatly upstepped in the offspring of these souls.

In the area of speech few human mortals are able to speak more than one language. However, ovan souls reaching the first circle will have the ability to speak interuniversal languages. Fanoving (Centaurian) languages, Avalonian (Pleiadian) languages, and Wolvering (Ursa Major) languages will begin to come back to them.

The planets within these universes that have developed into the higher stages of light and life have developed higher language forms, and the language of those particular planets on which the ovan souls have once been will begin to be remembered. This is necessary for interuniversal communication. The language that is an interuniversal language of a particular planet must be learned in order to communicate with those on that planet who are still in mortal reality.

It should also be noted that some on these planets have developed very high technological abilities. Many of these relatives are now in physical spacecraft, and it is the language of the mother planet that these beings presently speak. In order to communicate with them in the future, they will not be learning English, for instance, even though English will be the language of the first stage of light and life on Urantia. Those in the higher administrative functions of the Machiventa

Melchizedek Administration will eventually have to learn the languages of their ancestors, particularly those who have come into the higher stages of light and life. That is because these languages are higher than the English that is on Urantia. At some point, hopefully around 2010 on Urantia, there will be classes and training in these areas of interuniversal languages.

Also in the frontal lobe are the frontal areas concerned with emotion, judgment, and behavior. It should be noted here that many **first-time Urantians** and ovan souls alike who become very judgmental and cannot handle their emotions or are emotionally scarred in some way exhibit very noticeable behavior in this area and develop diseases of the body and sometimes, if they become iniquitous, develop tumors in this area of the brain.

Urantian scientists have not understood this correlation as of yet. They may have discovered that a personality may be under tremendous pressure and be overburdened emotionally, and they may think that this has caused the tumor, but a further investigation by a spiritual healer might disclose that even though this person may be a university professor, in some area in his life he may be teaching iniquitous principles and ungodly, nonabsolute reality to his students to such a degree that the circuits within his brain pattern are blocked in this particular area, causing a malfunction of the circuitry of that area, blocking higher healing from taking place by Deo-atomic cellular reality.

Continual abuse by a husband of a wife over a period of time, preventing her from growing into the spiritual personality she is meant to be, can also cause a brain tumor in the frontal lobe of the brain of that specific male. Unless a change of behavior is realized by that male, any healing will be temporary, and the brain tumor or another form of disease will occur in some other part of the body.

The Temporal Lobe

Moving on to the temporal lobe and the hearing section of the brain, it is written that those who can truly hear hear by a higher sense or a spiritual sense. Many hearing problems, which have been discussed in some of the previous transmissions, are the result of a problem in hearing from God or an unwillingness to hear from others. If you think that no one else has anything to say, then you actually block off certain channels within the ears that are meant to correlate with other parts of the brain because that is how the brain is set up, based upon a virtue sensor called humility. If that virtue sensor within the humility structure of the Pons area is blocked, then many hearing problems will develop that can actually be transferred even to the offspring of that person, particularly if he or she has children in the later years of life.

Also, in hearing interpretation, what one hears can be interpreted in many different ways. Something said may be understood at various levels by personalities, and if it is not heard at the very highest of levels, then this can actually change the decision process of a person, or even of a family, a nation, or a planet. When personalities within the first circle hear at the same level, that is one reality; when they all hear within the second circle, that is another; within the third circle, that is another; within the fourth, fifth, sixth, and seventh, that is another.

Presently on Urantia there are only a dozen or fewer personalities whose hearing interpretation of God's will in relation to the **primal absolute Paradise circuit wave** is within the first circle. Only Gabriel of Urantia/TaliasVan of Tora and **Niánn Emerson Chase** are stabilized on the first circle. When there can be hundreds hearing within the level of the first circle, so many changes can take place on Urantia that we would need a volume to discuss them. This has to do with those of the Cosmic Reserve Corps of Destiny understanding Continuing Fifth Epochal Revelation regarding the administration of Machiventa Melchizedek, and then for them to teach the Urantian Reserve Corps of Destiny. It is the Cosmic Reserve Corps of Destiny that will have a higher developed area within the temporal lobe of their brain.

Let us move on to the sensory areas. As mentioned in the previous transmissions, all throughout the human body are sensor locations. The sensing of each individual in relation to moment-to-moment realization depends upon a large variety of things, all too complicated to get into at this time. For instance, the sense of smell can be a strong driving force in relation to recreation for some personalities, whereas on Urantia very few think of recreation being involved with the sense of smell. Although flowers are enjoyed for their fragrances to some degree, very few Urantian personalities can enjoy fragrances enough to realize it as a form of recreation. On planets where the sense of smell is more highly developed, the use of the nose in this area can also trigger cellular responses to intrauniversal and interuniversal realities that are different from cellular memory. The use of the sense of smell can also be correlated in relation to soul travel, whereas on Urantia it is impossible to do this.

Reading ability is located in the temporal lobe area of the brain. At this time on Urantia, reading ability is greatly based upon the evolutionary age of the soul, the genetic inheritance of the first-time Urantian, and the willingness of the soul, either first-time or ovan, to align themselves with the Machiventa Melchizedek Administration. Ovan souls who have aligned themselves will begin to function with higher mindal abilities because of the opening up of circuitry, which you are now beginning to learn about regarding brain functioning.

It could be the will of Christ Michael to open up circuits without you knowing what is happening. However, we have found out that it is quite dangerous. It is like giving you a key to a high technological device, and you turning it on, and it harming you in some way because you did not know how to step out of its way in an instant or to use the power properly.

The opening up of the circuits on Urantia is a gradual process up into the second and third stages of light and life for specific individual personalities. It will not happen all at once. This is based upon an individual's ability to align himself or herself with the purposes of God on Urantia, and the purposes of God on Urantia are the purposes of the Machiventa Melchizedek Administration and the functioning of it.

The Divine Administration on Urantia will be established gradually, with individuals gradually. Even after the final change point it will continue to be a gradual opening up of circuits and a gradual coming into the first stage of light and life and above. For those individuals who walk into Continuing Fifth Epochal Revelation now, the gradual opening of their own circuitry, of their own memories, and of their own mindal and other abilities will greatly change their realities in many ways.

Reading ability is accelerated by the understanding of higher cosmic terminology; in this sense on Urantia, the Continuing Fifth Epochal Revelation is the highest cosmic terminology now being presented to Urantian mortals in the form of language. Unless disciplined souls are willing to invest their time and mental effort into studying and learning this terminology, this part of their brain will not develop to the point necessary to enable them to be used in Divine Administration. They may function within the Divine New Order in other capacities, but they will not be able to be used in administrative positions or any position of authority.

Regarding personalities who have reading disabilities on Urantia, it should be discovered even now that in underdeveloped countries those who are unable to read can easily develop diseases in the temporal lobe area of the brain. Scientists will discover more correlation between disease in the central nervous system and the temporal lobe area, and this should be discovered by those who study Fifth Epochal Revelation in third world countries. Even in Western civilization, those who have not developed the temporal lobe section of the brain will be discovered to have diseases associated with this underdevelopment. Their inability to read will be associated with a coordinating function of the central nervous system, which will be elaborated upon in a future transmission.

Speech understanding is also located in the temporal lobe. It has been discussed in a previous transmission that on Urantia it is very difficult for people to understand one another and that languages have developed based upon Luciferic reality and relative thinking. On planets where rebellion has not touched the one-, two-, and three-brained types, they have such an understanding in relationship to speech that intrauniversal and interuniversal communication can take place between individuals, and intra- and interuniversal languages can be learned at such a rapid rate that this area of the brain then corresponds with the central nervous system, promoting a higher artistic ability.

Celestial artisans and musicians will begin to coordinate intrauniversal and interuniversal harmonic and melodic patterns indigenous to other planets, which they may not have visited but can tune into, and formulate symphonic structures including those harmonic patterns. Sensitive personalities can actually begin to hear the music of the planets themselves.

Planets have a musical tone and vibration to them. Planets can be actually listened to musically, as well as the rhythmic patterns created by the inhabitants of those planets. Each solar system has its own voice pattern as well as each planet. One can tap into the symphonic orchestra of the physical planets in relationship to their central sun. Those solar systems that are functioning in the first stages of light and life and above have a unique symphony to them. Speech of the citizens of such planets is in correlation to the sound patterns of the physical planet itself. This has more to do with pitch than with vocabulary.

When pitch can be used to the degree necessary in relationship to the primal absolute Paradise circuit wave resonant to that particular planet in Paradise time sequence (meaning sequence that is not disturbed by rebellion in any way), that tone, if it can be duplicated by the personality who hears it, can be used in many ways, such as: lifting heavy objects, traveling from one place to another on that planet, helping another more material personality travel from one place to another, healing of a disease of the body, and for many other usages that are beyond your English vocabulary to describe.

The Parietal Lobe

Bodily-awareness functions are located in the parietal lobe. The correlation of mind with the various moveable parts of the body—such as the toes, feet, legs, fingers, and arms—is also functioning at far below the normal level of the evolutionary purposes designed for this planet. Because of this, the very architecture on Urantia is much different from, and far below, the norm of other planets that have not defaulted. Physical transportation also falls below the design of what it could be, and the bulk of transport machinery is much heavier and formulated in forms of cubes and squares rather than in more graceful patterns.

On architectural worlds, architectural designs of both organic and inorganic reality greatly influence the brain patterns, and when a personality goes to planets that are architecturally designed to the higher usage of brain thoughts, interuniversal cultural realities are more presently realized in moment-to-moment sequence. This helps visitors to various planets stabilize themselves in a greater understanding of the native personalities.

Urantia is not at all functioning with interuniversal architectural reality. Because of that, personalities who are genetically connected to interuniversal ancestry are living in architectural designs that are not best suited to them as individual ascending sons and daughters. In the sector areas of the Divine New Order to come, the architecture, particularly in the sector administrative areas, will be more resonant with interuniversal architectural reality based upon the planets of origin and systems of origin that are in the higher stages of light and life.

Writing ability, which requires the correlation of mental and physical abilities in communication, is located in the lower part of the parietal lobe. This subject could take a whole transmission, but those on Urantia who are used to bring automatic-writing messages to the degree necessary to receive from those beings they are receiving from have a somewhat clearer parietal lobe channel. But because other parts of their body are malfunctioning to various degrees, the automatic writing is not the highest form of interdimensional extraterrestrial communication. That is why we are speaking to an **audio fusion material complement** in audio reality at this time. However, on planets that have not defaulted, intercommunication by reflective personalities through automatic writing can be just as valid as the audio fusion material complement communication technique we are presently using with Gabriel of Urantia/TaliasVan of Tora.

The Occipital Lobe

Visual interpretation is located in the occipital lobe. There have been schools of thought based upon philosophical reasoning that ask, "Is what you see something that really exists?" The fact that what you see can be touched and then realized does not necessarily mean that what you touch and see is actually what another sees to the same degree. Colors for instance may be perceived by one a little differently than others. Although there may be some standardized reality of recognition, the higher that one becomes spiritually, the more clearly one begins to interpret colors and the more colors one can begin to see.

Urantians, from the **fourth dimension** and above within the first stages of light and life, will see many more colors and have greatly advanced visual perception, which also originates in the occipital lobe reception area. It is already happening with those at the First Planetary Sacred Home, particularly among the Eldership where visual perception is beginning to become upstepped.

Depending upon many circumstances, it will be the Eldership of Divine Administration—beginning with Gabriel of Urantia/TaliasVan of Tora and Niánn Emerson Chase and the **Mandate of the Bright and Morning Star**, then the Liaison Ministers, the other Elders, the **First Assistants**, and Vicegerent **First Ambassadors**—who will first see Machiventa Melchizedek and others of the staff, particularly those of the other three universes concerned, personalities from those universes that will also be seen at increasing levels of perception. Midwayers, possibly sanobim and cherubim, will also be perceived by those within the First Planetary Sacred Home of Urantia. Certain others who are part of the seven planetary sacred home sector areas will also begin to be able to perceive celestial personalities at a higher level.

If Christ Michael decides to return, then of course, what I have just said will greatly change in many ways. We ourselves can only speculate, based upon our experience and information that we have, about the kinds of changes that Christ Michael's return will bring with it. We give information at this point in reference to the fact that He is not here and what will begin to happen with the Eldership and possibly First Assistants until He does return.

If Machiventa Melchizedek is given permission to materialize, basically it will be the Elders and First Assistants who will see him first for some time, even before he becomes visible to others in the community of Divine Administration. This is because it will be a gradual and not an instant visual realization of **rematerialization**. We have already been informed that this will be the manner in which Machiventa Melchizedek will materialize, if indeed he is given permission to do so by Christ Michael. And so, this is one of the reasons for learning these higher principles of Continuing Fifth Epochal Revelation, because the perception visually is not just the perception of what you now presently see, but what you do not see.

The three-brained types all function in a higher relative capacity, coordinate to the seven superuniverses. Urantia at this time coordinates with only two superuniverses. One-brained types usually coordinate with only one superuniverse. It is not impossible for two-brained types to coordinate with more than two superuniverses, but these realities are beyond the scope of this transmission.

Because of the interuniversal cellular genetics of Urantia reality, the physical formation of the human head of contemporary Urantians has its prototypes. Upon keen observation you can and should be able to see that various head formations differ in form and size. Paleontology of the future will discover that the offspring of the higher spiritual complements of the Divine New Order will form a new head type on Urantia that will be much different than the physical head type now present on Urantia.

September 14, 1992

Paladin, Chief of Finaliters
in cooperation with interuniversal Life Carriers, interuniversal Master Physical Controllers, a Master Architect now resident on Urantia on the staff of Machiventa Melchizedek, and interuniversal unrevealed personalities

As transmitted through
the Pre-Level-One Audio Fusion Material Complement,
Gabriel of Urantia/TaliasVan of Tora

PAPER 258

Psychochemical Behavior Responses Of The Brain In Relationship To Deo-Atomic Mind-Soul Causal Current, Deo-Atomic Receptor Units, And Causal Memory Circuits Within The Family Of Neurotransmitters

BRAIN and behavior are intimately interwoven in a tapestry of infinite complexity. Cerebellar stimulation and environmental stimulation, or lack of it, are ways that can determine whether or not an immature brain will develop normally. By the implementation of cerebellar stimulation or a pacemaker, which causes a short-circuiting phenomenon in pleasure pathways of the brain with violent patients, complete remissions have occurred.

Continuing Fifth Epochal Revelation, however, states that other behavioral problems will develop if the spiritual root of the problem is not understood by the patient through psychospiritual methods of counseling. Ovan souls, especially with pacemaker healing of a particular problem, will recircuit another psychopathological disturbance.

Tron therapy is necessary in these situations to recircuit and rechannel Deo-atomic reality into specific pathways so that they can be realigned with the appropriate receptors. The brain, being a physical system, can be modified by physical agents. Psychochemical agents such as tranquilizers and antidepressants have been established as the most common means of treating the major mental illnesses. Continuing Fifth Epochal Revelation states again that this transition from psychological to psychochemical treatments only recircuits pathways to disturb other behavioral areas.

Lithium, although seemingly successful with manic-depressive behavior, causes the blockages of the neurotransmitters of appreciation and satisfaction sensors, causing patients to fall out of love with spouses and become apathetic in other formerly enjoyable areas or other things of life. Even though seemingly normal and appropriate behavior will occur while using lithium, other more dangerous side-effects affecting decision-making in the mind have as yet been undetermined by present-day Urantian scientists, although there have been a few who have theorized about other inappropriate behaviors in relation to satisfaction, appreciation, and normal love of spouse and children.

Urantian research has determined that neurons in reality are separate cells that communicate with each other but are never in direct physical contact. The brain is activated by electrical circuits. Scientists have developed a theory of brain action as being both electrical and chemical. Generators of weak electrical currents lie on the surface membrane of nerve cell bodies as well as along the dendrites and axons. With electron microscopes, surface structure of the neuron can be observed to possess many points where the axons of one cell approach very closely, but do not touch, the dendrites of other cells.

Communication between neurons is achieved when electrical potential is generated in one cell and travels along its axon at a constant rate in a coded sequence. When the signal reaches the next axon, it is ready to transfer to the next neuron. Nerve communication by a chemical process is about to take place. These neurotransmitters cross the synaptic cleft and selectively alter the membrane of the second cell by linking to a specific receptor. Scientists refer to the match between a neurotransmitter released from the first cell (the synaptic membrane of the axon) and its special receptor site in the second cell (postsynaptic membrane of the dendrite) as a lock-and-key arrangement. This is quite appropriate.

Psychobiologists have identified a family of chemicals with different molecular structures that exist throughout the brain and are important in normal and abnormal mental functioning. Of course, this family of chemicals is the **Deo-atomic cell** inheritance of the seven **cosmic-family** genetics of neurotransmitters at a mapped distribution throughout the brain and relative central-nervous-system coordinates.

I would like now to talk about neurohumoral transmission across the synapse. The transmitter molecule fits only specific receptors. A neurohumoral transmitter molecule seeks out and searches for its complementary polarity within a specific area or a designated home. Earth scientists understand at some level this specific method within the brain, but they do not understand it from the viewpoint of psychospiritual reasoning. Just as it is understood that this takes place at a very physical level, this reality also takes place in what is understood to some degree by Earth scientists as a second messenger system.

This second messenger system actually is a dual relationship with the unseen **causal coordinate body**. The various occurrences that take place unseen are a correlation with what is taking place that is seen and presently misunderstood. These receptors, besides having a very physical and motor response capability, are also very much in reality connected to **memory circuits**. They are also very much connected to the Paradise Trinity circuits of the Universal Father, of the Eternal Son, and of the Infinite Spirit.

The neurochemical process must be rapid in the thinking process in dealing with everyday life. The diverse functions of the brain are called upon to react instantly to circumstantial reality. Avoiding accidents, for example, calls upon an instant mediating neurochemical rapid process. Memory, on the other hand, depends on the rapid alignment of a former transmitter-receptor molecule for change, set to present-moment circuitry.

Deo-atomic mind-soul causal current is completely inhibited by blockages of **diotribes** within the neurochemical circuitry of your brain's 100 billion neurons. Thoughts that lead to beliefs of nonabsolute reality form the attitude that causes distortion in personality traits. This begins the blockage or short-circuiting of the causal current.

With fallen ovan souls, it has taken thousands of years and many **repersonalizations** to open up even one **causal memory circuit**. The causal memory circuit is the memory blueprint of ovan souls that was aligned with the ascending son or daughter before the fall. It is within the **point of origin reconstruction at time of fall** time-past blueprint with which all fallen souls need to realign.

Everything has a blueprint. Memory also has blueprints. That is how holograms are reconstructed in the transfiguration process. Somewhere in the person involved in doing the transfiguration are those memories. All we do is tap into those memory circuits and reconstruct them at whatever level we can, based upon that person's ascension. Everything that is nonmaterial can become material; everything that is matter can become spirit.

When we speak of a causal blueprint, a causal coordinate blueprint, we do speak of an identity. It may not be alive, but it has design and identity and has a form of energy in itself. If this blueprint is coordinated in its design to an ascending son or daughter, or any other being who has not defaulted, then it has in its own way motion—eternalized motion, an eternalized motion system.

Permanent memory trace is dependent upon a specific coming together or alignment of Deo-atomic receptors in order for a memory to become clear, for past-present eternalized memory must be joined in the present moment in time by a sufficient number of corresponding **Deo-atomic receptor units**.

I will try to paraphrase briefly what I just said in a more factually scientific manner. When a certain memory or a realization becomes more presently realized, that is an alignment between a transmitter and a receptor that come together and becomes a set unit or a receptor unit of Deo-atomic reality.

In order for that moment of time and space to become a more presently eternalized memory, it takes the association of hundreds of other receptor units. If that past memory has within its **home range area** only one receptor unit, then that particular memory based upon that one receptor unit will be vague, dim, or doubtful. With the joining of other complementary Deo-atomic units, the memory becomes stronger and clearer. It becomes part of the causal coordinate and astral bodies and becomes a presently eternalized memory that now is part of your present reality.

For ovan souls, and particularly those at the **First Planetary Sacred Home**, as past-life memory is becoming present-eternalized memory, it is by the same principle as for a memory of something you have experienced in the past in this lifetime. Deo-atomic receptor units from the past, somewhere located in your past causal coordinate body are reassigned to the home range area of your present astral body. What takes place then is a union of your present astral body in relation to your causal-coordinate-body future and your causal-coordinate-body past.

One must remember that the morontia body is ever growing, ever becoming more perfect. The astral body is becoming, but ever present with the physical body, or whatever body that you happen to be in. The **causal body** is always complete. The causal body can be used as a diagram for the astral body.

In dealing with interuniversal minds we are also dealing with interuniversal mind circuits. When the causal current is allowed to flow properly within the specific areas, the neurotransmitter family circuitry begins to be distributed to those particular home range areas of individual universal abilities. This process becomes quite complicated and is far beyond the scope of these early transmissions. We can only begin to deal with a very elementary understanding of the interrelationship between the physical body, brain and central nervous system, astral body, morontia body, and causal coordinate body.

The thought processes in relation to the morontia body or morontia mota begin to activate an eternalized presence, an eternalized personality. The death experience is no longer feared by one who is consciously transcending into morontia reality. The death process is no longer a part of the present reality; therefore, in this transition sequence, many time factors in relation to memory circuits must be analyzed within Continuing Fifth Epochal Revelation understanding of fusing mind with spirit.

Mind and spirit cooperate with one another in a relationship based upon cosmic absolutes, facts, and laws—the mathematics of cosmic physics and genetics. Biological determinations in relation to the physical body also come into play. This has to do with psychochemical reactions.

Because all of these words bring into play Urantian scientific terminologies based upon Urantian sciences, all of these definitions fused together can cause you to become confused in understanding the working of the brain in its psychospiritual reference frame. However, it is of the utmost importance that some understanding of what is presently known by modern research about the working of the brain be understood by students of Continuing Fifth Epochal Revelation, or it is impossible to bring psychospiritual and **ascension science** reality to the higher student of spiritual learning. One of the problems of the students of any discipline is that they want things to come to them a little easier than what it takes to become a true student.

All of the universities that exist in the ascension process to Paradise deal with individual bodies at every level and the relationship of those bodies to spiritual bodies or the final body of finality, which in a sense is post-existent to the causal body. However, there is much to be learned in the understanding of the causal body within the primal absolute Paradise circuit wave and the finality spiritual body, which is beyond the context of this transmission and beyond the context of some of the first volumes of *The Cosmic Family*.

When we can bring you some of the general understanding of human anatomy in relation to cosmic design and causal body, when you have a clearer perspective of the various bodies that exist in one particular moment of time, then you can have a better grasp of the functioning in the opening up of the circuits within ovan souls.

Because Urantian reality is based upon default and because you who read these transmissions are living in a defaulted reality at this time, Continuing Fifth Epochal Revelation will carry a completely different understanding after the final **change point** than it does now. To give you some example of what I am talking about, in a sense, the apostles at the time of Christ Michael as Jesus of Nazareth had some understanding of the Fourth Epochal Revelation when Jesus lived, walked, talked, and ate with them, but they had quite another understanding of Fourth Epochal Revelation when the resurrected Jesus talked to them. They became, in a sense, more eternalized, but it has taken several other repersonalizations even for those first-century ovan souls to become further eternalized. This is based upon the ascension growth, the evolution of the mind, and the rejoining of the mind to cosmic reality.

There is such a thing as mass-consciousness reality. It is based upon a certain vibrational sequence, you might say a vibrational pattern of the majority of souls on any one particular planet. Urantia has a measured **cosmologic vibration pattern** that is quite different from any of the planets in its own system. This is because of the **interuniversal genetics** of Urantia. A balancing out within the cosmologic vibration pattern between negative or diotribe reality and Deo-atomic reality is highly upstepped because of the growth in ascension of the ovan souls who are now beginning to find themselves with cosmic stamina.

Because of the growth of these ovan souls in stabilizing themselves to some degree, and because some of them have actually been able to be brought together again in a higher union of souls than they have ever been brought together before, the very fabric of the oxygen in the air, as spoken about in former transmissions, is changing.

This leads to complicated science and physics, which is unnecessary to get into at this time, but it should be understood that the very air you breathe triggers certain chemical reactions in the brain and the central nervous system, and also is quite influential in helping the receptor units and transmitters in the neurological system within the brain to find each other.

One of the primal reasons that the sacred areas are sacred and protected is because they help the human Eldership and those who are aligned to the Machiventa Melchizedek Administration at the First Planetary Sacred Home learn at a more rapid rate, and the very air breathed works upon the neurological system of the human brain at a higher rate. This is particularly true within the First Radius, and then outward from the Second to Third Radii where there is a higher or lower activation rate based upon the oxygen in the air in these different levels. This will also become the reality in the other sacred areas on the planet.

In the appointed sacred areas at the present time, there is a change taking place within those individuals who are living in them, and certain ovan souls are being brought to these areas, or are there already, and are under a different oxygen intake reality. They are also under a different neurochemical response in the pathways of their brains. Children being born in these areas to higher **complementary polarities**, at whatever level, already are also quite different from the children who were born in the previous generation, particularly since December 1989 and the arrival of the present Planetary Prince of this planet. Almost immediately, these protected areas became isolated at some level from interference by diotribe reality in relation to any diotribes that would hinder the destiny purposes of Cosmic Reservists.

Certain Cosmic Reservists who are functioning on a higher level of destiny purpose are more highly protected than others. This is based upon many circumstances including their present ascension levels, their loyalty to the purposes of God, and their ascension status upon transcending this planet in past repersonalizations.

Upon their alignment to the First Planetary Sacred Home, many members of the **First Cosmic Family** and the other cosmic families can and will find themselves going through tremendous psychological healing processes of the mind and the emotions in an upstepped process to almost miraculous circumstances brought about by those trained in tron therapy. Almost instantaneous metamorphosis of cosmic family members from the fifth psychic circle to the third in therapy sessions will be a normal occurrence at the First Planetary Sacred Home.

This will be based upon the ability of those trained in tron therapy and the willingness of cosmic family members to benefit from what the Elders and tron therapists have learned. Tron therapy cannot work without the aid of seraphim, and so, only those who remain on the third psychic circle can be tron therapists. Tron therapists who have been on the first psychic circle for at least one year will have the highest potential of making instantaneous changes within the personality receiving therapy.

Memory circuits can be instantaneously opened, hundreds of complementary receptor units can be brought to home range areas within the body and remain there, whereas previously it might have taken hundreds, or even thousands, of years to reactivate these circuits within a home range area of the brain.

Tron therapy upsteps the opening of memory circuits. Upon the opening of memory circuits, a personality becomes eternalized and morontial. Tron therapy should not be used with just anyone. Those who are chosen to be recipients of tron therapy will be chosen by Celestial Overcontrol alone. Tron therapy can be used in various degrees, but when it comes to the opening up of circuits, that is a mandate of Christ Michael alone. Within that mandate, Celestial Overcontrol and the present staff of the Planetary Prince make those decisions. The Planetary Prince, Machiventa Melchizedek, cannot make those decisions alone.

The opening up of memories in and through ovan souls is a precious gift. Knowing who one was in the past is a gift of eternity and should not be taken lightly. Because of the importance of this, Caligastia likes to make light of the reality of this past-present eternalized memory. And so, he invents ingenious methods to belittle or discredit the fact of past-present eternalized memory. He has done it in a very clever way, based upon the breakdown of the ascension process and of the understanding of God-reality—God-reality being a personal relationship with the Universe Father and the Universe Mother and the understanding of the Paradise Eternal Father.

The very molecular makeup of one's existence in all of its diverse circuitry is a time-present reality. Who you are in relation to eternity is based upon what you think and how you respond to negative thoughts. The brain with which you function on any physical level functions by the computer of the soul and mind. It is not diseased or damaged by physical chemical process, for within the body structure there are millions and millions of antibodies capable of coming against any negative poison chemical and redirecting it to nonabsolute hurt unless, of course, you decide by freewill choice to ingest poison to end your life by suicide.

Because of all of the various toxic chemicals in foods and in the air you breathe, Urantia today has its negative influence upon the circuitry of the brain. But all of these negative influences caused by ingesting toxins would have less effect upon the body if the soul itself became more spiritually ascended. It is indeed mind over body.

The **protected areas** can be referred to in a sense as a divine hospital, and you are the patients; first the Cosmic and Urantian Reservists are set aside and put into a sterilized area. Although there are certain viruses that do exist in these areas, these viruses also would have no effect upon the ovan soul if the ovan soul's thoughts were more highly coordinated with absolute reality and absolute fact. If you are in a sacred area and a virus triggers a disease within the body, then you are allowing it by your thought processes, and changes need to be made.

Each time a new cosmic family member enters a sacred area anywhere within the Third Radius, this triggers receptor units to find their home range area within the body. They are looking for the memory. The cells of the receptor units in the body of the other person with whom you have once associated in a past life form a kind of magnetic flow from their astral body to your astral body within a distance of approximately five miles.

In turn, this triggers a disturbance within the body. The closer this person comes to be within your frame of reality, the higher the disturbance. Those who are clairvoyantly attuned, those who have learned to use other Continuing Fifth Epochal Revelation realities, can know by sensor feelings when a cosmic family member is within the Third Radius even though they have not seen nor met them yet.

When you meet that individual based upon the moment-to-moment alignment of both being in the will of the Eternal Father, the memory circuits in particular will be more highly activated, and there will be a transference of cells from one body to the other as soon as you are within an aural radius of one another. This triggers not only the opening up of memory circuits but very physical responses in the body itself, such as sexual desire, home and family memories that may trigger the desire for foods that you ate at that time, experiences that you had together, and activities that you participated in together. You may find yourself thinking about things that you normally would not think about or desiring things that you would not normally desire.

This kind of behavior takes place on Urantia with Urantian personalities to some degree based upon social conduct and memories of this life that trace themselves back to pleasant times and experiences associated with joy and pleasure. When an ovan soul meets another ovan soul, the same functioning takes place. The brain pathways that are associated with past memories become reactivated, and cells, located in certain areas of the body that have been dormant and have not been able to be drawn out by causal current, now are drawn out of those areas and are searching for their primal or home range areas within the body.

If they are able to stabilize themselves within the body and remain there, based upon many circumstances having to do with mind and soul ascension, then an opening up of a memory circuit that now becomes eternalized can be both pleasurable and painful, and it means that certain experiences you had with that person have reactivated that memory circuit.

Because the reactivation of memory circuits can take place with ovan souls within the cosmic family, it is an undetermined factor that we ourselves are observing moment to moment of how ovan souls who have known each other in the past will respond to one another based upon all of the circumstances of present-day Urantia, and in particular at the First Planetary Sacred Home.

We have already observed inappropriate behavior by community members within the Divine Administration due to thoughts or judgments based upon normal tendencies of jealousy and envy of other cosmic family members that have no reference to present-day reality but are solely a memory of past-life experience. However, the present-day person, who has such thoughts and does not understand why or misunderstands those thoughts of envy, jealousy, or whatever about another cosmic family member, can make an inappropriate judgment.

It is one thing that a substantial amount of receptor units can be realigned at one particular thought-moment in relation to a past life, but when it is in relation to a past circumstance within that life, it is another. In order to remember everything about one particular past life, it would take the association of hundreds of thousands of specific memory receptor units in one particular location of the brain.

At the present time, those who have come to some understanding of who they were in past repersonalizations still only have a few receptor units functioning in their point of origin and other home range areas. Based upon the causal body's influence on those few receptor units, those individuals are becoming more eternalized. At the present time this is being highly observed within the Eldership of Divine Administration.

Keep in mind that Urantia is an experimental planet, and what is happening on Urantia is an experimental process. Using human complements and giving them divine mandates within the third dimension and having those human complements working towards the goal of transcending the death experience as a group of individuals is a first on Urantia. So we ourselves are in moment-to-moment observance, and many decisions that Celestial Overcontrol makes are based upon a moment-to-moment decision making on our part. Therefore, together we become a part of present-day eternity.

In order for you to understand the workings of the human brain, we must bring in cosmic philosophy. Philosophy and psychospiritual reality are primal factors in the movement of the cells to their appropriate physical location within the body. Thoughts in alignment with cosmic absolutes and cosmic virtues within the personality circuits are the most powerful force in the master universe. This subject is immense in scope and eternal in understanding.

As you begin to put it all together in the ascension-science process and begin to formulate cosmic philosophy and cosmic psychospiritual reality based upon the physiology of your present body in your ascending minds and souls, you are able to transcend not only the death experience but time and space itself. The mass consciousness of the whole planet is determined by each individual's level of acquiescence to these factors. If individuals outgrow others to such a degree that they cannot communicate higher cosmic reality, they could, like Enoch, transcend the world by Thought Adjuster fusion.

Thought Adjuster fusion for those presently within the First Planetary Sacred Home will not be allowed to occur, for they are needed in the administration of the planet after the final change point. Another cosmic reality is occurring, and in a sense it is a fusion, but it is being done in a slower process. Instead of a spontaneous combustion, you might say, it is being done by a process that is much more meaningful, based upon the destiny purpose of Reservists to function in administrative policy in and through a new *fourth-dimensional* reality on Urantia.

Certain memory circuits in relation to talents and abilities, if eternally realized and past-present eternalized, would actually hinder the destiny purposes of certain souls on the planet until those souls can be more highly trusted to better control their own thoughts in relation to destiny purpose within the will of God. The circuitry of the body must be slowly opened, and seraphim actually inhibit the opening up of certain circuits.

When the **Caligastia Sixty** rebelled against the Universal Father and Universe Father, their memory circuits were left intact, but other behavioral and functional circuits in relation to talents and abilities were blocked. The descendants of these supermortals have the latent abilities within the genetic coding. The reopening of these circuits would restore talents and abilities to those who have inherited former Deo-atomic cells; so great care is taken by Celestial Overcontrol that these cells not be recircuited until the soul finds himself or herself within divine will.

Instances in the past on Urantia, when certain latent circuits have been opened, have created imbalances within certain individuals who have been known as geniuses in the realm of music or art but are quite imbalanced in the actualities of life itself. With Cosmic Reservists we cannot allow this to happen. The growth of Cosmic Reservists must be slow and methodical up to this point. That is why it has taken countless repersonalizations to even begin to open up or to stabilize understanding such realities as being from another planet or another universe and believing it, based upon their reality existence on Urantia. Those who have come to that conclusion have not come to it overnight or in one lifetime. It has been a slow and arduous process.

When tron therapy can be used in its highest potential for the opening of memory circuits and other abilities, it will be used for the benefit of all humankind and not just for the individual. Tron therapy is a necessary instrument within an adjudication on any rebellious planet in order to upstep the healing process, the opening of the memory circuits, the actualization of the latent abilities, and the bringing of souls into a normal interuniversal causal reality.

The causal reality of interuniversal exchange differs from universe to universe. The methods of appropriating causal reality in relation to present reality also differ from universe to universe. They never differ from system to system or planet to planet, for they are the interuniversal prerogatives based upon the Creator Son and the mandates of that particular Creator Son. All ovan souls are under the causal reality of Christ Michael of Nebadon. All ovan souls are repersonalized and given life in Nebadon by Christ Michael.

Any past reality in association with a Creator Son of another universe is a time factor strictly under the authority and prerogative of Christ Michael to reactivate. The Creator Son of the past universe has no jurisdiction over your present reality. The Creator Son of your past reality has given complete sovereign authority to Christ Michael for the present ascension of your soul, and it is the prerogative of Christ Michael to reassign your ascension process within the scope of Nebadon, not the scope of your preceding universal existence. The pathways of your brain itself become Nebadon-eternalized, Nebadon-structured.

When you return to your planet of origin, except perhaps as a visitor, it will probably be as a finaliter, never again as an ascending mortal. You have in a sense disenfranchised yourself from your universe of origin and have realigned yourself to the ascension process of Nebadon with one difference. You have been allowed to repersonalize over and over again on the fallen worlds where your ancestors once fell. You can get to such a level and to such a point that you can ascend within the ascension process of Nebadon having complete memories not only of your repersonalizations on Urantia but the memories of your former universe embellishments and the cultural realities that formed you and are a part of you.

Based upon this pre-existence, you need to ascend to a former cultural norm as an ascending son or daughter. This you will do in a fourth-dimensional reality on Urantia and not on the mansion worlds of Satania. Nevertheless, at some point, some of you who fall into different classifications will be given a choice as to whether or not you want to continue in the Nebadon ascension process or resume your ascension in your native universe. This would depend on many factors, but the majority of starseed will have to go through the entire ascension process in Nebadon. Interuniversal visitation, however, will be an option for all starseed at various points in their Nebadon ascension process.

Urantia itself will be a type of mansion world for ascending mortals within the system of Satania with equal and lower evolutionary realities than previous **third-dimensional** Urantia. Urantia will take its place then as another first mansion world, and ascending sons and daughters can come to Urantia just as well as they could come to the first mansion world of Satania. Interuniversal ascenders, with the genetic inheritance of the Creator Son of another universe, can be assigned by that Creator Son to Urantia by the process of repersonalization, which has been the case for more than 200,000 years now. The difference is that rebellion will be over, but the prerogative of the Creator Sons, because Urantia is an interuniversal reality, will continue ad infinitum as far as we understand it.

It is estimated that it will take thirty to fifty years of Urantia time for ovan souls to completely fulfill their mortal desires as interuniversal citizens before they can transcend in the ascension process. Those with various mandates within the union of souls and their cosmic families will ascend at different times, but eventually they will end up together. Because they may not ascend by human death, it will be very much like a short vacation from one another. In Urantian years it may be up to ten years, but in time-and-space reality it is perhaps only a few weeks' time.

The master universe consists of one harmonic pattern. In the understanding of higher cosmic genetics, cellular structures, the ultimaton and so on, one thought leads to another, one reality complements another, one truth seems to be linked to another, and mathematics joins philosophy; therefore, it is of the utmost importance that certain truths and philosophic realities based upon cosmic absolutes be withheld from lesser minds and those of lesser persuasion.

Jesus said, "Don't cast your pearls before swine." And so at this time we again remind you who hold this transmission in the scope of your empirical vision, that if it has come to you, it has come to you by the will of God, but that does not mean you should share it with just anyone. It has been sent to you by the command of Celestial Overcontrol. It should not be given indiscriminately to another. An individual must obtain it by freewill choice.

This is procedure, and it is divine procedure. If for any reason you disregard this divine procedure, you will find that the very cellular flow within your own brain that you have just read about will begin to malfunction. You will find yourself forgetting things at a higher rate, and as you say on Urantia, spacing out. This is all a part of divine justice and the separating of the good seed and the bad seed in the **adjudication of the Bright and Morning Star versus Lucifer**, and it is our prayer that you can find yourself on the right side.

September 28, 1992

Paladin, Chief of Finaliters
in cooperation with a Divine Counselor, a Paradise Master Force Organizer, and an Architect of the Master Universe working in liaison with the Chief of Seraphim and the heads of the twelve seraphic corps on Urantia in correlation with the mandates of the present Planetary Prince, based upon Paper 215, for the implementation of the Divine Administration on Urantia in and through the present Planetary Prince, Machiventa Melchizedek

As transmitted through
the Pre-Level-One Audio Fusion Material Complement,
Gabriel of Urantia/TaliasVan of Tora

PAPER 259

The Present Planetary Administration Of Machiventa Melchizedek In Interuniversal Personality Representation In Administrative Function On Urantia

URANTIA—being a unique planet in the superuniverse of Orvonton, with **interuniversal genetics** and **repersonalized ovan souls** throughout its history since the fall of Lucifer and its Planetary Prince, Caligastia—has evolved to the place of uniqueness by the simple fact of this interuniversal genetic makeup and by the fact of the repersonalized ovan souls who have, time and again, repersonalized to learn the results of error, sin, and iniquity and to bring the concept of higher truth to the people of the planet. On some level of spiritual attainment they can do that as individuals and as a team, and, much more appropriately, as a **cosmic family** unit.

With the appointment of its Planetary Prince, Machiventa Melchizedek (who has been on this planet before), Urantia now has the unique opportunity of implementing representative government. This not only involves the brilliant representation of Melchizedek administrations, but also interuniversal representation based upon personalities who are presently joined with the staff of the present Planetary Prince to function as Overcontrol with human mandated personalities who are also representative of Overcontrol.

It is the first time in Nebadon that human personalities have been representatives of Celestial Overcontrol at this level in divine administration procedure. This experiment has been sanctioned by the Creator Son, Christ Michael Himself, and will be allowed to proceed on course as long as those human elders do not default from their destiny purpose. The significance of the few who have come to the first circle of attainment together within a representative human administration is beyond the scope of your understanding at this time. For this reason, we will not attempt to elaborate on the consequences of possible default by one or more of these human personalities. We are optimistic that they will proceed in their destiny purpose.

I, Paladin, Chief of Finaliters, along with interuniversal ascendant mortal finaliters, am not resident on Urantia at this time, October 23, 1992. We function strictly as the Revelatory Commission of Continuing Fifth Epochal Revelation and as advisors to all levels directly under the Bright and Morning Star of Salvington. Evacuation procedures are under the command of the finaliter, Ashtar, who, since December 1989, no longer communicates with human contacts, with the exception of **Gabriel of Urantia/TaliasVan of Tora** on a few occasions. He may directly contact Gabriel of Urantia/TaliasVan of Tora if deemed necessary, but I will be Ashtar's voice and the voice of all of Celestial Overcontrol.

There may be exceptions from time to time, mostly by the Planetary Prince, Machiventa Melchizedek, or the head administrator of Nebadon, the Bright and Morning Star, who will personally come to Urantia on a once-per-month basis to meet with Machiventa Melchizedek and staff and speak through his **Audio Fusion Material Complement**, Gabriel of Urantia/TaliasVan of Tora, in reflectivity through his body. This experience is for the spiritual uplifting of the cosmic families resident at the **First Planetary Sacred Home**.

Transport Areas

The staff of Machiventa Melchizedek is located at the **energy reflective circuit** of Cathedral Rock, which is identified as a square, following the example of the Jerusem administrative area. This square encompasses all of the land mass area of Cathedral Rock, where the Planetary Prince and the chiefs of all the orders of beings of whom I will speak in this transmission are located, and that is also an energy reflective circuit of transport for the celestial personalities listed below:

- the Bright and Morning Star
- the Melchizedeks
- the Lanonandeks
- sixth and seventh mansion world progressors
- Solitary Messengers

The area of Bell Rock is an energy reflective circuit for midwayers who use it to travel from one place to another on the planet at a more rapid rate. All of them are under the direct jurisdiction of Machiventa Melchizedek. Presently added to the Urantia midwayers are 4,000 primary midwayers, 4,000 secondary midwayers, and 4,000 midwayers of an unrevealed order, all from the universes of Avalon, Wolvering, and Fanoving, and all under the jurisdiction of the Chief of Midwayers of Urantia.

The areas of transport transition are:

- Boynton Canyon, the archangels' headquarters where all angelic orders enter this planet
- Cathedral Rock, where nonangelic orders enter
- Bell Rock, where midwayers, both interuniversal and planetary, enter[1]

The Staff of Machiventa Melchizedek

Along with Machiventa Melchizedek, there are one dozen Melchizedek Sons from the Melchizedek worlds functioning in cooperation with the twelve seraphim of planetary supervision under the direct jurisdiction of the Father Melchizedek functioning from Jerusem headquarters. The twelve seraphim group leaders are under the planetary jurisdiction of the Chief of Seraphim. The Melchizedeks' role along with the Chief of Seraphim is that of governmental counsel in relation to implementing the necessary procedure on the physical level to get things done from point A to point Z in the most rapid way when time is essential, both now and in the future.

Also on the staff of Machiventa Melchizedek are Material Sons and Daughters of the universe of Avalon from the planets of Tora, Celano, Alcyone, and Taygate. There are eight Material Sons and Daughters (four Daughters and four Sons), a pair from each of the Avalonian (Pleiadian) planets mentioned. From the Fanoving worlds are one Material Son and Daughter and also one pair from the Wolvering worlds.

Machiventa Melchizedek's staff also includes 1,000 Lanonandek Sons, all proven loyal, as well as two repentant Lanonandek Sons who, since the beginning of the adjudication in 1911, have reversed their rebellious path and have now rejoined forces with their Universe Sovereign, Christ Michael. These Lanonandek Sons are under the jurisdiction of Lanaforge. The two repentant ones are on probation and will be until the adjudication is over, but they do make autonomous decisions, are trusted, and are presently working solely in the area of Argentina and Chile in South America.

The seven cosmic family areas on the planetary level will be presided over by elders of the Council of Twenty-four, some of whom have returned to Urantia. All but one are presently invisible and in morontia form.

- *Onamonalonton,* of the red race, will be in the sector of the United States and presently is located at the First Planetary Sacred Home.

- *Singlangton,* of the yellow race, will be located in Maui, Hawaii, and will be part of the Machiventa Melchizedek Administration when the first human representatives from the First Planetary Sacred Home are mandated to be sent to Maui. At this time he is not permanently on Urantia, but he comes and goes. Some time after the final change point Singlangton may be transferred to the Central Asia sector.

- *Orvonon*, of the indigo race, presently comes and goes and will also become a permanent resident as soon as two mandated human representative personalities can be sent to Jerusalem.

- *Enoch* is resident on Urantia at the First Planetary Sacred Home with Machiventa Melchizedek and will be assigned at a future date to a sector area.

- *Moses* is present on Urantia and is an unrevealed repersonalized starseed. He will be revealed at a later time. Moses will be in overcontrol of the New Jerusalem at approximately A.D. 2040–2050 or before. The New Jerusalem will be a headquarters sector encompassing the area of what is now the four states of Arizona, New Mexico, Colorado, and Utah. If Moses does not remain on Urantia and other Urantians do not meet First Ambassador leadership, Amadon will rule the New Jerusalem and the planet.

- *Elijah* is back on Urantia and is also at the First Planetary Sacred Home. Elijah will be in overcontrol of the Yucatan area, which at that time will encompass a different sector administration.[2]

- *John the Baptist* is resident at the First Planetary Sacred Home and will be in overcontrol in the lower part of Central Asia, which would be in the area of present-day China. In the future John will switch places with Singlangton in the Maui, Hawaii sector.

If there are no human personalities mandated to go to the other administrative sectors before the final change point, those members of the Council of Twenty-four mentioned above will become permanent residents of Urantia regardless.

At the First Planetary Sacred Home, within the circle of the **First Cosmic Family** of Urantia, including representatives of all the other cosmic families resident within the Third Radius, the Chief of Midwayers and the Chief of the Seraphim of the Races will function within overcontrol.

In the circle of the First Cosmic Family and cosmic family representatives on the first psychic circle resident within the First Radius, the seraphim Destin (who is a destiny guardian) is in overcontrol.

In the circle of the First Cosmic Family and the representatives of the seven cosmic families on the third psychic circle within the Second Radius, the Chief of Mind Planners will function in overcontrol, along with midwayers (representative of all four universes) whose number will fluctuate.

In the circle of the First Cosmic Family and the representatives of the seven cosmic families on the fourth to seventh psychic circles within the Third Radius, the Chief of Seraphim will function in overcontrol, assisted by seraphim of the **World Council** of Government Administration.

These three circle areas represent the residential areas of human mortals in representative governmental administration on Urantia. They also represent the three concentric circles of Christ Michael and the bestowal gift of the Threefold Spirit to Urantia natives and repersonalized sojourners. It also is a representation of Paradise sovereignty on a human mortal level.

On the staff of Machiventa Melchizedek are Administrator Seraphim of the fourth order of the seraphic hosts of the local universe, consisting of:

- 1,000 Administrative Assistants
- 1,000 Justice Guides
- 1,000 Quickeners of Morality

Of the fifth order seraphim, the Planetary Helpers, there are:

- Solonia, the Voice of the Garden
- 1,000 Spirits of Brotherhood
- Vevona, Chief of the Souls of Peace
- 1,000 Souls of Peace
- 1,000 Spirits of Trust
- 100 Transporters

Also on the staff of Machiventa Melchizedek are seraphim of the sixth order, the Transition Ministers, including:

- 12 *Racial Interpreters* who work with each of the twelve groups of planetary seraphim.
- 1,000 *Morontia Counselors* to teach morontia mota to those Cosmic and Urantian Reservists who have been able to maintain themselves in the first circle for at least one year. At present they are working only with the Eldership of Divine Administration.
- 100 *Mind Planners* from the Seraphic Corps of Completion who, under the Chief of Mind Planners, facilitate the grouping of souls for assignment or advancement. This also has to do with personality reflectivity. They will work with the twelve World Councils listed below, under the Bright and Morning Star Mandate and with the Seraphic Chief of Mind Planners and the human Gabriel of Urantia/TaliasVan of Tora over the human representatives, and later, one human personality who will be in reflectivity to the Chief of Mind Planners. This person will be an administrative overcontrol assistant to Gabriel/TaliasVan at this level. At this time, **Niánn Emerson Chase**, as Gabriel's/TaliasVan's highest pair unit complement, is most likely to receive this; of reflectivity, Amadon is next. The human Gabriel/TaliasVan will work as overcontrol chief with

all appointed chiefs and sub-groupings of six mandated humans on each council, equaling seventy-two in all.

The **Mandate of the Bright and Morning Star**, and in human reflectivity, Gabriel of Urantia/TaliasVan of Tora in overcontrol, at some point in the future will be presiding over all of the twelve World Councils. His procedure will be to advise and counsel, but not necessarily to administer policy unless he deems it necessary. He can at any time take a necessary and appropriate action to remove any and all appointed representatives, but usually that will be left up to the chief of those groups if an appointed subordinate administrator is not functioning in proper capacity.

The overcontrol policy is to work with groups and not with individuals. At that point in time, the subgroups in the World Council of Governmental Administration will be more autonomous, working on a more individual basis with ambassadors and ambassadors' assistants, and Gabriel's/TaliasVan's overcontrol of that particular council will be the same type of overcontrol that he is functioning with regarding the other eleven.

It should be understood that the Bright and Morning Star Mandate as an overcontrol mandate has authority over all subgroups and all administrative appointees. That of course would be understood by anyone who understands the administration of the Bright and Morning Star in representative government of Nebadon. The representative government of Urantia in and through Melchizedek representation, seraphim representation, Brilliant Evening Star representation, and any reflectivity of Nebadon government, functions in the same manner as the government of Nebadon, but on a planetary level.

It should also be understood that working with Gabriel of Urantia/TaliasVan of Tora in overcontrol will be the appointed Elders, and some of those Elders are **Liaison Ministers** at the First Planetary Sacred Home. These Elders may or may not also serve as chiefs of one of the World Councils. In this instance one of the Vicegerent First Ambassadors will serve as chief of the World Council of Governmental Administration by becoming a First Ambassador. They will be Urantians, as Urantians will be trained to be leaders of their sector. It may be necessary that a starseed will have to serve as chief of two or more councils until a replacement can function as chief.

If Gabriel of Urantia/TaliasVan of Tora is away from the First Planetary Sacred Home, Niánn Emerson Chase, his highest **complementary polarity**, who shares his mandate, assumes all authority and responsibility of that mandate and works with the highest Liaison Minister. When the highest Liaison Minister is also away, Niánn would work with the next highest Liaison Minister(s). Representative authority is delegated whenever necessary to maintain the ongoing administrative authority at the First Planetary Sacred Home at all times.

Members of the Liaison Ministers' board at the First Planetary Sacred Home also most likely will serve as human chiefs on the various World Councils. Community leaders of the other six sector areas will first be appointed in accordance with their availability to serve on the councils. Some time after the final change point they will be assigned to the international areas according to their reflectivity to their personal angel of enlightenment based upon their ability to remain on the first circle for one year.

The male and female couples will most likely be mandated as Vicegerent First Ambassadors, but not always. Because of the disturbed reality of Urantia and the unpredictable circumstances at this time, whatever pair-unit classification can be sent, will be sent, even if they are not ambassadors. This would be unfortunate, but it may be necessary. Later, perhaps before and definitely after the final change point, they would be replaced by ambassadorship positions.

The twelve administrative groups functioning on the staff of Machiventa Melchizedek are the:

1. World Council of Agriculture
2. World Council of Architecture
3. World Council of Music and Art
4. World Council of Scientific Inquiry
5. World Council of Cosmic Philosophy
6. World Council of Race Genetics
7. World Council of Aquatic Life
8. World Council of Industry
9. World Council of Transportation
10. World Council of Government Administration
11. World Council of Animal Husbandry
12. World Council of Human and Nonhuman Relations

Cosmic and Urantian Reservists who are assigned to these councils must reflect a Spirit of Trust and a Spirit of Brotherhood. They will become human chiefs and directors in counseling on family and cultural life. Because the members of all groups on Urantia have interuniversal genetics and therefore will have varied interuniversal cultural needs regarding family organization, procreation, architecture, foods, philosophy, and human relations, counseling will be invaluable at this point in Urantia evolution.

Cherubim and sanobim on Machiventa Melchizedek's staff will be under his personal direction. Since the adjudication began in 1911, several hundred thousand angelic and other personalities who have repented their rebellious actions have now realigned with Christ Michael and have been assigned to these twelve groups under the personal direction of Machiventa Melchizedek.

Some time after the final change point they will come under the direction of the mandated human chiefs of the councils. The cherubim and sanobim will be visible to the chief human overseer and his or her human staff. The human chiefs will be in reflectivity of either a Brilliant Evening Star or the Father Melchizedek and under direct human supervision of either Gabriel of Urantia/TaliasVan of Tora or the First Ambassadors, depending upon whether they are reflective of the overcontrol function and mandate of either the Bright and Morning Star or Machiventa Melchizedek.

Those formerly rebellious personalities now on probation will be completely adjudicated based on their performances by approximately the year 2050 or before. Those under Machiventa Melchizedek will be subject to the decision of First Ambassadors as far as their being removed from the planet in case of their default. All twelve chiefs will have the prerogative to suggest evacuation of a personality from the planet upon the approval of the First Ambassadors, who will have the power and authority to do so without consulting Overcontrol if it is deemed necessary that an immediate departure of this personality must take place. Celestial Overcontrol action will take place after a decision has been made to remove a personality, but not necessarily before.

Autonomous authority will be given to Gabriel of Urantia/TaliasVan of Tora and the First Ambassadors some time after the final change point to make these decisions of removal when they are necessary. First Ambassadors can make this decision without the approval of Gabriel of Urantia/TaliasVan of Tora, but Gabriel/TaliasVan, or any personality of liaison mandates, can reverse that decision upon inquiry into the case and send the personality back. However, the personality can be removed from the planet at any time by the request of the First Ambassadors. This includes interplanetary or interuniversal personalities who are visiting Urantia and human mortals who interfere in any way with planetary procedure. If it is determined by First Ambassadors that a personality is in immediate danger from someone or something, then that someone or something will be removed.

The following is a further elaboration of administrative functions in relation to the twelve councils.

1. *The World Council of Agriculture.* The mandated human chief will appoint subdirectors of each administrative sector, who will in turn appoint a staff of six to serve in each of the other sectors.

2. *The World Council of Architecture.* The human mandated Head Architect of Urantia will be in charge of architecture and construction in all sector areas, including recreational areas. All physical and technical equipment needed for construction will be under his jurisdiction. There will be six subdirectors, one over each sector in charge of all construction workers. The Chief Engineer will approve all that is built. Construction will be based upon Satania design and functions for residential and administrative areas on Jerusem regarding the various circles, squares, rectangles, and triangles.

3. *The World Council of Music and Art.* This council functions under the overcontrol of the Bright and Morning Star Mandate with the Brilliant Evening Stars resident on Urantia. Other Brilliant Evening Stars will come to Urantia as more ascending daughters, who attain capacity for reflectivity to them, align with this administration. If there are 1,000 ascending daughters of Brilliant Evening Star reflectivity capacity, there will be 1,000 Brilliant Evening Stars in residence. It is very unique for many Brilliant Evening Stars to serve on a planet. Even if there were only 10 of them, Urantia would give off more light than any other planet in Nebadon.

    Gabriel of Urantia/TaliasVan of Tora will be in human overcontrol of all music programs until 2050 and will appoint representatives of all forms of artistic endeavors past and present. All technical equipment and studios for reproduction will be at the First Planetary Sacred Home. Individuals with music talent who have potential and ability will be given all they need to develop that potential based upon their willingness to spiritually present the universal character of God in and through their music.

Those with the ability to be leaders in various forms of music, such as ensembles, bands, and orchestras, automatically and instantaneously will be given instruments and programming needs so that all forms of artistic expression may be fulfilled. All kinds of music will be represented on Urantia, including interuniversal celestial art forms. Technicians involved in these productions will also be under the administration of Gabriel of Urantia/TaliasVan of Tora and his appointed staff.

4. *The World Council of Scientific Inquiry.* This will be headed by a human who reflects a Master Physical Controller under the supervision of a local universe Supreme Power Center. There will also be six subgroups appointed by the Chief.

5. *The World Council of Cosmic Philosophy.* A Urantian descendant of the sons of Han will reach a sixth- or seventh-stage mansion world consciousness. It is hoped that visitation of mansion world progressors at this level can return briefly to Urantia to serve on a council in which this Urantian descendant will be Chief. If this does not occur, a starseed descendant of that genetic line will be Chief. This line has included Lao-Tse, Mahatma Buddha, and Lao Shou Hsing. The official title of the Urantian descendant chief will be a Vicegerent First Ambassador. A starseed with a higher title cannot hold this title.

6. *The World Council of Race Genetics.* This council works in conjunction with interuniversal Material Sons and Daughters and the Chief of the Race Commissioners on Urantia. The human head of this

council would be mandated in reflectivity to the highest Material Son or Daughter of his or her planet of origin and would assign a subgroup of six to the other residential sectors.

7. *The World Council of Aquatic Life.* The human mandated head of this council would be in reflectivity of a finaliter, such as Kumatron or Kalacortex, who has ascended from a sea mammal, and would supervise any and all mortal species ascended from the sea. Under him would be six subgroups for each sector.

8. *The World Council of Industry.* This council would be headed by a human mandated in reflectivity to a seraphim among the progress angels. There will also be subgroups of six for each sector.

9. *The World Council of Transportation.* The human administrator of this council is in reflectivity of the Chief of the Midwayers and works with the appointed chiefs of the other sectors and subgroups of six for each sector in regard to physical transportation.

10. *The World Council of Government Administration.* This council is headed by a First Ambassador who comes into reflectivity of a Melchizedek Son and under the human supervision of Gabriel of Urantia/TaliasVan of Tora. He will appoint a system of subgroups in each of the administrative sectors, the elaboration of which will be the subject of another transmission. A starseed cannot hold this title but would function in it with a higher title.

11. *The World Council of Animal Husbandry.* The human representative head of this council works in conjunction with Life Carriers and other interuniversal representatives who have implanted interuniversal and native life forms now extinct on

Urantia but that will be re-established. There will also be six subgroups, one in each sector.

12. *The World Council of Human and Nonhuman Relations*. The head of this council will be appointed to work in direct conjunction with the Chief of morontia counselors and other morontia counselors, with a subgrouping of six in each sector.

Urantia is to become a transcendent school of interuniversal ascension attached to the seven mansion worlds of Satania. It has not yet been revealed as to which ascendant mortals will be sent to Urantia versus who will go to the first mansion world.

Scattered all over present-day Urantia are Cosmic Reservists and Urantian Reservists who have not come into the realization of who they are or what their destiny purpose is on Urantia at this time. If you are one of these, perhaps you have come into the Urantia movement to a high degree and have served Christ Michael loyally and to the best of your ability, based upon an understanding of the first one-tenth of the Fifth Epochal Revelation published as *The URANTIA Book*.

Now you must go further and come to understand yourself as a cosmic representative of an interuniversal reality. You must believe in your past as well as your future. You must recognize who you were, who you are, and who you are to be. You must understand that the Divine Administration on Urantia is now being set up under representative government using humans just like yourself and that you yourself are possibly being called to serve in positions of authority. You must understand that you are needed and that your decisions either hinder or help the implementation of this administration in the years leading up to the final change point. You must realize that you are important in the infrastructure of this Divine Administration. You can be replaced, but time is of the essence.

Ultimately and eventually the Divine Administration will come into completion. In an instant of time and in the twinkling of an eye the change will come to Urantia. Unfortunately, a Reservist who has not met his or her destiny will be unable to take part in the Divine Administration that will be established here in totality. You will transcend by physical death and may be on the mansion worlds wishing that you had responded appropriately to this message. You will be separated from your loved ones, which is not a pleasant thing.

Furthermore, once you are awakened on a mansion world, every relationship with those with whom you were formerly associated in past lives on Urantia in other spiritual renaissances will be remembered. We have tried to inform you of these things, but if you have obstinately refused to accept this reality, you will look down upon Urantia and its spiritual administration, and you will miss being with those you were supposed to be with. You will desire to be a part of that administration and the blessing it will be to the planet, but will be unable to help it in the way that you could have, had you heeded this transmission when it first came to you.

You cannot stop the establishment of this administration, but you can delay it. Your will to obey the will of God and the leading of the Spirit of Truth that is trying to reach you at this time is important. Your decision must be made over and above your false loyalties to the human interpretation of the first one-tenth of the Fifth Epochal Revelation that keeps you from accepting the continuing revelation. This acceptance is not only for your own benefit but for the good of all the people of Urantia.

As Reservists, you are a necessary link, a vital and important part in the design for this planetary Divine Administration. You can choose to align yourself with a misplaced loyalty to organizations such as those that are a part of the Urantia movement that presently do not recognize Continuing Fifth Epochal Revelation, but this shortsightedness can only limit your relationship and loyalty to Christ Michael.

However, soon you will be shaken from your obstinacy and be awakened to the fact that what is happening at the First

Planetary Sacred Home, in and through the Machiventa Melchizedek Administration, using human representation, is indeed of God. Yet you still may stubbornly reject it because of your pride. If that becomes the case, even the mansion worlds may not be an option for you upon transition from this planet. For those of you who can break that pride, we need you; your God needs you; the people of this planet need you, and we bid you come.

October 23, 1992

Paladin, Chief of Finaliters
in cooperation with the Bright and Morning Star of Salvington, the System Sovereign, Lanaforge, and other interplanetary and interuniversal personalities for the implementation of the Divine Administration in and through the present Planetary Prince, Machiventa Melchizedek

As transmitted through
the Pre-Level-One Audio Fusion Material Complement,
Gabriel of Urantia/TaliasVan of Tora

PAPER 260

The Clarification Of The Process In The Use Of An Audio Fusion Material Complement Pre-Level-One As Opposed To Deo-Audio Coupling (Pre-December 1989) And Dio-Audio Coupling (Channeling)—Reflectivity Personality Pattern And Higher Levels Of Audio Fusion

SINCE we are dealing with a fusion of semi-spirit and spirit reality in relation to interdimensional reality, both material and nonmaterial, and other variables, we speak of fusion as a degree between all of these various fields of flow. Many criteria come into play in order to bring about the highest quality of this kind of transmission, particularly when we are dealing with an **audio fusion material complement** meant to hear and learn what we are saying, such as **Gabriel of Urantia/TaliasVan of Tora**.

Depending upon what order of being is speaking from our side to yours brings into play various prerogatives and various laboratory procedures because a lot of it is experimental, with various applications that are known facts, which have been tried on other planets with nonhuman personalities. So we deal much with the unknown.

One thing that we would like to make perfectly clear is that fusion with an audio fusion material complement is just that; it is a fusion of one entity with another in the complete molecular reality of the lower being. Everything about that material reality becomes in part the lower reality of the higher being. Because of that, this brings into play many variables, mostly dealing with the ascension of the individual at any particular time in the processing within his or her mind, this individual's relationship with his or her own God, and circle attainment of the individual.

All of these factors affect quite prominently what is being said, how it is being said, when it can be said, and to whom it can be said. The reflectivity personality pattern of the audio fusion material complement is also a prominent factor in interdimensional communication. With higher ascension of the audio fusion material complement comes a higher level of fusion with a higher personality pattern.

Walk-ins, as they have become known on Urantia, involving those who are considered interdimensional teachers (and many, particularly within the New Age movement, claim to be these teachers), are in reality fusions of the particular levels of **ovan souls**' higher selves of the past, their highest self before their fall, a lower self, or it is a fallen entity fusing with them.

Another category is **mortal soul transference** when brain injury occurs and a variety of interuniversal personalities of equal or lower ascension may enter that body. They are not meant to be teachers, but they may teach many things of lesser ascension in their lower form, just like any human can teach another something. The reasons for this are many and will be the subject of a future transmission.

Where **diotribe** reality exists within the ovan souls who have telepathic abilities to some degree and can tap into an aspect of their astral selves, they bring into the Urantia dimension aspects of that self and knowledge of that self at the particular level at which they were in a past **repersonalization**. This could be either on this planet or most likely on a higher world, taking into consideration that at that time they may also have been in a fallen state already having Luciferic tendencies within them.

The human soul who is experiencing this fusion of a past astral self and knows that he or she is getting information from a higher source will many times label it an entity separate from himself or herself; this is the mind at mischief for many. Some have come to the conclusion that it is indeed themselves at a higher plane in a past repersonalization and make no claim that it is a separate entity. These are more accurate in the realization of what is happening to them.

Others who are more iniquitous in motive allow fallen midwayers and other unrevealed personalities within the Lucifer Rebellion to **dio-couple** with them, incorporating the diotribe reality of both entities. The human personality knows that someone else is speaking through them but may have little understanding of the validity of the information coming through them because they themselves have accepted the false teachings at some point in their own evolution, and it may sound good to them and pleasing to some aspect of them based upon their past experience. In these circumstances Caligastia and his staff are able to bring continued delusion and Luciferic thought to the people of Urantia.

Dio-audio coupling (as opposed to **Deo-audio fusion**) is:

- an integration of either the former higher self of a **starseed** at a molecular level
- or it is a coupling of a lower self at an ultimatonic level
- or it is a dio-audio coupling of a fallen entity on the ultimatonic to atomic level, depending upon the **dio** power of the order of being with whom the rebellious human mortal is coupled

All channeling since December 1989 and the beginning establishment of the present Planetary Prince, Machiventa Melchizedek, and the human complement, Gabriel of Urantia/TaliasVan of Tora with the **Mandate of the Bright and Morning Star**, is dio-audio coupling. Previous to 1989 Deo-audio coupling was a reality with the administration of the Bright and Morning Star, using various orders of beings with whom human mortals were Deo-coupled in and through the mandates of Christ Michael.

Always these channelers were complementary pairs (husband and wife) or ascending son/daughter teams even though they had no knowledge of the Fifth Epochal Revelation. One such team was Mark and Elizabeth Clare Prophet. After his death the information became dio. Even the Deo-audio coupling was only at a level of the fourth psychic circle.

Dio-audio coupling with a former higher self is only an opening of a **memory circuit** of a former higher memory. When the channeler does not even realize that it is himself or herself, even that memory circuit is short-circuited, and only partial truth can be received and given; that is why it is still dio, even though it is a former higher self of an **ovan soul**.

Basically, much ego is involved when the human channeler tries to make it more than it is. This is the mind at mischief and the soul in rebellion to God. Even though they may claim to be serving Christ Michael, they are at some level of error, sin, or iniquity. Today the Teaching Mission is an example of such rebellion in the Urantia movement as well as all dio-audio coupling channelers of the New Age movement.

We realize that many of you would like to experience us in our finality, in our Melchizedek reality, in our angelic reality, but at this time on Urantia this cannot be so. Until it is, we deal with communication through the audio fusion material complement and hopefully a visual material complement some time in the future in the manner in which we can, technically and spiritually, to the degree in which these individuals themselves are capable of ascending to higher virtue.

With an audio fusion material complement candidate such as Gabriel of Urantia/TaliasVan of Tora, once we are in (be it the Bright and Morning Star, a finaliter, Melchizedek, angel, or midwayer), it is not the human being speaking but whoever is in. We use everything about that human being, everything about Gabriel of Urantia/TaliasVan of Tora that he is. We use the knowledge of his mind; we use his emotions; we use his attitudes; we use his humor, his outlook on life, and the various perspectives of his individual perceptions of life. Everything that he is, we become. We cannot, under the mandate of Christ Michael, interfere in the process of this individual's personal relationship with his God by our own prerogative or in any way that would endanger the status of an agondonter. If we did so, we would not only jeopardize his individual status, but we would jeopardize those around him.

The value of an agondonter in the universes of time and space is beyond your comprehension at this time. You are like a precious gem that is being created. Because of that we allow certain mistakes to be made. We allow this because they are not mistakes on our side; they are mistakes on yours. Of course we can tell you with exactness, with unqualified absoluteness, the distance from one place to another, or we can correct a mistake in any procedure or any known fact, but we do not correct what is obvious by human intervention and human research. That is not why we are here, and it is not within our jurisdiction to do so.

So we not only allow these mistakes to go on, but sometimes we allow you to think certain things. We have found out that sometimes in thinking something that is not quite correct, it will lead you to discover what is correct a lot sooner than if the correct thought was brought to your mind. In this discovery you become more knowledgeable.

That which is learned by reading is not experientially learned by life inspiration and experience, and so Jesus taught His apostles through the method of practical friendship and discovery by empirical observation as in the normal process of life. It was by empirical observation of the apostles trying to substantiate in their own minds what Jesus said to them that they discovered much of the truth. Much of what He said at the time went right over their heads, as it is now with many of you. Truth does not resonate with the soul and the mind until it becomes applied and connected to experience and sequence in relation to change.

Lucifer, full well knowing these things, tried to make the ascension process appear illogical to various orders of beings in relation to their own will, desires, and thinking processes in whatever level of consciousness they were, which in Urantian terms (if terminology could be used) we would call narrow-mindedness. All of you suffer from this. One may think that one is more narrow-minded than the other; sometimes it is quite obvious, and sometimes it is not. In politics you have your conservatives and your liberals; in spiritual reality it is the same.

We have discovered throughout the worlds of time and space that those with the greatest diversity of mind are the ones we can speak through and use in the highest manner, and eventually they can become mandated as audio fusion material complements.

Yes, we do use Gabriel of Urantia's/TaliasVan of Tora's emotions, and you will recognize that we use his emotions. This process becomes even more complicated when we are speaking to Gabriel's/TaliasVan's cosmic relatives or to ours. For instance, where did Gabriel/TaliasVan get his emotions from? Who am I? Am I not his cosmic father? Am I not your grandfather? In your superconsciousness, could it be perhaps when I correct you, you hear me as you did as an Avalonian (Pleiadian) child who is being scolded by his cosmic father or grandfather?

How we say what we say is limited by the emotions of Gabriel of Urantia/TaliasVan of Tora, but what we say in relation to counseling is accurate. This must be understood and accepted by all on the human side within the Divine Administration of Machiventa Melchizedek. At whatever level it is misunderstood, it is the failure of these listeners to process more rapid changes within themselves in whatever area we are trying to reach them.

If we had been ordered by Michael to materialize in front of you at a safe distance and speak to you in our finality reality, our angelic reality, our Melchizedek reality, or the reality of any of the orders of beings who speak through Gabriel of Urantia/TaliasVan of Tora, that perhaps would change you for a day or a week. Perhaps you would even discipline yourselves for years at a time, but the old habits of so many centuries would still be there, so we have to deal with you at your level of reality change, particularly ovan souls who are in transition.

Some of you have actually been higher in spiritual value and character virtue in other lives than you are in this present repersonalization. That is why we use the apostle John's first century name, for in that lifetime he was actually higher in virtue than he is in this one. His mindal ability was not as high then or his comprehension of spiritual reality, but in virtue he was higher.

In Gabriel of Urantia's/TaliasVan of Tora's early years as Francis of Assisi he was higher in virtue characteristics and balanced stabilization than he was in his early years in this life. It has taken Gabriel/TaliasVan forty years in this life to reach the level Francis was able to reach in his early twenties in relation to the balance of the Father/Mother circuitry. Francis was also more in control of his emotional body, much more so than Gabriel/TaliasVan has been in this present life, even in Gabriel's/TaliasVan's present forties.

These are examples of why Gabriel of Urantia/TaliasVan of Tora and others at times do not understand the interrelationships between one another. In spite of this we mandate you anyway. We mandate all of you with your faults, and we do so by the order of Christ Michael who sees the end results. We, who have also observed you and know what you are capable of, are optimistic that in all areas of soul growth all of the ministers who are mandated in Divine Administration will come back into their **point of origin reconstruction at the time of fall**. A more detailed elaboration of this point-of-origin-reconstruction process will be given in a future transmission.

It is you who are now discovering certain things that you need to discover about yourselves so that you can stabilize and not fall back into lower tendencies either from past lives on this planet or others. In the first century many of the ovan souls became more stabilized in a transition, but none of you, not one of you, have been able to stay there. It is easier for a **first-time Urantian** to come to the first circle and stay there than it is for some of you starseed who are mandated with administrative authority, with higher spiritual knowledge and higher mindal capability, as ovan souls have more of a history of past lower tendencies into which you can regress.

You may discover that if you do not come to higher virtue characteristics, some of those who have transcended in the past to the mansion worlds will return some time after the final change point, by seraphic transport and not by repersonalization, to be leaders above you. The first shall be last and the last first. So, it is much more complicated than you may think.

When we use emotions to try to get through to you, we are not speaking so much to Gabriel of Urantia/TaliasVan of Tora or to **Niánn Emerson Chase**, or any Cosmic Reservist, we are speaking to that little child from Avalon (Pleiades) who is still trying to get his or her own way, and we are also speaking to that adult Avalonian (Pleiadian) who fell in the Lucifer Rebellion who is still a child in many ways, and all of you have fallen.

There are only fifteen ovan souls out of the 170,000,000 fourth-order ovan souls born before approximately 1988 who have chosen to come back this time, and fourteen of those have had to return to Urantia on an average of ten times previously and one only three times.

We are not disappointed in your recent transactions among each other at the **First Planetary Sacred Home** or in the Urantia movement at large; we are not discouraged; we knew that this was going to happen. As a matter of fact, we were told by Christ Michael Himself, who does give information at times to us in positions of higher authority, regarding time-and-space events. Knowing some of the things that would transpire did not stop us from working with all of you in the manner in which we do, with humor, with love, and with concern, but mostly very optimistically, believing in the end result that all of you would overcome your childish ways and stabilize in the virtues of God, which is much more important than any mindal ability at which any of you have arrived.

We remind all of you that Lucifer, Caligastia, and many other orders of beings of the angelic realms were brilliant in mind but fell to pride or error. Now it is time for all of you to become beautiful in spirit and soul. It is the virtue of God that you must ascend to and stay in, in every aspect. You must put away your childish tendencies and put yourself under a microscope, each and every one of you. You must view yourself through this microscope daily. Stop pointing the finger at the other person. Will the one who has no sin pick up the first stone and cast it, please.

Because this is the **adjudication of the Bright and Morning Star versus Lucifer**, we first are working with those with whom we have closest contact and can work with most effectively, which are the Elders, **First Assistants**, Vicegerent First Assistants, **Second Assistants**, Vicegerent Second Assistants, and students of **The Schools of Melchizedek on Urantia** [the **Global Community Communications Schools**].

What is happening from our side to your side can only be understood at the highest level by those Elders, First Assistants, Vicegerent First Assistants, Second Assistants, Vicegerent Second Assistants, and students through experiential reality and not just by reading words from a book. Until the majority of the Urantia movement begin to understand **Continuing Fifth Epochal Revelation** at a necessary level of psychic circle attainment on third-to-first circle reality, their own soul growth will be greatly hindered, and they will most likely have to experience the death process to make their transition to the mansion worlds.

For those who can attain the ascension level necessary for the understanding of Continuing Fifth Epochal Revelation, it will then be possible for the evolving changeless, but yet potentially growth-activated, personality to transcend without experiencing death in order to become unified within the primal causal design in relation to the unification of the Thought Adjuster and the evolving soul here on Urantia.

As Urantia has been and is a decimal planet, Urantia being an experimental planet—twice fallen through the miscarriage of trust by planetary supervisors and consisting of interuniversal genetics—the uniqueness of the unification of personality, soul, and spirit taking place among and in the ovan souls on Urantia is unqualifiedly without precedence. Words are quite inaccurate at this time to communicate from our side to yours what is happening.

What will become known to those throughout the Urantia movement who have attained a stabilization on the third circle for approximately one year, and to those at the First Planetary Sacred Home who have stabilized themselves on the third circle and received an angel of enlightenment, is that the interdimensional communication that is taking place through the mandated Audio Fusion Material Complement, Gabriel of Urantia/TaliasVan of Tora, is the highest on the planet and that he is the only one mandated by Christ Michael at this time, and since December of 1989, to do so.

It will become increasingly evident when Continuing Fifth Epochal Revelation is dispersed around Urantia and as it is compared with other channeled information, which will be either of Caligastia and his staff or the higher or lower selves of those ovan souls presenting this information who themselves are still deceived by Luciferic thought. Although certain truths may evolve through these channelings, there will be no comparison between this other information and Continuing Fifth Epochal Revelation coming through Gabriel of Urantia/TaliasVan of Tora in relation to the **ascension science** process and the growth of the soul within the adjudication.

Since this is a unique experience taking place, it will take the ability of the Elders involved in this interplanetary audio communication process to come to the level where they themselves begin to be able to ask questions within their own minds that will elicit appropriate answers from us. It is a process that cannot be accomplished overnight. We cannot just bestow upon any of them complete, absolute, and unqualified knowledge without the experiencing happening in the life-experiment process. So, in the questioning and the pursuit of understanding comes the actualization of the reality taking place at the First Planetary Sacred Home.

If those who are presently channeling in the Urantia movement would realize that it is their higher selves who are talking to them, their astral selves, their once higher third-to-first circle superconsciousness and not another entity, then they may be able to come into their own cosmic mind. If their motives are impure or if they are in any manner controlled by others less pure than themselves, Caligastia or any of his forces can also enter their consciousness. They should come to the First Planetary Sacred Home and let Paladin, formerly of the Pleiades (Avalon), tell them just who their higher selves were, give them their real **cosmic names** and pertinent information to set them on their true course as Cosmic Reservists. Error can lead to iniquity if humility does not rule your heart. I quote from *The URANTIA Book*:

> . . . Not until the cock crowed did it occur to Peter that he had denied his Master. Not until Jesus looked upon him, did he realize that he had failed to live up to his privileges as an ambassador of the kingdom.
>
> Having taken the first step along the path of compromise and least resistance, there was nothing apparent to Peter but to go on with the course of conduct decided upon. It requires a great and noble character, having started out wrong, to turn about and go right. All too often one's own mind tends to justify continuance in the path of error when once it is entered upon.
>
> Peter never fully believed that he could be forgiven until he met his Master after the resurrection and saw that he was received just as before the experiences of this tragic night of the denials. [*The URANTIA Book*, pp. 1981–1982]

Peter was indeed forgiven. You should see him now!

February 11, 1993[1]

Paladin, Chief of Finaliters
in cooperation with the Bright and Morning Star of Salvington, the Melchizedek Revelatory Director responsible for the Life and Teachings of Jesus (Part IV of *The URANTIA Book*) and Gabron, primary midwayer, for the calling forth of Cosmic Reservists for the human implementation of the administration of the present Planetary Prince, Machiventa Melchizedek

As transmitted through
the Pre-Level-One Audio Fusion Material Complement,
Gabriel of Urantia/TaliasVan of Tora

PAPER 261

Similectic (Semi-Electric) Genetic Alignment Transference In Relationship To The Aquarian Age, Which Is The Alignment Of Urantia With Planets In The Highest Stages Of Light And Life In The System Of Satania Within The Context Of The Adjudication Of The Bright And Morning Star Versus Lucifer Which In Its Upstepped Energies Has Occurred Since The Arrival Of The Planetary Prince In December Of 1989

IN 1967, the activation of the Holy Spirit of the Universe Mother Spirit to the planet as a whole and to individuals on Urantia was greatly upstepped, as mentioned in a previous transmission. This began the alignment of Urantia with the highest planets of **auhter energy** in the later stages of light and life in the system of Satania.

This manifestation of synchronicity has to do with the beginning alignment in 1967 of certain individuals of the **cosmic families** who were beginning to receive in their personal relationships with God the activation of the Spirit of Truth of the Bestowal Son and the activation of the Universe Mother Spirit, which in actuality is the activation of the Infinite Spirit circuitry from Paradise in and through the Universe Mother Spirit to individuals on Urantia. At that time, however, none of the cosmic family members knew of **Continuing Fifth Epochal Revelation** or, for some, not even of *The URANTIA Book*.

It began a consciousness on Urantia wherein the group, community, or planet began to become more important to the individual than the mere individual self. This was more highly understood by the spiritually-minded. At that time, spiritually-minded psychologists and scientific astrologers also understood that great archetypal energies, correlated by time–space realities that they little understood, were bringing about a change in consciousness on Urantia, but that is basically all that they understood. In their lower understanding they believed that this had something to do with the alignment of physical planets. As mentioned in *The URANTIA Book*, this understanding is ignorant and superstitious.

However, there is an associated reality in which time–space correlation of both physical and spiritual energies in nature are activated by seraphim at the beginning of an age. It is these seraphim along with other celestial personalities that begin this energy activation at the beginning of various ages pertinent to the consciousness needs of that particular evolutionary planet, imparting to beings of that planet both inner and outer message patterns, affecting major world events as well as individual private lives.

In the Aquarian Age, or first stage of light and life, humankind will regain the value of the feminine principle. Again we must be reminded that the Universe Mother Spirit energies are activated on an individual level and on a worldwide conscious level. Fusion of mindal abilities and intellectual knowledge with heart is a necessity to activate the circuitry of the Universe Mother Spirit. The Father circuits must provide the structure and administration to fuse the feminine and the artistic.

Aquarian energies promote the desire in **ovan souls** to know of their past and for **first-time Urantians** the desire to better understand the collective history of Urantia's past, both historically and spiritually. The Aquarian Age is the fusion of science and spirituality that has been termed **ascension science** in previous transmissions. It is the higher understanding of what formerly has been, at times, erroneously called the supernatural, and includes such concepts as:

- subatomic particles

- the nature of light
- parapsychology
- psi phenomena
- alternative healing
- radionics
- Kirlian photography
- telepathy
- exploration of the causal, astral, and etheric or bioplasmic bodies

The Aquarian mind develops a hunger for the knowledge of energies and systems of universal law that control all life and creation of the master universe. This **ascension astrology**, which I will elaborate upon later in this transmission, is understood in terms of statistical research and ascension science investigation into Continuing Fifth Epochal Revelation. God, to the Aquarian mind, is the First Source and Center of energies, both physical and within the psyche. God is the intelligent principle behind all laws.

Aquarian energy, which is **interuniversal auhter energy**, is concerned with the group or **cosmic genetic** families or union of souls. It is understood in the Aquarian mind that this Aquarian Age is to be one of cooperation rather than competition, but a much higher understanding must be reached by New Age thinkers as to family cooperation and coordination in genetic relationships.

The Aquarian Age is the elevation of women in society to positions of leadership operating in feminine Paradise-circuit energies that will designate the Aquarian Age as truly unique and Universe Mother-circuited. It is the emergent energy of the Father circuits of creative individuality and authority fused with motherly intuition and the intrinsic values of the individual for the benefit of the group or planet, and not just for the self or a capitalist corporation in which the ego is trying to succeed.

The Aquarian mind is logical, consistent, and principled. The whole is more important than the parts that compose it. One must find his or her genetic cosmic family and heritage and give his or her talents to that group rather than sell them to the highest bidder. Organization and discovery is vital to the Aquarian mind coming into the first stages of light and life. The Aquarian mind has a higher connection to the Thought Adjuster, the God within, as this mind begins to see God as a Father and not just as a force or an energy.

Aquarian air is higher **Deo-atomic oxygen**, and humankind is no longer subject to the rebellion of past ages of earth, fire, and water. The first stage of light and life brings the Aquarian **Deo-atomic air** that opens the memory circuits of ovan souls and brings higher understanding to first-time Urantians. It begins at the **First Planetary Sacred Home** and spreads out to the other sectors and areas of the planet according to the consciousness on the planet. It can be extended to millions. If it does not happen to that degree before the final **change point**, it will happen at some time in the future all over this planet.

As we have said, the planet will go through the change, and millions will go through the death process to transcend this planet. Humankind will only find themselves by looking inward in order to change and actualize the words of Jesus, the Fourth Epochal Revelation, who said, "For whosoever would save his life selfishly, shall lose it, but whosoever loses his life for my sake and the gospel's, shall save it." [*The URANTIA Book*, p. 1760] Then one must look to the Father for help to make those changes. This help comes by energy transference of various potencies from Salvington by way of a vast administration to the evolving mind through the brain's neural networking. It has spiritually become known as grace.

Individual destiny has nothing to do with Urantia's wobbling on its polar axis as it orbits around the sun and its position in the heavens in relationship to other planets or stars.

It does have a correlation with the personality circuit of the Universal Father and the changing eras of man's development of consciousness, which usually precede the arrival of an epochal revelation and continued minor revelations of energy potency at approximately 2,000 year intervals pertinent to **similectic genetic alignment transference** stages in the mortal evolutionary mindal development on two-brained-type planets. One-brained and three-brained planets differ in these stages of similectic (semi-electric) genetic alignment transference.

The statement by the midwayers in *The URANTIA Book* that "the courses of the stars in the heavens have nothing whatever to do with the events of human life on earth" is true, but an archangel of Nebadon also stated that "the frank, honest, and fearless search for true causes gave birth to modern science: It turned astrology into astronomy, alchemy into chemistry, and magic into medicine." [*The URANTIA Book*, p. 1680 and p. 901]

If Earth astronomers had, with spiritual insight, incorporated a primal absolute God into their science, they would have discovered many secret universal cosmic facts, secret because only a spiritual mind can discover such truths. Astronomy would have become interuniversal similectic genetic alignment transference, which we have also termed ascension astrology for the sake of scientific astrologers who are discovering certain cosmic realities.

Is this not the way in which Christ Michael taught and lived as He took the truths of all evolutionary religions and built upon them? Should we now not also do the same in this era of human existence with the more scientific astrology of the 1990s that is beginning in its ascension science infancy to realize certain factual cosmic realities?

After certain general statements were made by the midwayers and a Melchizedek Son about astrology on Urantia, it was decided by the then-acting Resident Governor General, in cooperation with the Melchizedek director and the Revelatory Commission, that certain other transmissions should be given. These transmissions would include an increased understanding of similectic genetic alignment transference and also repersonalization. A brief instruction on these subjects would be given in these transmissions. What transpired was an unfortunate reality to present-day Urantia in relation to what has been written and incorporated into *The URANTIA Book*.

William Sadler, Sr.[1] was vehemently against the idea of reincarnation at any level, even before he came to the URANTIA Papers. He was also vehemently against astrology. He agreed very highly with what was first given, but when the second group of papers came, shedding more light upon these areas, he had a very difficult time incorporating these papers into what was already given. This was coupled with the fact that an assistant of his, rather than he personally, was present when these papers came through. He then began a systematic degradation of these papers to the point that he argued with his own staff for many years as to the validity of these papers, making irrational statements to the effect that the staff member himself incorporated them into the text.

We ourselves were working with an interplanetary receiver at that time who was not the type of receiver that **Gabriel of Urantia/TaliasVan of Tora** is, where we are able to deal with the moment-to-moment personality disputes, so we could not correct the situation that developed after 1935. All that we could do was to pray that these papers would be put into the book and incorporated with all the other papers given.

Unfortunately, this was not done, and those papers were eventually destroyed by those who feared truth. We were unable to rectify the situation until a Continuing Fifth Epochal Revelation vessel was found. The loss of these presentations of the higher realities of similectic genetic alignment transference (ascension astrology) and repersonalization in regard to Cosmic Reservists has complicated our present task. Many souls who could have benefited from *The URANTIA Book*, and now Continuing Fifth Epochal Revelation, have been left in confusion and doubt because of these unfortunate omissions.

Those who studied astrology in its higher God-connected inspirational aspects studied it for the purpose of understanding the psyche. The word psychology comes from the Greek words for soul (psyche) and reason or divine wisdom (logos). One of the problems with astrology today is the lack of understanding of the cosmic definitions of mind, soul, and personality. The compatibility between psychology and astrology has always been evident when the astrologer was one who understood a God-oriented universe. When astrology is void of the Universal Father and His personality bestowals, astrology becomes superstitious ignorance and confusion. But whenever astrology was incorporated with a Father-centered universe, astrology became enlightening.

It is unfortunate at this time that the higher aspects of present-day astrology, which are actually ascension astrology and similectic genetic alignment transference reality, are not understood in the context of a light-and-life planet. Urantia, now coming into the energy frequencies and space potencies of these higher planets, has nothing to do with physical alignment and conjunctions; it has to do with energy alignments with the higher consciousness or auhter energy created by the souls on those planets who are of intrauniversal or **interuniversal genetic** relationships. On a **third-dimensional** planetary level, your Urantian physicists who deal with electricity in motion call these phenomena electrokinetics.

Throughout the system of Satania, these energy alignments are charted, and maps are written for higher celestial personalities to work out their own destiny purposes and functions and for other administrative personalities of celestial orders to work out their own administrative functions. On higher planets of light and life, these charted maps are actually given to evolutionary mortals who understand them, just like you understand your own maps in relation to geographic locations of countries, continents, and so on. On Urantia there is also an electronic navigational system that establishes the approximate position through the coincidence in amplitude of two radio signals called the elektra system.

Urantia is now being included into this space-energy-potency process. A coordination begins on Paradise, and it goes outward to the created universes. Some of these energy maps are so intricate that it takes dozens of Urantian years to even begin to understand them. Higher celestial personalities use these charts to make massive decisions in relation to universal structure, and Creator Sons use these charts to create universes, based upon the prior understanding and enlightenment of former ages and planetary, system, constellation, universe, and superuniverse ethics.

Similectic genetic alignment transference contains genetic reality on an ultimatonic level and below. It cannot be understood by the evolving Urantian mind at this time. We can only bring this information to you in generalities, step by step, precept upon precept, and concept by concept.

Continuing Fifth Epochal Revelation will begin to bring these concepts and principles to you on a continuing basis so that at some point you too will begin to understand these higher genetic energy realities so that you can understand who you are in relation to the cells that make up your body. In the future you will also be given these charts on this planet when any of you are able to have a high enough understanding of them that they can be incorporated into your intrauniversal and interuniversal space travels, for which some of you will become eligible.

There is an ordered and patterned transference of interuniversal genetic reality that is a superuniverse reality and has nothing to do with the visitation and **repersonalization** of interuniversal personalities from one system or one universe to another. This has more to do with Paradise circuitry that functions in all of the seven superuniverses that gives life to all the mortals and evolutionary races of these planets. It has to do with the stages of light and life development on these planets. Here on Urantia, because of the adjudication, I, the Chief of Finaliters, have been given my status. This is based upon similectic genetic alignment transference reality. It is also based upon my seed who are on Urantia, which is explained in other transmissions.

This reality has also been able to bring Adam and Eve back to this planet, unseen but now ever-present in administrative functioning on Urantia. It soon will also bring Christ Michael back to this planet as He promised, and/or the Trinity Teacher Sons, which is the orderly process when the auhter energy at this level is created by personalities of intrauniversal and interuniversal genetic combinations. This is happening now at the First Planetary Sacred Home because of the spiritual ascension and union of souls who are now functioning as a corporate unit, exemplifying the beginning stages of light and life. It is not so much the quantity of these personalities that matters; what matters more is the quality of these personalities.

It must be remembered that the ever-present but unseen celestial staff has worked on Urantia with less than 100 members. The staff of Caligastia was 100. If the community of Divine Administration can come to that number, the potential to change this planet and bring in the Trinity Teacher Sons will be just as real as the events that took place at the beginning evolutionary mind levels when Caligastia first came to this planet. Now on Urantia, the members of Divine Administration are of a much higher evolutionary mind consciousness, which greatly adds to the power of the auhter energy that is now being created at the First Planetary Sacred Home.

With just a few at the First Planetary Sacred Home, great and marvelous things can happen on Urantia, but it must be ever understood that each and every one of you who reads this transmission is dependent upon each one at the First Planetary Sacred Home in the administration and Eldership who also are ever so dependent upon one another. No one member, no one personality can bring in the Trinity Teacher Sons. There must be a consciousness and an auhter energy of corporate, non-competitive reality, for this is what the first stage of light and life is.

Similectic genetic alignment transference patterns in space are important, even to evolutionary mortals in the system of

Satania who travel by physical spacecraft. Just like it is on Urantia when roads are constructed, those who understand the maps can travel on the better highways for more speedy travel from one place to another. In space it is the same way. Planets that are more aligned to genetic reality in the higher ascension status create a higher light in the seemingly dark universe. These lights are seen by evolutionary mortals and are read by meters much like your radiation meters, and it is known by the evolutionary mortals aboard these spacecraft that they can depend upon these energy paths that have even become known on your planet at lower levels as star routes.

Energy reflective circuits are star routes from various planets to Urantia, and certain student visitors from these planets can come to and go from Urantia because of these star routes or energy reflective circuits. There can be a star route from one planet to another without an energy reflective circuit, but there cannot be an energy reflective circuit without the personalities to create the interdimensional transference. Neither audio communication, astral material fusion (walk-in), or etheric visual communication can take place without the alignment of genetically-aligned personalities. The genetic reality that is incorporated in the aligned personalities on the higher circles of attainment actually is in alignment to the majority of personalities of the other planets.

In a sense, you can say that the whole universe is one; each planet is one with another planet. Eventually this becomes a great science that is too complicated to explain here but that Continuing Fifth Epochal Revelation will begin to teach in the future. This is due to the fact that all subatomic particles—intrauniversal or interuniversal, organic or inorganic—in the first stage of light and life begin to be pulled to their complementary elements or point-of-origin reality. This creates a higher electromagnetic charge in the human body, particularly high in ovan souls and extraterrestrial-genetic strains. This process is similar to dedifferentiation and differentiation.

Dedifferentiation is a special process wherein certain cells retrace their steps from a mature, specialized state to a more primitive, even primordial, unspecialized form. It is the de-repressing of repressed genes. Differentiation is acquisition or possession by maturing cells of specialized characteristics or functions by restricting or repressing all genes for other cell types.

For those who read this transmission and who may have doubts about this ascension astrology, we ask you this question: If you truly think that you are a first-time Urantian and are not a Reservist, what good is it if you have learned the first one-tenth of the Fifth Epochal Revelation and are unable to bring true actualization and true fulfillment into your life? You are still trapped in sheer existence—keeping a roof over your head, working at jobs or careers that you may dislike, tied down to the mundane realities of life, and unable to meet your destiny. If you truly look at yourself, you will find that you are unfulfilled and perhaps afflicted with the many diseases that are affecting you and have already taken some of your friends and loved ones from this planet.

Continuing Fifth Epochal Revelation was not brought to this planet to bring death, for death is no longer necessary. It was given to this planet to bring life and fulfillment. You must not look at the first one-tenth of it in *The URANTIA Book* as the final source of all your answers and the answers of all humankind, as it states within it that it is not a complete revelation. Throughout all of the morontia worlds in the universe of Nebadon you will be receiving continual revelation. The Fifth Epochal Revelation is not over on Urantia. It may not be over for another 50 or 60 years.

We remind you that the Fourth Epochal Revelation lasted on Urantia from the time that Jesus could speak and teach as a little child to His last word on the cross, which was more than 30 years, and He was the Creator Son Himself. Why do you then think that the Fifth Epochal Revelation would only have been from 1934 and 1935, or for that matter, from 1911 to 1935, when the Third Epochal Revelation was 94 years, the

Second Epochal Revelation was 117 years, and the First Epochal Revelation was 300,000 years? Do not put yourself into the box of your own smallness. Humble yourselves and continue to learn, or you will suffer the consequences of your narrow-mindedness and false loyalties.

January 7, 1993[2]

Paladin, Chief of Finaliters
in cooperation with Adam and Eve, presently resident on Urantia, and the Chief of Seraphim to bring about the calling forth of the Cosmic and Urantian Reservists to the First Planetary Sacred Home to be instructed in Continuing Fifth Epochal Revelation at the schools of Melchizedek [the Global Community Communications Schools] for the sake of Urantia and all its inhabitants, as this is the adjudication of the Bright and Morning Star versus Lucifer

As transmitted through
the Pre-Level-One Audio Fusion Material Complement,
Gabriel of Urantia/TaliasVan of Tora

NOTES

Foreword

[1] All of *The Cosmic Family* volumes are published by Global Community Communications Publishing in Arizona, USA. *The Cosmic Family, Volume I* was first published in 1993. Although *Volume II* was not published until 1997, the transmissions that comprise this volume were transmitted between March 1992 and March 1993. However, the transmissions were immediately available for study at the time of transmission for qualified students in the Global Community Communications Schools. Succeeding volumes will be printed as they are made available to the public. For more information contact:

>Global Community Communications Publishing
>P.O. Box 4910, Tubac, AZ 85646 USA
>Phone: (520) 603-9932
>e-mail: info@GlobalCommunityCommunicationsPublishing.org

[2] All *URANTIA Book* quotes used in *The Cosmic Family* volumes are quoted from the edition of *The URANTIA Book*, published by the Urantia Foundation. At present, other companies have begun to publish the contents of *The URANTIA Book*, but no such versions have been quoted in this text.

Continuing Fifth Epochal Revelation Terminology

[1] As of the publishing of this second edition of *The Cosmic Family, Volume II*, Gabriel of Sedona is now Gabriel of Urantia, Urantia being the name celestial personalities use for Earth.

Copyright from a Cosmic Perspective

[1] For a detailed explanation of Gabriel of Urantia's other name, TaliasVan of Tora, see the section titled "Concerning Van" in the back of this book.

Introduction

[1] Gabriel of Urantia/TaliasVan of Tora, *The Cosmic Family, Volume I* (Sedona: Global Community Communications Publishing, 1993).

[2] As of 2009, Niánn Emerson Chase is the highest material complement of a Brilliant Evening Star. Centria, Tiyiendea, Celinas, and Marayeh are beginning to move into reflectivity of Brilliant Evening Stars, each at the level of their current ascension status. Santeen reached the beginning reflectivity of Machiventa Melchizedek 1,000 years ago. More than 3,000 years ago, Gabriel of Urantia/TaliasVan of Tora reached that status during his lifetime as Ikhnaton (Akhenaten), and Niánn Emerson Chase, as Nefertiti, became reflective of a seraphim.

[3] Niánn Emerson Chase had to work outside Divine Administration in the beginning years but has not done so for more than 18 years, as of Autumn 2009.

[4] At that time Gabriel of Urantia/TaliasVan of Tora was not yet a level-one audio fusion material complement. However, even as a pre-level-one audio fusion material complement, he brought through much higher information than any "channel" on the planet.

[5] At some point the present *Cosmic Family* volumes will be combined into a larger book, like *The URANTIA Book*.

[6] "These assistants to the Planetary Prince seldom mate with the world races, but they do always mate among themselves. Two classes of beings result from these unions: the primary type of midway creatures and certain high types of material beings who remain attached to the prince's staff after their parents have been removed from the planet at the time of the arrival of Adam and Eve. These children do not mate with the mortal races except in certain emergencies and then only by direction of the Planetary Prince. In such an event, their children—the grandchildren of the corporeal staff—are in status as of the superior races of their day and generation. All the offspring of these semimaterial assistants of the Planetary Prince are Adjuster indwelt." [*The URANTIA Book*, p. 574]

[7] "4. THE LIMITATIONS OF REVELATION

Because your world is generally ignorant of origins, even of physical origins, it has appeared to be wise from time to time to provide instruction in cosmology. And always has this made trouble for the future. The laws of revelation hamper us greatly by their proscription of the impartation of unearned or premature knowledge. Any cosmology presented as a part of revealed religion is destined to be outgrown in a very short time. Accordingly, future students of such a revelation are tempted to discard any element of genuine religious truth it may contain because they discover errors on the face of the associated cosmologies therein presented.

Mankind should understand that we who participate in the revelation of truth are very rigorously limited by the instructions of our superiors. We are not at liberty to anticipate the scientific discoveries of a thousand years. Revelators must act in accordance with the instructions which form a part of the revelation mandate. We see no way of overcoming this difficulty, either now or at any future time. We full well know that, while the historic facts and religious truths of this series of revelatory presentations will stand on the records of the ages to come, within a few short years many of our statements regarding the physical sciences will stand in need of revision in consequence of additional scientific developments and new discoveries. These new developments we even now foresee, but we are forbidden to include such humanly undiscovered facts in the revelatory records. Let it be made clear that revelations are not necessarily inspired. The cosmology of these revelations is *not inspired*. It is limited by our permission for the co-ordination and sorting of present-day knowledge. While divine or spiritual insight is a gift, *human wisdom must evolve*.

Truth is always a revelation: autorevelation when it emerges as a result of the work of the indwelling Adjuster; epochal revelation when it is presented by the function of some other celestial agency, group, or personality.

In the last analysis, religion is to be judged by its fruits, according to the manner and the extent to which it exhibits its own inherent and divine excellence.

Truth may be but relatively inspired, even though revelation is invariably a spiritual phenomenon. While statements with reference to cosmology are never inspired, such revelations are of immense value in that they at least transiently clarify knowledge by:
1. The reduction of confusion by the authoritative elimination of error.
2. The co-ordination of known or about-to-be-known facts and observations.
3. The restoration of important bits of lost knowledge concerning epochal transactions in the distant past.
4. The supplying of information which will fill in vital missing gaps in otherwise earned knowledge.
5. Presenting cosmic data in such a manner as to illuminate the spiritual teachings contained in the accompanying revelation." [*The URANTIA Book*, pp. 1109–1110]

[8] In July 1992 there were only four Elders. Since then, their numbers have steadily increased. As of Autumn 2009 there are ten Elders.

Paper 230

[1] *Merriam-Webster's Collegiate® Dictionary*, 10th ed., 1993

[2] Some Master Architects are interuniversal, and there are also Nebadon types of a variety of orders. There is, for example, a Master Architect who is a Lanonandek Son and who is now assigned to Urantia.

Paper 232
[1] *The Cosmic Family, Volume I*, Paper 223
[2] *The Cosmic Family, Volume I*, Paper 215

Paper 233
[1] John 1:14

Paper 236
[1] First Timothy 3:5
[2] Deuteronomy 5:21

Paper 239
[1] Matthew 19:14

Paper 240
[1] Continuing Fifth Epochal Revelation teaches the concepts of spiritual unity in the midst of vast and creative diversity, all supported by God-oriented complementary relationships. With this in mind, it becomes clearer that Fifth Epochal Revelation (*The URANTIA Book*) and Continuing Fifth Epochal Revelation teachings on the eventual amalgamation of evolving races on evolutionary worlds and the complementary roles of men and women are visions of higher spiritual realities, reflected in uniting the best of each race and sex and identifying the interdependence each has with the others in ascending together as cosmic family. Continuing Fifth Epochal Revelation celebrates the divinely-orchestrated diversity and beauty each soul contributes, evolving into a group dynamic to attain higher levels of spiritual genetics and quality of life for all souls on the planet.

Paper 241
[1] Isaiah 53:6
[2] The editors would like to point out that absolute perfection and absolute constancy occur in stages and levels. For example, attaining perfection on Urantia for a mortal is different from attaining perfection for a mortal who has ascended to Edentia status.

Paper 242
[1] The sugar molecule referred to here is sucrose, common table sugar derived from sugarcane.
[2] Matthew 13:33

Paper 244
[1] At the time of the printing of this book, Autumn 2009, Avalon Organic Gardens, Farm, and Ranch™ at the First Planetary Sacred Home is supplying at least 90% of the animal and plant foods for the community.
[2] Matthew 28:19

Paper 247
[1] John 9:41

Paper 249
[1] See "Regarding Copyright from a Cosmic Perspective" at the beginning of this book for clarification.

Paper 250
[1] *McGraw-Hill Encyclopedia of Science & Technology*, 7th Edition, 1992
[2] Philippians 4:8

Paper 251
[1] Romans 10:17
[2] Matthew 6:33

Paper 255
[1] The following was transmitted by Paladin on August 2, 2005: "This statement would be true if there had not been the defaults of Destiny Reservists who had been called to align with Divine Administration at the First Planetary Sacred Home. As a result of the defaults, the timetable has been lengthened and greater planetary tribulation continues. If those Destiny Reservists had not defaulted, many potentialities of higher reality could have manifested into actualities, but at this time they remain potentialities."

Paper 256

[1] The term generics is an introductory concept for understanding the relationships between groups and circuitry. Generics refers to characteristics relative to a whole group such as ovan souls on Urantia. Modern neuroscience and quantum physics are at the threshold of visualizing the interdependence of molecular (particle) reality with the circuitry-in-toto (wave function) principle.

Paper 259

[1] As of the publishing of this book (Autumn 2009) in lieu of the current relocation of the First Planetary Sacred Home from Sedona to Tumacácori, Arizona, Paladin revealed that the archangels' headquarters, as well as Machiventa Melchizedek's celestial headquarters, are in the process of relocating from their former Sedona locations to energy reflective circuits in and around Tumacácori.

[2] As of November 1993 Elijah has left Urantia and will return at a future date.

Paper 260

[1] From September 14, 1992 through February 11, 1993 a total of twelve transmissions for *The Cosmic Family* volumes were received. The sequence of their inclusion in *Volume II*, beginning with Paper 260, was determined by Celestial Overcontrol. Hence, seven of the transmissions received during this time interval are included in *Volume III* rather than *Volume II*.

Paper 261

[1] William Sadler, Sr. (1875–1969) was an innovator in medicine, psychiatry, and religion, displaying extraordinary abilities beginning in early childhood. At age eight Sadler gave a commencement address on "Crucial Battles of History" at a high school graduation. Leaving home at fourteen to work in the Battle Creek Sanitarium, directed by Dr. John Harvey Kellogg, Sadler simultaneously attended Battle Creek College. He went on to become a surgeon and later became a psychiatrist, studying in Vienna under Dr. Sigmund Freud. Sadler is credited with originating what he referred to as the school of "American Psychiatry." He started a magazine with an eventual circulation of 150,000 in the late 1800s and authored 42 books,

including *Theory and Practice of Psychiatry*, which long served as a major textbook for schools of psychiatry.

He became a leading figure in popularizing preventative medicine and was a professor of medicine at the University of Chicago. He was a well-known favorite lecturer at Lyceum and Chautauqua meetings. He also taught at the McCormick Theological Seminary for twenty-five years. Dr. Sadler's most significant achievement was his role as the central figure in the Contact Commission responsible for receiving the Fifth Epochal Revelation and later publishing it in 1955 as *The URANTIA Book*. Throughout his adult life, Sadler worked intimately with his wife and spiritual complement, Lena Kellogg Sadler, who was also a physician and played an instrumental role with him in receiving and publishing *The URANTIA Book*.

[2] Paper 261 was transmitted on January 7, 1993 and is the only transmission in *The Cosmic Family, Volume II* that is not sequentially dated in relation to the other transmissions in *Volume II*. This rearrangement of the sequence of the transmissions at the end of *Volume II* is based on instruction from Celestial Overcontrol.

GLOSSARY

NOTE: The definitions in this glossary are limited. For further information, we recommend that the reader study this volume of *The Cosmic Family*, as well as other volumes, and *The URANTIA Book*. Glossary references to papers in these books are those papers that would be most useful to study, but are not necessarily all inclusive.

"Although these definitions are as exact as they can be in relation to the students who are studying this revelation, updated information can change the definition to some degree. The content of the meaning will still be there. We are limited, based upon language, from our side to yours, and hindered by your own ability to understand such a massive volume of information of specific details.

Sometimes definitions have many meanings, and some terms are very similar. Whenever we can, we will try to introduce them but may not be able to clearly differentiate the terms at the time. If you can somewhat begin to understand 10% of these definitions in total, we can expand on them and go from there. It could take years to completely comprehend these very cosmic technical terms in ascension science until it becomes second nature to you. Two-brained types such as are now on Urantia, both native and ovan soul, have the ability of complete comprehension at some point in their future evolution."

September 29, 1994

Paladin, Chief of Finaliters on Urantia

7-dehydrocholesterol A provitamin found just under the skin that, when exposed to sunlight, is converted to cholecalciferol or Vitamin D_3. See Paper 247

Glossary 463

7,22-didehydrocholesterol See ergosterol.

ACTH (adrenocorticotropic hormone) A pituitary hormone that stimulates the adrenal cortex.
See Paper 248

Adam and Eve The Material Son and Daughter, father and mother of the violet race, who came to Urantia approximately 38,000 years ago to biologically uplift the evolutionary races.
See Papers 229, 240; *The URANTIA Book*, Paper 74; and *The Cosmic Family, Volume I*, Paper C

Adamson and Ratta High complementary pair who gave origin to a great line of the world's leadership and also became the grandparents of the secondary midwayers. After the default of Adam and Eve, their first-born son, Adamson, left the Garden of Eden and mated with Ratta, a pure-line descendant of the Caligastia One Hundred with interuniversal genetics.
See Paper 240; *The URANTIA Book*, Paper 77; and *The Cosmic Family, Volume I*, Paper 208

adjudication of the Bright and Morning Star versus Lucifer The combined celestial and mortal judicial process, led by the Bright and Morning Star (Gabriel of Salvington), representing the final determinations and conclusion of the Lucifer Rebellion throughout the planetary system of Satania.
See Introduction, Papers 229, 247, 254, 258, 260; *The URANTIA Book*, Paper 53; and *The Cosmic Family, Volume I*, Paper 213

adjutant mind spirits Offspring of the local Universe Mother Spirit who extend the mind ministry of the Infinite Spirit to ascending evolutionary mortals. The seven adjutant mind spirits are: the spirit of intuition, the spirit of understanding, the spirit of courage, the spirit of knowledge, the spirit of counsel, the spirit of worship, and the spirit of wisdom.
See Papers 229, 240, and *The URANTIA Book*, Paper 36

adrenal glands A pair of endocrine glands located just above the kidneys, each consisting of two glandular parts, the cortex and the medulla, responsible for releasing various steroid hormones and adrenaline.
See Paper 233

adrenaline (epinephrine) Hormone produced by the medulla of the adrenal gland for the "fight, fright, or flight" response. It also functions as a neurotransmitter.
See Paper 249

adrenocorticotropic hormone See ACTH.

agondonter An evolutionary will creature "who can believe without seeing, persevere when isolated, and triumph over insuperable difficulties even when alone." [*The URANTIA Book*, p. 579]
See Introduction and Paper 260

Amadon Human hero from the Andonite race 500,000 years ago who, as an associate of Van, remained loyal to Christ Michael throughout the Lucifer Rebellion and who has now repersonalized on Urantia during the final phase of the adjudication of the Bright and Morning Star versus Lucifer.
See Papers 237, 259; *The URANTIA Book*, Paper 67; and *The Cosmic Family, Volume I*, Paper 207

Ambassadors (First and Second, including Vicegerents) Mandated to serve as ambassadors to the world, representing Machiventa Melchizedek's Administration within the human Divine Administration under the Mandate of the Bright and Morning Star.
See Papers 236, 254, 257, and 259

amino acid An organic compound so named because it has both a basic amine group ($-NH_2$) and an acidic carboxyl group ($-COOH$). Proteins are strings of amino acids.
See Papers 242 and 244

amylases Enzymes that specialize in hydrolyzing starches and glycogen and that are basically Father-circuited non-personality life forms.
See Paper 244

ancestral dyad units Mortal ancestral pairs who can direct divine circuitry flow to deserving good seed to assist them in their attempts to align themselves to the will of God.
See Paper 239

Ancients of Days Trinity-origin beings who rule a superuniverse and, as Trinity representatives, are the judges of all personalities of origin in that superuniverse. There are three Ancients of Days in every superuniverse.
See Papers 229, 231, 240, 253; *The URANTIA Book,* Paper 18; and *The Cosmic Family, Volume I,* Paper C

Andon and Fonta The first two human beings on Urantia, fraternal twins (male and female). Thus, they became the parents of all humankind, having nineteen children together, beginning the race called the Andonites.
See Papers 240, 243, 254 and *The URANTIA Book,* Paper 62

Andonites The pure-line offspring of Andon and Fonta. Their numbers diminished down to barely 100 families approximately 500,000 years ago when there suddenly arose from the Andonites— the Sangik family, the ancestors of all six colored races of Urantia.
See Paper 240 and *The URANTIA Book,* Paper 63

androgens One of a group of male sex hormones that stimulate development of the testes and of male secondary sexual characteristics (such as growth of facial and pubic hair in men). Testosterone is the most important. Androgens are also produced in smaller amounts in women.
See Paper 248

anemia A lack of vitality arising from a condition in which the blood is deficient in red blood cells, in hemoglobin, or in total volume.
See Paper 246

angels of enlightenment Seraphim who have ascended to Paradise-level attainment. Angels of enlightenment first arrived on Urantia at Pentecost. Some of these angels are assigned today as the personal seraphim for Reservists stabilized on the third psychic circle.
See Papers 232, 259; *The URANTIA Book,* Paper 114; and *The Cosmic Family, Volume I,* Paper 212

apostles The first-century apostles (including Matthias, Luke, and Paul) who have repersonalized in the twentieth century. They are a mixed group of starseed and second-time Urantians. An apostle is one who is in full-time spiritual ministry in contrast to a disciple, who is in part-time ministry.

See Introduction, Papers 233, 237, 258, 260; *The URANTIA Book*, Paper 139; and *The Cosmic Family, Volume I*, Paper 218

Aquarian reality The reality of the Aquarian Age or first stage of light and life wherein the Aquarian mind fuses science and spirituality into ascension science. It is a reality based upon cooperation rather than competition.
See Paper 231

arbor vitae ("tree of life") A tree-like structure of white substance in the longitudinal section of the cerebellum.
See Paper 256

archangels They are a high order of local universe personalities created by the Creator Son and Universe Mother Spirit. They are an order separate from angels. "They are dedicated to the work of creature survival and to the furtherance of the ascending career of the mortals of time and space." In recent times a divisional headquarters of the archangels has been maintained on Urantia and is presently located at the First Planetary Sacred Home in Arizona, USA. There are no archangels communicating with humans at present.
See Papers 233, 259, 261; *The URANTIA Book*, Paper 37; and *The Cosmic Family, Volume I*, Introduction

ascension astrology The knowledge of energies and systems of universal law that control all life and creation of the master universe. While the frank and honest search for the First Cause turned astrology into astronomy, astronomers themselves have essentially failed to promote spiritual insight and incorporate a primal absolute God into their science. Had they done so, they would have discovered many secret universal cosmic facts, secret because only a spiritual mind can discover such truth. Astronomy would have become what Continuing Fifth Epochal Revelation terms "ascension astrology."
See Paper 261

ascension science A universally spiritual science that fuses the spiritual with the scientific. On Urantia, it is very much the physics of rebellion.
See Papers 229, 237, 242, 251, 258, 260-261 and *The Cosmic Family, Volume I*, Paper 217

Assistants (First and Second, including Vicegerents) Mandated to assist Gabriel of Urantia/TaliasVan of Tora and Niánn Emerson Chase, under the Mandate of the Bright and Morning Star of Salvington, functioning in various aspects of reflectivity of Celestial Overcontrol.
See Papers 236, 254, 257, 260, and *The Cosmic Family, Volume I*, Papers 209 and 218

Assuntia Name of a neighboring planetary administrative system to our system of Satania, within the constellation Norlatiadek.
See Paper 249 and *The URANTIA Book,* Paper 41

astral body A composite of the bodies a personality has existed in before at any point in time and space, each existence having a separate body connected to it. The astral body in the present is ever growing; that of the past is in inactive form, yet not separate from the present physical body. The astral body of a second-time Urantian does not begin to form until death.
See Papers 235, 251–253, 255, and 258

astralology reconstruction An ascension science process for the repersonalization of the reflective images of the Paradise Trinity Personalities through the creation process of the Creator Sons and to humans through the individual circuits of the premorontia body and the glands of the flesh body. It is a process within the creation process by the Creator Sons in the seven superuniverses whereby the reflective images of the sevenfold aspects of the Paradise Trinity personalities are reconstructed, rematerialized, and repersonalized. In the forming of the lower bodies in relation to ascending sons and daughters, the seven aspects of God in and through the Master Spirits are reconstructed within the ascension science process through the individual circuits of the premorontia body. The glands of the flesh body very much function in correlation with certain energies coherent with Master Spirit reflectivity.
See Paper 235

astralology reconstructive circuitry A fusion in the thinking processes needed to create the morontia body on a third-dimensional level.
See Paper 235

astral psychoanalysis A method of analysis for therapeutic purposes in astral healing, especially in relationship to astralology reconstruction and the

counseling of ovan souls, based upon the premise that specific spiritual problems lead to the abnormal mental reactions that cause particular diseases that afflict the human body.
See Paper 235

atom The smallest particle of an element that retains the properties of the element.
See Paper 242

audio fusion material complement The mortal soul component in a fusion between a celestial being and a mortal. This fusion of one entity with another occurs in the complete subatomic-to-cellular reality of the lower being.
See Introduction, Papers 257 and 259-260

audio motion That aspect of kinetic energy relating to the sense of sound.
See Paper 230

auhter energy The higher force-energy synergetic field resultant from cosmic nuclear fusion created by the joining or rejoining of spiritual cosmic families or groups based upon the personality bestowal of the Universal Father and each individual's acquiescence to His personality and the group consciousness in relationship to Celestial Overcontrol.
See Papers 230, 237, 239, 243, 245, 250, 257, and 261 and *The Cosmic Family, Volume I*, Paper 228

automaton coding Higher intrinsic signal transference of genetic information that takes place with higher reception and response to the Paradise commands from God. When one hears and then responds in a higher way to God's perfect instructions, new and more powerful genetic codes become available to provide the ascender with new subcellular and cellular regulatory networks of higher capacity. In the understanding of higher cosmic genetics, cellular structures, the ultimaton, etc., the sequencing codes of function-and-form go like this: one thought leads to another, one reality complements another, one truth seems to be linked to another, and so forth, such that one's growing, loving, and living philosophy actually formulates his/her ever-changing physical form.
See Paper 230

automaton communication An interdimensional communication that is a fusion of auhter energy and kinetic energy creating motion that allows the reception of communication by ascended souls by pure impression or audio motion.
See Paper 230

automaton sequence The ordered and directionalized movement and positioning of creative thoughts and instructions from higher to lower beings who are all actively willing and able to manifest God's will in God's perfect timing. Available to all worlds that are settling to any degree in light and life and is a perfectly designed proper sequence of reflective Paradise communication leadership commands of Paradise Father/Eternal Son/Infinite Spirit orchestrated thought. In potential and in fact, right on down to the ascending evolutionary worlds, the pure thought responses of an individual, group, or even the mass consciousness of millions can activate and direct particle reality into higher motion, form, and fulfillment. Worlds that have entered the field current streams of the automaton sequence become self-governing proportional to the extent of their ability to fulfill the perfect will of God.
See Paper 230

automaton sounding The truly awe-inspiring ways and means by which the Paradise Father converts His creative thoughts and desires into perfect motion and sound, which moves down through a whole hierarchy of perfect and perfecting beings who translate the Father's song into exquisitely perfect and diverse forms. The Perfect First Sound from the Paradise Father is received by the Eternal Son and Infinite Spirit and sent forth to the Creator Sons and Universe Mother Spirits who hear the first causation and tap into it to create their universes. This sounding goes on even down to the humblest worlds of time and space such that, from the tiniest particle to whole magnificent continents, oceans, and worlds, the perfect Paradise pattern of God the Father can become manifest to all inhabitants and visitors therein.
See Paper 230

Avalon Name of a neighboring universe whose nucleus is the region of the Pleiades. Most of the starseed from the First Cosmic Family come from Avalon.
See Papers 241, 256, 259; *The URANTIA Book*, Paper 66; and *The Cosmic Family, Volume I,* Paper 213

axon The conduction portion of the neuron that can carry nerve impulses away from the cell body towards either a target organ or the brain and communicates with other neural structures by releasing a neurotransmitter substance.
See Papers 256 and 258

bacteria Unicellular microorganisms that usually multiply by cell division and have cell walls that provide a constancy of form.
See Papers 242 and 246

basal metabolic rate (basal metabolism) The minimum rate of energy turnover in an awake but resting individual. The three hormones most directly involved in basal metabolism are thyroxin, insulin, and adrenaline.
See Paper 248

binaural Of or relating to two ears.
See Paper 255

Boilermakers' Disease Deafness previously found associated with excessive sustained noise but actually more applicable to starseed children from dysfunctional families and environments whose loss of hearing may develop at an early age due to their sensitivity to the rebellious frequencies of Urantia.
See Paper 255

brain, the three planetary physical types The three basic organizations of the brain and nervous system encountered throughout the grand universe, classified as one-, two-, and three-brained types. The human brain can be viewed as an organ that receives and processes mind energy and makes willed-actions capable of increasing its intellectual and spiritual capacities. The three primal brain areas for increasing brain function (based upon higher soul and spirit pursuits) are called the forebrain, the midbrain, and the hindbrain. Urantians are currently a two-brained species. The ability to eventuate three-brained types on a two-brained world such as Urantia depends upon a shift in the mass consciousness of the planet, the challenge being to collectively help one another in destiny fulfillment and actualization such that all planetary citizens can achieve higher areas of brain usage in relationship to the causal brain.
See Papers 250, 261, and *The URANTIA Book*, Paper 49

Bright and Morning Star First-born personality creation of Christ Michael and the Universe Mother Spirit, called Gabriel of Salvington, who is the Chief Administrator of the universe of Nebadon. He now visits Urantia in overcontrol of the adjudication of the Bright and Morning Star versus Lucifer and periodically speaks through the mandated Audio Fusion Material Complement, Gabriel of Urantia, manifesting in reflectivity through this mortal vessel.
See Introduction, Papers 231, 249-251, 259-260; *The URANTIA Book*, Paper 33; and *The Cosmic Family, Volume I*, Papers 200 and 213

Bright and Morning Star Mandate See Mandate of the Bright and Morning Star.

Brilliant Evening Stars An order of local universe aids, created by the Creator Son and Universe Mother Spirit, who function mainly as liaison officers for and under the direction of the Bright and Morning Star. They frequently also function as teachers. The human Liaison Ministers, who hold the second highest mandate on the planet, are in reflectivity to these Brilliant Evening Stars.
See Papers 259, 261; *The URANTIA Book*, Paper 37; and *The Cosmic Family, Volume I*, Statement of Purpose

Caligastia The former Planetary Prince who arrived on Urantia 500,000 years ago with a staff of one hundred rematerialized ascending sons and daughters (the Caligastia One Hundred) to bring the First Epochal Revelation to Urantia. Caligastia followed Lucifer in a rebellion 200,000 years ago. Although shorn of all administrative authority, he has been allowed to remain on the planet for unrevealed reasons pertinent to the ongoing adjudication.
See Introduction, Papers 241, 258-261; *The URANTIA Book*, Papers 66-67; and *The Cosmic Family, Volume I*, Paper C

Caligastia Forty The forty supermortal members of Caligastia's staff who did not fall in the Lucifer Rebellion with Caligastia.
See Paper 240

Caligastia One Hundred Fifty male and fifty female ascending ovan souls, each from a different planet, brought by seraphic transport from the system capital Jerusem 500,000 years ago and rematerialized on Urantia to be

Caligastia's administrative staff on the physical level. During the Lucifer Rebellion, 40 remained loyal and 60 fell. The rebellious ones mated with the evolutionary races and created the Nodite race, so-named after their leader Nod. A select few ascending sons and daughters repersonalized on Urantia since the fall of Caligastia belong to this unique group of ovan souls who were first embodied here as the Caligastia One Hundred, and some Urantians have their interuniversal genetics.
See Introduction, Papers 256–257; *The URANTIA Book*, Papers 66-67; and *The Cosmic Family, Volume I,* Paper 208

Caligastia Sixty The sixty supermortal members of Caligastia's staff who fell in the Lucifer Rebellion with Caligastia.
See Paper 258

carbohydrates Organic compounds (such as sugars, starch, and cellulose) with the general formula $C_x(H_2O)_y$ and forming an important class of foods that supply energy to the body. The Trinity association of carbohydrates in the body is the family of the Infinite Spirit.
See Papers 244–245

catalyst Generally speaking, a particle, substance, or entity that seems to propel others near it to increase in speed or intensity of change and energy exchange. Chemically and biologically speaking, a substance or agent that initiates a chemical reaction and enable it to proceed under milder conditions than otherwise possible.
See Paper 242

causal body The first personality blueprint framed and perfect within the primal absolute Paradise circuit wave; that spirit-body that is perfect from its source, the body of the First Cause. The perfection itself is progressive throughout the ascension career and does not become full reality until an ascender becomes a finaliter. In relation to the human body, the causal body is the body of the future. It never changes, and it is constant.
See Papers 240, 253, and 256–258

causal brain The nonmaterial brain of causal design wherein the personality and spirit circuits draw the evolutionary mind to connect with the divine mind.
See Paper 256

causal coordinate body The body that begins to be formed in the fourth-dimensional reality based upon the astral ascension of the ovan soul. It is not material or semi-material but a blueprint derived from the causal body for each time–space experience.
See Papers 253, 256, and 258

causal coordinate ear Blueprint ear, predetermined by the Universal Father, which an ovan soul coordinates with his or her present repersonalization in order to build a morontia ear.
See Paper 255

causal memory circuit The causal memory circuit is the blueprint of ovan souls that was aligned with the ascending son or daughter before the fall. It is within the point-of-origin reconstruction time-past blueprint with which all fallen souls need to realign. Everything has a blueprint. Memory also has blueprints. That is how holograms are reconstructed in the transfiguration process. Somewhere in the person involved in doing the transfiguration are memories. All Overcontrol does is tap into those memory circuits and reconstruct them at whatever level they can, based upon that person's ascension. Everything that is nonmaterial can become material, everything that is matter can become spirit.
See Paper 258

causal wave line The connection to the causal coordinate body that must be established on the highest level for reflectivity between the destiny guardian and the soul's level of ascension. For the sake of analogy, envision the causal wave line as an umbilical cord, seeing the destiny guardian as the placenta in this case and the growing embryo as the soul's level of ascension.
See Paper 253

celestial mechanics The branch of astronomy in which theoretical mechanics is used to calculate motions of celestial bodies under the action of their mutual gravitational attractions." Continuing Fifth Epochal Revelation stresses the difference between disturbed motion and reflective cellular magnetic motion polarity at all levels of ascension. As spirits and particles increasingly arrange themselves in accordance to the Father's perfect will, disturbed motion begins to vanish and celestial mechanics tends toward the arrangement and circuitry of the architectural worlds, patterned after Paradise itself.

See Papers 250 and 252-253

Celestial Overcontrol Celestial Overcontrol is the term designating orders of beings who function on higher levels of universe administration, guiding and overseeing the human mandated personalities on a planetary level of functioning in cooperation with the Planetary Prince, Machiventa Melchizedek—the final authority in planetary affairs. These beings typically reside in the fifth dimension and above here on Urantia, and include (but are by no means limited to) the Bright and Morning Star (Gabriel of Salvington) and the Chief of Finaliters on Urantia (Paladin). Throughout this book the terms "Celestial Overcontrol" and "Overcontrol" have been used interchangeably when referring to this administrative body of celestial beings.
See Papers 229, 236, 250, 258-259; *The URANTIA Book*, "The Overcontrol of Supremacy," p. 115; and *The Cosmic Family, Volume I*, Preface and Foreword I

cell Organically speaking, the smallest unit of living structure, usually composed of a membrane-enclosed mass of protoplasm and containing a nucleus; in the more generic sense, a greater unit.
See Papers 235, 243, 250, 255-256, 258, and 261

cell structure Biologically speaking, the architecture of a living organic cell. When Continuing Fifth Epochal Revelation refers to cell structure, it is envisioning an omnipresent pattern throughout the entire master universe, whether it be a tiny ultimaton, a blazing star, a whirling nebulae, or even the central or superuniverses. In organic terminology the primal blueprint is called a casual body.
See Paper 250

cellular sound wave frequencies The Continuing Fifth Epochal Revelation term for universal life force or the vibrations coming from the First Source and Center. Cellular sound wave frequencies at first come into a source-center in the body by the primal absolute hearing assent capacity and must be understood at some level by each and every person or he/she simply will not be healed.
See Paper 251

censorship command center Station of censoring circuitry between the ear and the brain, which acts to separate will sound from nonwill sound, and which censors out that which is imperfect and nonabsolute.
See Paper 252

central nervous system The part of the nervous system that coordinates all neural functions. In human mortals, it consists of the brain and spinal cord.
See Paper 256

cerebellum Within the brain an integrating and coordinating relay organ of the rhombencephalon or hindbrain. Urantian neuroscience is not cognizant of the part the cerebellum plays in the perception and appreciation of conscious sensations or in intelligence. However, Continuing Fifth Epochal Revelation teaches that the cerebellum has much to do with the regulation of thought and is, in fact, like a clearing house between absolute and relative reality.
See Paper 256

cerebral cortex (cerebrum) The so-called "thinking cap" of the brain, derived from the telencephalon and including mainly the cerebral hemispheres (cerebral cortex and basal ganglia). The cortex is responsible for the control and integration of voluntary movement and the senses of vision, hearing, touch, etc. It also contains centers concerned with memory, language, thought, and intellect. Continuing Fifth Epochal Revelation teaches that the brain can actually become lighter and more compact and still show an increase in mindal activity. The cerebral cortex would be better viewed as a "soft-wired" radio receiver/transmitter used and modified by the mortal mind in communicating with God and His cosmic family.
See Paper 256

cerebrospinal fluid The lymph-like fluid that is secreted by the choroid plexus into the ventricles of the brain, filling these and other cavities in the brain and spinal cord, and which is reabsorbed by veins on the brain surface. Continuing Fifth Epochal Revelation teaches that cerebrospinal fluid has important interuniversal cultural characteristics, and in fact, the Avalonian (Pleiadian) personalities function with a much higher usage of this medium.
See Paper 256

change agent A present-day apostle who is in full-time ministry, aligned and functioning under the Mandate of the Bright and Morning Star.
See Papers 232, 239, 257, and 260

change point The term change point used throughout *The Cosmic Family* volumes can have multiple meanings. The reader should understand that there is not just one particular moment, day, or year that is the change point, but rather the change point unfolds over time, with many smaller change points (both personal and collective) contributing to the ultimate shift of the planet into the first stage of light and life, which would be the final change point.
See Introduction, Papers 238, 242, 244-245, 249, 254, 257-259, 261; *The Cosmic Family, Volume I,* Statement of Purpose and Paper C; and the Global Change Teaching by Niánn Emerson Chase titled "The Change Point: The Continuing Saga," (June 24, 2001).

cherubim The lowest order of angels. They serve with a complementary polarity, called a sanobim, and are faithful and efficient aids of the seraphic ministers. The cherubim is positively charged, and the sanobim is negatively charged.
See Papers 233, 257, 259; *The URANTIA Book*, Paper 38; and *The Cosmic Family, Volume I,* Foreword I

chief of seraphim A primary supernaphim from Paradise who first arrived on Urantia at the time of Pentecost and is now stationed at the First Planetary Sacred Home of Urantia, in command of the twelve corps of Master Seraphim of Planetary Supervision and the seraphic hosts.
See Papers 233, 259; *The URANTIA Book*, Paper 114; and *The Cosmic Family, Volume I,* Paper 201

cholecalciferol Vitamin D_3, or activated 7-dehydrocholesterol, produced by the action of sunlight on a cholesterol derivative in the skin.
See Paper 247

Christ Michael A Paradise son who is the Universe Father, Sovereign, and Creator Son of this local universe of Nebadon. He bestowed on Urantia two thousand years ago to portray the nature of the Universal Father, fulfilling the Fourth Epochal Revelation to this planet in the life of Jesus of Nazareth. After this seventh bestowal, He poured out the Spirit of Truth for the benefit

Glossary 477

of His entire universe. He is expected to soon return to this planet, as He promised.
See Introduction, Papers 243-244, 247, 253, 257-261; *The URANTIA Book*, Paper 119 and Part IV; and *The Cosmic Family, Volume I*

chromatid Each of a pair of new sister chromosomes formed during the early stages of mitotic cell division.
See Paper 243

chromosome A structure composed of DNA and proteins that bears part, but not all, of the genetic information of the cell.
See Paper 243

circuit The circle of complete function and influence of specified interrelated realities such as force, energy, power, or personality in accordance with universal law, respecting each and every source even and always unto the First Source and Center. The word circuitry usually connotes the detailed plan of a circuit that addresses as much as possible all of the components and subdivisions of that circuit.
See Papers 232, 256-257, and 261

circumstantial reality As energy follows thought, physical reality is manipulated by the totality of your thoughts and the thoughts of others pertinent to all kinds of life situations. The future is not determined; it is decided thought upon thought and moment-to-moment right or wrong action.
See Papers 233, 251 and 258

cochlea A spiral tube in the inner ear that contains the sensory cells involved in hearing.
See Papers 252 and 255

coenzyme An organic nonprotein molecule that plays a role in catalysis by an enzyme. The coenzyme may or may not be part of the enzyme molecule. Many vitamins are precursors of coenzymes.
See Paper 246

competitive inhibition The result of loss of desired function when the appropriate species loses its place to a competitive inhibitor. Chemically

speaking, a competitive inhibitor is a substance, similar in structure to an enzyme's substrate, that binds the active site and inhibits a reaction.
See Paper 246

complementary polarities Entities (from particles to personalities) created to operate in pairs. Within human beings, the highest complementary polarities are male and female pairings. In ascension science, complementary polarities (photons of any relationship but particularly pair-units) are beginning to activate circuitry within the neural pathways of the brain especially when they are operating within divine will for divine purposes.
See Papers 244–245, 250, and 258

compound A substance made up of atoms of more than one element.
See Papers 242 and 245

Constellation Fathers Name for those Vorondadek Sons (local universe Sons of God) who rule the constellation governments of the universes. There are one million Vorondadeks in our local universe of Nebadon. Our constellation, Norlatiadek, is ruled by 12 Vorondadek Sons.
See Paper 233 and *The URANTIA Book*, Paper 35

Continuing Fifth Epochal Revelation The ongoing continuation of the revelation found in *The URANTIA Book*, which is the first one-tenth of the Fifth Epochal Revelation. Between 1934 and 1935 the body of information in the Urantia Papers came through, but since 1947 new means of continuing revelation have come to this planet climaxing in 1988 with the attainment of the audio fusion material complement through which Continuing Fifth Epochal Revelation now reaches this planet. Gabriel of Urantia/TaliasVan of Tora is the only audio fusion material complement on Urantia.
See Introduction, Papers 257–261; *The URANTIA Book*, Paper 92; and *The Cosmic Family, Volume I*, Foreword I

corticoids (corticosteroids) Steroid hormones produced and released primarily by the cortex of the adrenal glands.
See Paper 249

cosmic brothers/sisters Males and females who had the same cosmic father or cosmic mother, or both cosmic parents, in a former life.

See *The Cosmic Family, Volume I*, Paper D

cosmic family Generically speaking, the divine family of living beings, constituting the patterns for personality manifestations and relations in the grand universe. Genetically speaking, a cosmically extended family of ascending sons and daughters (usually related to a finaliter). On Urantia, cosmic family members who have various local universe origins including Nebadon and three nearby sister universes. There are presently seven cosmic families on Urantia from the following four universes: Avalon, Fanoving, Wolvering, and Nebadon.
See Papers 229, 239, 246, 256-259, 261 and *The Cosmic Family, Volume I*, Paper 228

cosmic genetics The higher (more cosmic and absolute) genetic material and functioning potentials that are added to the evolutionary gene pool, usually beginning on an evolutionary world by the contribution of the violet race. Cosmic genetics on Urantia is more unique in that it also has interuniversal genetic reality, first introduced by the fallen Caligastia Sixty and subsequent starseed repersonalized souls.
See Papers 240-241, 245, and 258

cosmic husbands/wives Reuniting marital couples in the present repersonalization; pair-unit complements who have had higher circuitry and higher dimensional relationships in former lives and who are capable of bringing in higher new offspring or former cosmic children, for special purposes in this life.
See Introduction and *The Cosmic Family, Volume I*, Paper D

cosmic name A new and more spiritually potent name attributed to an ascending soul by a qualified cosmic ancestor, such as the finaliter Paladin or his son Gabriel of Urantia/TaliasVan of Tora. The new name can open the consciousness of the benefactor and significant-others to a higher state of ascension in a former life or to a higher destiny purpose in the present life, or both. There are very distinct characteristics carried in the sounds, accents, and syllables of the spoken cosmic name including personality bestowal, genetic heritage, and cosmic family relationships.
See Preface, Paper 260; *The URANTIA Book*, p. 2062; and *The Cosmic Family, Volume I*, Paper D

cosmic parents The parents a soul has in its very first life, whether originating on this planet or on another world.
See Paper 235 and *The Cosmic Family, Volume I*, Paper 211

cosmic relatives Cosmic family members linked through their interuniversal genetics from various Creator Sons, Material Sons and Daughters, and finaliters.
See Papers 239, 243, 246, 250, and 260

cosmic son or daughter The children that one has been the biological parent of in their very first life, whether on this planet or in another universe.
See Introduction and *The Cosmic Family, Volume I*, Paper 226

Cosmic Reserve Corps of Destiny A group of starseed on Urantia who function under the guidance of various entities such as midwayers and seraphim to bring cosmic consciousness to the planet. They are called to serve in the Machiventa Melchizedek Administration in various capacities in order to fulfill their destiny purpose. These ovan souls are members of one of the seven cosmic families presently sojourning on Urantia. All cosmic reservists are called to the First Planetary Sacred Home for further training.
See Paper 230; *The URANTIA Book*, Paper 114; and *The Cosmic Family, Volume I*, Paper E

cosmologic vibration pattern The normal vibrational pattern that resonates in Paradise harmony among the unfallen planets of any universe. It signifies the divine plan for that universe.
See Papers 232, 258, and *The Cosmic Family, Volume I*, Paper 216

Council of Twenty-four A council of 24 former spiritual leaders from various ages on Urantia who function under Christ Michael in relation to affairs arising from the Lucifer Rebellion in Satania. Each fallen planet in the system of Satania has a similar council, but the Urantia council is in overcontrol of them all.
See Papers 233, 247, 256, 259; *The URANTIA Book*, Paper 45; and *The Cosmic Family, Volume I*, Foreword I

coupling Mutual transference between two or more cellular entities creating a greater complex unit that may become fusion-responsive depending upon the purity and degree of the cohesive interchange. Coupling at the molecular

level is a chemical reaction in which two or more atoms maximize their intermolecular attractions. At the ultimatonic level, coupling is the synchronization of fields of vibration and flow into electronic configurations and motions. At the subultimatonic level, coupling is the spirit-particle transference from a seraphim to the neural pathways of a mortal ascender, the quality and quantity of the exchange depending upon many factors including the godly virtues, the psychic circle, and the soul age of the ascender.
See Paper 260

Creator Son A personality of Paradise origin, created by the Universal Father and the Eternal Son, belonging to the order of Michael. Together with a Creative Daughter, a Creator Son is the creator of a local universe of time and space. There are 700,000 local universes in the grand universe. To gain full sovereignty over His universe, a Creator Son bestows Himself seven times in the likeness of the created personalities on various levels in His own creation, reflecting one of the aspects of the Paradise Trinity, after which He earns the title of "Master Son." In our local universe of Nebadon, our Creator Son bestowed on Urantia as Jesus of Nazareth.
See Introduction, Papers 243, 248, 251–252, 258–259, 261; *The URANTIA Book*, Paper 21; and *The Cosmic Family, Volume I*, Introduction

crown circuit The first of seven circuits of the third-dimensional body, associated with the pituitary gland. It is the complement to the heart circuit and has 1,000 subcircuits corresponding to the inhabitable worlds of Satania. It is located on the top of the head and is the circuit through which the soul and spirit enter the next plane and is the travel route for transcendence. This circuit enables clairvoyant reception to these inhabitable planets of Satania, and imagination and inspiration enter through it. The crown circuit resonates with the first superuniverse, the superuniverse of the Universal Father.
See Papers 233–235, 251–253, and 255

Dalamatia The original Planetary Sacred Headquarters founded by Caligastia, Urantia's first Planetary Prince, 500,000 years ago on a peninsula that has since submerged in the Persian Gulf. Dalamatia was named after Daligastia, Caligastia's assistant. Many of the legends about Atlantis and the sons of God mating with the daughters of men go back to the time of Dalamatia.

See Introduction; *The URANTIA Book*, Papers 66-67; and *The Cosmic Family, Volume I*, Paper 223

decimal planet See experimental planet.

dendrite The receiving portion of a neuron that resembles a branch of a tree and forms connections with the axons of other neurons and transmits nerve impulses from these to the cell body.
See Papers 256 and 258

Deo good; godly; of God.
See Papers 251 and 257

Deo-atomic Atomic reality whose structure and function is in alignment with God.
See Papers 233, 250, 256, and 258

Deo-atomic air The higher atmospheric vibration, movement, and gatherings of Deo-ultimatons that become activated in the surroundings where complementary polarities of higher ascension status, who have been together before in higher spiritual endeavors, begin to function near one another in a geographic location on a more daily basis, in a moment-to-moment reality, all hearing within the divine mind.
See Paper 245

Deo-atomic cells Cells that are aligned with Paradise absolutes and are the cells of the morontia or light body.
See Papers 233, 242, 245, 250, 253-256, and 258

Deo-atomic genetics The genetics of Deo-atomic cosmic families or trisector families. Such genetic implantation, inheritance, and encoding, based upon deeper sub-atomic vibratory harmonics, can only be appropriated to those in divinely protected areas who are aligned with Divine Administration and procedures.
See Papers 242 and 250

Deo-atomic hydrogen Deo-ultimatonic vibratory, electrokinetic arrangement that carries either the Universal Father or Eternal Son motion

and patterned configuration. In the Deo-atomic H_2O molecule, which Deo-atomic hydrogen atom is representing the Father and which atom is representing the Son cannot be so easily distinguished, even by high ascending observers, because "He who sees the Son, sees the Father."
See Paper 242

Deo-atomic inheritance Higher genetic fusion capacity received from ancestors who have achieved high spirit level status in material bodies. The Trinity circuitry in the ascension of the parents translates into the substance and potential of genetic matter in evolutionary offspring. Although the spiritual ascension of the individual offspring is mandatory for full gene expression, inheritance from Deo-atomic parents greatly augments the rate of soul growth of the inheriting ascending son or daughter.
See Paper 242 and *The URANTIA Book*, p. 848

Deo-atomic mind-soul causal current The current from the causal body to the neurochemical circuitry of the brain. This causal current is inhibited by diotribes, and it affects the ability of past-life memories to be clear in the present.
See Paper 258

Deo-atomic offspring Progeny of parents who have stabilized on the third psychic circle and are in fourth-dimensional and higher relationships with one another, and who are seeking and expressing divine will in their moment-to-moment lives. Such parents and offspring have often lived together before on other worlds in cosmic-family relationships that were highly reflective of the Threefold Spirit reality inherent in the Paradise Trinity.
See Paper 254 and *The Cosmic Family, Volume I*, Paper 221

Deo-atomic oxygen A higher form of oxygen exhaled in carbon dioxide by higher personalities on Urantia, particularly those mandated in Divine Administration.
See Papers 245, 254, and 261

Deo-atomic parents Fourth-dimensional complementary polarities who replicate physical offspring after they have both reached the fourth stage of a fourth-dimensional reality or higher and are daily fusing with God while living high levels of Threefold Spirit reality.
See Paper 254 and *The Cosmic Family, Volume I*, Papers D and 224

Deo-atomic proton A form of proton created wherever a higher resonating order of God exists within aligned bodies in any one particular planet, system, constellation, or universe.
See Paper 244

Deo-atomic reality The higher God-reality manifest in the personality, spirit, mind, physical circuitry, and environs of individuals who are creating a union of souls in harmony with cosmologic vibration pattern.
See *The Cosmic Family, Volume I*, Paper 217

Deo-atomic receptor units Receptor sites in the brain for the activation of memory circuits. Past-memory traces depend upon specific alignments of certain minimal numbers of these units. Deo-atomic receptor units from the past, located in your past causal coordinate body, are reassigned to the home range area of your present astral body.
See Paper 258

Deo-atomic structure God-patterned, God-oriented nuclear structure within the ultimatons of souls working together with one another within the divine mind for divine purposes, through which the primordial Paradise relationships in the Paradise Trinity can transform physical molecules into Deo-atomic molecules in and around all such God-knowing souls.
See Papers 230, 240, 245–247, 249–251, 254, 256–258, and *The Cosmic Family, Volume I*, Paper 217

Deo-audio coupling A subatomic fourth-to-seventh-circle form of interdimensional communication (audio channeling) between the spirit and non-spirit mind used by Celestial Overcontrol to complementary male/female spiritual teams prior to December 1989.
See Paper 260

Deo-audio fusion World- and universe-destiny-fulfilling level of soul-spirit fusion between an ascending evolutionary mortal and a higher loyal celestial being in which the mandated mortal ascender is diligently hearing and practicing the will of God in concomitant and parallel incremental fusion responses to the indwelling Thought Adjuster leadings.
See Paper 260

Deo function A function in administration based upon one's virtue and desire to serve. The value of the Deo function and the Deo power within that function depends upon experience, wisdom, and higher ascension as well as the Deo function power of those in authority above one.
See Paper 251

Deo power Power used within divine mandates and administration in accordance with the character and will of God.
See Paper 251

Deontology The study of duty and loyalty in relationship to God and His cosmic family; the theory of moral obligation with respect to the privilege of serving.
See Paper 231

Deotonic Of or relating to levels of ethics and morality in regards to spiritual authority.
See Paper 231

Deotonic reality A recognition of the spiritual authority of another personality of higher ascension, and the beholder's reaction to the higher personality regarding the acceptance of certain decisions that may be contrary to one's own.
See Paper 231

Deo-ultimatonic The ultimate matter-energy structure and function that is in perfect alignment with God-order and God-purpose, as manifested when ascending mortals fuse virtue and fact in the formation of meridian circuits interlinked to the first morontia brain dynamics.
See Paper 250

desoxycorticosterone (DOC) A steroid precursor of corticoids that illustrates relationships in the Father and Mother circuits in regards to genetic predisposition and expression in and by the offspring.
See Paper 249

diencephalon The posterior subdivision of the forebrain that together with the telencephalon constitutes the prosencephalon.
See Paper 256

dimensional coordinate placement Divine absolute principles of celestial physics and orbital mechanics in relation to planetary placement correlated with personality placement according to interplanetary cellular reality and other factors.
See Paper 250

dio erroneous; evil; ungodly; not of God; out of divine pattern.
See Papers 251, 257, and 260

dio-audio coupling Audio interchange with a former higher self, a lower self, or a fallen entity who is operating outside of divine will.
See Paper 260

dio-couple The dio-magnetic drawing together, or conglomerating, of two or more unpurposed individuals or lower mind–soul stagnation states, wherein diotribe reality is being allowed or even practiced. Since any dio-couple is actually a non-reality transition zone, the stronger the diotribe magnetic coupling, the more disturbing and self-negating will be the vicinity in which such an unholy alliance is taking place.
See Paper 260

diotribe A negative or harmful particle manifesting in the body as the result of wrong thinking induced by the individual's acquiescence to Luciferic thought patterns.
See Papers 235, 240, 243, 250, 252–253, 255–256, and 258

diotribe intraction cells Diotribe cells from other universes that have found themselves in material or semi-material individuals.
See *The Cosmic Family, Volume I*, Papers 220 and 222

diotribe sensory way station A sort of rectifier station adjoining each of the seven circuits of the body and the meridian circuits, which censor out diotribe realities.
See Paper 253

disturbed motion A gravitational perturbation in the apparent physical motion of astronomical bodies, which illustrates the disturbance that results when any particle in the cosmos interacts exclusively with other particles rather than by merit of its relative ratio of motion to the other particles in

terms of the absolute ratio of each and all particles to the First Source and Center.
See Paper 250

Divine Administration Personal and authoritative outreach of God and His laws to all His creation and creatures via a vast and marvelous hierarchy of divine and celestial beings. Divine Administration begins in the perfect relationships within the Paradise Trinity and the divine family of beings, is coordinated on Paradise, and directed outwards to the created universes. It is the ministry of Paradise love, regard, and guidance poured out upon Havona, superuniverse, local universe, constellation, planetary system, and even planetary levels. With the appointment of Machiventa Melchizedek as Planetary Prince, Urantia now has the unique opportunity of implementing human representative government in reflectivity to, and coordination with, Divine Administration.
See Paper 235

divine counselors Coordinate Trinity-origin beings who are the perfection of the divine council of the Paradise Trinity.
See Paper 234 and *The URANTIA Book*, Paper 19

divine mind The mind of God the Father, the First Source and Center. All beings, spirit and mortal, derive their mind from the divine mind. Within the divine mind there is always the perfect plan for the unfolding master universe and all will creatures.
See Papers 229, 236, 241, 252–253, and 257

Divinington One of the 21 sacred spheres of Paradise, and one of the 7 worlds in the circuit of the Universal Father Himself. This world is home to the Thought Adjusters along with a host of other entities and personalities who reside there. Divinington is presided over by a corps of ten Trinitized Secrets of Supremacy.
See Paper 229 and *The URANTIA Book*, Paper 13

DNA (deoxyribonucleic acid) The fundamental hereditary material of all living organisms, stored primarily in the cell nucleus; a nucleic acid using deoxyribose rather than ribose.
See Papers 250–251

dyad unit A pair unit or group of cosmic relatives in alignment with the First Planetary Sacred Home who periodically join for the purpose of common prayer or establishing a secondary protected area.
See Paper 237

Eldership Hierarchy of human leadership on Urantia under the authority of the Bright and Morning Star and the human overcontrol of Gabriel of Urantia/TaliasVan of Tora and Niánn Emerson Chase, including the Liaison Ministers at the top, then those titled as Elders, First Assistants, and Vicegerent First Ambassadors.
See Papers 236, 253-254, and 257-259

Elektra system An electronic navigational process for finding a position in space-energy potency through the coincidence in amplitude of two radio signals.
See Paper 261

electron Orbital material complement of the proton, usually functioning within organizations called atoms and molecules.
See Paper 250

element The simplest form of electronic matter, which, under laboratory conditions, cannot be separated into simpler substances by chemical reactions.
See Papers 237 and 242

Elijah A Hebrew prophet and fearless warrior for righteousness, in the ninth century before Christ, who was compared by many in the first century A.D. to John the Baptist, both of whom were subsequently assigned as members of the Council of Twenty-four on Jerusem.
See Paper 259 and *The URANTIA Book*, Papers 45 and 97

emotional body (etheric body) The body between the physical and the astral, related to the morontia body of the ovan soul.
See Papers 244 and 260

endocrine gland One of the seven major glandular systems, such as the adrenal, that secretes hormones into the body through the blood.
See Paper 248

Glossary

energy constant The energy made available by the activation of the lower-body and meridian circuits such that constant reflection upon them equals constant energy.
See Paper 233

energy reflective circuits Energy fields of flow on a planet, known in lower level terminology as "vortexes" or "star routes," which allow for interdimensional communication and transportation and within which humans exhibiting morontia mota consciousness and above will draw higher cellular reality and unrevealed elements into their bodies.
See Papers 235, 237, 247, 257, 259, and 261

Enoch First son of Cain and Remona who became the head of the Elamite Nodites and was the first mortal on Urantia to fuse with his Thought Adjuster. Member of the Urantia advisory Council of Twenty-four.
See Papers 234, 258-259, and *The URANTIA Book*, Papers 45 and 76

enzyme A protein that is modified by chemical groups on its surface to make that protein a catalyst for a chemical reaction.
See Papers 235, 242, and 244

enzyme, heme An enzyme that reacts with iron porphyrins for electron transport and vital energy exchange in the body.
See Paper 246

enzyme, hydrolyzing An enzyme that catalyzes reactions in the presence of water, such as amylase, lipase, and proteinase, which are related respectively to the Father, Son, and Infinite Spirit.
See Paper 244

enzyme, neutronic An enzyme associated with the Universe Mother and more prevalent in females.
See Paper 244

enzyme, protonic An enzyme associated with the Universal Father and more predominant in males.
See Paper 244

enzyme, specific An enzyme that catalyzes a specific reaction with a specific type of molecule, some of which are so specific that they cannot be fooled by any substitution. A Deo-atomic enzyme is such an example, demonstrating that until personalities find their perfect destiny purpose, they will not be complete or wholly actualized.
See Paper 243

epochal revelation A revelation designed for the uplifting of an entire planet as distinguished from revelation to specific individuals or groups. There have been only five epochal revelations on Urantia to date, all having to do with the sorting and censuring of the successive religions of evolution, each ever expanding and more enlightening.
See Introduction, Papers 254, 261, and *The URANTIA Book*, Paper 92

ergosterol (ergosterin) 7,22-didehydrocholesterol, the most important of the provitamins D_2, which when exposed to sunlight is converted to ergosterol or Vitamin D_2.
See Paper 247

estrogen Any of several steroid hormones, produced chiefly by the ovaries in females.
See Paper 249

eternal present body The physical body or cellular manifestation in which the soul finds itself at any moment in its ascension.
See Papers 255–256

Eternal Son The second person of the Paradise Trinity, co-creator with the Universal Father and Infinite Spirit; not to be confused with a Creator Son of a local universe.
See Papers 232, 242, 246, 254, 258; *The URANTIA Book*, Paper 6; and *The Cosmic Family, Volume I*, Paper C

etheric body The body between the physical and the astral, sometimes called the emotional body, but is related to the morontia body of the ovan soul.
See Papers 253 and 256

exergonic reaction A synthesis reaction in which free energy is released and the interacting components move into a more stable position by conversion. Auhter energy, created by a union of souls, is a result of an exergonic reaction.
See Paper 243

experimental planet (decimal planet) One planet out of every ten inhabited planets in the grand universe designated for experimental purposes directed mostly for the production of new and improved variations in the evolutionary life plasm. Urantia is a decimal planet and is also unique in having humans who are being trained in Divine Administration.
See Paper 234

famotor movement A mechanized and spiritualized characteristic body movement that is the result of the strong correlation between the morontia and the physical body of an ovan soul and the way that that soul within the body responds to its spiritual ascension. Famotor movement usually dictates to the body its physical form in the long run.
See Papers 234–235

Fanoving Name of a neighboring universe in the general direction of Centaurus. Some starseed of certain cosmic families on Urantia come from Fanoving.
See Papers 241, 256, 259; *The URANTIA Book*, Paper 32; and *The Cosmic Family, Volume I*, Paper 228

Father-circuited Representing the qualities of the Universe Father, much like a human father, in responses: strong, decisive, leading, protecting, guiding, etc.
See Papers 233, 234, 240, 244, 247, 249, and 252

fats A living system found in nature as a mixture of lipids, chiefly triglycerides, whose function is energy storage, formation of membranes, and cell identification. The Trinity association of fats in the body is reflective of the communion of the Eternal Son with the Creator Sons. The enzymes that hydrolyze fats are basically from the Eternal Son.
See Paper 244

field Generically speaking, the mode or domain of bestowal or transference of any set of laws, relationships, or properties from the higher reality to the less absolute one. For example, the laws of force-charge between particles are derived from the field equations of wave motion.
See Papers 230, 237, 250, 254, and 256

fifth dimension See third dimension.

Fifth Epochal Revelation The revelation found in *The URANTIA Book*, which is the first one-tenth of this current epochal revelation. *The Cosmic Family, Volume I* is the beginning of Continuing Fifth Epochal Revelation, which will contain the other nine-tenths and is now in progress through the Audio Fusion Material Complement, Gabriel of Urantia/TaliasVan of Tora. This living revelation is furthermore being actualized in the lives of the ascending sons and daughters who have aligned with the Divine Administration of Machiventa Melchizedek under the Mandate of the Bright and Morning Star of Salvington and are trying to walk in the perfect will of God on a moment-to-moment basis.
See Introduction, Papers 241, 259-261, and *The URANTIA Book*, Paper 92

finaliters Ascending mortal or nonmortal sons or daughters who have ascended from their planet of origin through the local universe, the superuniverse, the central universe of Havona, and have reached Paradise. After having been embraced by the three Paradise Trinity personalities, they have been mustered into the Mortal Corps of the Finality. Finaliters are sent off on assignments in the superuniverses of time and space and are always involved when a planet is about to move into the first stage of light and life. Paladin became Chief of Finaliters on Urantia in January 1992. He is the head of the First Cosmic Family.
See Papers 229, 236, 243, 252, 258-260; *The URANTIA Book*, Paper 31; and *The Cosmic Family, Volume I*, Paper 226

First Ambassadors See Ambassadors.

First Assistants See Assistants.

First Cosmic Family A family of ascending sons and daughters, mostly of origin in Avalon (Pleiades), but containing interrelated members from the other six cosmic families presently on Urantia, and first- and second-time

Urantians with interuniversal genetics. The First Cosmic Family is the most closely aligned with planetary administration and is responsible for gathering the other six cosmic families. The First Cosmic Family is headquartered at the First Planetary Sacred Home in Arizona, USA. The finaliter Paladin is the head of the First Cosmic Family.
See Papers 229, 239, 247, 258-259, and *The Cosmic Family, Volume I*, Papers 227-228

First Epochal Revelation The first of five epochal (planetary) revelations to Urantia. Occurred beginning 500,000 years ago when the first Planetary Prince of Urantia, Caligastia, arrived with his staff of 100 ascendant citizens and established Planetary Headquarters in Dalamatia. For 300,000 years the planetary staff, which included a large number of angelic cooperators and a host of other celestial beings, worked to advance the interests and promote the welfare of the human races. This revelation to the primitive people centered on the First Source and Center (God the Father) and was promulgated until the Lucifer Rebellion broke out.
See Papers 254, 261, and *The URANTIA Book*, Paper 92

First Planetary Sacred Home Planetary Headquarters of the celestial divine administration. The first of these headquarters on Urantia was Dalamatia at the time of Caligastia's arrival 500,000 years ago. The second planetary headquarters was the Garden of Eden at the time of Adam and Eve 38,000 years ago. The third was the schools of Salem at the time of Machiventa Melchizedek approximately 4,000 years ago. The fourth was wherever Jesus was 2,000 years ago. At present, it is located where the Planetary Prince, Machiventa Melchizedek, resides in Arizona, USA.
See Introduction, Papers 239, 253-254, 257-261, and *The URANTIA Book*, Paper 92

First Source and Center The creator, controller, upholder, and God of all creation; the primal cause of the universal physical phenomena of all space. Without the First Source and Center, the master universe would collapse. He is also the Universal Father of all personalities. He unqualifiedly transcends all mind, matter, and spirit. A fragment of this First Source and Center lives within the normal human mind and is the spirit pilot to help find the Father on Paradise.
See Papers 229, 232, 247, 251, 253, and 261

first stage of light and life The first of seven successive stages of an inhabited, evolutionary world becoming progressively more settled in spiritual attainments and refined existence levels reflecting divine pattern in all ways.
See Papers 231, 251, 257, and 261

first-time Urantians New souls whose planet of origin is Urantia and whose present life is the very first existence of that soul. Most people on this planet are first-time Urantians.
See *The Cosmic Family, Volume I*, Paper A

folic acid (folate) A vitamin and coenzyme in DNA synthesis important for healthy cell division and replication.
See Paper 246

force-energy Force of energy frequencies and harmonies in alignment with higher consciousness.
See Papers 237, 239, 247, and 250

forebrain See prosencephalon.

fourth dimension See third dimension.

Fourth Epochal Revelation The fourth of five epochal (planetary) revelations to Urantia. Began approximately 2,000 years ago with the birth of Jesus of Nazareth, who is in reality Christ Michael, Creator Son of this universe called Nebadon. This bestowal of Christ Michael centered on teaching the world of the Fatherhood of God and the brotherhood of humankind, focusing on service to others. The Fourth Epochal Revelation lasted approximately 35 years, Jesus' life span.
See Papers 251, 258, and 261

Fragment of the Father See Thought Adjuster.

frequency Rate of vibration from say one cycle per billion years to billions of cycles per second. When the mind is in a higher frequency, these vibrations are the vibrations of harmony. Harmony is the vibration of absoluteness, and absoluteness is the vibration coming from the First Source and Center in relation to order and presence.

See Papers 234, 251–252, 254–255, and 257

frontal lobe The foremost of the four lobes of the brain, with the prefrontal cortex anterior and the primary motor cortex posterior, primarily involved with motor planning and activity.
See Papers 256–257

fusion Merging of diverse essences, entities, phenomena, or elements into a unified whole. In the ascension process, there can be a soul-spirit fusion between an evolutionary mortal and a higher celestial being, or a personality fusion between an ascender and a Thought Adjuster. It can involve a fusion of the past and the present in relationship to the experiential reality, or a fusion of semi-spirit and spirit reality in relationship to interdimensional reality, both material and non-material.
See Papers 229–230, 232, 251, 254, 258, 260–261 and *The URANTIA Book*, Paper 112

Gabriel of Salvington See Bright and Morning Star.

Gabriel of Urantia/TaliasVan of Tora Co-founder and leader of Divine Administration (Global Community Communications Alliance and its affiliates), head of the First Cosmic Family on Urantia, and holder, with his complement Niánn Emerson Chase, of the highest mandate of God for mortals on the planet, the Mandate of the Bright and Morning Star. He is the only audio fusion material complement on Urantia.
See Papers 236, 257, and 259

Gabron and Niánn Primary midwayers on the present staff of Machiventa Melchizedek assisting in the implementation of the Divine Administration in and through human personalities.
See Paper 239

gene The unit of inheritance observable at the molecular level. However, molecular genetics is fragmented and disjointed without fusing with neuroscience and quantum physics, and quantum physics has not penetrated the ultimatonic domain of mind-energy exchange much less the subultimatonic orbital mechanics wherein spirit-genetic transference takes place. Hence, ascension science will have to be much more advanced before genetic inheritance and gene splicing can be correctly understood.

See Paper 243

generics The term "generics" is an introductory concept for understanding the relationships between groups and circuitry. Generics refers to characteristics relative to a whole group such as ovan souls on Urantia. Modern neuroscience and quantum physics are at the threshold of visualizing the interdependence of modular (particle) reality with circuitry-in-toto (wave function) principle.
See Paper 256

glandular circuit receptivity formation motions The way in which body parts form as a result of the astral-mind thinking in the ovan soul or the development of the new soul in the first physical body.
See Paper 252

Glantonia Name of a neighboring planetary administrative system to our system of Satania, within the constellation Norlatiadek.
See Paper 249 and *The URANTIA Book,* Paper 41

glial cells See neuroglia.

Global Community Communications Alliance See section titled "Global Community Communications Alliance and Divine Administration" at the back of this book.

Global Community Communications Schools Formerly called The Extension Schools of Melchizedek and later The Starseed and Urantian Schools of Melchizedek, these schools focus on Divine Administration principles reflective of the self-governing taught by the Melchizedeks. Adult courses incorporate the highest truths from many world religions as well as continuing epochal revelation. The two school programs for teens and children are a home school cooperative and a parochial school.
See Introduction and Papers 230, 241, 244, 249–251, 255, and 260

glucose A monosaccharide (sugar) of the carbohydrate family that is crucially important in the energy metabolism of living organisms.
See Papers 244–245

gonads The sexual glands, the male being the testes that produce spermatoza (sperm cells), and the female being the ovaries that produce ova (egg cells). These organs also produce hormones that regulate secondary sexual characteristics of the individual.
See Papers 234 and 248-249

Governor General (Resident Governor General) A formerly rotating one-hundred-year assignment amongst the Council of Twenty-four (prior to December 1989 when Machiventa Melchizedek was officially inaugurated as Planetary Prince of Urantia) wherein the designated council member served as the mortal coordinator of all superhuman planetary affairs, acting more as a fatherly advisor than a technical ruler.
See Paper 233

grand universe The inhabited part of the master universe, which includes the eternal central universe of Havona of one billion unique and perfect worlds and the seven evolutionary superuniverses of time and space, which include 700,000 local universes, created by the Creator Sons and Creative Daughters.
See Papers 229, 232, 236, 247, 250, 253, and *The URANTIA Book*, Paper 15

gray matter Neural tissue of the brain and spinal cord that has a brownish gray color. At the cellular level, the paucity of neuroglial companion cells that myelinate the neurons for improved electrical conduction is the most noteworthy contributor to the gross gray appearance.
See Paper 256

Havona The name of the central universe surrounding Paradise, which functions as the pattern for the time-space universes. It is part of the destiny of ascending mortals to go through all of the one billion perfect worlds of Havona before reaching Paradise.
See Papers 229, 232, 236, 256, and *The URANTIA Book*, Paper 14

heart circuit The fourth of seven circuits of the third-dimensional body, associated with the thymus gland. It is centrally located in the thorax and contains 12 subcircuits connected to the 12 Vorondadek Sons of Norlatiadek. Within it is a second subcircuit of 1,000 circuits connected to the inhabitable worlds of Satania, within which subcircuit is a third subcircuit of

10 million circuits connected to the inhabitable worlds of Nebadon. It is also known as the Salvington Circuit and is connected to the fourth superuniverse, reflecting the Father-Son.
See Papers 232-235, 248-249, and 251

helper (helpmate) molecule Molecules of elements such as magnesium or iron in fusion with protein enzymes that create a synergy that equals a form of auhter energy. The drawing power of the helper molecule to the enzyme is, in type, a form of morontia magnetic field flow.
See Paper 246

heme enzyme See enzyme, heme.

hippocampus A curved ridge extending over the floor of the descending horn of each lateral ventricle of the brain, associated with the ability to make new memories or to retrieve old ones and also related to the search for novelty.
See Paper 256

Holy Spirit The ministering spirit of the Universe Mother Spirit; the first of three distinct spirit circuits to function in the local universe. Not to be confused with the Infinite Spirit on Paradise or the Spirit of Truth of the Creator Son, poured out at Pentecost.
See Introduction, Papers 244, 249, 251, 257, 261, and *The URANTIA Book*, p. 2062

home range area An area in the brain where receptors for memory circuitry regarding a particular past-life memory or past talents and abilities are reassembled and reassociated in the present astral body to become a present-eternalized reality.
See Paper 258

hormone A substance produced in one part of the body and transported to another part where it exerts its specific effect on the physiology or biochemistry of the target cells.
See Papers 235 and 248-249

impedance The ratio of the pressure to the volume displacement at a given surface in a sound-transmitting medium. A clear understanding of how

impedance is matched between sound waves in the air and in the cochlear fluid depends upon the fusion of past teachings of celestial mechanics, cellular and Deo-atomic cellular reality, diotribe cellular reality within the body, force-energies from Paradise, and many other factors.
See Paper 252

Infinite Spirit Third person of the Paradise Trinity. Not to be confused with the Holy Spirit, which is the spirit circuit of the Universe Mother Spirit of a local universe. The Infinite Spirit is the Creator of the local Universe Mother Spirits and the Mother-aspect of God.
See Papers 230, 242, 246, 254, 258, 261, and *The URANTIA Book*, Paper 8

inhibitor A substance that interferes with a catalyzed reaction.
See Paper 246

interuniversal auhter energy (Aquarian energy) Auhter energy that is interuniversal in scope, concerned with the group or cosmic genetic families or union of souls.
See Paper 261

interuniversal corporate membrane gland A combination of the hair and skin glands connected to the seven superuniverses. This gland has to do with the coordination of sense perceptions such as touch and feeling in relation to the Paradise Trinity personalities, beginning on the evolutionary world and inward to Paradise relative to bodies prior to pure spirit form.
See Paper 248

interuniversal Deo-atomic cellular transference A unique phenomenon now happening at the First Planetary Sacred Home wherein Creator Son combinations (from Nebadon, Avalon, Fanoving, and Wolvering) are fusing in cellular existences. These inherited integrated Creator Son cellular combinations are making Urantia (Earth) interuniversally unique, a likely prototype of higher evolutionary mortal development and unrevealed personality development in mortal form far beyond even the highest civilizations of the other six superuniverses.
See Paper 242

interuniversal genetics The higher and deeper genetic reality available to evolutionary mortals on designated planets such as Urantia, which is now

benefiting from the exchange and transference of Deo-reality from higher worlds, dimensions, and beings of time and space and beyond. Urantia is particularly unique because of the interuniversal reality of the starseed present today who have either finaliter fathers or the genetics of such fathers, from the spiritually-strategic neighboring universes of Avalon, Wolvering, and Fanoving.
See Paper 235 and *The Cosmic Family, Volume I*, Paper 226

interuniversal supermortal genetics The God-personality bestowed, spirit-born genetics available first from the three primordial persons of the Paradise Trinity all the way down to mortal evolutionary beings on worlds of time and space such as Urantia. Included in these supermortal genetics on Urantia today are special Creator Son combinations from Avalon, Wolvering, Fanoving, and Nebadon, as transmitted through the Material Sons and Daughters of the Creator Sons of those respective universes.
See Paper 261 and *The Cosmic Family, Volume I*, Paper 228

intraction Incorporation of thoughts, sounds, and perceptions that are imperfect, non-absolute, and inharmonious with the true nature and will of God.
See Papers 236, 237, and *The Cosmic Family, Volume I*, Paper 223

intraction cell reality Diseased cell reality at any level from inharmonic thought patterns of disturbed spirit, mind, or physical reality, which then creates further inorganic and organic disturbances in the primal vibratory reality needed for the generative and regenerative frequencies of wholeness and wellness from the First Source and Center, the Paradise Father.
See Paper 240 and *The Cosmic Family, Volume I*, Papers 223 and 225

intraction language Language inharmonic with cosmologic vibration pattern and cosmic truth (e.g. Luciferic thought), which disorganizes frequency circuits from various headquarters worlds causing emotional, psychological, and physical disease.
See Paper 251 and *The Cosmic Family, Volume I*, Paper 223

invariable septum stratum force An intermediate designated force-energy coordinate with personality circuitry of Paradise function in relation to cellular reality in like-mind brain formation and auhter energy. The mindal process and development of one planet depends upon the nearest inhabited planets

that surround it that are coming into the higher stages of light and life. At the First Planetary Sacred Home, invariable septum stratum force acts as an opposing force to eliminate all diotribe reality in the air, water, and food.
See Paper 250

iodothyronines Two important naturally occurring thyroid hormones that are actually a cooperative creation of the Creator Son and Universe Mother Spirit to increase the spiritual capacity of the evolving evolutionary mortals.
See Paper 248

Islets of Langerhans Small groups of cells in the pancreas that secrete insulin.
See Paper 248

Jesus The man of Nazareth, Son of Man, incarnated Creator Son Christ Michael of Nebadon, who bestowed Himself upon Urantia 2,000 years ago to earn His sovereignty and to portray the nature of the Universal Father, fulfilling the Fourth Epochal Revelation to this planet. The spirit identity of Jesus was built up during His lifetime in the flesh, first by the direct efforts of His Thought Adjuster and later by His own adjustment between the physical necessities and the spiritual requirements of the ideal mortal existence, as it was effected by His never-ceasing choice of the Father's will. It is not known whether the spirit reality of Jesus returned to become part of His resurrected personality, but there are those in the universe who hold that His soul-identity now reposes in the "bosom of the Father," to be subsequently released for leadership of the Nebadon Corps of the Finality in their undisclosed destiny in connection with the uncreated universes of the unorganized realms of the master universe. In any event, for 40 days after His death and Resurrection, Jesus met all the requirements of the system soul ascension, communicated and worked with the superhuman beings on Earth, and made 19 apparitions to reliable witnesses in the human cosmic family. Then, from the western slope of Mt. Olivet, He departed for the constellation capitol Edentia by way of the system capitol Jerusem. There the Constellation Fathers, under the observation of the Paradise Son, released Jesus of Nazareth from His soul-form and, through the spirit channels of ascension, returned Him to the status of Paradise Sonship and supreme sovereignty of this universe. And He literally ascended to the right hand of the Father, there to receive formal confirmation of His completed sovereignty of the Universe of Nebadon. And it is also literally true that this

Paradise Creator Son of God, when He was Jesus of Nazareth, promised that He would someday return to Urantia.
See Paper 231 and *The URANTIA Book*, Part IV

John the Baptist The forerunner of Michael's mission on Urantia and, in the flesh, distant cousin of the Son of Man. John was the extraordinary Jewish preacher and prophet of the first century who dressed like Elijah of old and thundered admonitions for all to repent and make ready for the end of the age, proclaiming that the kingdom of heaven was at hand. After the death of John the Baptist, Jesus began His public work. John the Baptist along with Elijah and Enoch are members of the Twenty-four Counselors on Jerusem who are now resident at the First Planetary Sacred Home on Urantia.
See Paper 259, and *The URANTIA Book*, Papers 45 and 135

Kalacortex A finaliter who is a pair-unit classification complement for the finaliter Kumatron. As pair-unit complements, they have participated in the transmission of some Continuing Fifth Epochal Revelation.
See Paper 238

kinetic energy Energy associated with motion that also occurs within humans or other mortal bodies when pair units are thinking of one another, being affectionate, or are in sexual union.
See Papers 230 and 245

kinetic fusion The fusion of the union of souls of the third and fourth dimensions from one side to another, creating a closer communication link between seen and unseen personalities.
See Paper 230

kliteus Represents cosmic truth in relation to the Eternal Father and Infinite Spirit. It is either Father-factual or Infinite Spirit-relative. Kliteus behavior accelerates spiritual growth when balanced.
See Paper 234

Kumatron A finaliter now working with Paladin, Chief of Finaliters, for the regathering of their seven cosmic families on Urantia today. Kumatron's planet of origin was a water planet where mortal ascenders lived in cities under the ocean.

See Paper 238

Lanaforge Primary Lanonandek Son of Nebadon and System Sovereign of Satania. He replaced Lucifer 200,000 years ago. Lanaforge is a gracious and brilliant ruler who remained loyal to Christ Michael in a previous rebellion. He takes great interest in the affairs of Urantia and regularly visits our planet.
See Papers 231, 259, and *The URANTIA Book*, Paper 45

Lanonandek Son An order of local universe Sons who function in system administration. They are best known as System Sovereigns and Planetary Princes.
See Introduction, Paper 259, and *The URANTIA Book*, Paper 45

level one audio fusion material complement A level of molecular fusion as a material complement to a spiritual being for the purpose of audio communication on a third-dimensional world as achieved by Gabriel of Urantia on March 25, 1993. In March 2007 Gabriel of Urantia/TaliasVan of Tora reached level eight.
See Paper 260

Liaison Ministers Those holding the second highest Mandate of the Bright and Morning Star in reflectivity to Brilliant Evening Stars, who act as liaison officers in human overcontrol between the Bright and Morning Star and the Machiventa Melchizedek mandated personalities. The Liaison Ministers also function as elders on the inner board of directors at the First Planetary Sacred Home.
See Papers 251, 257, 259, and *The Cosmic Family, Volume I*, Foreword I

life carriers Local universe Sons of God who implant and foster life on the evolutionary worlds. They are created by the Creator Son, Universe Mother Spirit, and one Ancient of Days.
See Papers 243, 245–246, 250; *The URANTIA Book*, Paper 36; and *The Cosmic Family, Volume I*, Paper D

light and life One of the marvelous successive ages of physical security, intellectual expansion, and spiritual achievement for evolutionary worlds to be settled in as the inhabitants achieve more heavenly values and relationships in God. There are typically seven stages of light and life that an

evolutionary world evolves through; our world Urantia is currently in the prestages of light and life.
See Paper 232 and *The URANTIA Book*, Paper 50

limbic system   A network identified mainly in the brain that mediates between thought processes and emotional behavior as expressed through the endocrine, visceral, and somatic activities. Just as the limbic system holds the key to the memory of the species, so it is also the key to the ovan soul for gaining access to past-life experiences. Also called the rhinencephalon.
See Paper 257

lipases   Enzymes that digest fat, which are basically from the Eternal Son and give an energy form to presubstance that is a submissive substance that brings a balance to the protein enzymes in the body.
See Paper 244

Lucifer   A Lanonandek Son, the fallen System Sovereign of Satania, who led a rebellion against his Creator Father, Christ Michael, which involved thirty-seven planets in the system of Satania, including Urantia. Lucifer's manifesto was about unbridled personal liberty, rejection of universe allegiance, and disregard of fraternal obligations and cosmic relationships, even denying the existence of the Paradise Father. Since the bestowal of Christ Michael on Urantia as Jesus of Nazareth 2,000 years ago, Lucifer has been imprisoned and awaits his final adjudication.
See Papers 230, 251, 259-260, and *The Cosmic Family, Volume I*, Foreword II

Lucifer Rebellion   A rebellion led by Lucifer 200,000 years ago in Satania; 37 of the 619 inhabited worlds in the system participated. It involved many personalities of various celestial orders as well as mortals. On Urantia, an adjudication of the Bright and Morning Star began early in the twentieth century and is expected to be completed in the twenty-first century. Many fallen starseed had to repersonalize on Urantia at the present time for this adjudication.
See Papers 229, 251, 256-257, 260; *The URANTIA Book*, Paper 53; and *The Cosmic Family, Volume I*, Paper C

Glossary 505

Machiventa Melchizedek Planetary Prince of Urantia since December 1989. This same Melchizedek Son incarnated in the likeness of mortal flesh and lived on Urantia for 94 years during the time of Abraham, and was known as the Prince of Salem. He came on an emergency mission when the spiritual light on Urantia was almost extinguished, and taught the one-God concept. He brought the Third Epochal Revelation to this world. He established a school where missionaries were trained who later brought his teachings to all parts of the world. Now Global Community Communications Schools at the First Planetary Sacred Home in Arizona, USA, are again training teachers to bring the Fifth Epochal and Continuing Fifth Epochal Revelation to the rest of the planet.
See Introduction, Papers 239, 254, 257, 259-260; *The URANTIA Book*, Paper 93; and *The Cosmic Family, Volume I*, Papers 213-214

magnet Polarized object with an electrokinetic field that attracts power.
See Paper 250

magnetic transpositional force-energy Creative force and power of interdimensional circuitry that is tapped into when the appropriate cosmic family members are moving into their proper personality-patterned positions in relation to divine purpose.
See Paper 244

Mandate of the Bright and Morning Star The universe directive from Christ Michael, Creator and Sovereign of the Universe of Nebadon, authorizing His Chief Administrator, Gabriel, the Bright and Morning Star of Salvington, to adjudicate the Lucifer Rebellion, beginning with our planet Urantia. Under this mandate is the authority to reinstate Divine Administration on the planet through the highest complementary-polarity couple on the planet, his Audio Fusion Material Complement, Gabriel of Urantia/TaliasVan of Tora, and Niánn Emerson Chase, in cooperation with the present Planetary Prince, Machiventa Melchizedek. This mandate includes bringing through Continuing Fifth Epochal Revelation, healing of the various bodies, and the authority to train and mandate humans to administrative positions in Divine Administration.
See Introduction, Papers 236, 251, 257, 259-260, and *The Cosmic Family, Volume I*, Preface and Foreword I

mansion worlds Morontia training worlds in the system of Satania that souls normally go to some time after their physical death. Those worlds are

situated near the system capital functioning with the purpose of helping ascenders to overcome mortal deficiencies. After the change point Urantia will function as another mansion world.
See Papers 229, 241, 249, 253, 258-260; *The URANTIA Book*, Paper 47; and *The Cosmic Family, Volume I*, Foreword I

Master Architects Transcendental beings who are the administrators of the master universe as a whole, from Paradise to the fourth and outermost space level, prior to the appearance of certain specific rulers. They are not only architects but also artists, the great composers of physical matter. They incorporate the harmonious melodic patterns of Deo-atomic reality and fuse them with pre-existent substance of a nonlife variety, thus endowing nature with exquisite physical stability along with boundless biologic elasticity. Some Master Architects are interuniversal, and there are also Nebadon types of a variety of orders. There is, for example, a Master Architect who is a Lanonandek Son and who is now assigned to Urantia.
See Papers 230, 257, and *The URANTIA Book*, Paper 31

Master Force Organizers Two orders of transcendental energy regulators (Primary Eventuated Master Force Organizers and Associate Transcendental Master Force Organizers) resident on Paradise but who function throughout the master universe, more particularly in the domains of unorganized space. These two mighty orders of primordial-force manipulation work exclusively under the supervision of the Architects of the Master Universe, and at the present time they do not function extensively within the boundaries of the grand universe.
See Paper 252 and *The URANTIA Book*, Paper 29

Master Physical Controllers A unique group of living beings having to do with the intelligent regulation of energy throughout the grand universe. They are the direct offspring of the Supreme Power Centers. They often function in batteries of hundreds, thousands, and even millions. They can upstep and accelerate the energy volume and movement, and detain, condense, and retard the energy currents. The Master Physical Controllers on Urantia today are under the command of the Divine Executioner, a quasi-material "fourth creature" of the Conciliating Commission, who has great power and range of activity on an inhabited world.
See Papers 230, 259; *The URANTIA Book*, Paper 29; and *The Cosmic Family, Volume I*, Paper 200

Master Spirits The seven primary personalities of the Infinite Spirit whose sevenfold self-duplication exhausted the associative possibilities inherent in the functional existence in the three persons of Deity. The Master Spirits have many functions, but at the present time their particular domain is in the central supervision of the seven superuniverses.
See Papers 230, 232, 235, 240, 248, 250 and *The URANTIA Book*, Paper 16

master universe The universe of universes, including the eternal central universe of Havona, the seven evolutionary superuniverses of time and space, plus the presently mobilizing (but uninhabited) four outer space levels.
See Papers 231-232, 250-251, 258, 261; *The URANTIA Book*, Paper 12; and *The Cosmic Family, Volume I*, Paper D

material complement The highest order of interplanetary and interdimensional receiver of communication; one mandated in reflectivity to a celestial personality. Material complements also function as conduits of universal energies transmitted to them by higher celestial personalities.
See Introduction; *The URANTIA Book*, Paper 109; and *The Cosmic Family, Volume I*, Paper 209

Material Sons and Daughters The highest type of sex-reproducing beings in a local universe, the Adams and Eves, who are the biological uplifters of the evolutionary races, physically present in administrative capacity under a Planetary Prince. They are the founders of the violet race. Usually only the progeny of the Material Sons and Daughters procreate with mortals.
See Papers 229, 259; *The URANTIA Book*, Paper 51; and *The Cosmic Family, Volume I*, Papers C, 216, 221, and 228

medulla oblongata (myelencephalon) See rhombencephalon.

Melchizedeks Local universe Sons of God who function in many capacities but mainly as teachers and emergency ministers. Ever since the Lucifer Rebellion and the Caligastia betrayal, twelve Melchizedek Sons have been guarding the spiritual evolution on our planet. In 1989 one of these twelve Melchizedeks, Machiventa Melchizedek, became our new Planetary Prince.
See Introduction, Papers 252, 259-261; *The URANTIA Book*, Paper 35; and *The Cosmic Family, Volume I*, Paper C

memory circuits Pathways of the mental processing system that registers, modifies, stores, and retrieves that which is being, or has been, experienced or learned.
See Introduction, Papers 258 and 260

Meniere's Syndrome A manifestation of deafness and loss of equilibrium in adults due to damage of the inner ear and diotribe realities linked to wrong thinking and an imbalance in the Father and Mother circuits.
See Paper 255

meninges Membranous coverings (usually threefold) of the brain and spinal cord.
See Paper 256

meridian center A subcircuit and geographic location created by a group or circuit of people who have formed their own individual meridian circuits and then joined together in a union of souls.
See Paper 232

meridian circuits Circuits of the morontia mind beginning in those who are coming into the first stages of light and life. Morontia mota begins in the meridian formation of the eighth, ninth, and subsequent circuits of the body that resonate with the superuniverses and with subcircuits connected to the major and minor sector headquarters as well as to system and planetary headquarters.
See Papers 232-233 and 253

meridian telepology A higher form of clairvoyance predicated upon the forming of the Third Source and Center within the meridian triad and used for interplanetary and interuniversal communication through the mind circuits.
See Paper 232

meridian triad Three meridian-activated souls linked to a particular celestial entity forming a higher cosmologic vibration pattern on a planet.
See Paper 232

mesencephalon (midbrain) The region of the brain called the midbrain that does not form subdivisions and is central to all thought-life functions, and considered the "heart" of the brain.
See Paper 256

messenger RNA See RNA.

metabolism Generically speaking, the matter-energy exchanges in the interactions between particles and wave-function. Chemically speaking, the changes in living cells by which energy is provided for vital processes and activities, and new material is assimilated to repair the waste.
See Papers 235 and 256

metencephalon See rhombencephalon.

Michael An order of Paradise Creator Sons, created by the Universal Father and Eternal Son, who in cooperation with the local Universe Mother Spirits create the 700,000 universes of time and space. The Michael Sons are named after the first being created of their order, whose name was Michael.
See Introduction, Papers 249, 260; *The URANTIA Book*, Paper 21; and *The Cosmic Family, Volume I*, Paper 207

midwayer commission A delegation of 12 midwayers from the Brotherhood of the United Midwayers of Urantia, who were officially assigned to portray the life and teachings of Jesus (Part IV of *The URANTIA Book*). Now they are working in cooperation with Celestial Overcontrol to help bring through the Continuing Fifth Epochal Revelation.
See Introduction; *The URANTIA Book*, pp. 1322 and 1343; and *The Cosmic Family, Volume I*, Paper 197

midwayers Unique beings about midway between mortals and angels, who are the permanent citizens of an evolutionary world. Primary midwayers are the offspring of the rematerialized staff of the former Planetary Prince, Caligastia. Secondary midwayers on Urantia are descendants of Adamson (firstborn of Adam and Eve) and Ratta (pure-line descendant of the Caligastia One Hundred). During the time of the Lucifer Rebellion the majority of the primary midwayers went into sin, and later many of the secondary midwayers also failed to align with the rule of Michael of Nebadon.

See Introduction, Papers 251, 254–255, 257, 259–261; *The URANTIA Book*, Papers 38 and 77; and *The Cosmic Family, Volume I*, Paper C

mind Organized consciousness that can be classified as physical, mindal, or spiritual. In human life, the adjutant mind spirits and celestial beings associate with the mindal mind, the Thought Adjuster associates with the spiritual mind, while the physical mind is involved in the physical aspects of life. It is in the physical mind that the power of choice has developed.
See Papers 229–230, 233, 244, 248, 258 and *The URANTIA Book*, Paper 110

mind gravity circuits Circuitry of the Third Source and Center that links the absolute mind of the Infinite Spirit to the spirit mind of the Seven Master Spirits to the adjutant mind spirits of the local Universe Mother Spirits even unto the pre-mind reality of new ascending souls. It is complementary to the personality-spirit gravity circuits of the Father-Son circuitry and makes communication with the divine mind of the First Source and Center possible. The coordination of the mind gravity circuits from the Infinite Spirit with reception of the Father-Son circuits by individuals on Urantia at this time on the planet is imperative. However, when alignment of thought processes are outside of divine mind through selfishness and self-assertion, then the evolution of the soul, which is a kinetic response to God purpose, cannot happen, and therefore destiny fulfillment for all is delayed.
See Paper 230 and *The URANTIA Book*, Papers 5–9

mitochondria Energy-generating organelle that, in each human cell, contain copies of cytoplasmic DNA. The sacred areas of Urantia are like mitochondria that will produce the final molecule and a new seed of a morontia body.
See Papers 243 and 245

molecule A bonded group of atoms that act as a unit. When two atoms are drawn together as complementary polarities, they fuse together at the higher molecular level resulting in a higher flow of orbiting electrons.
See Papers 242, 254, and 258

morontia A level of local universe reality between the material and spiritual levels of creature existence. The human soul is an experiential acquirement that is created by a creature choosing to do the will of the Father in heaven.

This resulting new reality is a morontia reality that is destined to survive mortal death and begin the Paradise ascension.
See Introduction, Papers 241, 259; *The URANTIA Book*, Paper 48; and *The Cosmic Family, Volume I*, Paper 197

morontia body The various body forms of the 570 ascending morontia levels of creature existence an ascending soul uses within the local universe. It is also known on Urantia as the light body. While souls usually receive a morontia body after death, it is possible to construct one by moving into Deo-atomic reality while living at Planetary Headquarters, being aligned with the Divine Government of the present Planetary Prince, Machiventa Melchizedek, and living in the perfect will of God moment-to-moment. Many variables are needed in order to attain a morontia body without passing through the death experience.
See Papers 232, 243, 248, 250, 253–254, 256, 258; *The URANTIA Book*, Paper 48; and *The Cosmic Family, Volume I*, Paper 197

morontia counseling A form of counseling that is concerned with spiritual progression, fulfillment of destiny purpose, and personality actualization of an ascending mortal, especially important to ovan souls during this time of adjudication to bring them back to their spiritual proficiency prior to their fall.
See Paper 235

morontia counselors On Urantia in the first stages of light and life, those mandated mortals trained and assigned to counseling particularly ovan souls. On the mansion worlds, those transition seraphim assigned to teach, direct, and counsel the surviving mortals from the worlds of human origin.
See Papers 238, 259, and *The URANTIA Book*, Paper 48

morontia ear The ear of the morontia body, which is connected to the causal coordinate body after the formation of the morontia eye.
See Paper 253

morontia eye The second organ formation after the morontia heart that is connected to the causal coordinate body. Unlike the morontia heart, which is pre-existent and time-present, the morontia eye must will-created and will-continued.
See Paper 253

morontia heart Construct of the eighth meridian circuit, which is the beginning of the morontia body.
See Papers 232 and 253

morontia heart circuit Eighth meridian circuit, also called the morontia circuit, which is unique to each individual ascender.
See Paper 233

morontia magnetic field flow A higher flow of auhter energy between cosmic family members one to another opening a divine circuitry path to system and universe headquarters and above, and creating a magnetic drawing power to the First Planetary Sacred Home, and is available to those who know about the activation of thought energy in connection to divine circuitry.
See Papers 239 and 246

morontia magnetic force energy The divine flow of open circuitry in relation to memory that draws cosmic family members to one another. In essence, this morontia magnetic force energy is equivalent to the higher thoughts of cosmic family members, which allows them to recognize apparent strangers upon their initial contact on an evolutionary world such as Urantia.
See Paper 239

morontia mota Philosophy and brotherhood at the morontia level of creature existence. The thought processes in relationship to the morontia body.
See Paper 231 and *The URANTIA Book*, Paper 48

morontia progressors Ascending souls on any of the 570 levels of morontia life before they become full-fledged spirits. The morontia career actually begins on the planet of origin, and in the Nebadon ascension scheme there are 8 morontia body changes in the planetary system, 71 in the constellation, and 491 during the sojourn on the spheres of Salvington. All along the way, these souls are becoming more spiritual and less material in their natures.
See Paper 233 and *The URANTIA Book*, Paper 30

Glossary 513

morontia seraphim coordinators (and reconstructive coordinators) Previously unrevealed personalities resident on Urantia designated to coordinate certain celestial personalities with certain Cosmic and Urantian Reservists to aid in the higher understanding of the ascension science process and for purposes of destiny alignment.
See Paper 252

morontia temple A planetary temple built to system capital specifications by morontia power supervisors and master physical controllers at the capital of an inhabited world as it enters the settled stages of light and life. Besides hosting its other special planetary ceremonies, the morontia temple also serves as the place of assembly for witnessing the translation of living mortals to the morontia existence.
See Papers 237, 253 and *The URANTIA Book*, Paper 55

mortal soul transference A phenomenon of soul transference (related to "walk-ins") in which, as a result of brain injury, a variety of interuniversal personalities of equal or lower ascension may enter the body.
See Paper 260

Moses Hebrew prophet, lawgiver, and liberator of the Israelites from Egypt who lived approximately B.C. 1000 and is considered one of the greatest historical characters between Melchizedek and Jesus. The greatness of Moses lies in his wisdom and sagacity. Other men have had greater concepts of God, but no one man was ever so successful in inducing large numbers of people to adopt such advanced beliefs.
See Paper 259 and *The URANTIA Book*, Papers 95–96

Mother-circuited Representing the qualities of the Universe Mother Spirit, much like a human mother, in responses: gentle, soft, submissive, yielding, kind, giving, patient, etc.
See Papers 233, 247, and 249

myelencephalon (medulla oblongata) See rhombencephalon.

Mystery Monitors See Thought Adjusters.

navel circuit The sixth of seven circuits of the third-dimensional body, associated physically with the functions of the adrenal gland. It resonates

with the sixth superuniverse, which reflects the Eternal Son and Infinite Spirit. The dominant outer subcircuits represent the six aspects of Father-Mother reality on lower worlds. It has one thousand subcircuits connecting to the inhabitable worlds.
See Papers 233–235

Nebadon The name of our local universe, created by Christ Michael and the Universe Mother Spirit. Salvington is its headquarters.
See Introduction, Papers 241, 253, 256, 258–259, 261; *The URANTIA Book*, Part II; and *The Cosmic Family, Volume I*, Foreword I

neuroglia (glial cells) Support cells that are housekeepers and overcontrol for the nerve cells and their branches.
See Paper 256

neurohumoral transmitter A chemical substance formed in a neuron to activate or modify the functioning of a neighboring neuron or a specific target organ elsewhere in the body.
See Paper 258

neuron An interlinking life-force communication system whose generic and genetic relay unit is called the "nerve cell," consisting of cell body, dendrites, and axon. While the neural network mediates the living energy system of the lower physical body, the glial network is the more spiritual mediator particularly in relation to astral and morontia realities.
See Papers 250, 253, 256, and 258

neurotransmitter A chemical that mediates the transmission of a nerve impulse across a synapse.
See Paper 258

neutron The complementary polarity of the proton.
See Paper 244

neutronic enzyme See enzyme, neutronic.

New Jerusalem A triune particle city that will also be the planetary headquarters of Urantia when the planet enters the first stage of light and life. Although the arrival of the New Jerusalem must await the whole planet's

entrance into the settled age of light and life, implementation of the architectural design for the triune particle city is already in motion and will be realized at the First Planetary Sacred Home within the Machiventa Melchizedek Administration some time after the final change point.
See Paper 230

Niánn Emerson Chase Co-founder of Global Community Communications Alliance who shares the Mandate of the Bright and Morning Star with her complement Gabriel of Urantia/TaliasVan of Tora. Just as the highest Son/Mother representation and ministry in the local universe of Nebadon is that of the Bright and Morning Star of Salvington bonded with the highest Evening Star, so is the highest dual ministry of administrative divine power on Urantia reflected in the complementary polarity of Gabriel of Urantia/TaliasVan of Tora bonded with Niánn Emerson Chase.
See Papers 236, 257, and 259

Nodite and Andite amalgamations Genetic hybridization resulting from first the illicit sexual procreation of fallen members of the Caligastia One Hundred (led by Nod) with the evolutionary races, then the inappropriate direct mixing of Adam's and Eve's plasmas with the evolutionary races, with the subsequent intermingling of these two blood lines in the evolving mortals. The resulting genetic incompatibilities and mutations have caused great complexities on Urantia, yet throughout the centuries repersonalized starseed (descendants from Adamson and Ratta) have been used as Reservists in preparation for a great spiritual recovery and unprecedented cosmic family reunion, which is now being witnessed today at the First Planetary Sacred Home in the dawning stages of light and life.
See Paper 240; *The URANTIA Book*, Paper 81; and *The Cosmic Family, Volume I*, Paper 208

nonvirtue sensors Those sensors of personality that allow for diotribe reality such as abilities of control and manipulation.
See Paper 252

nonwill sound Sound that is imperfect, nonabsolute, and inharmonious with the primal absolute Paradise circuit wave.
See Paper 252

Norlatiadek Our local constellation in the universe of Nebadon. Norlatiadek consists of 100 local systems. Edentia is Norlatiadek's headquarters world. The constellation is administered by 12 Vorondadek Sons.
See Papers 233, 236 and *The URANTIA Book*, Paper 15

nucleus Generically speaking, the center of energy that acts like a magnetic pull and command center to all wave and particle reality in its jurisdiction sphere. Biologically speaking, that part of the cell that holds most of the DNA and is in charge of cell division.
See Papers 243–244 and 250

occipital lobe The posterior segment of the brain primarily concerned with the reception and processing of the visual sense and understood to deal with reason.
See Papers 256–257

Onamonalonton A leader of the red race in the distant past who advocated veneration of the Great Spirit and who subsequently became one of the Twenty-four Counselors on Jerusem.
See Paper 259 and *The URANTIA Book*, Papers 45 and 64

one-brained type planets See brain.

ontology Study of the nature and relations of being or kinds of existence.
See Paper 255

orbit Path described by one object in its revolution about another.
See Paper 250

Organ of Corti (spiral organ) Structure in the inner ear that transforms mechanical forces produced from pressure waves ("sound waves") into action potentials that are sensed as sound.
See Papers 252–253 and 255

Orvonon Leader of a great spiritual awakening among the indigo people of ages past, who led them in the worship of the "God of Gods" and who is now a member of the Council of Twenty-four on Jerusem.
See Paper 259 and *The URANTIA Book*, Papers 45 and 64

Orvonton The name of superuniverse #7 out of the seven superuniverses comprising the grand universe, the Milky Way Galaxy being roughly equivalent to its observable nucleus. Orvonton is ruled by three Ancients of Days, and Uversa is its headquarters. Orvonton is destined to reflect the nature and wills of the three Paradise Deities. Because it is more difficult to do this, Orvonton has had more rebellions than any other superuniverse and has been called the "superuniverse of mercy."
See Paper 229; *The URANTIA Book*, Paper 15; and *The Cosmic Family, Volume I*, Foreword II

otology The study of the ear, its physiology, its functions, and disorders.
See Paper 255

otosclerosis A conductive disease of the ear caused by distorted sound frequencies that block the circuitry of the virtue sensors.
See Paper 255

oval window (fenestra ovalis) The flexible membrane that, when moved by the bones of the middle ear, produces pressure waves in the inner ear.
See Paper 252

ovan souls Souls who have survived the initial experience of mortal planetary existence and who have attained the morontia-consciousness equivalent of the first mansion world and the realization of Paradise circuitry in a morontia body.
See Papers 229, 240–241, 255, 258, 260–261 and *The Cosmic Family, Volume I*, Papers D and 219–221

oxidation That aspect of chemical coupling involving the sharing of electrons with substances having a greater affinity for them, such as oxygen. Most oxidation, including biological ones, are associated with the liberation of energy.
See Papers 245–246

pair-unit classification A classification of ascending sons and daughters who are complementary polarities and mating pairs. Each of the children will inherit a particular original personality and form based on the first cosmic parents, which reflect the Paradise Deities at that moment in time in which he/she first became a potential mortal soul. Many ovan souls look alike in

some way and have the same personality traits but may be from different nationalities or races. This is the result of the Deo-atomic inheritance in relationship to their first cosmic-family parents.
See Introduction, Papers 229, 236, 243, 245, and 259

Paladin, Chief of Finaliters Chief of a group of interuniversal ascendant mortal finaliters who are currently functioning as the Revelatory Commission of Continuing Fifth Epochal Revelation and acting as advisors to all levels directly under the Bright and Morning Star of Salvington. While one or more companies of mortal finaliters are in service on Urantia, there are certain mortal finaliters from different universes and superuniverses of origin designated to assemble on Urantia as finaliter fathers to regather their cosmic families for grand-universe supreme purposes. Paladin became Chief of Finaliters on Urantia in January 1992 because of the spiritual ascension of his cosmic son Gabriel of Urantia/TaliasVan of Tora. Paladin is the head of the First Cosmic Family now gathering at the First Planetary Sacred Home where some of those family members are becoming administratively functional to the Divine Administration of the Planetary Prince of Urantia.
See Papers 229, 259; *The URANTIA Book*, Paper 31; and *The Cosmic Family, Volume I*, Paper 226

pancreas A gland near the stomach that secretes digestive enzymes into the small intestine and releases insulin into the blood stream.
See Papers 235 and 248

Paradise The abiding place of the Universal Father, Eternal Son, and Infinite Spirit. This Eternal Isle is the absolute source of the physical universes—past, present, and future. It is the universal headquarters of all personality activities and the source-center of all space-force and energy manifestations. Paradise is the geographic center of infinity and the only stationary thing in the master universe. It is the goal of all ascending sons and daughters to ascend to Paradise.
See Papers 230, 232, 236, 242, 244, 248–253, 255–258, 261 and *The URANTIA Book*, Paper 11

Paradise Trinity An association and union of the three infinite persons on Paradise: The Universal Father, the Eternal Son, and the Infinite Spirit, functioning as a corporate entity in a nonpersonal capacity but not in contravention of personality.

See Papers 233–234, 242, 249–250, 254, 258; *The URANTIA Book*, Paper 10; and *The Cosmic Family, Volume I*, Paper 219

parathyroid glands Four glands on the posterior surface of the thyroid that produce and release parathormone involved in controlling the amount of calcium in the blood.
See Paper 235

parietal lobe The sensory portion of the brain situated posterior to the frontal lobe, anterior to the occipital lobe, and superior to the temporal lobe. In higher brain types, the parietal area should be able to detect the presence of celestial personalities within one mile.
See Papers 256–257

Perfections of Days Order of Supreme Trinity Personalities who are the triune rulers of the major sectors of the grand universe and peculiarly perfect in the mastery of administrative detail. They were trinitized for the special work of assisting the superuniverse directors, and they rule as the immediate and personal vicegerents of the Ancients of Days.
See Paper 233 and *The URANTIA Book*, Paper 18

Perfectors of Wisdom A specialized creation of the Paradise Trinity, designed to personify the wisdom of divinity in the superuniverses. There are exactly seven billion of these beings in existence, and one billion are assigned to each of the seven superuniverses. They do not reflect the wisdom of the Paradise Trinity; they are that wisdom.
See Paper 251 and *The URANTIA Book*, Paper 19

personality The presence of the Universal Father in His personality circuitry that is destined to have an endless love affair with Deity and which, like Deity, is characterized by volition and unity. As unifiers, Deity and personality each act at the level of the total. Deity always seeks manifestation as personality, and it does this on the levels of the prepersonal, personal, and superpersonal, all of which manifest phases of volition. While personality strives to unify the physical, mindal, and spiritual realities within the realm of its influence, Deity endeavors to join the personality of its association with other Deity-associated personalities and with itself.

See Papers 229–232, 234–239, 242, 245, 251–252, 254–255, 257, 259 and *The URANTIA Book*, Papers 55 and 56

photon ("electron photon") Pair-unit quantum of physical light.
See Paper 244

pineal gland A small appendage in the brain that functions as a part of the time-measuring system and appears to process light through the skull as a vestigial third eye and endocrine organ.
See Papers 230 and 235

pituitary gland (hypophysis) A small gland attached to the base of the brain whose hormones control the activities of other glands. Also known as the master gland.
See Papers 235 and 248

planetary headquarters The administrative geographic center where a Planetary Prince administers and advances an evolutionary world. In Nebadon, the Planetary Princes are under the universe administrative jurisdiction of Gabriel of Salvington, while in immediate authority they are subject to the mandates of the System Sovereigns. Also referred to as Planetary Sacred Home.
See Papers 232–233, 255 and *The URANTIA Book*, Paper 50

Planetary Prince The spiritual ruler of an inhabited world in time and space, usually of the order of Lanonandek Son. The first Planetary Prince of Urantia was Caligastia who arrived approximately 500,000 years ago and ruled faithfully until he chose the side of Lucifer during that rebellion of 200,000 years ago. Christ Michael earned the title of Planetary Prince of Urantia after His seventh bestowal 2,000 years ago, having lived the life of the human mortal Jesus of Nazareth. In 1989 A.D., Machiventa Melchizedek became Planetary Prince and has his headquarters in Arizona, USA.
See Introduction, Papers 250, 257, 259–260; *The URANTIA Book*, Paper 66; and *The Cosmic Family, Volume I*, Statement of Purpose

Planetary Sacred Home Planetary center of the celestial divine administration. The First Planetary Headquarters was Dalamatia at the time of Caligastia 500,000 years ago; the second was the Garden of Eden, 38,000 years ago; the third was the schools of Salem at the time of

Machiventa Melchizedek 4,000 years ago; the fourth was wherever Jesus of Nazareth was 2,000 years ago. Today it is located where the Planetary Prince, Machiventa Melchizedek, resides in Arizona, USA. All Destiny Reservists are called to Planetary Sacred Headquarters to receive further training at Global Community Communications Schools under the Mandate of the Bright and Morning Star.
See Papers 232–233, 239; *The URANTIA Book*, Paper 66; and *The Cosmic Family, Volume I*, Statement of Purpose

point of origin reconstruction at the time of fall The reconstruction of the complete memory and Deo-atomic structure of an ovan soul at the level attained before the incorporation of Luciferic thought into the circuitry.
See Papers 258 and 260

polypeptide Some multiple combination of peptides such as a di-, tri-, or tetra-peptide, depending upon the number of amino acids in the molecule. Peptides form the constituent parts of proteins, and it is the simpler polypeptides that are usually involved in the main work of living.
See Paper 242

polypeptide loops Long and complex loops of amino acid chains making up globular proteins. Some of these loops are superfluous and can actually burden life-functions.
See Paper 242

pons (pons Varolii) A neural network and subdivision of the rhombencephalon situated in the anterior portion of the metencephalon that functions to regulate thought and relay impulses between different parts of the brain.
See Paper 256

Porogia Name of a neighboring planetary administrative system to our system of Satania, within the constellation Norlatiadek.
See Paper 249 and *The URANTIA Book*, Paper 41

power direct field A field of morontia magnetic flow that becomes pregnant when higher cosmic-family relatives are geographically within a radius of one another within one acre.
See Paper 239

prefrontal lobe Anterior portion of the frontal lobe of the brain that connects thought content to emotional response; also involved in long-range planning and moral integrity.
See Paper 256

presbycusis The loss of sensitivity to high-frequency sounds due to the varying degree to which people become set in their ways and in their thinking.
See Paper 255

primal absolute hearing assent capacity The capacity of each individual ascending personality at any level to hear the primal absolute Paradise circuit wave from the Thought Adjuster.
See Paper 251

primal absolute Paradise circuit wave The primal circuit wave sung into existence by the Universal Father in the harmonics of the Paradise center. Creator Sons and Universe Mother Spirits hear this first causation pattern and tap into it to create their universes.
See Papers 235, 251–255, and 257–258

primal brain flow circuitry patterns Patterns of circuit flow in the brain that act like fingerprints of each complex personality based upon the personality bestowal of the Universal Father.
See Paper 251

Primary Eventuated Master Force Organizers See Master Force Organizers.

primary midwayers See midwayers.

prosencephalon Forebrain, consisting of the telencephalon and the diencephalon.
See Paper 256

protected areas Geographic locations around the planet, including the First Planetary Sacred Home in Arizona, USA, where gatherings of cosmic-family members align under the proper Eldership. Some protected areas will

become sectors of Divine Administration into the twenty-first century and provide safe areas to live, due to celestial and human cooperation.
See Papers 236, 238–239, 255, 257–258 and *The Cosmic Family, Volume I*, Papers E, 201, 214–215, and 227

protein An organic compound composed of amino acids, providing cellular structure, enzymatic action, and immunity.
See Papers 235 and 242–244

proteinases Enzymes that specialize in hydrolyzing proteins and which are a fusion of the Father and the Son. They are the Mother-oriented energies and molecules that create within the body the flowing, the allowing, and the energizing.
See Paper 244

proton The Father-polarized field of force in the nucleus of the atom whose material complement is the electron.
See Paper 244

proton photon A specialized wave packet of light emitted from a Deo-atomic proton. Creator Sons can use proton photons collectively to produce new life forms.
See Paper 244

proton sequential force energy A proton photon energy-force created by a union of souls, wherein the Divine Administration is functioning corporately through human personalities all in the will of God.
See Paper 244

provitamin A substance such as ergosterol or carotene that can be converted into a vitamin in the body.
See Paper 247

psychic circles The seven levels of personality realization on a material world. Entry on the seventh psychic circle marks the beginning of true human personality function. Completion on the first psychic circle denotes the relative maturity of the mortal being. Destiny reservists at the First Planetary Sacred Home who are stabilized on the third psychic circle receive an angel of enlightenment. Psychic circle attainment and stabilization is an

enormous subject and will be more thoroughly explored in *The Cosmic Family Volumes III* and *IV*.
See Papers 229, 239, 256, 258–260; *The URANTIA Book*, Paper 110; and *The Cosmic Family, Volume I*, Preface

psychobiology The study of how the mind at all levels creates and extends biology or life.
See Paper 256

psychochemical Pertaining to electrical and chemical flows in the brain having to do with mind, emotions, and behavior.
See Paper 258

psychophysics The relationship between mind and sensation in terms of stimulus and response. A stimulus is considered to be any change in external or internal energy that gives rise to excitation of the nervous system sufficient to arouse a response in the person concerned. The psychophysical experience—be it in tone, color, sentience, or any combination thereof—involves many related components, such as physical, chemical, physiological, spiritual, or personal aspects.
See Paper 254

psychoschizophysiology The relationship between the dio- and Deo-neurotransmitters and the central nervous system, and their relationship responsive to the systems of the body, and the physical body itself, to the cellular levels, functioning primarily coordinate to the Conjoint Actor, although qualitatively and quantitatively responsive to the Father-Son circuitry.
See Paper 257

psychospirituality Spiritual psychophysiology attentive to behavioral and physical interactions in the ascension process of alignment of the Threefold Spirit of God, and adjustments to interrelationships between other ascenders and celestial beings in higher authority.
See Paper 256

pure impression A sense impression created when the human ear resonates with the instruction given by a higher source and is understood by the mind of a higher receptive channel.

See Papers 230, 239, and 252–254

quantum physics Subatomic physics of mind and matter which holds that all matter-energy and its motions can be analyzed and altered in terms of fundamental frequencies by adding or subtracting them as finite quanta.
See Paper 251

race commissioners Spirit-fused ascending mortals who have been enrolled in the Nebadon Corps of Perfection and in service on the evolutionary worlds for interpreting the viewpoints and portraying the needs of the various human races. Some time after the final change point on Urantia, they will work in close coordination with interuniversal Material Sons and Daughters and the World Council of Race Genetics.
See Papers 244, 259 and *The URANTIA Book,* Paper 37

Rantulia Name of a neighboring planetary administrative system to our system of Satania, within the constellation Norlatiadek.
See Paper 249 and *The URANTIA Book,* Paper 41

reconstructive coordinators See morontia seraphim coordinators.

reflective cellular magnetic motion polarity A mutual magnetic attraction on the level of subcellular cosmic physics in which Deo cells recreate Deo-atomic reality in personality structure and is the principle of the attraction of celestial beings to one another.
See Paper 250

Reflective Image Aids Children of the 49 Reflective Spirits, each Reflective Spirit creating his own Aid. They are true images and constantly function as the channel of communication between the Reflective Spirits and the superuniverse authorities. The Image Aids are not merely assistants; they are actual representations of their respective Reflective Spirit ancestors.
See Paper 233 and *The URANTIA Book,* Paper 17

Reflective Spirits Children of the Paradise Trinity and Master Spirits who variously reflect the natures and characters of the seven possible combinations of the association of the divinity characteristics of the Universal Father, the Eternal Son, and the Infinite Spirit. One of each type was assigned to service in each of the seven superuniverses. These groups of

seven dissimilar Reflective Spirits maintain headquarters on the capitals of the superuniverses at the reflective focus of each realm.
See Paper 233 and *The URANTIA Book*, Paper 17

reflectivity The phenomenon of the mind levels of the Infinite Spirit, the Supreme Being, and the Master Spirits that is transmissible to all beings concerned in the working of the vast scheme of universal intelligence. One important attribute of reflectivity is the power of a lower universe creature to become reflective of the nature, and to some extent the presence, of a higher, and often times ancestral, being or beings. As an ascending son or daughter on Urantia becomes consistently reflective of his or her celestial counterparts, he or she begins to build the morontia and higher bodies, and such reflectivity gives the ascending son or daughter the Deo-power of that or those celestial beings.
See Paper 260 and *The URANTIA Book*, Paper 17

reflectivity personality pattern Pattern of progressive associative reflectivity of an ascending mortal at some cellular level to higher universe creatures. For example, when Gabriel of Urantia/TaliasVan of Tora reaches a certain audio fusion material complement level, he becomes the fullness of the Bright and Morning Star. Just as Jesus was the incarnated Son of the Universal Father, Gabriel of Salvington has continued to fuse with Gabriel of Urantia/TaliasVan of Tora in repersonalized particle union.
See Paper 260

rematerialization One of several techniques providing a physical body for a personality of another dimension.
See Papers 235, 248, 257; *The URANTIA Book*, Papers 66 and 67; and *The Cosmic Family, Volume I*, Papers 200 and 206

repersonalization A form of reconstruction that a Creator Son can authorize that a certain personality be reconstructed on a world within that same Creator Son's universe for the purposes of His ascension plan. Repersonalizations may also be done on an interuniversal basis when two Creator Sons from two different universes decide that a personality should be reconstructed on a world that is in a universe other than that soul's point of origin.
See Introduction, Papers 236, 247–248, 252, 258, and 260–261

Reserve Corps of Destiny A corps of living men and women who have been admitted to the special service of the superhuman administration mainly to assure against breakdown of evolutionary progress. There are Cosmic Reservists (starseed from other worlds) and Urantian Reservists (natives of this world). Since the coming of the new Planetary Prince, Machiventa Melchizedek, all Destiny Reservists are called to the First Planetary Sacred Home in Arizona, USA, to receive further training in Divine Administration at Global Community Communications Schools.
See Papers 230–231, 257; *The URANTIA Book*, Paper 114; and *The Cosmic Family, Volume I*, Paper E

Resident Governor General See Governor General.

rhinencephalon Region of the brain related to the sense of smell, including the olfactory cortex, the hippocampus, and the amygdala. At a subultimatonic level, a seraphim can transmit certain signals to the memory section in the rhinencephalon, and the resulting spiritual exchange can register as a scent. That is, the making and recovery of memories can be accompanied by a certain aroma.
See Paper 257

rhombencephalon The region of the brain called the hindbrain, including the medulla oblongata (metencephalon), pons, and cerebellum; the experiential clearing house between relative and absolute thinking, and a relay station for the coordination between brain and body. It is an experiential manifestation of the existential relationship between the Infinite Spirit and the Paradise Trinity. Nebadon personalities function with a higher usage of the rhombencephalon.
See Paper 256

RNA (ribonucleic acid) A nucleic acid using ribose. Messenger RNA is a class of RNA that transcribes the genetic information in DNA. Transfer RNA transfers a particular amino acid to a growing polypeptide chain at the site of protein synthesis during translation.
See Paper 250

root circuit The seventh of seven circuits of the third-dimensional body, associated physically with the gonads. It is a creation circuit located near the base of the spine and its four subcircuits are related to the Universal Father, the Eternal Son, the Infinite Spirit, and the Creator Son and Creative Spirit

acting as one. This circuit of birth is also the source-center for Deo-atomic cells in relation to mortals and is connected to the seventh superuniverse in reflectivity to the Father-Son-Spirit.
See Papers 231 and 233–235

Salvington The headquarters sphere of the universe of Nebadon, situated at the exact energy-mass center of the local universe. It is the destiny of ascending sons and daughters to sojourn on Salvington as a part of their training and Paradise ascension. When a soul leaves Salvington, it is a full-fledged spirit.
See Introduction, Papers 232, 241, 247–248, 257, 259, 261; *The URANTIA Book*, Paper 32; and *The Cosmic Family, Volume I*, Introduction

Sandmatia Name of a neighboring planetary administrative system to our system of Satania, within the constellation Norlatiadek.
See Paper 249 and *The URANTIA Book*, Paper 41

Sangik races Six races derived from the Sangik family, belonging to the Badonite tribe 500,000 years ago. Nineteen children of superior intelligence later mated with their tribesmen, and all of their children had the skin color of the Sangik parent, forming the six Sangik colored races on the planet. Today, only portions of the red, yellow, blue, and indigo races have survived. Furthermore, the violet race (derived from the line of Adam and Eve) has been genetically mixed mainly with the blue race to create the present day "white" race.
See Introduction and *The URANTIA Book*, Paper 64

sanobim Complementary polarity to a cherubim. Every fourth cherubim and sanobim are morontial. They are wonderfully intelligent, marvelously efficient, touchingly affectionate, and almost human.
See Paper 233

Satania The twenty-fourth local system in the constellation Norlatiadek, of which our planet Urantia is number 606. This system was named after Satan, Lucifer's assistant, long before they both went into rebellion 200,000 years ago.
See Papers 229, 236, 255, 258–259, 261; *The URANTIA Book*, Paper 45; and *The Cosmic Family, Volume I*, Foreword I

Glossary 529

secondary midwayers See midwayers.

Second Ambassadors See Ambassadors.

Second Assistants See Assistants.

Second Epochal Revelation The second of five planetary revelations to Urantia. Occurred approximately 38,000 years ago with the arrival of Adam and Eve, a Material Son and Daughter, who established Planetary Headquarters in the Garden of Eden (now submerged under the eastern Mediterranean Sea), with intentions of promoting the welfare of the human races through education and the strategy of genetically upstepping the mortal races via the admixture of these races with their own children. Unfortunately, the mission on Urantia ended prematurely with the default of Adam and Eve by their mating directly with the mortals of the realm. Hence, the Second Epochal Revelation lasted only 117 years.
See Papers 254, 261 and *The URANTIA Book*, Paper 92

second messenger system Cellular communication networking between the unseen causal coordinate body transmitting Paradise Trinity command signals via Deo-atomic cells (first messengers) to receptor molecules on the cell surface whereby mindal acquiescence to the will of God releases enzymes (second messengers) within the cell that activate genes encoded for cellular reconstruction.
See Paper 258

Second Source and Center The Eternal Son, the second person of the Paradise Trinity. He is the pattern personality and emanates the spirit-gravity circuit throughout the grand universe.
See *The URANTIA Book*, Papers 6–7

second-time Urantians A unique group of Urantians numbering less than 2,000 who were sleeping survivors, and who, for the first time in the history of Urantia by decree of Christ Michael, have for undisclosed reasons been allowed to repersonalize on Urantia since the beginning of this century. Some of the first-century apostles have repersonalized and are second-time Urantians.

See Papers 229, 241, 244, 246, 253, and *The Cosmic Family, Volume I*, Paper D

sensor units Relay units in various Deo-atomic cellular parts of the anatomy that resonate with the divine blueprint for the higher body. These sensor units are essential to the development of the next body form in that if the body cannot be built according to the divine blueprint, then the body's growth and development are also hindered. There are generic Deo-atomic unit locations within the body that connect causal design to psychospiritual reality based upon the body absolutes of the causal body, which will be discussed in future papers, particularly in *The Cosmic Family, Volume III*.
See Paper 256

separation from the supreme primal The separation that occurs when the causal coordinate body is placed at a distance from the energy line of the crown circuit of an individual due to blockages created by that individual.
See Paper 253

septuplicate planetary invariable septum stratum force The combined invariable septum stratum force functioning and stabilized in the seven safety areas including the First Planetary Sacred Home. Those areas will then have an affinity with six other planets that have already reached the first stages of light and life in Satania.
See Paper 250

sequential force-energy The force-energy created by a union of souls for a common purpose within divine will, different from auhter energy because it is created by various personalities, human and celestial, at various levels of reality engaged in prayer.
See Paper 237

seraphic transport Mode of transport of beings from the lowest morontia to the highest spirit forms by ministering spirits specialized for that task.
See Papers 232, 253, 260 and *The URANTIA Book*, Paper 39

seraphim Local universe angels who are of origin in the Universe Mother Spirit and are designated Ministering Spirits of the local universe. Seraphim are created slightly above the mortal level. Those assigned to the watch care

of ascending mortals are called Seraphic Guardians of Destiny. An angel of enlightenment can also serve as a destiny guardian.
See Introduction, Papers 252, 257–258, 261; *The URANTIA Book*, Paper 38; and *The Cosmic Family, Volume I*, Paper 212

Seraphim of the Races The group of Master Seraphim of Planetary Supervision specifically designated to Cosmic and Urantian Reservists for the purpose of their coming together within their original cosmic family linkage. These seraphim are closely associated with the ministry of the Race Commissioners.
See Paper 243; *The URANTIA Book*, Paper 114; and *The Cosmic Family, Volume I*, Paper 212

similectic genetic alignment transference An ordered and patterned transference of interuniversal genetic reality having to do with Paradise circuitry that functions in all of the seven superuniverses that gives life to all mortals and evolutionary races of the planets. This astrological transference depends upon the higher consciousness or auhter energy created by the souls on those planets who are of intrauniversal and interuniversal genetic relationships.
See Paper 261

sine wave Wave form described by the trigonometric sine function that is the fundamental quantum of harmonic motion and the basis for the physics of wave mechanics and wave motion as applied accurately and practically to sound and music as well as to the basic infrastructure and electrokinetics of matter.
See Paper 251

Singlangton One of the yellow men who, approximately 100,000 years ago, assumed leadership of the yellow tribes and led his people in the worship of the "One Truth" instead of many. He is a member of the Council of Twenty-four.
See Paper 259 and *The URANTIA Book*, Papers 45 and 64

solar plexus circuit The fifth of the seven circuits of the third-dimensional body, associated physically with the functions of the pancreas. It is a vast network of the Universe Mother Spirit and the Infinite Spirit and is a circuit of emotions, empathic abilities, nurturing, and healing. It is associated with the

fifth superuniverse and reflects the Father-Spirit aspect of the Trinity. It has 10 subcircuits that are connected to the major sectors of Orvonton, beginning for us with subcircuit #5, connected to Splandon and its headquarters world, Umajor the fifth.
See Papers 233–235

Solitary Messengers The first children of the Infinite Spirit. Spirit personality messengers who travel alone through time and space at incredible speeds, thereby being great timesavers for those beings involved with universe administration.
See Papers 229, 259 and *The URANTIA Book*, Paper 23

somatotropic hormone (STH) A hormone secreted by the pituitary gland that stimulates protein synthesis and growth and repair within the body. Also called Growth Hormone (GH), it is related, but not identical, to Growth Stimulating Hormone (GSH), which is produced by certain glial cells in the brain to increase neural networking and activities.
See Paper 248

Son-circuited Representing the qualities of the balance between the Universe Father and Mother with strong human father traits and gentle human mother qualities in responses.
See Paper 249

Sortoria Name of a neighboring planetary administrative system to our system of Satania, within the constellation Norlatiadek.
See Paper 249 and *The URANTIA Book,* Paper 41

soul A growing formulation of identity between the physical and the spiritual, also known as character, which is contactable by other souls but cannot be discovered by exclusive physical or spiritual testing. Growth of the soul (development of spiritual character) comes from the conscious attempt to follow the leading of the Thought Adjuster. Survival comes as personality relocates its seat of identity from the physical mind to the soul.
See Papers 231, 234, 247, 260 and *The URANTIA Book*, Paper 111

sound waves Longitudinal waves propagating through and vibrating particles such that audio sensations are produced in the cochlea of the ear and then transmitted as electrical signals to the brain.

See Papers 251–252 and 255

source cells The higher subatomic particle reality of the higher body before the fall into rebellion of the fallen starseed in relation to the ascension of the soul.
See Paper 252

source center For evolutionary mortals, the circuits or subcircuits in which beginning Deo subatomic-to-cellular reality is stored from various other circuits within the body (including the meridian circuits) according to the ascension level of the soul. All mortals begin with the root center as the source-center. At some point, the throat circuit becomes the source-center for the ascending son. With the ascending daughter, there can be fluctuations between the root and throat, but the root is always the main source-circuit in the ascending daughter in evolutionary bodies. The throat circuit becomes the main source-circuit in ascending sons as they become stabilized on the third circle and move in attunement with the Father above.
See Paper 233

spirit Supernatural extension of God's presence such as the indwelling Father Fragment that adjusts the human mind to progressively divine attitudes, along with the everywhere active presence of the divine spirit of the Eternal Son. All pure unfragmented spirit and all spiritual beings and values are responsive to the infinite drawing power of the Eternal Son. Although all divine beings can be referred to as spirits, in the Infinite Spirit's functional family, the term 'spirit' is confined to the seven Supreme Spirit groups and the Ministering Spirits of Time. In general, spiritual beings occupy spirit space charged by spirit potency and inhabit spirit form made of spirit substance, carrying out numerous spirit activities, but they also inhabit material spheres and exist in relationship to physical space.
See Papers 229–230, 235, 238, 250–251, 253–255, 260 and *The URANTIA Book*, Papers 5–6 and 8

Spirit of Truth The spirit left by Christ Michael after His bestowal on Urantia at Pentecost. It is experienced in human consciousness as the conviction of truth and needs to be continually activated by soul growth through a relationship with God and His will as opposed to religious doctrine. The Universe Mother Spirit acts as the universe focus and center of truth as well as Her own personal influence, the Holy Spirit.

See Introduction, Papers 232, 237, 249, 251, 257, 259, 261; *The URANTIA Book*, Papers 180–181; and *The Cosmic Family, Volume I*, Paper 210

spiritual inbreeding A process that takes place when mortal personality fuses with threefold divine personality at any level. Spiritual inbreeding takes place long before Thought Adjuster fusion. Spirit of Truth reception is the beginning of inbreeding on normal worlds, but in Orvonton inbreeding is not complete until the reception of the Spirit of Truth and actualization of the activation of the Holy Spirit.
See Paper 234

spiritualized mind The totality of experience in absolute truths pertinent to the decision-making process and relating to circumstantial reality at any point or sojourn in time and space. It takes into account all lives lived, genetic inheritance, and interuniversal genetics.
See Papers 233 and 254

stapes (stirrup) The innermost of three bones responsible for passing sound vibrations on to the oval window, the opening to the cochlea within the ear.
See Paper 252

starseed A term generally used on Urantia to designate mortals originally from another universe born of human parents through the repersonalization technique. There are 7 orders of starseed. Much of the understanding of starseed in New-Age circles in relation to "walk-ins," soul transference, space visitors, etc. who are presently on Urantia referred to as starseed is Caligastia's confusion.
See Papers 229, 232, 234–235, 238, 240–241, 243–245, 249, 251–253, 256, 259, and 260

Starseed and Urantian Schools of Melchizedek See Global Community Communications Schools.

steroid Any of a group of lipids containing the carbon ring cycle of cholesterol and including the sterols and various hormones and glycosides.
See Paper 235

Glossary 535

subcells Cells within cells, subultimatonic groupings of various levels of particle reality. Subcells are always Deo cells.
See Papers 249 and 256

sulci Shallow furrows on the surface of the brain separating convolutions.
See Paper 257

sulfanilamide The first of the sulfonamides, which has antibiotic properties by merit of the fact that it neutralizes folic acid uptake in certain bacteria.
See Paper 246

supernaphim The ministering spirits of Paradise and the central universe who are the highest of the lowest group of the children of the Infinite Spirit— the angelic hosts. Such ministering spirits are to be encountered from the Isle of Paradise to the worlds of time and space.
See Paper 253 and *The URANTIA Book*, Paper 26

superuniverse One of seven inhabited galaxies in the grand universe, each superuniverse being composed of 100,000 local universes that are created by the Creator Sons of God and the Universe Mother Spirits. Each superuniverse is ruled by three Ancients of Days.
See Papers 233, 235, 242, 248, 250, 256–257, 259, 261 and *The URANTIA Book*, Paper 15

sympathetic vibration A vibration produced in one object by a vibration of the same frequency in another object.
See Paper 255

synapse The narrow gap between the terminal bouton of one neuron and the dendrite or cell body of another.
See Paper 258

syntonic impressions Ordered and godly impressions responding to oscillations adjusted or tuned to a particular frequency. The people of Urantia, ovan souls or otherwise, need to syntonize themselves to the frequencies of the Universal Father, the Eternal Son, and the Infinite Spirit.
See Paper 254

system (generic grouping) A consistent and complex whole made up of correlated and interdependent parts. For example, a biological system can be the entire organism, a complex of structures anatomically and physiologically related, or a member or group within a species.
See Papers 232 and 256

system (planetary grouping) An administrative grouping of evolutionary planets within time and space. A system ultimately will have one thousand inhabited worlds settled in light and life. Each system is ruled by a System Sovereign, usually of the order of Lanonandek Sons. There are 100 local systems in a constellation. Jerusem is the headquarters world of our system, Satania, which is system number 24 in the constellation Norlatiadek. Sandmatia, Assuntia, Porogia, Sortoria, Rantulia, and Glantonia are six planetary systems in the neighborhood of Satania whose System Sovereigns are working closely with Lanaforge, System Sovereign of Satania, for the implementation of the first stages of light and life for our planet Urantia.
See Papers 231–232, 249–250, 261 and *The URANTIA Book*, Paper 15

System Sovereign The administrative head (usually a primary Lanonandek Son) of a local system of approximately 1,000 inhabited planets. Our system Sovereign in Satania is Lanaforge, who replaced Lucifer after his fall 200,000 years ago.
See Papers 231, 250 and *The URANTIA Book*, Paper 45

TaliasVan of Tora See Gabriel of Urantia/TaliasVan of Tora.

telencephalon The anterior portion of the prosencephalon of the brain whose functions are: the highest level of all sensory integration and perception; memory association with personality; the highest level of somatic motor control; and receiving nerve impulses from, and sending through nerve fibers to, all lower areas. Personalities from the universe of Avalon function with a higher usage of this part of the brain.
See Paper 256

temporal lobe A large lobe of each cerebral hemisphere that is situated in front of and underneath the parietal lobe, which contains a sensory area associated with the organ of hearing, understanding of speech, and reading ability.
See Papers 256–257

testosterone A male hormone (complementary polarity to the female hormone estrone) that is responsible for inducing and maintaining male secondary sex characteristics.
See Paper 249

third dimension, fourth dimension, and fifth dimension Three currently available and contemporary levels of individual and mass consciousness in the fusion between mind and spirit, which can be clearly differentiated today as Urantia moves from the pre-stages of light and life into higher planetary dispensations.
— The third dimension is the time-present level of self-consciousness in growing comprehension of breadth, height, and depth of mathematical and logical coordination; the pre-mind dominated time-and-space orientation.
— The fourth dimension is the time-coordinate level of group-consciousness that merges mathematics and logic with morality and brotherhood; mind-spirit directed space-time orientation.
— The fifth dimension is the time-transcending level of spirit awareness that integrates the spirit and non-spirit mind into organic and inorganic coordinate purpose; spirit-mind and body fusion within causal design. Even though Continuing Fifth Epochal Revelation can bring fourth-, fifth-, sixth-, and higher dimensional reality to ascenders on Urantia, one cannot formulate a higher body on any level until one begins to spiritualize in some form of three-dimensional thought.
See Papers 230 and 254

third ear See morontia ear.

Third Epochal Revelation The third of five planetary revelations to Urantia, arriving at the time of Abraham (approximately 4,000 years ago) with the rematerialization of Machiventa Melchizedek (called the Sage of Salem). Machiventa Melchizedek rematerialized on Urantia as a temporary man of the realm, bestowing himself as an Emergency Son of world ministry. He carried forth his mission of the revelation of truth and the reality of God for 94 years near the city of Salem, in Palestine, later to be called Jerusalem, at a time when the world's religions and peoples had nearly lost sight of the one-God concept altogether.
See Paper 261 and *The URANTIA Book*, Paper 92

third-eye circuit The second of the seven circuits of the third-dimensional body, associated physically with the functions of the pineal gland. Located behind the forehead, this circuit has 100 subcircuits corresponding to the 100 systems in the constellation Norlatiadek and to the System Sovereigns. Subcircuit #24 is the link to Lanaforge, the System Sovereign of Satania. This circuit is also used for clairvoyant prophetic purposes in relation to events, interdimensional communication, and celestial personality observance. It is connected to the second superuniverse and the reflectivity of the Eternal Son.
See Papers 233–235 and 255

Third Garden of Eden Geographic location of the present First Planetary Sacred Home, wherein complementary polarities of higher ascension status function near one another on a daily basis tapping into Paradise circuitry coming out from Paradise to create a new reality in which ascending mortals on Urantia can achieve kinetic fusion with higher dimensional reality and higher celestial beings and settle into the first stages of light and life.

The First Garden of Eden was prepared by Van (TaliasVan of Tora) and his associates as the place of abode for the arriving Material Son and Daughter (Adam and Eve), biological uplifters, to begin their sojourn and work on evolutionary Urantia. The Second Eden was the cradle of civilization for almost 30,000 years. The Third Eden, founded by Gabriel of Urantia/TaliasVan of Tora and Niánn Emerson Chase, is the regathering site for all seven cosmic families of Urantia wherein personalities within the higher circles of attainment can come to understand each other at a fourth-dimensional and higher level, thereby stabilizing their personalities within the mind circuit for the opening of memory circuits, the activation of certain abilities, and the recovering of certain talents for the good of all in the system of Satania.
See Paper 246 and *The URANTIA Book*, Papers 73 and 78

Third Source and Center The Infinite Spirit, the third person of the Paradise Trinity, from whom emanates the mind-gravity circuit throughout the grand universe.
See Paper 232 and *The URANTIA Book*, Papers 8–9

Thought Adjusters Prepersonal fragments of the Universal Father that indwell normal minds of human mortals. It is through the Thought Adjusters that the Universal Father has personal communion with mortal beings.

Fusion with the Thought Adjuster guarantees eternal survival. Also called Mystery Monitors.
See Introduction, Papers 229, 246, 249, 251–252, 255–258, 260–261; *The URANTIA Book*, Papers 1 and 5, and *The Cosmic Family, Volume I*, Foreword I

three-brained type planets See brain.

Threefold Spirit Three separate manifestations of the Paradise Trinity functioning within a mortal: the Thought Adjuster (Universal Father), Spirit of Truth (Eternal Son / Creator Son), and Holy Spirit (Infinite Spirit / Universe Mother Spirit).
See Papers 233, 244, 255, 257, 259 and *The Cosmic Family, Volume I*, Paper D

throat circuit The third of the seven circuits of the third-dimensional body, associated with the thyroid and parathyroid glands. This circuit is connected to the third superuniverse and the Infinite Spirit. It has 210 subcircuits that coordinate with the 210 Perfections of Days on the major sector headquarters of the seven superuniverses. It is the circuit of coordination of the will of humans with the will of God and the hearing of that will as reflected through personalities reflective of the First Source and Center. These subcircuits are related to the Salvington Circuit.
See Papers 233–235 and 248

thymus gland A glandular portion of the lymphoid system (connected to the heart circuit), involved in development and maintenance of the immune system.
See Paper 235

thyroglobulin A protein that binds with the thyroid hormones, exerting a buffering or moderating effect that permits a gradual response to the metabolic requirement of the body.
See Paper 248

thyroid gland A two-lobed gland that produces the thyroid hormones that control the rate of all metabolic processes in the body and influence physical development.
See Paper 235

thyroxine The principal hormone of the thyroid gland. Just as the Infinite Spirit is the God of motion (promoting all the activities of the Universal Father and the Eternal Son), so is thyroxine the molecule that mediates both growth and metabolism throughout the human body.
See Paper 235

time-coordinate consciousness A level of consciousness in which all things relative to the coordinate exist simultaneously.
See Paper 254

Tora The third planet from Alcyone in the Pleiades and the point of origin, at least in the superuniverse of Orvonton, of the finaliter Paladin and certain members of the First Cosmic Family on Urantia.
See Paper 259 and *The Cosmic Family, Volume I*, Paper D

transfer RNA See RNA.

transpositional visualization sequence A creative force and power in relationship to human and celestial personalities who align themselves with a common purpose within divine will.
See Paper 237

triad-unit I A complementary relationship between an ascending son and two ascending daughters in which the ascending son has children with both.
See Paper 234

triad-unit II The same thing as triad-unit I, without children with one or both.
See Paper 234

trimonad unit A complementary relationship between an ascending son and two ascending daughters in which the ascending son is not sexually involved with one of the ascending daughters.
See Paper 234

Trinity Teacher Sons Paradise Sons of Trinity origin who appear on an evolutionary world when the time is ripe to initiate a spiritual age. They are the exalted teachers of all spirit personalities.

See Introduction, Papers 244, 249, 261; *The URANTIA Book*, Paper 20; and *The Cosmic Family, Volume I*, Paper 218

tron therapy A psychospiritual therapy that restores broken circuitry within the body, removes diotribes, and is a touch therapy that is destined to replace surgery. It is done only in conjunction with psychospiritual counseling and involves the permanent healing of all bodies (the astral, etheric, and physical) for those who are in alignment with their God. Tron therapy is available only at the First Planetary Sacred Home through mandated tron therapists.
See Papers 235, 251, and 258

twelve seraphic orders of Urantia See twelve Seraphim of Planetary Supervision.

twelve Seraphim of Planetary Supervision Twelve Master Seraphim who are the heads of the twelve seraphic corps of planetary supervision on Urantia. Master Seraphim have graduated on Seraphington, a Paradise satellite world for angels, and been assigned to certain planetary services under the immediate direction of the Chief of Seraphim and the Planetary Prince. The Master Seraphim insure planetary progress against vital jeopardy through the mobilization, training, and maintenance of the Reserve Corps of Destiny.
See Paper 259; *The URANTIA Book*, Paper 114; and *The Cosmic Family, Volume I*, Paper 212

two-brained type planets See brain.

ultimatonic membrane cells Hair and skin cells that corporately form the tissues of the interuniversal corporate membrane gland, which coordinate in relationship to the heart center and pituitary gland to form a new duct upwards to the eighth and ninth glands being incorporated into the morontia body and placed in the area above the heart center.
See Paper 248

ultimatons The basic units or first measurable form of emergent energy, the ultimate 'quanta' of quantum physics, which have Paradise as their nucleus and respond only to circulatory Paradise gravity pull, one hundred ultimatons being mutually associated in a typical electron.

See Papers 232, 242–243, 246, 256 and 258

union of souls A group consciousness reflecting the ideals and status of ethical relationships and functioning in the realm of harmonious teamwork. Also the name of a group of ministering spirits of the order of secondary seconaphim.
See Introduction, Papers 237, 242, 255, 258, 261; *The URANTIA Book*, Paper 28; and *The Cosmic Family, Volume I*, Foreword I

unit factors Factors that measure the degree to which freewill humans are able to function in relation to the spiritualizing efforts of their assigned celestial personalities in coming into reflectivity of them.
See Paper 252

Universal Censors Beings created by the Paradise Trinity who are the judgment of Deity.
See Paper 229 and *The URANTIA Book*, Paper 19

Universal Father The first person of the Paradise Trinity, who is the Creator, Controller, and Upholder of all creation. The Universal Father desires to have communion with mortals through the prepersonal fragments of Himself, the Thought Adjusters, who indwell the normal human mind. He also has reserved the prerogative to bestow personality and maintains personal contact with His creatures through the personality circuit.
See Introduction, Papers 244, 246–247, 249, 253–254, 261; *The URANTIA Book*, Papers 1–5; and *The Cosmic Family, Volume I*, Paper C

universal ontology and otology Study of the patterns and personalities of grand-universe and master design in relation to the primal absolute hearing assent capacity of ascending and descending beings.
See Paper 255

universe An astronomical and administrative unit of creation, made by a Creator Son and Creative Daughter, there being 700,000 such units in the grand universe. Each universe is subdivided into 100 constellations; each constellation is divided into 100 local systems; and each system is destined to have 1,000 inhabited evolutionary planets. Our local universe of Nebadon is relatively young and is far from finished. Urantia has seven cosmic

Glossary 543

families from four different universes: Avalon, Fanoving, Wolvering, and Nebadon.
See Introduction, Papers 247, 251, 257–259, 261; *The URANTIA Book*, Part II; and *The Cosmic Family, Volume I*, Introduction

Universe Father A Creator Son of a local universe. Christ Michael of Nebadon is our Universe Father and was created by the Universal Father and the Eternal Son on Paradise.
See Papers 236, 258; *The URANTIA Book*, Paper 21; and *The Cosmic Family, Volume I*, Preface

Universe Mother Spirit A Creative Daughter, created by the Infinite Spirit; co-creator of a local universe and complementary polarity to a Creator Son.
See Papers 231, 244–245, 247, 252, 261; *The URANTIA Book*, Paper 34, and *The Cosmic Family, Volume I*, Introduction

unstabilized incongruent personality pattern A peculiar or characteristic pattern developed from the incorporation of all of the noises of relative thinking, blocking harmonic reception, and causing incoherent, unsynchronized, and cosmically aberrant behavior.
See Paper 251

Urantia The cosmic name of our planet Earth. Urantia is planet #606 in the system of Satania, which is system #24 in the constellation of Norlatiadek, which is constellation #70 in the universe of Nebadon. Urantia is also the planet that Michael of Nebadon chose among all the planets in Nebadon for His seventh and final bestowal.
See Introduction, Papers 245, 247, 253, 255–256, 258–261; *The URANTIA Book*, Part III; and *The Cosmic Family, Volume I*, Statement of Purpose

Urantians Ascending sons and daughters whose planet of origin is Urantia. Most people in this category are experiencing their very first life on this planet, but there is also a group of Urantians who are here for the second time. At times, the term "Urantians" refers more generally to the current population of Urantia (which includes both native Urantians and starseed, whose souls are of origin on another planet or in another universe).
See Introduction, Papers 229, 231, 254–255, 257, 259, 261 and *The Cosmic Family, Volume I*, Paper D

Urantia Reserve Corps of Destiny See Reserve Corps of Destiny.

vector Directional energy or motion mathematically best represented by an ordered tetrad (or quaternion) always ultimately referenced to Paradise as the absolute point and system of origin. On Urantia today, the idea of a vector should always be in terms of coordinating the will of God with the will of humans.
See Paper 254

vector field A field of pre-emergence for accommodating directional motion.
See Paper 254

vector space The ability of the consciousness to create a field of flow coordinate with a field of reality; the spiritual with a present mind.
See Paper 254

vector thought A thought that correlates a present moment with an assent to a spiritual concept. In so doing, it draws Deo-atomic cells to a particular area within the physical, etheric, and morontia body according to the depth, height, and width of the God-presence in the third dimension relative to the Universal Father, Eternal Son, and Infinite Spirit circuits.
See Paper 254

ventricles (of the central nervous system) The four linked fluid-filled cavities of the brain.
See Paper 256

vestibulocochlear nerve The eighth pair of cranial nerves, also known as the acoustic or auditory nerve. The vestibular branch conveys impulses having to do with equilibrium, and the cochlear branch conveys impulses having to do with hearing.
See Paper 253

virtue sensors Sensors placed at various appropriate parts of the body that discriminate will sounds from nonwill sounds and are protective sensors of the glands and of all the seven circuits. Virtue sensors allow higher messages of God to pass through to bring healing to the body.
See Papers 252–255

Glossary 545

virus A vector of virulence or pathology with the apparent force of disturbed motion or chaos. Generically speaking, viruses are diotribes, the microscopic agents of mutiny and murder, a result of the Lucifer Rebellion.
See Paper 242

vitamins Organic substances that are essential in minute quantities to nutrition, which act in the regulation of metabolic processes but do not provide energy or serve as building units.
See Paper 247

Vorondadek Sons Local universe Sons, created by the Universe Father and Mother, who often serve at the constellation level as the head of each constellation government. Also known as Constellation Fathers or the Most Highs.
See Paper 233 and *The URANTIA Book*, Paper 35

white matter The white nervous tissue appearance of the network of myelinated neurons in the brain manifesting the quality of associative unified communication in God. At the tissue level, the contrasting gray-matter appearance may relate to regions of unmyelinated neurons, but at the deeper levels it appears as a landscape of mental and emotional blockages in spreading residues or other such viruses. All gray matter must be removed from the brain before the morontia body can be received.
See Paper 256

will freeze A process within the adjudication procedure that can be implemented upon the will of Christ Michael in relation to iniquitous personalities whose wills can thereby be suspended.
See Paper 246

will sound The perfect harmonics of the primal absolute Paradise circuit wave. Reception begins in the Organ of Corti whose receptor cells are grouped into various sensing networks. Each sensing separator directs will sound and nonwill sound to a particular part of the brain. There are various receiver stations between the ear and brain that alert the ascending son or daughter to perfect absolute sounds.
See Paper 252

will-sound personalities Personalities when they speak truth aligned with the perfect harmonics of the primal absolute Paradise circuit wave.
See Paper 252

Wolvering Name of a neighboring universe located in the general direction of Ursa Major, from which some starseed of the cosmic families on Urantia have originated.
See Papers 241, 259; *The URANTIA Book*, Paper 32; and *The Cosmic Family, Volume I*, Paper 228

World Councils The twelve human administrative units functioning on the staff of Machiventa Melchizedek in planetary administration under the overcontrol of celestial personalities. Cosmic and Urantian Reservists who are assigned to these councils must reflect the Spirit of Trust and the Spirit of Brotherhood, and they will become human chiefs and directors in counseling on family and cultural life.
See Paper 259

ABOUT THE
AUDIO FUSION MATERIAL COMPLEMENT
GABRIEL OF URANTIA /
TALIASVAN OF TORA

Gabriel of Urantia/TaliasVan of Tora has been an ardent student of metaphysical/spiritual truth for more than thirty years. Born in Pittsburgh, Pennsylvania, he studied theology at Duquesne University and became one of the first students involved in the charismatic renewal of the Catholic Church, exploring priesthood in Benedictine and Franciscan monasteries in three states.

He has worked as an ordained minister and counselor at various spiritual communities across the United States, including the Nicky Cruz/Teen Challenge organization and Youth with a Mission in Hollywood, California. On the campus of the University of Arizona, he founded a student spiritual organization and became chaplain of the Pima County Sheriff's Department in southern Arizona. For eleven years he worked with the homeless and destitute by providing shelter and counseling. He has explored the writings of all major religions, denominations, and metaphysical sects. After becoming a Reiki Master, he progressed on to *The URANTIA Book* and became the vessel to bring through the Continuing Fifth Epochal Revelation (*The Cosmic Family* volumes).

Gabriel of Urantia/TaliasVan of Tora was a human Planetary Prince of several worlds in other universes, with the title Melfax. His story on this world goes back 500,000 years to the staff of the fallen former Planetary Prince, Caligastia, at which time the soul of Gabriel of Urantia/TaliasVan of Tora was the soul of Van—the loyal supermortal who stood firmly against the Rebellion (see *The URANTIA Book*, page 759). Throughout history his soul has returned to Urantia with the soul of his complement, Niánn Emerson Chase, to start many spiritual renaissances, which include those of Ikhnaton (Akhenaten), Pharaoh of Egypt; Peter, the apostle; Francis of Assisi; and Martin Luther, to name but a few.

Presently, Gabriel of Urantia/TaliasVan of Tora is a level-eight audio fusion material complement for the Chief Executive of our local universe, the Bright and Morning Star of Salvington/Gabriel of Salvington. As Gabriel of Salvington's material complement, Gabriel of Urantia/TaliasVan of Tora holds the Mandate of the Bright and Morning Star, which is a multidimensional, superuniverse, broadcast-circuit link that various celestial personalities are permitted to use and speak through. A human audio fusion material complement is the highest form of interplanetary and interdimensional communication. Some would call these special fusion appearances a "walk in."

Gabriel of Urantia/TaliasVan of Tora is the head human administrator of the Divine Administration as well as being considered one of the most ascended spiritual teachers and leaders on our planet. As a serious, disciplined student of scientific fact and theory, he has become a theoretical physicist. Gabriel of Urantia/TaliasVan of Tora is in contact with and is currently being used by celestial personalities to bring through the Continuing Fifth Epochal Revelation that is a continuation of the 196 Papers of *The URANTIA Book*. These continuing papers, collectively known as *The Cosmic Family* volumes, are fundamental as a basis for understanding the current state of our planet and our relationship to the physics of rebellion, ascension science, and the cosmic community.

Gabriel of Urantia/TaliasVan of Tora and his highest spiritual complement, Niánn Emerson Chase, founded Divine Administration in 1989 and are Global Community Communications Alliance's spiritual leaders. He is the author of *The Divine New Order* (his autobiography) and the audio fusion material complement of *The Cosmic Family* volumes.

He is also an accomplished songwriter/singer/performer. He pioneered the first New Age "Vocal" album, *Unicorn Love*, in 1985. Now he has introduced another unique style of music, CosmoPop®, to the world, performing major outdoor concerts nationwide. As of the publishing of this book, Gabriel of Urantia/TaliasVan of Tora has produced five CDs and on-going is in the recording studio working on future albums and projects. He has an award-winning concert DVD (which won an Aurora Award Gold Award for "Musical Live Concert") featuring his accomplished eleven-piece band, The Bright & Morning Star Band.

Gabriel of Urantia/TaliasVan of Tora lives with his present wife of 12 years, Tiyiendea, and his family at the Divine Administration community. Tiyiendea is also a spiritual complement and past-life wife of many lives, and she is from the universe of Fanoving. His family includes his four children SanSkritA, DeleVan, Amadon (with Niánn Emerson Chase), and Ellanora (with Tiyiendea).

CONCERNING VAN

"Van" is also pronounced as "Son/Sen" on the planet Tora of Avalon, the local universe of which the Pleiades is part. Van of the Caligastia One Hundred in Dalamatia was actually TaliasVan, meaning of the universe of Avalon and of the Creator Son of Avalon, TaliasSon. On Urantia the name later became Taliesen and Taliesin in the Arthurian legends of ancient Glastonbury (also rightfully known as Avalon). It seems that the suffix "sin" was adopted to explain the fall from the universe of Avalon of the fourth-order starseed and TaliasVan's role in the adjudication of the Rebellion on Urantia. King Arthur of Camelot, "The Once and Future King," was also known as TaliasVan, also pronounced Taliesen—a name Arthur correctly thought was of his ancestry, but he had no idea it was his cosmic name.

The prefix "Dele" in front of a name on Tora of Avalon means "of the ancestry line of." DeleVin would mean "of the daughters of Van." DeleVan would mean "of the sons of Van." On higher worlds where more efficient genetic ancestral records are kept, an ascending son could have the higher genetic link to the first trisector family of the first cosmic mother. Therefore his name would be DeleVin/Van and not DeleVan. On Urantia the word Van is often used in the last name of many ancestral links without the full knowledge that this is an ancestral link to the descendants of Van himself. In Van's present life his maternal grandmother's ancestry was English and the genetic line actually goes back to ancient Glastonbury (Avalon). From his paternal grandfather comes the line of the Amadonites of Urantia. Thus Van's son in this life is Amadon Dell Erba in Italian, which means "of the grass or earth." *The URANTIA Book* says: "What of Amadon of Urantia [Earth], does he still stand unmoved?" (*The URANTIA Book*, p. 762)

TaliasVan's name was shortened to Van when the first one-tenth of the Fifth Epochal Revelation came through, known as *The*

URANTIA Book, which primarily discusses the ascension plan of Nebadon and the first-light souls of native Urantians. He would discover his identity and his point of origin when he was chosen to become an audio fusion material complement for Continuing Fifth Epochal Revelation as TaliasVan of Tora/Avalon with the mandate in Nebadon from the Creator Son Christ Michael. The Continuing Fifth Epochal Revelation is for the fourth-order starseed to begin to reawaken their memory circuitry.

The Mandate of the Bright and Morning Star also has to deal with the adjudication of all those who fell in the Rebellion. Who should rightfully have this mandate other than the loyal Van of the Caligastia One Hundred? A new name was given to him, the same as the firstborn son and first administrator of Nebadon, Gabriel of Salvington. Therefore, TaliasVan of Tora became Gabriel in 1985 and Gabriel of Sedona in 1990. He is presently known as Gabriel of Urantia. Sedona, Arizona, USA was the archangels' headquarters of Urantia and has been since before 1989. It was in 1989 that this energy reflective circuit area became the fifth-dimensional and above headquarters of the administration of the present Planetary Prince, Machiventa Melchizedek, upon the arrival of the Mandate of the Bright and Morning Star to Sedona. When the Mandate of the Bright and Morning Star moved to Tubac/Tumacácori, Arizona, it became the new headquarters of the archangels, Machiventa Melchizedek the present Planetary Prince, the Mandate of the Bright and Morning Star, and Divine Administration.

Global Community Communications Alliance and Divine Administration

Global Community Communications Alliance is a church supporting: a religious order and EcoVillage of 100+ international members living in community (with thousands of local and international supporters); Avalon Organic Gardens, Farm, and Ranch; Personality Integration Rehabilitation Program for Teens and Adults; Global Family Legal Services. In addition Global Community Communications Alliance's affiliates and supporting nonprofit organizations—Soulistic Medical Institute and Soulistic Hospice, and Global Change Multi-Media—also support ministry programs.

Founded in 1989 by Gabriel of Urantia (www.GabrielOfUrantia.info, www.GabrielOfUrantia.net, www.GabrielOfUrantia.com) and Niánn Emerson Chase, Global Community Communications Alliance is located in southern Arizona in the charming, historic southwest towns of Tubac and Tumacácori—a sacred area known as "the Palm of God's Hand."

Find out more about our many local and global related humanitarian efforts, services, and church programs listed:

World-Wide Sunday Services[SM]
Open to the public and webcast via Internet.
(520) 603-9932

Avalon Organic Gardens, Farm, & Ranch[SM]
165-acre farm and ranch in southern Arizona, using spiritually-based principles and permaculture practices.
Also a Community Supported Agriculture (CSA) provider.
www.AvalonGardens.org • (520) 603-9932

Soulistic Medical Institute & Soulistic Hospice
Offers healthcare by professionals whose expertise involves
various healing modalities that encompass
the soul, mind, and body.
www.SoulisticMedicalInstitute.org • (520) 398-3970
www.SoulisticHospice.org • (520) 398-2333

Personality Integration Rehabilitation Program^{SM}
for Teens and Adults
Assisting socially-disappointed souls
in their psychospiritual healing process.
www.pirp.info • (520) 603-9932

Friendly Hands Vocational Training
Spiritual Training Apprenticeship Programs in
a wide range of career fields.
(520) 603-9932

Global Family Legal Services
Legal aid in various fields focusing on immigration for
low-income individuals and families in need.
www.GlobalFamilyLegalServices.org
(520) 730-0984 or (928) 282-2590

Global Community Communications Publishing^{TM}
Publishing continuing epochal revelation and related
materials as well as Global Change Teachings
and other spiritually-oriented texts.
www.GlobalCommunityCommunicationsPublishing.org
(520) 603-9932

Alternative Voice^{TM}
Quarterly periodical that addresses the many crises of our
world, fusing spirituality with activism.
www.AlternativeVoice.org • (520) 603-9932

Spirit Steps Tours^{SM}
Offering enlightening tours for the seeking
sojourner and eco-tourist.
www.SpiritSteps.org • (520) 398-2655

Global Community Communications Schools^{SM}
Incorporating the highest truths from many world religions
as well as continuing epochal revelation.
www.GlobalCommunityCommunicationsSchools.org
(520) 603-9932

Out of the Way Galleria^{SM}
An eclectic blend of created art contributed
by local artisans and donors.
www.OutOfTheWayGalleria.org • (520) 398-9409

CosmoArt Studio^{SM}
Blending the talents of many artists in creating spiritually-
inspiring art through humility and cooperation.
www.CosmoArt.org • (520) 603-9932

Planetary Family Services^{SM}
Provides services to create, embellish, and bring Godly
energy to your home environment.
www.PlanetaryFamilyServices.org • (520) 403-4207

Magic Land Realty & Investment, Inc.
Licensed Real Estate Agents who aid others in finding their
sacred home/work environments.
www.magiclandrealty.com • (520) 403-6271

Global Change Multi-Media
www.GlobalChangeMultiMedia.org • (520) 398-2542

Divisions of Global Change Multi-Media:
Future Studios^{SM}

Recording studio and live-entertainment venue, presenting performers from around the world in a dynamic and positive environment, free from smoke, alcohol, and drugs. Events can be viewed live on-line through World-Wide Webcasts.
www.FutureStudios.org • (520) 398-2542

Global Change Music^{SM}

Nonprofit record label offers musicians recording opportunities using professional world-class equipment for voice and instrumental training.
www.GlobalChangeMusic.org • (520) 398-2542

The Musicians That Need To Be Heard Network^{SM}

Provides opportunities for musicians to communicate their music messages without spiritual compromise.
www.MusiciansThatNeedToBeHeardNetwork.org
(520) 398-2542

Global Change Radio^{SM}

Internet radio station broadcasting live and on-demand audio webcasts, including talk radio on various religious and social themes.
www.GlobalChangeRadio.org • (520) 398-2542

Global Change Television^{SM}

Internet television station offering live webcasts worldwide with a variety of programs of spiritual content, on demand.
www.GlobalChangeTelevision.org
(520) 398-2542

Global Change Films[SM]

Presenting educational, mind-expanding, and thought-provoking films that strive to raise the consciousness of the planet. Soon Global Change Films will produce major motion pictures with a spiritual emphasis.
www.GlobalChangeFilms.org • (520) 398-2542

Future Studios Cinema[SM]

Working with filmmakers and distributors of independent, activist, and educational films and documentaries that motivate spiritually thought-provoking group dialogue for the public at Future Studios.
www.FutureStudiosCinema.org • (520) 398-2542

Global Change Theater Company[SM]

Dedicated to writing, performing, and staging plays and various higher-consciousness, inspirational, dramatic productions where students receive training and opportunities to participate in theatrical shows and workshops. • (520) 398-2542

Global Change Multi-Media Distribution Company[SM]

Distributes music, DVDs, books, magazines, and any product that would be considered by its parent company to be a Global Change Tool for the dissemination of revelation and spiritually-uplifting information through media materials.

Global Change Multi-Media Productions[SM]

Professional audio, video, and Internet service producing spiritual and educational message media, via Internet video streaming, live webcasting, graphic design, and CD and video/DVD media production.
(520) 398-2542

Global Community Communications Alliance
P.O. Box 4910, Tubac, AZ 85646 USA
(520) 603-9932
e-mail:
info@GlobalCommunityCommunicationsAlliance.org
www.GlobalCommunityCommunicationsAlliance.org
www.GlobalChangeTools.org

INDEX

Terms listed in this index do not necessarily reflect every occurrence of that term within the book but rather indicate "significant" references or usage of the term on the pages listed.

7-dehydrocholesterol, 224, 225, 228
Abraham, xx
Adam and Eve, xviii, 20, 146, 188, 189, 206, 255, 375, 451, 454
Adamson and Ratta, 147
adjudication of the Bright and Morning Star versus Lucifer, xix, 104, 172, 341, 443
adrenal glands, 75, 100, 237, 250
adrenaline (epinephrine), 250
adrenocorticotrophic hormones (ACTH), 238
agondonters, 14, 435
AIDS, 160, 178
Akhenaten. *See* Ikhnaton
alignment, 25, 54, 72, 194, 409, 443, 449
allergies, 183
Amadon, 118, 418, 549
Amadonites, 549
Ambassadors, 109, 346, 422, 424
amino acids, 166, 168, 187, 241
amylases, 184
ancestral dyad units, 132
Ancients of Days, 17, 51, 295
Andon and Fonta, 141, 148, 179, 339
Andonites, 140
androgens, 238, 254
anemia, 213
angel of enlightenment, xxvii, 53, 65, 422
apostles, 12, 39, 61, 115, 117
Aquarian Age, 444

Aquarian reality, 40
arbor vitae, 367
archangels, 62
archangels' headquarters, xix, 416, 550
Architect of the Master Universe, 413
architectural planet, 194
Arthurian legends, 549
ascension astrology, 445, 448, 453
ascension science, xxvii, 16, 93, 202, 288, 374, 402, 440, 444
Ashtar, 415
astral body, 95, 323, 327, 407
astral psychoanalysis, 101
astralology reconstruction, 93, 99
astralology reconstructive circuitry, 102
astrology, 96, 449
astrophysics, 344
atoms, 163, 164, 169
audio fusion, xxvi
audio fusion material complement, xv, xix, xxvi, 1, 3, 69, 316, 343, 431, 440, 550
audio motion, 26
auditory cortex, 351
auhter energy, 25, 26, 28, 30, 107, 116, 118, 135, 170, 193, 197, 211, 256, 274, 384, 451
automatic writing, 394
automaton communication, 26
Avalon, xxviii, 12, 160, 371, 417, 549
axons, 366, 398

bacteria, 164, 214, 231
basal metabolic rate (BMR), 240
binaural, 350
body chemistry, 163
Boilermakers' Disease, 354
brain tumors, 379
Bright and Morning Star, xix, xxiii, xxvi, 14, 40, 238, 284, 303, 420, 421, *See also* Gabriel of Salvington
Caligastia, xviii, 3, 6, 30, 282, 328, 374, 547
Caligastia Forty, the, 147
Caligastia One Hundred, the, 8, 147, 549
Caligastia Sixty, the, 410
Camelot, 549
carbohydrates, 182, 197, 211
catalysts, 166, 167, 175
causal body, 322, 376
causal brain, 368
causal coordinate body, 322, 330, 331
causal coordinate ear, 350
causal ear, 332
causal memory circuit, 399
causal wave line, 335
Cayce, Edgar, 66, 72
celestial artisans and musicians, 392
celestial harmonics, 286
celestial mechanics, 266, 308, 332
celestial musicians, 357
Celestial Overcontrol, xvi, xxiv, xxvi, 23, 109, 111, 138, 187, 215, 226, 266, 327, 424
cell function, 270
cell structure, 270
cells, 98, 176, 270, 271, 273, 360
cellular affinity, 271
cellular and genetic implantation, 174
cellular reality, 117, 272

cellular sound wave frequencies, 297
cellular structures, 265
censorship command center, 308
central circuit, 84
central nervous system, 60, 174, 290, 366, 403
cerebellum, 367, 370, 372, 373
cerebral cortex, 365, 367, 374
cerebrospinal fluid, 365
cerebrum, 365
chain of command, 161
chakras, 43, *See also* crown circuit, third-eye circuit, throat circuit, heart circuit, solar plexus circuit, navel circuit, root circuit
change agents, 47, 134, 253
change point, xvi, 8, 170, 257, 259, 346, 347, 422
chemical, 25, 164, 240, 398, 403
cherubim, 62, 116, 319, 423
Chief of Finaliters, xxi, 415
Chief of Seraphim, 65, 417, 419
cholecalciferol, 224
Christ Michael, xvii, xix, xxiii, 3, 19, 110, 172, 194, 228, 236, 276, 395, 411, 417, 451, 550, *See also* Michael of Nebadon
chromatid, 176
chromosomes, 176, 177
circuit, 46, 60, 102, 239, 250, 252
circuit reflectivity, 34
circular function, 49
circular velocity, 51
circularize, 51
circulatory reality, 50
circulatory system, 53, 54, 57
circumcision, 56
clairvoyance, 244
cochlea, 307, 318, 351
coenzymes, 214
colored races, 146
competitive inhibition, 213

559

complementary polarities, 4, 197, 211, 212, 264
compounds, 237, 290
consciousness, 342, 344, 443, 447
Constellation Father, 62
Continuing Fifth Epochal Revelation, xiii, xv, xx, xxiii, xxvi, 5, 6, 9, 452, 550, *See also* Fifth Epochal Revelation
coordinate harmonic compliance, 275
cornea, 221
corticoids, 250, 254
cosmic, 41, 66, 81, 107, 169, 187, 253
cosmic ancestors, 50
cosmic biochemistry, 179
cosmic circulatory system, 57
cosmic clairvoyance, 244
cosmic design, 50
cosmic family, xvii, xxvi, 107, 135, 137, 138
Cosmic Family volumes, The, 548
Cosmic Family, Volume I, The, xxvii
cosmic genetics, 141, 147, 148, 149, 155, 412
cosmic language, 50
cosmic mind, 441
cosmic mother, 549
cosmic name, xxviii, 549
cosmic parents, 94, 278
cosmic philosophy, 409
cosmic relatives, 137, 138, 181, 186, 193, 280
Cosmic Reserve Corps, 25
Cosmic Reservists, xxvi
cosmic son, xxvi
cosmic stamina, 403
cosmologic vibration pattern, 53, 54, 403
cosmology, 238

Council of Twenty-four, 63, 375, 417, 418
coupling, 433
Creator Sons, 14, 17, 111, 172, 276, 329, 549
crown circuit, 65, 79, 97
Dalamatia, xviii, 9, 549
David of Israel, xxiii
deafness, 350
déjà vu, 380
dematerialization, 334
dendrites, 366, 398
Deo, xviii
Deo function, 301
Deo power, 301, 303
Deo-atomic, 273, 275, 342, 377, 397
Deo-atomic air, 446
Deo-atomic cells, 82, 205, 266, 375, 410
Deo-atomic enzymes, 175
Deo-atomic generics, 364
Deo-atomic genes, 174
Deo-atomic genetics, 168, 266
Deo-atomic hormones, 237
Deo-atomic inheritance, 163
Deo-atomic mind-soul causal current, 399
Deo-atomic molecules, 215
Deo-atomic motion, 275
Deo-atomic offspring, 342
Deo-atomic oxygen, 208, 347, 446
Deo-atomic parents, 342
Deo-atomic proton, 193
Deo-atomic receptor units, 400
Deo-atomic/ultimatonic circuitry, 91
Deo-audio coupling, 434
Deontology, 34
Deo-subatomic to cellular reality, 70, 76
Deotonic, 34, 40
Deotonic reality, 34
Deo-ultimatonic, 225

Deo-ultimatonic reality, 274
desoxycorticosterone (DOC), 254
Destiny Reservists, xxviii
diabetes, 178, 241, 242
diencephalon, 370, 371
digestion techniques, 182
digestive enzymes, 184
dimension, xxvi
dimensional coordinate placement, 279
dimensional reality, 339
dimensional reality, higher, 343
dio, xviii, xxvii
dio-audio coupling, 433, 434
diotribe magnetism, 273
diotribe sensory way station, 336
diotribes, 102, 118, 273, 336, 366, 375
disturbed motion, 268, 282, 283
Divine Administration, xix, 104, 136, 216, 234, 420, 451, 548, 551
Divine Counselor, 92
divine mind, 22, 55, 56, 115, 116, 154, 185
Divinington, 17, 22
DNA, 270, 296
dyad units, 121
Earth. See Urantia
Earth Mother, 56, 76, 141, 144, 180, 252, *See also* Universe Mother Spirit
Eldership, 109, 337, 346, 384, 404, 420
electrochemical, 383
electrokinetics, 449
electrons, 264
elektra system, 449
elements, 119, 163, 170, 185
Elijah, 418
emotional body, 106, 191, 437
endocrine glands, 238
energy constant, 81
energy reflective circuits, 97, 120, 169, 452

Enoch, 91, 409, 418
enzyme molecule, 211
enzyme reaction, 211
enzymes, 100, 166, 171, 182, 183, 184, 211, 212
epochal revelation, 5, 447
ergocalciferol, 222
ergosterol, 222
esophagus, 100, 186, 252, 356, 374
estrogen, 238, 254
estrone, 254
Eternal Son, 45, 85, 87, 97, 103, 184, 341, *See also* Second Source and Center
eternal-present body, 376
evacuation procedures, 415
evil, sin, and iniquity, xxvii
exergonic reaction, 176
experimental planet, 91
famotor movement, 94, 133, 326
Fanoving, 160, 371, 417
fats, 182, 184, 211
field, 26, 115, 116, 136, 137, 138, 265, 340
Fifth Epochal Revelation, xiii, xv, xx, 1, 161, 202, 284, 453, 549, *See also* Continuing Fifth Epochal Revelation
fifth-dimensional and above, 550
finaliters, xxi, xxvi, 22, 46, 69, 122, 411, 415
First Assistants, 109, 346, 439
First Cosmic Family, 19, 136, 150
First Epochal Revelation, 342, 454
First Garden of Eden, 234
First Planetary Sacred Home, xviii, xxiii, xxvii, 5, 13, 108, 137, 151
First Radius, xx
First Source and Center, 22, 47, 54, 61, *See also* Universal Father

first-dimensional reality, 342
first-light souls, 550
five-mile radius, xx
folic acid, 214
force field, 116, 118
force-energy, 117, 133, 177, 218, 273
forebrain, 370
Fourth Epochal Revelation, 302, 403, 453
fourth-dimensional, 59, 323, 327
fourth-dimensional reality, 345
fourth-order starseed, 550
Fragment of the Father, 141, *See also* Thought Adjusters
Francis of Assisi, 547
frequency, 88, 341, 342, 347, 348, 351, 353, 356
frontal lobe, 368, 371, 373, 380, 386, 388
fusion, xv, 16, 22, 26, 46, 47, 68, 293, 339, 409, 431, 432, 444
Gabriel of Salvington, xix, 56, 550, *See also* Bright and Morning Star
Gabriel of Urantia/TaliasVan of Tora, xv, xix, xxiv, 109, 395, 421, 547, 548, 551
Gabron and Niánn, 139
Gandhi, 304
Garden of Eden, xviii
gene splicing, 174
generic Deo-atomic unit locations, 376
genes, 177, 178
genetic breeding, 378
genetic inheritance, 174
glandular circuit receptivity formation motions, 311
Glastonbury, 549
Global Community Communications Alliance, xix, xxiv, 551

Global Community Communications Publishing, xxiii
glucose, 183, 197, 198
gonads, 91, 237, 238
grace, 446
grand universe, 17, 46, 48, 91, 99, 113, 280
grand universe deity, 53
gray matter, 366, 375
harmonic patterns, 291
Havona, 42, 112, 116, 377
heart circuit, 47, 60, 80, 98, 251, 252, 290
heartbeat, 82
helper (helpmate) molecules, 212
heme enzyme, 212
hindbrain, 370, 372
hippocampus, 371
Holy Spirit, 4, 18, 289, 383, 443
home range areas, 400, 401, 405
hormones, 97, 237, 248, 254
hydrolyzing enzymes, 184, 193
hypoglycemia, 178, 242
Ikhnaton (Akhenaten), 547
impedance, 307
Infinite Spirit, 30, 70, 85, 88, 95, 98, 103, 184, 341, *See also* Third Source and Center
inhibitor, 212
inner ear, 321
innerdimensional, 339
interdimensional, 59, 431
interdimensional and interplanetary communication, 365
interdimensional extraterrestrial communication, 394
interdimensional transference, 452
interplanetary and interuniversal travel, 318
interuniversal ancestry, 393
interuniversal and intrauniversal Life Carriers, 210

interuniversal architectural reality, 393
interuniversal auhter energy, 445
interuniversal communication, 387
interuniversal compliance, 276
interuniversal corporate membrane gland, 237, 239
interuniversal Deo-atomic cellular transference, 169
interuniversal digestive systems, 192
interuniversal diotribes, 174
interuniversal enzymes, 182
interuniversal genetics, 414
interuniversal headquarters circuits, 34
interuniversal language, 387
interuniversal laws, 154
interuniversal reality, 280, 318
interuniversal representation, 414
intraction infusion, 118
intraction-cell, 147
intraplanetary communication, 365
intrauniversal and interuniversal harmonic and melodic patterns, 392
intrauniversal and interuniversal space travels, 450
invariable septum stratum force, 272, 274
invisible yet ever-present city, 179
iodothyronines, 241
iris, 221
Islets of Langerhans, 238
Jesus, xviii, xxiii, 38, 39, 49, 64, *See also* Michael of Nebadon
Jesus Christ Michael, xxviii, *See also* Michael of Nebadon
John the Baptist, 418
Joseph, 148
Kalacortex, 427
kidney, 250

kinetic energy, 25, 198
kinetic fusion, 26
King Arthur, 549
Kumatron, 122, 427
Lanaforge, 40, 53, 68, 417, *See also* System Sovereigns
Lanonandek Sons, 9, 417
lens, 221
level-eight audio fusion material complement, xxvi, 547
Liaison Ministers, 303, 395, 421
Life Carriers, 174, 182, 208, 222, 265, 375
life implantation, 94
light, 53, 194
light and life, 43, 53, 221
light patterns, 53
limbic system, 380
lipases, 184, 193
liver cells, 179
Lucifer, xix, 30, 82, 115, 373
Lucifer Rebellion, xix, xxvii, 17, 30, 150, 368
lungs, 198, 207
Luther, Martin, 547
Machiventa Melchizedek, xviii, xx, xxiii, 105, 110, 152, 162, 347, 395, 414, 415, 550
magnetic cells, 265
magnetized, 205
magnets, 264
major sectors, 73
Mandate of the Bright and Morning Star, xix, xxiv, xxix, 3, 109, 152, 291, 298, 395, 421, 433, 547, 550
mansion worlds, 20, 45, 116, 429, 430
Mary (Jesus' mother), 148
Master Architects, 28, 104, 396
Master Physical Controllers, 33, 396, 426
Master Spirits, 28, 53, 93, 140, 239, 264
master symphony, 291

master universe, 40, 256, 279
material complement, 2, 5, 434, 547
Material Sons and Daughters, 20, 60, 148, 189, 417
medulla oblongata, 368, 371
Melchizedek. *See* Machiventa Melchizedek
Melchizedeks, 8, 414
Melfax, 547
memory circuitry, 550
memory circuits, 2, 399, 434
Meniere's syndrome, 354
meninges, 365
meridian center, 53
meridian circuitry, 47
meridian circuits, 42, 45, 47, 53, 59, 77, 78, 102, 274, 323
meridian telepology, 52
meridian triad, 53
mesencephalon, 370, 371
messenger RNA, 270
metabolism, 97, 240, 366, 373
metencephalon, 370, 372
Michael of Nebadon, 2, 117, 280, 284, 378
midbrain, 370
Midwayer Commission, 12
midwayers, xix, 2, 116, 319, 382, 416
mind, 21, 29, 79, 188, 242, 339, 402
mind-gravity circuits, 25
mitochondria, 175
modern astrology, 221
molecular structure of human mortals, 163
molecules, 163, 171, 198, 254, 286
Monmatia, 73, 378
morontia, 9, 102, 179
morontia body, 57, 69, 78, 102, 189, 262, 326, 327, 329, 336, 369
morontia counseling, 101

morontia counselor, xxvii, 123, 127, 420
morontia ear, 325, 338
morontia eye, 326
morontia heart, 64, 326
morontia heart circuit, 78
morontia magnetic field flow, 132, 133, 212
morontia magnetic force field, 136
morontia magnetic force-energy, 133
morontia mota, 34, 52, 67, 102, 420
morontia organs, 327
morontia personalities, 179
morontia progressors, 69
Morontia Seraphim Coordinators, 320
morontia temple, 121, 343
morontian brain, 274
mortal soul transference, 432
Moses, 418
Most Highs, 61
musical notes, 290
myelencephalon, 368, 371, 372
Mystery Monitors, 21, *See also* Thought Adjusters
navel circuit, 74, 80, 81, 86, 100
Nebadon, xxiii, 1, 5, 12, 16, 40, 280, 372
Nebuchadnezzar, 245
neural pathways, 383
neurohumoral transmitter, 399
neurons, 273, 398
neurotransmitters, 398, 401
neutronic enzymes, 187
neutrons, 188
New Age, xxviii, 328, 374, 445
New Jerusalem, 23, 33, 151, 194, 343, 418
Niánn Emerson Chase, xxvii, 109, 395, 422, 547, 551
Nodite and Andite amalgamations, 140

nonvirtue sensors, 316
nonwill sound, 308
Norlatiadek, 61, 113
nose brain, 380
Nostradamus, 66
nuclear family, 166
nucleus, 174, 176, 179, 188
obesity, 185
occipital lobe, 367, 371, 380, 394
Onamonalonton, 417
one-, two- and three-brained personalities, 273
one-brained type, 273, 447
one-mile radius, xx
open circuit, 381
orbits, 268, 275
Organ of Corti, 308, 318, 321, 351
Orvonon, 418
Orvonton, 17, 38, 95, 101
otosclerosis, 353
oval window, 307
ovan souls, xxi, 2, 105, 214, 224, 256, 295, 404
ovum, 180
oxidation, 197, 212
oxidized, 201
pair-unit classification, 2, 19, 110, 148, 150, 199, 211
Paladin, xxvi, 23, 415
pancreas, 99, 237, 238, 241
Paradise, 43, 45, 46, 244, 248, 254, 264, 290, 308, 326, 360, 376, 402, 443
Paradise constant, 154
Paradise time sequence, 392
Paradise Trinity, 71, 84, 91, 164, 237, 261, 265, 340, 399
paralysis, 225, 333, 379
parathyroids, 98, 237, 238
parietal lobe, 367, 380, 393
Perfections of Days, 71
Perfector of Wisdom, 305

personalities, 26, 43, 108, 115, 123, 132, 169, 208, 313, 346, 357, 384, 414
personality, 16, 34, 91, 95, 203, 287
personality circuit linkages, 87
personality circuits, 87
personality structure, 265, 272
personality types, 85
Peter, the Apostle, xxviii, 547
phosphate bonds, 198
photons, 194
physics of rebellion, xxvii, 548
pineal gland, 28, 97, 237
pitch, 392
pituitary gland, 97, 237, 243, 251
planetary headquarters, xviii, 53, 77, 359
planetary mortal epochs, 273
Planetary Prince, xix, 13, 48, 62, 138, 151, 156, 255, 277, 347, 383, 414, 433, 547, 550
Planetary Sacred Headquarters, xx
Planetary Sacred Home, 138, 168, 169
plastic surgery, 84
Pleiades, 12
point of origin, xxviii
point of origin reconstruction at time of fall, 400, 437
polypeptide loops, 166
polypeptides, 167, 271
Pons (Pons Varolii), 367, 370
positive protein enzymes, 167
power direct field, 136
prefrontal lobe, 373
pre-level-one, 431
presbycusis, 353
primal absolute hearing assent capacity, 287, 297
primal absolute Paradise circuit wave, 103, 287, 308, 317, 322, 331, 341, 352, 389, 402

primal brain flow circuitry patterns, 298
Primary Master Force Organizers, 320
primary midwayers, 139, 342, 416
prosencephalon, 370
protected areas, 106, 123, 135, 137, 189, 234, 354, 383
protein, 99, 164, 168, 179, 182, 211
proteinases, 184, 193
proton photon, 193
proton sequential force-energy, 194
protonic and neutronic enzymes, 186
protonic reality, 187
protons, 188, 193
provitamins, 222, 234
psychic circle, xxviii, 18, 53, 132, 142, 372, 373, 405, 419, 434
psychobiology, 364, 365
psychochemical, 397
psychophysics, 339, 341, 364
psychoschizophysiology, 381
psychospiritual, 365, 374, 376
psychospirituality, 364
pupil (of the eye), 221
pure impression, 26, 135, 314, 320, 334, 342
purification of Urantia, 56
quantum physics, 288, 293
Race Commissioners, 196, 426
ratio, 50
realignment, 310
Reconstructive Coordinators, 320
reflective cellular magnetic motion, 275
reflective cellular magnetic motion polarity, 274
Reflective Image Aids, 71
reflective lighting, 54
Reflective Spirits, 71

reflectivity, xxvi, 53, 218, 220, 223, 248, 380, 431
reflectivity personality pattern, 432
reincarnation, 10, *See also* repersonalization
rematerialization, 102, 246, 395
repersonalization, xxvi, 3, 30, 59, 106, 149, 170, 246, 295, 316, 408, 410, 411, 412, 432, 437, 438, 448
Reserve Corps of Destiny, 41
Resident Governor General, 447
retina, 221
rhinencephalon, 380
rhombencephalon, 371, 372
root circuit, 40, 74, 75, 80, 86, 101
root races of Urantia, 182
Salem, xviii, xx
Salvington, 222, 238, 384, 415
Salvington circuit, 59, 343
Sangik races, 9
sanobim, 62, 116, 319, 423
Santeen, xxvi
Satania, xix, 17, 60, 113, 118, 329, 361, 411, 428, 443
Second Epochal Revelation, 341, 454
second messenger system, 399
Second Radius, xx
Second Source and Center, 22, 220, *See also* Eternal Son
secondary glands, 237
secondary midwayers, 342, 345
second-dimensional reality, 342
second-time Urantians, xx, xxi
Sedona, Arizona, 550
semi-spirit, 431
sensor units, 369
separation from the supreme primal, 330
septuplicate planetary invariable septum stratum force, 275
sequential force-energy, 115, 117

seraphic guardians of destiny, 208
seraphic orders of Urantia, 172
seraphic transport, 46, 79, 332, 438
seraphim, 11, 116, 314, 382, 416, 444
seraphim of planetary supervision, 416
Seraphim of Race Commissioners, 210
Seraphim of the Races, 181, 419
seven primary glands, 237
significant others, 50
similar mind-brain formation, 272
similectic genetic alignment transference, 447, 448, 450, 451
sine wave, 290
Singlangton, 417
solar plexus, 99
solar system, 73, 378
solar-plexus circuit, 72, 80, 86
Solitary Messengers, 20, 23, 416
Solomon, xxiii
somatotropic hormone, 238
soul, 84, 225, 227, 341, 432, 439
soul surgeon, xxvii
sound, 286, 307, 347, 350, 357
sound waves, 287, 307, 352
source cells, 311
source-center, 70, 76, 297
spacecraft, 194
specific enzymes, 175
spermatozoa, 180
spirit, 23, 28, 102, 125, 292, 323, 339, 361, 402, 431, 439
Spirit of Truth, 4, 18, 49, 106, 115, 249, 284, 289, 383, 429, 443
spirit-brain, 274
spiritual bodies, 211, 218
spiritual implantation, 94
spiritual inbreeding, 91

spiritual purification, 56
Splandon, 73
stapes, 307
star routes, 452
starseed, xx, xxii, 23, 30, 58, 81, 92, 95, 147, 159, 178, 297, 376, 412, 426, 433, 438
steroid, 100
subcells, 248, 365, 377
subcircuits, 60, 72, 77
sulci, 380
sulfanilamide, 214
summons date, 138
supernaphim, 338
superuniverses, 59, 77, 103, 170, 246, 280, 377, 396, 414, 450
sympathetic vibration, 356
symphonic orchestra, 392
synapse, 399
syntonic impressions, 341
system, 16, 23, 38, 48, 53, 192, 262, 277, 443
System Sovereigns, 40, 68, 70, 277
TaliasSon, 549
TaliasVan of Tora. *See* Gabriel of Urantia
telencephalon, 370, 371
temporal lobe, 371, 380, 389, 390
testosterone, 254
third dimension, 343
third ear, 323, 338
Third Epochal Revelation, 453
Third Garden of Eden, 217
Third Radius, xx
Third Source and Center, 22, 52, *See also* Infinite Spirit
third-dimensional perspective, 59
third-dimensional reality, 342
third-dimensional world, 340
third-eye circuit, 66, 79, 97
Thought Adjusters, 4, 16, 17, 141, 287, 289, 294, 327, 352, 377, 409, 439, *See also* Fragment of the Father

three-brained type, 273, 447
Threefold Spirit, 78, 92, 121, 135, 195, 360
three-mile radius, xx
throat circuit, 70, 80, 86, 98, 239
thymus gland, 98, 237
thyroglobulin, 241
thyroid, 98, 237
thyroxine, 98
time travel, 69
time-coordinate consciousness, 342
time-past, time-present, or time-future reality, 344
Tora of Avalon, 549
transfer RNA, 271
transfiguration, 400
transpositional visualization sequence, 115, 117, 121
triad-unit I, 87
triad-unit II, 87
trigonometric series, 50
trihedral, 50
trilateral, 50
trimonad units, 87
Trinity Teacher Sons, 14, 194, 451
trisector family, 549
tron therapy, 101, 296, 397, 405, 410
Tumacácori, Arizona, xix
two-brained type, 273, 447
ultimaton, 54, 95, 176, 213, 377, 412
ultimatonic level, 450
ultimatonic membrane cells, 239
Umajor the fifth, 73
union of existences, 166
union of molecules, 175
union of souls, xxvi, 5, 22, 23, 115, 175, 361, 403
unit factors, 310

Universal Censor, 23
Universal Father, 11, 22, 85, 87, 103, 184, 233, 236, 281, 341, 447, *See also* First Source and Center
universal ontology and otology, 350
Universe Father, xxviii, 106, 406
universe law, 56
Universe Mother Spirit, xix, 40, 197, 220, 443, 444
universes, xxiii, 1, 14, 16, 22, 23, 303, 318, 319, 329, 549
unstabilized incongruent personality pattern, 297
Urantia, xviii, xxiv, 1, 206, 218, 327, 414, 432, 443
URANTIA Book, The, 548, 550
Urantia movement, xxviii
Urantian, 380
Urantian Reserve Corps, 15, 25
Urantians, 38, 341, 361, 418, 444
Van, xxvii, 547, 549
vector, 340
vector field, 340
vector space, 340
vector thought, 340
ventricles, 371
vestibulocochlear nerve, 321
virtue sensors, 310, 329, 343, 353, 357
viruses, 164, 166, 205
vitamins, 211, 218
Vorondadek Sons, 61
water molecule, 165, 174
white matter, 366, 371
will freeze, 213
will sound, 309, 310
will-sound personalities, 308
Wolvering, 160, 371, 417
World Councils, 419, 420, 422, 423, 425, 426, 428

Other titles by Gabriel of Urantia available from
Global Community Communications Publishing

The Divine New Order
by Gabriel of Urantia/TaliasVan of Tora
Autobiography of Gabriel of Urantia/TaliasVan of Tora and
the history of beginnings of Global Community Communications Alliance.

The Cosmic Family, Volume I
as transmitted through Gabriel of Urantia/TaliasVan of Tora
Continuing Fifth Epochal Revelation,
Papers 197-228 succeeding *The URANTIA Book*.

Messages to Urantia, 1997−2000
as transmitted through Gabriel of Urantia/TaliasVan of Tora
A collection of 19 sacred messages
from celestial beings addressing the state of our world, Urantia.

***Global Change Teachings for the New Millennium,
Series One, Two, & Three***
by Gabriel of Urantia/TaliasVan of Tora and Niánn Emerson Chase
Teachings to assist the planet's transition
into the first stage of light and life.

Teachings on Healing, From a Spiritual Perspective
by Gabriel of Urantia/TaliasVan of Tora and Niánn Emerson Chase
Teachings focused on bringing about healing
on the physical, mental, emotional, and spiritual levels.

The Best of the Film Industry—Movies You Don't Want to Miss!
compiled by Gabriel of Urantia/TaliasVan of Tora
A list of films that educate, challenge,
and expand the consciousness.

***Making the Most of Media Exposure for Global Change
Versus Our Experience with the Media***
by Gabriel of Urantia/TaliasVan of Tora and Niánn Emerson Chase
Firsthand account of experiences with corporate-controlled media.

Spiritual Quotes
by Gabriel of Urantia/TaliasVan of Tora
A collection of spiritual insights and wisdom
addressing many of life's facets.

www.ingramcontent.com/pod-product-compliance
Lightning Source LLC
Chambersburg PA
CBHW051414290426
44109CB00016B/1300